EU DISTRIBUTION LAW

EU Distribution Law

Fourth Edition

JOANNA GOYDER

Freshfields Bruckhaus Deringer, Brussels

·HART·
PUBLISHING
OXFORD AND PORTLAND, OREGON
2005

Hart Publishing
Oxford and Portland, Oregon

Published in North America (US and Canada) by
Hart Publishing c/o
International Specialized Book Services
5804 NE Hassalo Street
Portland, Oregon
97213-3644
USA

Distributed in the Netherlands, Belgium and Luxembourg by
Intersentia, Churchillaan 108
B2900 Schoten
Antwerpen
Belgium

Hart Publishing is a specialist legal publisher based in Oxford, England.
To order further copies of this book or to request a list of other
publications please write to:

Hart Publishing, Salter's Boatyard, Folly Bridge,
Abingdon Road, Oxford OX1 4LB
Telephone: +44 (0)1865 245533 or Fax: +44 (0)1865 794882
e-mail: mail@hartpub.co.uk
WEBSITE: http//www.hartpub.co.uk

British Library Cataloguing in Publication Data
Data Available
ISBN 1–84113–550–X (hardback)

Typeset by Hope Services (Abingdon) Ltd.
Printed and bound in Great Britain by
MPG Books, Bodmin, Cornwall

For my father
(1938–2004)

Contents

Preface to the Fourth Edition

In one way this book remains what it was when it was first published in 1992. It is now, as it was then, a guide to European Union law aspects of distribution agreements, aimed in particular at legal practitioners and in-house corporate lawyers not necessarily already familiar with European Union institutions and procedures, or with competition law. It is intended to provide an approachable, readable and informative introduction to European Union competition law and the law on commercial agents as it affects distribution contracts and practices.

But since then competition law has been developing at a heady pace, and the last four years have been no exception. At the time the last edition was published, radical proposals to reform the entire enforcement framework of Articles 81 and 82 of the EC Treaty were barely a twinkle in the eye of some European Commission officials. Since then they have acquired the force of law and are now bringing about a quiet revolution. The European Commission has enhanced powers to investigate and impose fines, and national courts and competition authorities now have a greater role in enforcement. Business bears much more responsibility than before for assessing the legality of its own conduct. Companies need to monitor aspects of their business more closely: an increase in market share can render a previously legal agreement illegal. While block exemptions provide some with safe harbours in which to shelter, others have to adapt to the choppy seas of self-assessment.

Equally momentous is the enlargement of the EU in 2004 to embrace 10 new Member States. Though not changing the law as such, this changes the meaning of expressions such as 'an exclusive territory comprising all Member States of the EU', necessitating a review of many thousands of distribution contracts. It may also entail the redrafting of contracts that mentioned these countries by name, and the education of commercial staff who may need to change their practices to ensure they do not illegally hinder sales into these new EU territories. Similarly, the increased opportunities for parallel imports will have led producers to review their pricing strategies.

The revision of this book becomes more difficult each time it is updated, as a consequence of the relentless increase of the influence of economics on this area of the law. While it is clearly desirable that competition law be applied in accordance with the dictates of economics, this change of focus brings about a corresponding reduction in certainty, and the legality of given conduct depends increasingly on many factors beyond the actual terms of an agreement.

At the same time the development of electronic communications has raised new questions, many of which remain unanswered. The European Commission has taken the line that the traditional rules are sufficiently flexible to provide the answers, and has refrained from adopting specific guidance beyond the few paragraphs in its Guidelines on vertical restraints. Nor has there, so far, been much decisional practice in this area.

It is strongly advised that those new to EU competition law read Chapters 1, 2 and 3 before consulting any of the later chapters. These first chapters give a general overview of the EU legal order, and in particular competition law as applied to distribution. Without an appreciation of the background against which they operate it will be difficult to understand the more specific rules discussed in later chapters.

Each chapter except the first opens with a table of 'Key Points' which give a brief sketch of the areas covered in that chapter. They are necessarily simplified statements of the law, and as such need to be read together with the fuller treatment given in the body of the chapter.

Future developments will be noted in regular updates available free of charge at www.hartpub.co.uk/updates. In addition, relevant legislative materials are now so readily available electronically that this edition includes fewer Appendices than previous ones, on the assumption that most readers are able to find these texts through DG Comp's website.

Thanks go to my colleagues in the Antitrust, Competition and Trade Group at Freshfields Bruckhaus Deringer, who allowed me the time I needed to complete work on this new edition, and from whom I learn on a daily basis. I am particularly grateful to Günter Bauer and Alison Jones, both of whom read parts of the text and made many helpful suggestions for improvements. Any remaining imperfections are entirely my responsibility.

Thank you too to Rebecca Deakin for her secretarial assistance, and to all at Hart Publishing for taking on the book at short notice and efficiently bringing it to publication.

The law is stated as at 15 February 2005.

Finally, this edition is dedicated to my father, Dan Goyder, who has reviewed the text of previous editions in full, and is sadly no longer here to do so. His life was and is an inspiration to me far beyond the law.

Joanna Goyder
Brussels
February 2005

Table of Cases

Numerical

Court of First Instance

European Court of Justice

Commission Decisions

Table of Legislation

Treaties

Regulations

Directives

1

European Union Law

The European Community[1] was founded by the Treaty of Rome (or EC Treaty) and came into existence on 1 January 1958. At the same time the European Atomic Energy Community, often known as 'Euratom', was created. These two Treaties are together known as the European Communities. (Until recently there was also a third Treaty, the 1952 European Coal and Steel Treaty, which applied only to the coal and steel sectors. It expired on 23 July 2002.)

These Treaties created three separate Communities, with individual executive organs but sharing in common the European Parliament (originally called the European Assembly) and the European Court of Justice. However, since 1 July 1967 they have had common institutions. Thus, although two of the three original separate Treaties are still in force, there is now only one Council, one Commission, one European Parliament and one European Court of Justice.

On the entry into force of the Treaty on European Union (TEU) on 1 November 1993, the European Union (EU) was created and the then three European Communities became part of the EU. The other two parts of the EU are a common foreign and security policy, and co-operation in the fields of justice and home affairs. However, these two parts involve mainly intergovernmental co-operation at political level rather than legislative activity. It is therefore still correct to talk of 'Community law' rather than 'Union law'. Strictly speaking, all the law covered in this book is 'European Community' (or 'EC') law since it has its origin in that Treaty which contains rules of general application, and is not concerned with the sectoral Euratom Treaty.[2] Nevertheless, this book is called 'EU Distribution Law' in recognition of the fact that the term 'EC law' can appear outdated, now that 'EU law' has become widely accepted usage.

Since 1 May 2004 there have been 25 Member States of the EU. On that date, the existing 15 Member States—Austria, Belgium, Denmark, Finland, France, Germany, Greece, Ireland, Italy, Luxembourg, the Netherlands, Portugal, Spain,

---

[1] Its name was changed in 1993 from 'European Economic Community' (EEC) to 'European Community' (EC) by the Treaty on European Union (TEU or Maastricht Treaty).

[2] The institutional structure will change again if and when the new EU Constitution enters into force, but ratification requirements mean that this will not happen until 2007 at the earliest.

Sweden and the United Kingdom—were joined by Cyprus, the Czech Republic, Estonia, Hungary, Latvia, Lithuania, Malta, Poland, the Slovak Republic and Slovenia. Bulgaria and Romania are expected to join in 2007. The official languages of the EU are now Czech, Danish, Dutch, English, Estonian, Finnish, French, German, Greek, Hungarian, Italian, Latvian, Lithuanian, Maltese, Polish, Portuguese, Slovak, Slovenian, Spanish and Swedish. The different language versions of legislative texts all carry equal weight.

1.2 EU INSTITUTIONS

The main institutions are as follows.

Council of Ministers

The Council of the European Union is made up of a representative from the government of each Member State. When the representatives are the heads of state or government it is called 'the European Council'. Otherwise, it is referred to according to sectors of responsibility: for example, 'the Transport Council' is made up of Ministers of Transport. This means that it is possible for 'the Council' to have several different meetings at the same time. Competition law is handled by various Councils depending on the subject matter: for example, the recent procedural reform of competition law was discussed by the Industry Council, but the Transport Council would deal with competition measures specifically applicable to the transport sector.

In most spheres it is the Council, jointly with the European Parliament, that has responsibility for adopting secondary legislation, on the basis of proposals made by the Commission (though competition law is one of the few areas in which the Parliament's role is fairly limited). The Council also concludes agreements, which are generally negotiated by the Commission, between the European Communities and third countries.

Commission

As of November 2004 the Commission has 25 members or 'Commissioners' (one from each Member State), nominated by common consensus between the governments of all the Member States and the person whom they have previously agreed to nominate as Commission President. In principle the Commissioners perform their duties completely independently of the influence of national governments and national interests.

The Commission administration is divided up into 36 Directorates-General ('DGs') and specialised 'Services'. Of particular interest in the context of EU distribution law are the Competition DG or 'DG Comp'[3] (responsible for the application and enforcement of EU competition rules), the Internal Market DG (dealing with the internal market, including rules applicable to commercial agency) and the Legal Service, which is involved in all Commission acts of legal significance.

The Commission has responsibility for defending the general interest of the European Union. It makes legislative proposals to the Council and European Parliament and it has a duty to ensure within the limits of its powers that the rules of the Treaty are obeyed. It has some legislative powers delegated to it by the Council. It also administers Community policies and negotiates agreements between the European Communities and third countries.

In the field of competition law it has important enforcement powers: in particular it may impose fines of up to 10 per cent of a company's worldwide annual turnover. It also has broad powers to conduct investigations and inspections where it suspects breach of the competition rules. DG Comp is divided into nine Directorates. Directorate R deals with 'strategic planning and resources' and Directorate A is responsible for 'competition policy and strategic support', including the European Competition Network and international relations. The five Directorates B to F apply the Community rules on anti-competitive agreements, abuse of a dominant position and merger control to various industry sectors: Directorate B covers energy, water, food and pharmaceuticals; Directorate C covers information, communication and media; Directorate D covers other services; Directorate E covers industry, and Directorate F consumer goods. Directorates G and H are responsible for control of state aid.

European Parliament

The European Parliament has been a directly elected body since 1979 and now has 732 members.

Until 1993, despite the 1986 Single European Act which increased its powers, it remained essentially a consultative body (though its views were often influential). With the entry into force of the Maastricht Treaty in 1993, the Amsterdam Treaty in 1999, and the Nice Treaty in 2003 its powers have steadily grown. In most areas of legislative activity it now enjoys an equal role with the Council.

The Parliament also has powers with respect to the budget, the admission of new Member States to the European Union and the conclusion of association agreements with third countries. It has the right to approve the nomination of the Commission President and other Commission members. It also has the power to adopt a motion of censure of the Commission, requiring it to resign in its entirety.

---

[3] The Competition Directorate-General was known as DG IV until 1999 when Commission President Prodi abolished the use of the numbering system in favour of names based on the policy areas covered.

It thereby exercises a political control, which it wielded most famously during the crisis which brought down President Santer's Commission in 1999.

European Court of Justice and Court of First Instance

The European Court of Justice[4] (ECJ) is situated in Luxembourg. It has 25 judges and eight Advocates-General. Cases may be heard either by a 'full Court' (normally 11 judges, but more in exceptionally important cases) or by a Chamber of one, three, five or seven judges.[5]

It reviews the acts of the other institutions, makes findings of breaches against Member States in the case of their failure to observe their obligations under the Treaties, ensures the uniform application of Community law by giving authoritative interpretations of that law, and hears appeals on points of law from the Court of First Instance (see below). Cases may be brought by the Community institutions, Member States, and, in some circumstances, by companies and individuals. Cases brought directly to the ECJ, and requests for preliminary rulings (see below), take an average of around two years, and appeals from the Court of First Instance tend to take a few months longer.

Apart from the Court of Justice itself, there is also a Court of First Instance (CFI) of 25 judges who sit in Chambers of three or five, or as a single judge or, in exceptionally important cases, as a 'full Court' of 11 or more judges. It has jurisdiction over, among other things, competition law cases, where it reviews Commission Decisions when they are challenged by private parties. Cases before the CFI take an average of about two years. Appeal from judgments of the CFI lies, on questions of law only, to the ECJ.

The kinds of cases that may be of relevance in the context of EU distribution law are the following.

Judicial review

The CFI acts frequently in its judicial review capacity in the field of competition law under Articles 230 and 232 of the EC Treaty. It hears appeals from companies on whom the Commission has imposed fines or whose agreements it has declared void for breach of Article 81 or 82 of the EC Treaty. Both the finding of an infringement and the level of any fine may be reviewed.

Cases brought by private parties are always heard by the CFI, and those brought by a Member State or a Community institution are heard by the ECJ. Private

---

[4] Not to be confused with either the European Court of Human Rights in Strasbourg or the International Court of Justice in the Hague.

[5] A case must be heard by the full Court if the action is brought by a Member State or by a Community institution or if a Member State or a Community institution taking part in the case so requests: Art 221 EC Treaty.

parties appealing against measures that are not addressed specifically to them are always required to show that they are 'directly and individually concerned'.[6]

The Court can also review the adoption by the Commission of a block exemption Regulation (see p 32) if there are grounds for alleging that the Commission enacted such a Regulation illegally. A Member State can always make such a challenge, and the case will be heard by the ECJ. A company, on the other hand, will often have difficulty establishing the 'direct and individual concern' which is necessary to give it standing to bring such an action.[7]

Infringement proceedings

Infringement proceedings may be brought against a Member State or a Community institution for breach of European Union law. Proceedings might be brought, for example, by the Commission against a Member State for failure to implement or inadequate implementation of a Directive. This kind of case is preceded by an administrative phase during which the Commission attempts to persuade the Member State to rectify the situation. Only if this proves unsuccessful will the case be brought before the ECJ. The only Directive of direct relevance to distribution law is the Directive on commercial agents (see p 182).

Preliminary ruling

The EC Treaty allows (or, in the case of a court from which no appeal lies, requires) a judge sitting in a national court to ask the ECJ for a preliminary ruling on the interpretation[8] or validity of Community law.[9]

For example, a litigant in a national court might allege the invalidity of a contract being enforced against him on the grounds that the contract violates Article 81 of the EC Treaty. The national judge might be unsure whether or not, on a proper interpretation of Article 81, the contract is void. Either of the parties might suggest to the judge, or the judge might decide on his own initiative, to put a preliminary question of interpretation to the ECJ.

It takes an average of around two years to obtain an answer to a preliminary question. Such a delay may well be to the advantage of one party and to the disadvantage of the other, and so may be used by one party as a delaying tactic. It is up

---

[6] In Case C-70/97 *Kruidvat v Commission* [1998] ECR I-7183, [1999] 4 CMLR 68, Kruidvat had been sued by Givenchy for selling Givenchy products while not an authorised member of its network. Kruidvat tried to challenge the Art 81(3) exemption which had approved Givenchy's distribution arrangements, but was held to have no standing to do so because during the Commission's investigation it had only intervened through its trade association, and it had not at any point applied to become a member of the network. It was therefore not 'individually concerned' within the meaning of Art 230.

[7] Such a challenge to the block exemption Regulation on vertical restraints failed for this reason: Case C-341/00 *CNPA v Commission* [2001] ECR I-5263.

[8] Although in principle limited to performing an interpretative role, the borderline between interpretation and application can be hard to discern and the Court sometimes all but directs the national court on how to apply the law to the facts of the case.

[9] Art 234 EC Treaty.

to the national judge to decide on the basis of national procedural rules whether to grant any kind of interim relief in such circumstances.

1.3 WHAT ARE THE SOURCES OF EU LAW?

The main sources of EU law relevant to distribution law[10] are as follows.

Treaty of Rome

The Treaty of Rome or EC Treaty itself is primary EU legislation. It has been amended a number of times since it came into force in 1958, most importantly by the 1986 Single European Act, the Treaty on European Union which entered into force on 1 November 1993, the Amsterdam Treaty which entered into force on 1 May 1999, and the Nice Treaty which entered into force on 1 February 2003.

The Amsterdam Treaty effected a renumbering of the Treaty, which can make for confusion in discussing cases and texts dating from before the renumbering. In this book only the new numbering is used, but readers will need to be aware of the old numbering to the extent that they consult sources dating from or dealing with events before 1 May 1999.[11]

The most important Articles of the EC Treaty in the context of distribution law are Article 81 (formerly Article 85) and Article 82 (formerly Article 86) which contain the competition rules applicable to commercial enterprises. The rules contained in these two Articles are directly effective (see below) and so are part of national law in EU Member States. Breach of these Articles can render a party liable to a fine by the European Commission or a national competition authority, and may mean that a contract or some of its terms are void and unenforceable. It may also give rise to liability in damages.

Articles 28 to 30, setting out the Treaty rules on free movement of goods, are also relevant to distribution. They prohibit, with certain exceptions, national laws and regulations which hinder free trade between Member States.[12]

Regulations

Whether adopted by the Commission, or by the Council and European Parliament, Regulations are also directly applicable law in all Member States. Like

---

[10] A complete list of sources would include some other categories such as international law and internal administrative acts by the Community.

[11] The numbering will change again if and when the new EU Constitution enters into force, but ratification requirements mean that this will not happen until 2007 at the earliest.

[12] These rules are beyond the scope of this book. See eg Peter Oliver, *Free Movement of Goods in the European Community*, 4th edn (Sweet & Maxwell, 2003).

the Articles of the EU Treaty referred to above, they are also part of national law and are automatically binding on Member States, government agencies and companies and individuals. There is no need for any sort of act of transposition into national law:

> By reason of their nature and their function in the system of the sources of Community law, regulations have direct effect and are, as such, capable of creating individual rights which national courts must protect.[13]

In fact, transposing acts are not only unnecessary, but also illegal.[14] Regulations are always published in the Official Journal of the European Communities and they come into force 20 days after publication unless another date is specified in the Regulation itself.[15] Such publication is obligatory and is a condition of the Regulation's binding effect.

There are two main Commission Regulations specific to distribution. These are both 'block exemption' Regulations, enacted under Article 81(3) of the EC Treaty. They ensure the validity of various categories of agreement that might otherwise be void and unenforceable by virtue of the prohibition contained in Article 81(1).

Directives

Directives are usually adopted jointly by the Council and Parliament. They are addressed to Member States and require a certain legislative result to be achieved by a particular date. However, Member States are left free to decide how they wish to implement the Directive and to draft their own implementing legislation.

It often happens that a Directive is not implemented in time by some or all Member States. Even where this occurs it is still sometimes possible for an individual to benefit from some or all of the rules laid down in the Directive. In such a case, the Directive or part of it is said to have 'direct effect' (see below). Whether given terms of a Directive will be held to have direct effect depends essentially on whether they are precise and unambiguous enough to confer rights on private parties, and against whom it is sought to enforce the Directive.

The only Directive which will be considered in detail in this book is the Directive on commercial agents (see p 182).

Decisions

Decisions are binding on the party or parties to whom they are addressed, and they are required to be notified only to such parties.[16] They are of considerable

---

[13] Case 43/71 *Politi v Italian Ministry of Finance* [1971] ECR 1039, [1973] CMLR 60, para 9.

[14] Case 39/72 *Commission v Italy* [1973] ECR 101, [1973] CMLR 439.

[15] Art 254 EC Treaty.

[16] *Ibid.* However, it is sometimes provided in secondary legislation that Decisions are to be published. For an example in the field of competition law see Art 27 of Reg 1/2003 (Appendix 2).

importance in competition law. For example, if the Commission decides to impose a fine on a company for breach of Article 81 or 82 of the EC Treaty, it must do this through a formal Decision, which must be served on that company. A Decision is also adopted to impose interim measures pending a final decision, and to close an investigation on the basis of commitments given by a company, and is also required to oblige an undertaking to submit to an investigation on its premises.

Opinions, Recommendations, Communications and Notices

Unlike Treaty Articles, Regulations, Directives and Decisions, these other categories are not binding forms of law. An Opinion will be issued to a Member State before proceedings are taken against it in the ECJ, and Recommendations may suggest how a Member State's national legislation should be amended in order to bring it into line with Community law. Communications and Notices provide guidance on the position taken by the institution making the publication. They bind no one, though they may have legal consequences to the extent that they create legitimate expectations. For example, where a Commission Notice might have led a company to believe that its illegal conduct was in fact permissible, the ECJ has held that the Commission may not impose a fine in respect of this conduct.[17]

Judgments of the European Court of Justice and Court of First Instance

Decisions of the ECJ are the highest authority for interpretation of Community law. There is no appeal from a judgment of the ECJ. The CFI is a lower court with jurisdiction to hear certain types of case, including most competition cases, and its judgments are second in authority only to those of the ECJ. There is no formal doctrine of precedent and the ECJ is free not to follow its previous rulings. In practice this happens extremely rarely.[18] The Community competition rules, with which a large part of this book is concerned, have been the subject of many cases before the ECJ and the CFI.

Though not a source of law in the technical sense it is sometimes also useful to consult the Opinions of the Advocates-General. Before giving judgment in any case, the ECJ (but not the CFI) will almost always have the benefit of hearing the submissions of the Advocate-General assigned to that case. The Advocate-General suggests to the Court how it should decide the case, and his suggestion is backed up by full analysis of the case and often by extensive consideration of earlier relevant jurisprudence of the Court, much in the style of the judgment of an English

---

[17] Joined Cases 40–48/73 *Suiker Unie v Commission* [1975] ECR 1663, [1976] 1 CMLR 295, para 557.

[18] An example is Joined Cases C-267 and C-268/91 *Keck and Mithouard* [1993] ECR I-6097, [1995] 1 CMLR 101.

judge. He may even consider arguments which occur to him which were not put forward by the parties, and look at relevant principles in the national laws of EU Member States. This can be useful, since the ECJ's judgment itself may be quite short and, since there is no official doctrine of precedent, may not always fully cite earlier cases. Although the Advocate-General's Opinion may not be followed by the Court, in very many cases it is.

If the Court rejects the Advocate-General's Opinion in whole or in part then the rejected arguments are of little practical use. However, in the case of a point on which the Court has never stated its view, the Opinion may be of persuasive value and may contain arguments worth adopting when arguing the point, particularly when conducting a case before a national court or authority.

General Principles of Law

In interpreting Community law the ECJ has regard, amongst other things, to general principles, both those that can be deduced from the Community Treaties and those common to the laws of the Member States. These have proved a rich source in the field of fundamental rights, in particular in guaranteeing certain basic rights concerning the conduct of judicial and administrative proceedings. Both the European Convention on Human Rights and the Charter of Fundamental Rights of the European Union may be relevant in such cases.

An example of the invocation of a fundamental right in the context of competition law is the claim made by a company whose premises had been searched by the Commission without any prior warning. The company alleged that this action constituted an unlawful infringement of its fundamental right to freedom from invasion of its privacy. Although the Court rejected this argument, referring to the exception to this principle permitted by the European Convention on Human Rights (the case pre-dated the Charter) where interference with the right is necessary to protect the public interest, it accepted that in principle such fundamental rights had to be respected.[19]

The right to a hearing and legal professional privilege are also rights developed on the basis of general principles in the context of competition law, as is the right not to incriminate oneself. These are considered further in Chapter 2. Other important general principles upheld by the ECJ include the principles of legal certainty[20] and proportionality.[21]

---

[19] Case 136/79 *National Panasonic v Commission* [1980] ECR 2033, [1980] 3 CMLR 169. See further p 50.

[20] Case 81/72 *Commission v Council* [1973] ECR 575, [1973] CMLR 639.

[21] Case 114/76 *Skimmed Milk Powder* [1977] ECR 1211, [1979] 2 CMLR 83.

1.4 WHERE IS EU LAW TO BE FOUND?

The texts of the most important Treaty Articles and secondary legislation in the context of distribution law are reproduced in the Appendices to this book. These and all other official texts, and many unofficial texts, are available on the Internet, and in particular on DG Comp's website. Below are some key sources for further reference. Details of useful websites and other resources and suggested further reading are at p 199.

Official Journal of the European Union

The Official Journal[22] is made up of the 'C' (communications) and the 'L' (legislation) series. Binding legislative texts appear in the 'L' series and all other official documents in the 'C' series. It is published almost every day, with several issues usually appearing in one day.

It is in the Official Journal that are found the texts of all Regulations and Directives, and many Decisions, Recommendations and Communications. In addition, draft legislation and Notices of intention to take particular Decisions are published in it: this gives interested parties the opportunity to make their views known if they so wish before a final legislative text is approved or Decision adopted.

A subscription to the Official Journal is not expensive; the chief problem for subscribers is that, in paper form, it takes up a great deal of space. Many therefore use a CD-ROM or online service instead of or in conjunction with the paper form.

European Court Reports (Reports of Cases before the ECJ and CFI)

This series generally gives the full official text of the Court's judgment and, for cases before the ECJ, the Advocate-General's Opinion. However, some extremely long judgments are given in summary form only, and in such cases the full text can be obtained from the Court Registry. Unfortunately, the need to translate the reports into all official Community languages delays official publication, which lags behind judgment by about a year.

However, each language version is published on the Court's website as soon as it is available, so that at least one language version is always available the same day a judgment is given. Thus, where judgments are described in this book as 'not yet officially reported', they can nevertheless be found on the Internet.

---

[22] As a result of the entry into force of the Nice Treaty on 1 February 2003 its official name changed from Official Journal of the European Communities to Official Journal of the European Union (Art 254 EC Treaty).

Common Market Law Reports—Antitrust Reports (CMLR)

Although these are not official reports, they appear more promptly than the official European Court Reports: judgments appear about six months after they are delivered. They include not only ECJ and CFI judgments but also Commission Decisions and Notices, and other useful texts such as relevant questions put in the European Parliament. They are therefore a convenient source of reference in practice, and CMLR references are given throughout this book.

1.5 EU LAW AND NATIONAL LAW

In the area of distribution law, both EC rules and national laws co-exist, and there is a sharing of competence between the Community on the one hand and the Member States on the other. It is therefore crucial to understand the way in which the two interact. The general principle is that, in the absence of specific rules, national courts and authorities are free to take action provided such action does not conflict with the application of the Treaty rules.[23]

In order to understand the way in which this general rule works it is necessary to be familiar with the two key notions of (1) direct effect and (2) supremacy.

Direct Effect of Community Law

The fact that Community law is directly effective means that individuals may assert rights conferred upon them and be bound by duties imposed upon them by Community law, and that these rights and duties may be enforced in national courts. In this way, it differs fundamentally from traditional international law, which in some Member States cannot be invoked by individuals in national courts unless there has been some kind of national legislative implementing measure.

The principle of the direct effect of Community law was first established by the ECJ in *Van Gend & Loos*,[24] a case concerning an Article of the EC Treaty. An individual invoked the direct effect of the Article against a government which had failed to carry out its obligations under the EC Treaty. This was 'vertical' direct effect, operating between a private party and the state. It was later affirmed that the principle applies not only to Treaty Articles, but also to Regulations and Directives. Except in the case of Directives, and to a limited extent even then (see below), the principle applies also to relations between private parties ('horizontal' direct effect).

---

[23] In the competition law area see Case 14/68 *Walt Wilhelm v Bundeskartellamt* [1969] ECR 1, [1969] CMLR 100.

[24] Case 26/62 [1963] ECR 1, [1963] CMLR 105.

It is not all Treaty provisions or all secondary Community legislation that are directly effective. In order to be so the obligations imposed by them must be clear and unambiguous, and unconditional,[25] in that their operation must not be dependent on further action being taken by the Community or national authorities.

Direct Effect of Treaty Provisions

The main Treaty provisions on competition are Articles 81 and 82 of the EC Treaty. It was established in *Bosch*[26] that these two Articles are directly effective and that they may therefore be invoked by one undertaking against another in a national court.

The general issue of whether and under what circumstances damages may be claimed for breaches of the Treaty is a question of national law and has not yet been resolved in all jurisdictions. However, as far as Articles 81 and 82 are concerned Community law clearly requires that damages be available to injured parties (see further p 60).

Direct Effect of Regulations

EC Regulations are directly effective: this is stated explicitly in Article 249 of the Treaty.[27] This part of Article 249 has been interpreted by the Court as follows:

> Therefore, by reason of their nature and their function in the system of the sources of Community law, regulations have direct effect and are, as such, capable of creating individual rights which national courts must protect.[28]

Direct Effect of Directives

Perhaps surprisingly, given the absence of any statement in Article 249 that Directives can have direct effect, the ECJ has established that they can sometimes be directly effective.

The potential direct effect of Directives was established in *Van Duyn*.[29] It has since been described by the Court as follows:

> The binding effect of a directive implies that a national authority may not apply to an individual a national legislative or administrative measure which is not in accordance

---

[25] eg Case 14/83 *Van Colson and Kamann v Land Nordrhein-Westfalen* [1984] ECR 1891, [1986] 2 CMLR 430. This second requirement does not prevent a provision having direct effect even in the absence of the required action, if a deadline for such action has been laid down and that deadline has passed.

[26] Case 13/61 [1962] ECR 45, [1962] CMLR 1.

[27] For practical purposes, the expression 'directly applicable' which appears in Art 249 can be treated as equivalent to the expression 'directly effective' which is more often used by the ECJ.

[28] *Politi v Italian Ministry of Finance*, above n 13.

[29] Case 41/74 [1974] ECR 1337, [1975] 1 CMLR 1.

with a provision of the directive which has all the characteristics necessary to render possible its application by the court. . . . Likewise, a national authority may not apply to a
person legislative or administrative measures which are not in accordance with an
unconditional and sufficiently clear obligation imposed by the Directive.[30]

Even if a Directive has been implemented by a Member State, the validity of that
implementing legislation may be challenged by reference to the requirements of
the Directive.[31] For example, if a party considers that the Directive on commercial
agents has been incorrectly implemented, it may argue in a national court that,
insofar as it is incorrect, the national court should not apply it.

However, the direct effect of a Directive may not generally be invoked by a private party against another private party.[32] Nor may a Member State invoke the
direct effect of a Directive or unimplemented part of a Directive against a private
party if that Member State has not yet implemented the Directive or has not fully
implemented it.[33] However, the ECJ, at the same time as reiterating this rule, has
stated that unimplemented Directives should nevertheless be looked to in interpreting national law, even in a case brought against a private party.[34]

It has also held that someone suffering prejudice as a result of a Member State's
failure to implement a Directive should, under certain conditions, be able to
recover damages from that Member State.[35]

Supremacy of Community Law

European Community law forms a new and unique legal order. This legal order
has supremacy over the national legal orders of the Member States, and its rules
have primacy over the rules of the national legal order. National courts have a duty
not to apply national laws which are in conflict with Community law. In other
words, some element of sovereignty has been conferred by the Member States on
the Community. Thus, for example, the UK Parliament's sovereignty was cur-
tailed by the accession of the United Kingdom to the European Communities in
1973.

The principle of supremacy or primacy does not derive expressly from any of
the Treaties, but was established by the jurisprudence of the ECJ. One of the earliest and best known statements of the principle was made by the Court in the case
of *Costa v ENEL*. In this case it had been argued that a subsequently enacted Italian

---

[30] Case 158/80 *Rewe v Hauptzollamt Kiel* [1981] ECR 1805, [1982] 1 CMLR 499, para 41.
[31] Case 51/76 *Verbond der Nederlandse Ondernemingen* [1977] ECR 133, [1977] 1 CMLR 413.
[32] Case 152/84 *Marshall v Southampton AHA* [1986] ECR 723, [1986] 1 CMLR 688; Case C-91/92
Faccini Dori [1994] ECR-I 3325, [1995] 1 CMLR 665.
[33] Case 80/86 *Officier van Justitie v Kolpinghuis Nijmegen* [1987] ECR 3969, [1989] 2 CMLR 18.
[34] Case C-106/89 *Marleasing* [1990] ECR I-4135, [1992] 1 CMLR 305; Case C-334/92 *Wagner Miret*
[1993] ECR I-6911, [1995] 2 CMLR 49.
[35] Joined Cases C-6/90 and C-9/90 *Francovich v Italian Republic* [1981] ECR I-5357, [1993] 2 CMLR
66; Joined Cases C-46/93 *Brasserie du Pecheur* and C-48/93 *Factortame III* [1996] ECR I-1029; Joined
Cases C-178 etc/94 *Dillenkofer* [1996] ECR I-4845, [1996] 3 CMLR 469.

law had the effect of overriding a piece of national legislation incorporating the EC Treaty into national law in Italy and thereby overriding the provisions of the Treaty where the new law was inconsistent with them.

The Court rejected this reasoning:

> the law stemming from the Treaty, an independent source of law, could not, because of its special and original nature, be overridden by domestic legal provisions, however framed, without being deprived of its character as Community law and without the legal basis of the Community itself being called into question.[36]

In other words, Community law provisions always take precedence over national law provisions where the two conflict.

Regulation 1/2003 (Appendix 2) now sets out the way in which this principle applies in competition law. In the case of Article 81, it means that where this Article prohibits or permits specific conduct, that conduct cannot be respectively permitted or prohibited by national law. In the case of Article 82, the effect of this rule is to create a 'double barrier': an agreement or practice must be permitted by both Community law and the relevant national law if it is to be legal (see further p 41).

Although at one time there was resistance on the part of some courts in some Member States to the principle of supremacy, it now finds more or less total acceptance in all Member States.[37]

Directly applicable EU law is therefore part of the national law of all 25 Member States of the EU. This means that certain Articles of the Treaty of Rome, all EC Regulations and, in certain circumstances, EC Directives, may be invoked in national courts, conferring rights and duties on the state and on individuals.

In practice this may mean, for example, that a national court has to declare void a contract that would be perfectly valid according to the relevant domestic law. Alternatively, it might mean that a national court, or even a national competition authority,[38] was obliged to refuse to apply a domestic statute, if the statute was in conflict with EU legislation. However, note that in the context of Article 82 of the EC Treaty, which prohibits abuse of a dominant position, the rules operate to produce a 'double barrier' so that EU law does not have the effect of overriding more restrictive national law.

1.6 WHAT DOES EU DISTRIBUTION LAW CONSIST OF?

Most EU distribution law, and most of this book, is concerned with competition rules. The competition rules applicable to the distribution activities of private (as well as public) enterprises are contained in Articles 81 and 82 of the EC Treaty and

---

[36] Case 6/64 [1964] ECR 585, [1964] CMLR 425.

[37] For an example of a case in which the UK House of Lords reaffirmed its acceptance of the rule of supremacy of Community law see *R v Secretary of State for Transport, ex parte Factortame Ltd (No 2)* [1990] 3 CMLR 375.

[38] Case C-198/01 *CIF* [2003] ECR I-8055.

in secondary legislation adopted to implement those rules. Article 81(1) prohibits certain agreements and Article 81(2) states that they are void. Article 81(3) provides for exemption from this prohibition in certain circumstances. Article 82 prohibits abuse of a dominant position.

The relevant secondary competition legislation consists mainly of Regulations setting out detailed procedural rules and exempting certain categories of agreement from the prohibition contained in Article 81(1). There are also important Notices giving guidance on the interpretation of the Regulations, and on the competition law treatment of agreements of minor importance and vertical agreements.

Apart from competition law, another topic of particular relevance to distribution is the law relating to the protection of commercial agents. These rules are contained in a Directive and are discussed in Chapter 6.

Some other areas of legislation might legitimately be treated as 'distribution law'. For example, there is Community legislation on doorstep selling, and distance sales through means such as mail order and electronic commerce, as well as on advertising and liability for damage caused by defective products. Although manufacturers and distributors should be aware of these, they are concerned essentially with consumer protection and so are outside the scope of this book, which focuses on competition law and other rules specific to the relationship between supplier and distributor.

Similarly, the rules of free movement of goods contained in Articles 28 to 30 of the Treaty are of relevance to distributors. Member States are strictly limited in the restrictions they may impose on the circulation of goods from other Member States. The rules extend beyond direct import restrictions to any national laws which put goods imported from another Member State at a disadvantage. The impact of these rules on intellectual property rights is particularly important, since they may, for example, prevent, a supplier in one country from using his intellectual property rights to stop a third party distributor from repackaging his goods and selling them under a different name in another Member State. These rules are not covered in this book as they concern the restrictive effects of national legislation rather than those of agreements between suppliers and distributors. Thorough treatment of the whole of this area of the law is to be found in Peter Oliver's *Free Movement of Goods in the European Community*.[39]

In some situations distribution agreements may involve other aspects of intellectual property, such as knowhow, patent or software licensing, in which case more specialised texts should be consulted. Similarly, the broadcasting, telecommunications and utilities sectors are subject to regulatory regimes which are outside the scope of this book.

In 1991, at the request of the Council, the Commission drew up a document entitled *Towards a Single Market in Distribution*.[40] In this, the Commission

---

[39] Above n 12.
[40] COM(91)41 of 11 March 1991. See also the European Commission's Green Paper on Commerce COM(96)530.

outlined its plans for action to ensure that the distributive trades were able to meet the challenges of and take full advantage of the opportunities offered by the single European market. When discussing the way in which divergent national legislation and regulations may hamper developments in this direction, the Commission expressed a strong preference for as few regulatory constraints as possible. Instead, it preferred to rely on consultative mechanisms leading to self-regulation:

> National and local regulations affecting commercial activity are extensive and reflect the predominantly national or local character of the commercial sector . . . there is no case for community legislation except in very limited cases where differences between national rules threaten to inhibit the internationalisation of the sector—and in particular where the marketing method is intrinsically transnational in character.
>
> Even in these cases the Commission considers that the process of trade should be subject to as few regulatory constraints as possible. The best approach may therefore be to use consultative mechanisms to explore the scope for solutions based on self-regulation. This approach seems likely to prove particularly appropriate in dealing with new problems, where rapid changes in commercial methods and technology may give rise to a demand for regulation (para 3.1).

Two examples were cited of areas in which such self-regulation had already been introduced. One was the issue of precontractual preliminaries to the conclusion of franchise agreements which is the subject of a code of conduct adopted by the European Franchise Association in 1990. Another is the area of electronic payments: trade federations representing financial institutions and retailers have co-operated to produce codes of conduct governing the relations between card issue distributors and cardholders in line with the relevant Commission Recommendations.[41] (Recommendations are not legally binding.)

Since then legal developments specifically applicable to distribution (except for those concerned with competition) have tended to take the form of non-binding Recommendations, agreements and codes of conduct rather than binding Regulations, Directives or Decisions. Exceptions to this rule will occur where such 'soft law' proves ineffective, when the Commission is likely to propose binding legislation. An example of this is the decision to prohibit 'pyramid selling' through the proposed Directive on unfair commercial practices,[42] though this is mainly due to the fact that the prohibition is seen as a consumer protection measure rather than a measure regulating relations between business parties.

---

[41] Recs 87/598/EEC, OJ 1987 L365/72 and 88/590/EEC, OJ 1988 L317/55.

[42] COM(2003)356, 18 June 2003 is a proposed Directive concerning unfair business-to-consumer commercial practices and Annex 1 includes a prohibition on pyramid selling.

2

EU Competition Law

KEY POINTS

- EU competition law prohibits certain anti-competitive agreements which affect trade between Member States. For example, agreement terms banning exports or fixing prices will usually be void and the European Commission or national competition authorities may impose fines on the parties to them.
- Other anti-competitive agreements such as some exclusivity arrangements and non-compete clauses are exempted from this prohibition if they fall within the scope of a 'block exemption' or if they satisfy certain substantive criteria.
- EU law also prohibits abusive unilateral behaviour by businesses which have a dominant market position. No exemption from this prohibition is available.
- Such agreements and unilateral acts may infringe EU competition rules even though they only involve businesses in a single Member State, if they have an effect on inter-state trade.
- EU competition law is not applicable in situations where there is no appreciable effect on trade between Member States, but national competition law may apply.
- Responsibility for assessing whether their conduct infringes EU competition rules falls primarily on the parties themselves, subject to the control of the courts and authorities in the event of a dispute or complaint.
- Businesses which infringe EU competition law risk not only the imposition of fines and the unenforceability of any infringing contractual clause, but also damages claims which may be brought in national courts by injured parties.
- The European Commission and most national competition authorities have powers, if they suspect infringement of EU competition rules, to request information from businesses and to make unannounced inspections of company premises and records. In some cases private homes may be inspected.

Treaty of Rome (EC Treaty)

Articles 81 and 82 (Appendix 1)

EC Regulations

Council Regulation (EC) 1/2003 of 16 December 2002 on the implementation of
 the rules on competition laid down in Articles 81 and 82 (Appendix 2)
Commission Regulation (EC) 773/2004 of 7 April 2004 relating to the conduct of
 proceedings by the Commission pursuant to Articles 81 and 82 (implementing
 Regulation 1/2003) (Appendix 6)

EC Notices

Commission Notice on agreements of minor importance (*de minimis*) (Appendix 8)
Commission Notice on the definition of relevant market for the purpose of
Community competition law, OJ 1997 C372/5, [1998] 4 CMLR 177
Commission Notice on co-operation within the network of competition author-
 ities, OJ 2004 C101/43
Commission Notice on co-operation between the Commission and the courts of
 the EU Member States in the application of Articles 81 and 82, OJ 2004 C101/54
Commission Notice on the handling of complaints by the Commission under
 Articles 81 and 82, OJ 2004 C101/65
Commission Notice on informal guidance relating to novel questions concerning
 Articles 81 and 82 that arise in individual cases (guidance letters), OJ 2004 C101/78
Commission Notice–Guidelines on the effect on trade concept contained in
 Articles 81 and 82, OJ 2004 C101/81
Commission Notice–Guidelines on the application of Article 81(3), OJ 2004
 C101/97

2.1 INTRODUCTION

The competition provisions of the Treaty of Rome directly affecting private parties involved in distribution agreements are Articles 81 and 82. They deal respectively with anti-competitive agreements and with abuse of a dominant position. Their purpose is to ensure the maintenance, throughout the common market, of the benefits that flow from the existence of a competitive market environment. Certain kinds of agreements and behaviour are therefore prohibited and can be penalised.

Distribution contracts are normally 'vertical agreements': this means that the parties to the agreement are active at different stages of the production and marketing process and are therefore not direct competitors. Examples are distribution contracts between a manufacturer and a wholesaler, or between a wholesaler and a retailer. 'Horizontal agreements' are those made between competitors, such as an agreement between two or more retailers or between two or more manufacturers. Article 81 can apply to both vertical and horizontal agreements.

A very common way in which Article 81 is applied to distribution agreements is to prohibit export bans (where the distribution contract provides that goods are not to be sold outside a particular country or territory) or other provisions for market-sharing between different distributors, or arrangements granting absolute territorial exclusivity to distributors. Resale price-fixing will also infringe Article 81.

Article 82, on the other hand, is more commonly applied to producers or suppliers, for example, for refusal to supply or for operating unacceptable fidelity rebate schemes, or discriminatory pricing practices.

The political aim of market integration has had a strong influence on EU competition policy, which means that any agreement of any significance that tends to divide up markets along national boundaries will fall within the scope of the prohibition in Article 81. This, of course, includes many exclusive distribution, exclusive purchase, selective distribution and franchising agreements. Fortunately, many such agreements fall within the terms of one of the 'block exemption' Regulations. These exempt, among other things, a degree of territorial protection for parties to certain types of contract, though without ever permitting a complete ban on sales outside any given territory.

The summary that follows of the way in which these provisions are applied covers both substantive and procedural aspects of EU competition law but is necessarily concise and concentrates on those aspects of the law of direct relevance to distribution agreements. More detailed works on EU competition law should be consulted for further information on this subject (see p 199).

2.2 ARTICLE 81(1)

Article 81 begins by laying down a broad and general prohibition in Article 81(1):

The following shall be prohibited as incompatible with the common market: all agreements between undertakings, decisions by associations of undertakings and concerted practices which may affect trade between Member States and which have as their object or effect the prevention, restriction or distortion of competition within the common market

and goes on to give a non-exhaustive list of examples of violations of this prohibition; these are agreements which:

(a) directly or indirectly fix purchase or selling prices or any other trading conditions;
(b) limit or control production, markets, technical development or investment;
(c) share markets or sources of supply;
(d) apply dissimilar conditions to equivalent transactions with other trading parties, thereby placing them at a competitive disadvantage;
(e) make the conclusion of contracts subject to acceptance by the other parties of supplementary obligations which, by their nature or according to commercial usage, have no connection with the subject of such contracts.

'Agreements'

This concept covers both legally binding contracts as well as a wide range of informal arrangements which fall short of legally enforceable contracts. Although distribution agreements are usually legally binding agreements, it is not possible to avoid the application of the competition rules by not putting an agreement in writing or by relying on a so-called 'gentlemen's agreement'.[1] Similarly, standard conditions appearing on the back of each of a series of invoices will be regarded as terms of agreement between the parties, even if from the point of view of national contract law they were never terms of the individual contracts.[2]

Furthermore, the Commission has long treated as 'agreements' certain arguably unilateral measures taken by suppliers to restrict parallel trade in their goods, and until recently the European Court of Justice (ECJ) had upheld this approach. However, it is now clear that there are limits to this concept. In its *Bayer* Decision the Commission stretched the concept of 'agreement' further than ever before in order to fine Bayer €3 million for taking measures to prevent parallel imports between Member States of its heart drug Adalat. Bayer had set up systems to identify wholesalers in low-price countries who were engaging in parallel exports to high-price countries,[3] and reduced its supplies to them accordingly. The wholesalers resorted to various means of obtaining additional supplies, such as placing orders through smaller wholesalers who were not being monitored by Bayer. The Commission found that this de facto export ban constituted an agreement.

---

[1] Case 41/69 *ACF Chemiefarma* [1970] ECR 661, [1970] CMLR 43; *National Panasonic*, OJ 1982 L354/28, [1983] 1 CMLR 497, para 43.

[2] Case 277/87 *Sandoz v Commission* [1990] I ECR 45, [1990] 4 CMLR 242.

[3] In some Member States pharmaceutical prices are state-controlled and prices in these countries tend to be substantially lower than in countries where the market is freer, creating an incentive for purchasers in low-price states to export to high-price states. Manufacturers have therefore long wrestled with the question of what measures they may take to stop such 'parallel trade' which causes them a substantial loss of revenue and certain other problems.

The Court of First Instance (CFI), and later the ECJ, held that the Commission had stretched the notion of 'agreement' too far in this case, and that it had only shown unilateral conduct on the part of Bayer (reduction of supplies), so that Article 81 did not apply. It attached importance to the fact that although Bayer openly admitted that it intended to reduce parallel trade, the Commission had not shown either that Bayer had made any request, or communicated its policy, to its wholesalers, so that there was nothing that they could be said to have acquiesced in, even tacitly.[4]

The *Bayer* decision concerned a simple commercial relationship consisting of a series of orders for supplies. The issue may be more complex in the context of selective distribution, though the same basic principle applies. For example, in *AEG Telefunken*,[5] refusal by AEG to supply a particular dealer was held to infringe Article 81(1), on the grounds that such action formed part of an agreement between AEG and its distributors that only certain types of distributors should receive supplies of AEG's goods. This type of conduct is particularly common in the context of selective distribution and the 'agreement' issue will be considered again in Chapter 4.

The word 'agreements' covers not only horizontal arrangements, but also vertical arrangements. This is very important in the context of distribution networks and agreements, which normally involve vertical relationships. At one time it was argued by some that vertical arrangements were not caught by Article 81(1) at all, but it has long been established that, although horizontal agreements are normally treated more severely than vertical ones, both are potentially within the scope of Article 81.[6]

The borderline between 'agreements', 'decisions' and 'concerted practices' is not clearly delineated and it is not necessary that it be so, since Community law applies in the same way to all of them.[7]

'Decisions by Associations'

This expression includes not only the rules and regulations of the association that are accepted by its members, but also non-binding recommendations made by the association to its members.[8]

'Concerted Practices'

Virtually any kind of knowing co-operation between parties will amount to a concerted practice. The Court has defined the concept as:

---

[4] Cases T-41/96 [2000] ECR II-381, [2001] 4 CMLR 126 and C-3/01, 6 January 2004 (not yet officially reported), [2004] 4 CMLR 653.

[5] Case 107/82 [1983] ECR 3151, [1984] 3 CMLR 325.

[6] Cases 56 and 58/64 *Consten & Grundig v Commission* [1966] ECR 299, [1966] CMLR 418.

[7] See eg *Nintendo*, OJ 2003 L255/33, [2004] 4 CMLR 421, para 256.

[8] Case 8/72 *Vereeniging van Cementhandelaren v Commission* [1972] ECR 977, [1973] CMLR 7 (price recommendations). See also Case T-14/93 *Railway Tickets* [1995] ECR II-1503, [1996] 5 CMLR 40 though the Commission Decision was annulled on procedural grounds.

a form of co-ordination between undertakings which, without going so far as to amount to an agreement properly so called, knowingly substitutes a practical co-operation between them for the rules of competition.[9]

The principle is easy to state, but in practice it is extremely difficult to distinguish between independent response to competitors' behaviour, and collusion between competitors. This is particularly true in an oligopolistic market in which it is easy for the small number of competing firms to find out about each other's behaviour on the market and therefore to react to it almost immediately it occurs.

In the *Sugar* case the Court said that the rule against concerted practices did not 'deprive economic operators of the right to adapt themselves intelligently to the existing and anticipated conduct of their competitors' but that it did, however:

> strictly preclude any direct or indirect contact between such operators, the object or effect whereof is either to influence the conduct on the market of an actual or potential competitor or to disclose to such a competitor the course of conduct which they themselves have decided to adopt or contemplate adopting on the market.[10]

It is not clear precisely what the Commission is required to prove in order to establish such a concerted practice. However, in practice the Commission may make a presumption of a concerted practice in a situation in which it considers that there can be no other explanation in the circumstances.[11] Therefore, in practice a party should always be prepared to produce an alternative explanation of its conduct.

'Undertakings'

'Undertakings' include any independent economic actor or entity: a company, a partnership, an association, a trust company, an individual or a group of individuals may therefore be an undertaking for these purposes. An undertaking does not have to be profit-making. The precise legal characterisation that would be applied under national law is not of direct relevance, and certainly it is not necessary that an undertaking have legal personality. As is generally the case in the interpretation of Community competition law, an economic rather than a legal approach is taken: what is important is the fact that an independent economic activity is being carried out.[12]

Agreements with agents (unless they bear certain commercial risks) for some purposes fall outside the scope of Article 81(1). However, the notion of agency in this context is narrow and can therefore be relied on only in limited circumstances. This subject is covered in detail in Chapter 6.

Similarly, agreements between members of a single group of companies will not be caught, unless the individual companies enjoy a high degree of independence

---

[9] Case 48/69 *ICI v Commission* [1972] ECR 619, [1972] CMLR 557, para 64.
[10] Cases 40–48 etc/73 *Suiker Unie v Commission* [1975] ECR 1663, [1976] 1 CMLR 295, para 174.
[11] *Woodpulp* OJ 1985 L85/1, on appeal Cases 89 etc/85 *Woodpulp* [1993] ECR 1307, [1993] 4 CMLR 407.
[12] Case 170/83 *Hydrotherm v Andreoli* [1984] ECR 2999, [1985] 3 CMLR 224.

of action, since the group will be treated as a single undertaking, or 'one economic unit'.[13] Again, it is irrelevant that a subsidiary may have separate legal personality from its parent company: the crucial factor is whether it enjoys economic independence.[14] It is not independent if its parent company exercises a decisive influence on its commercial policies such as distribution and pricing.[15]

Nor can a contractual clause escape the application of Article 81(1) on the grounds that it was inserted by an officer of the company without proper authority.[16]

Market Definition

No requirement to define the relevant market appears in Article 81, and in some cases it will be clear that, even on the narrowest or widest view of the market that could reasonably be taken, the outcome of the application of Article 81 will be the same. However, in other cases the result of the Article 81 analysis may differ according to different views of market definition that may be taken. For example, conduct may affect competition appreciably on one market but not on a possible broader one, or the parties may have market shares falling beneath the thresholds of the *de minimis* Notice on the basis of one market definition, but not on the basis of a possible narrower definition. The concept is also extremely important in establishing whether a company is 'dominant' on the market for the purposes of Article 82.

Both the geographical market and the product market must be defined. They are subject to change over time, so that market definitions used in previous cases may not apply in a later case. The Commission has published a detailed Notice on market definition,[17] and market definition in the context of distribution is discussed in Chapter 3.

Geographical Market

The relevant geographical market is the area where the parties do business and in which the goods are subject to homogeneous competitive conditions. For example, in *United Brands*,[18] where the product in question was bananas, countries in which a special preferential regime applied to banana imports from certain countries were excluded from the relevant geographical market. Retail markets are frequently national, regional or even smaller, depending on consumers' purchasing habits.

---

[13] At one time it was also important that the agreement could be characterised as the internal distribution of tasks, but the Court of First Instance in Case T-102/92 *Viho Europe v Commission* [1995] ECR II-17, [1995] 4 CMLR 299 contradicted this and its judgment was upheld by the ECJ in Case C-73/95 [1996] ECR I-545, [1997] 4 CMLR 419. See also *Interbrew*, 1996 Annual Report on Competition Policy, p 136.

[14] See *Viho*, above n 13.

[15] Case 48/69 *ICI v Commission* [1972] ECR 619, [1972] CMLR 557; see also *AEG-Telefunken*, above n 5.

[16] See *Viho*, above n 13.

[17] Commission Notice on the definition of relevant market for the purposes of Community competition law OJ 1997 C372/3.

[18] Case 27//76 *United Brands Co v Commission* [1978] ECR 207, [1978] 1 CMLR 429.

Product Market

The relevant product market normally consists of the product or service in question and all products or services considered by the consumer to be substitutable for them, in view of their characteristics, price and intended use (this is the concept of 'demand substitutability'). So, in considering whether a distributor of bananas has a dominant position, the product market for bananas must be defined: for example, it must be decided whether, from the point of view of the consumer, apples can be considered a substitute for bananas.[19] In some circumstances 'supply substitutability' may also be taken into account: this will be the case where products are not substitutable from the user's point of view, but the supplier can with little difficulty switch to producing one rather than the other. An example is different grades of paper: most users require a specific quality, thickness and finish, but the supplier can fairly easily adjust his machines to produce the various different grades.

In practice the Commission has often defined markets very narrowly. For example, in *Boosey & Hawkes*[20] the relevant product market was defined by the Commission as brass band instruments for 'British-style' brass bands. A producer may even be dominant in the market of spare parts for its products if these spare parts are not available anywhere else, for example, because they are protected by intellectual property rights.[21]

'Which May Affect Trade Between Member States'

This element of Article 81 is of dual importance. It is an essential substantive requirement for establishing an infringement of Article 81(1). It also governs the choice of law (EU or national) in the context of proceedings in national courts and national competition authorities (see p 42). For this reason the Commission has published Guidelines on the effect on trade concept, which provide a detailed summary of ECJ and CFI case law and Commission practice on this point.[22]

An agreement satisfies this requirement:

> where it is possible to foresee with a sufficient degree of probability that it may have an influence, direct or indirect, actual or potential, on the pattern of trade between Member States.[23]

The requirement of an 'effect on trade between Member States' has been broadly interpreted by the Commission and ECJ. In the early case of *Consten & Grundig* it was said that:

---

[19] In *United Brands* the Court held that they could not.

[20] OJ 1987 L286/36, [1988] 4 CMLR 67.

[21] *Hugin/Liptons* OJ 1978 L22/23, [1978] CMLR D19 (reversed on appeal on another ground: Case 22/78 *Hugin v Commission* [1979] ECR 1869, [1979] 3 CMLR 345).

[22] OJ 2004 C101/81.

[23] Case 61/80 *Stremsel v Commission* [1981] ECR 851, [1982] 1 CMLR 240, para 14.

what is particularly important is whether the agreement is capable of constituting a threat, either direct or indirect, actual or potential, to freedom of trade between member states in a manner which might harm the attainment of the objectives of a single market between states. Thus the fact that the agreement encourages an increase, even a large one, in the volume of trade between states is not sufficient to exclude the possibility that the agreement may 'affect' such trade in the above-mentioned manner.

In other words, it extends not only to restrictions causing a reduction in the flow of trade, but also to any restrictions altering the pattern of trade that would otherwise exist, even if such an effect is only potential.

As a result of this broad interpretation, very many commercial agreements may be held to be within the scope of Article 81(1). Thus, although this requirement should always be considered, it is rare that an agreement of any economic importance is not held to satisfy it.

In order to establish whether trade between Member States is affected, it is necessary to look at the effect of the agreement as a whole rather than at particular clauses in isolation.[24] Thus, it is possible that an individual restrictive clause which in isolation would have no effect on inter-Member State trade can fall within the ambit of Article 81(1) when combined with other clauses in the agreement, if the agreement as a whole has such an effect.

As already stated, the requirement that there be an effect on trade between Member States has been applied so as to bring within the terms of Article 81(1) an unexpected range of contracts. This is true of many agreements that might appear to be of only national importance and not to affect trade with other Member States. For example, the Court has considered that an agreement between Belgian asphalt producers had such an effect.[25] Even a national newspaper distribution network has been found to fall within Article 81(1).[26] More recent cases involving retail banking services have had the opposite outcome,[27] and it may be that the Commission and the ECJ are being influenced by the fact that most Member States now have appropriate national laws for dealing with such situations. However, the more of a reality the Single Market becomes, the more likely it is that commercial practices in one Member State will affect trade in another.[28] In addition, in the *Dutch Industrial Gases*[29] cartel case the Commission held that although only Dutch subsidiaries were involved in the cartel, the effects of the conduct flowed through to the multinational parent companies through dividends paid up the group chain, which meant that there was an effect on trade between Member States. This approach could bring a very wide range of apparently local agreements within the scope of Article 81.

---

[24] Case 193/83 *Windsurfing v Commission* [1986] ECR 611, [1986] 3 CMLR 489, para 97.

[25] Case 246/86 *Belasco v Commission* [1989] ECR 2117, [1991] CMLR 96.

[26] Case 126/80 *Salonia v Poidomani* [1981] ECR 1563, [1982] 1 CMLR 64.

[27] Case C-215/96 *Bagnasco v BPN* [1999] ECR I-135, [1999] 4 CMLR 624; *Dutch Banks* OJ 1999 L271/28, [2000] 4 CMLR 137.

[28] See also Guidelines on the effect on trade concept OJ 2004 C101/81, paras 77–92.

[29] OJ 2003 L84/1, [2003] 5 CMLR 144, para 371.

Further, even if there is negligible export of the goods in question, it is sufficient to infringe Article 81(1) that those goods are used to manufacture other goods which are the subject of intra-Community trade.[30] Similarly, it is possible in some circumstances for agreements ostensibly not concerning EU territory, such as an export ban imposed on operators in Ukraine and Russia, to have the requisite effect on trade.[31]

The effect on trade must be 'appreciable'.[32] The Commission's Notice on the effect on trade concept includes quantitative criteria which will normally indicate the absence of an effect on trade, even if the agreement includes 'hard-core' restrictions (such as price-fixing clauses or clauses providing for absolute territorial protection):

- the parties are small and/or medium-sized undertakings[33] or
- the parties' aggregate market share on any affected market does not exceed 5 per cent and
  —horizontal agreements (eg between two suppliers): the aggregate annual EU turnover of the parties' corporate groups in the products covered by the agreement (or, in the case of joint buying, the parties' combined purchases of such products) does not exceed €40 million;
  —vertical agreements (eg between supplier and distributor): the supplier's aggregate annual EU turnover in such products (or, in the case of licensing, the aggregate turnover of the licensor and licensee or, in the case of several purchase agreements, the buyer's combined purchases) does not exceed €40 million.

In such cases there is a rebuttable presumption that trade is not affected and undertakings relying on these thresholds in good faith will not be fined. Note that in the case of distribution networks, sales throughout the entire network are taken into account.

In addition, where an agreement is by its very nature capable of affecting trade between Member States (eg agreements concerning imports or exports, or covering several Member States), an effect on trade is rebuttably presumed when these thresholds are exceeded. An exception to this rule is that the 5 per cent threshold does not apply where the agreement covers only part of a Member State.

'Object or Effect the Prevention, Restriction or Distortion of Competition'

This requirement overlaps to some extent with the requirement that there be an effect on trade between Member States, and has also been broadly interpreted by

---

[30] Case 123/83 *BNIC v Clair* [1985] ECR 391, [1985] 2 CMLR 430.

[31] Case C-306/96 *Javico v Yves St Laurent* [1998] ECR I-1983, [1998] 5 CMLR 172. See also Guidelines on the effect on trade concept OJ 2004 C101/81, paras 100–9.

[32] This is a separate question to that addressed by the Commission's *de minimis* Notice (see p 28).

[33] As defined in Commission Recommendation 2033/361/EC, OJ 2003 L124/36 (fewer than 250 employees and either an annual turnover not exceeding €50 million or an annual balance sheet total not exceeding €43 million).

the Court and Commission. However, there are indications in the Commission's Notice on the application of Article 81(3) that it may interpret it more narrowly in the future. Article 81 is applicable to both horizontal and vertical restrictions, but the Commission is particularly severe in its judgment of horizontal restrictions.[34]

Restrictions by Object

Some classes of restriction, such as resale price-fixing, market-sharing and non-compete clauses, are considered as having an anti-competitive object. In such cases an actual effect on competition need not be shown. It is enough that the purpose is clearly anti-competitive. Nor is it an object in the subjective sense that is required: the Commission is not required to give evidence of the actual intentions of the parties. Rather, the terms of the agreement itself are decisive.

Restrictions by Effect

Other types of restriction, which do not have an anti-competitive object, will only infringe Article 81(1) if they have an anti-competitive effect. This depends on the agreement itself, but also on the surrounding market circumstances.

The requirement that the economic and market situation surrounding an agreement must be taken into account in assessing its compatibility with Article 81(1) means that it is frequently extremely difficult to come to a firm opinion as to whether that Article is infringed or not. In any case, a meaningful assessment can only be made with the fullest possible knowledge of the precise market for the product, market structure and market trends in the Community Member States, individually and as a whole. The economic analysis required can be complex, and the European Commission and national authority officials dealing with such cases comprise economists as well as lawyers.

Also, the fact that a distribution contract is one of many making up a network may affect its legal status: an agreement between a Belgian brewery and a Belgian bar has been held to infringe Article 81(1), since it had to be considered in the context of a large number of similar arrangements making up the distribution network.[35] However, for an effect on competition to be found, the individual agreement in question must itself contribute significantly to such an effect.[36] Similarly, the existence of a number of similar networks on the relevant market must be taken into consideration.[37] (See also p 83).

---

[34] For an example in the beer distribution sector see eg IP 94/345 of 28 April 1994 re *Interbrew/Carlsberg*.

[35] Case 23/67 *Brasserie de Haecht v Wilkin No 1* [1967] ECR 407, [1968] CMLR 26.

[36] Case C-234/89 *Delimitis v Henninger Brau AG* [1991] ECR 1935, [1992] 5 CMLR 210; Case C-279/95 *Langnese-Iglo v Commission* [1998] ECR I-5609, [1998] 5 CMLR 933; Case T-9/93 *Schöller Lebensmittel v Commission* [1995] ECR II-1611, [1995] 5 CMLR 602.

[37] Case 26/76 *Metro v Commission (No 1)* [1977] ECR 1875, [1978] 2 CMLR 1.

Notice on agreements of minor importance

The requirement that there be an effect on competition is, however, subject to a *de minimis* limitation, which is generally expressed as the requirement that there be an appreciable effect on competition.[38] In order to provide guidance on the scope of this rule the Commission has published a Notice on agreements of minor importance which do not appreciably restrict competition (Appendix 8).

The Notice sets thresholds based on the parties' market shares, below which the Commission will not institute proceedings or impose fines. National authorities and courts are not legally bound by the Commission's Notice, but it states that it is intended to provided them with guidance, and in practice they can be expected to follow it. The thresholds are:

- horizontal agreements[39] (eg between two suppliers): the aggregate market share of the parties' corporate groups on any of the relevant markets affected by the agreement does not exceed 10 per cent;
- vertical agreements (eg between supplier and distributor): the market share of each of the parties' corporate groups on any of the relevant markets affected by the agreement does not exceed 15 per cent.

However, it should be noted that these thresholds do not apply to hard core restrictions such as price-fixing clauses or clauses providing for absolute territorial protection, which may infringe Article 81(1) however small the parties' market shares.

Alternatively, an agreement will be *de minimis* if the parties are small or medium-sized businesses.[40]

Where a number of parallel networks of supply or distribution agreements have a cumulative foreclosure effect (hindering competitors' access to distribution outlets) on the relevant market then the threshold is 5 per cent for horizontal and vertical agreements. Such an effect is said to be unlikely to occur where less than 30 per cent of the relevant market is covered by such similar networks.

Ancillary restrictions

Restrictive clauses have sometimes been held to fall outside the scope of Article 81(1) on the grounds that, though restrictive, they are 'ancillary' to the main agreement. This means that they are directly related and objectively necessary to the main transaction, which is not itself anti-competitive, and are proportionate to it. This will frequently be the case for certain types of restrictive clauses in the context of selective distribution (see Chapter 4) and franchising (see Chapter 5).

---

[38] Case 5/69 *Volk v Vervaecke* [1969] ECR 295, [1969] CMLR 273.

[39] The Notice defines 'potential competition' very widely, so that many agreements which one would not expect to be horizontal do in fact so qualify in this context.

[40] See above n 33.

Categories of restrictions

In the next chapter a number of specific clauses and practices of relevance to distribution agreements in general are considered in turn. Selective distribution, franchising and agency contracts will then be considered in detail in separate chapters.

2.3 ARTICLE 81(2)

Any contractual clause infringing the prohibition described above, and not exempted under Article 81(3) (see below) is declared by Article 81(2) to be void: it was confirmed early on by the ECJ that this paragraph is automatically effective, without the need for the Commission or any other authority to take any decision or even to know of the offending agreement.[41]

National courts are competent to declare an agreement void, so it is possible to raise Article 81(2) as a defence to a contractual action in a national court. The agreement is void not only as between the parties to the agreement but also with respect to third parties.[42] This means that a party may invoke as a defence to legal proceedings the nullity of an agreement to which he is not a party.[43]

Only the offending clauses are void under Article 81, and not the whole agreement.[44] The consequences of such partial nullity of an agreement depend on the relevant national law.[45] Under English law the essential question will be whether the void clause or clauses are severable from the remainder of the contract: in *Chemidus Wavin* Buckley LJ stated:

> It seems to me that in applying Article [81] to an English contract one may well have to consider whether, after the excisions required by the Article of the Treaty have been made from the contract, the contract could be said to fail for lack of consideration or any other ground, or whether the contract could be so changed in its character as not to be the sort of contract that the parties intended to enter into at all.[46]

Under English law there is no possibility for the Court to rewrite the offending contract term. This can lead to difficulties where, for example, a distribution agreement contains provision for an exclusive territory for the distributor. If the exclusivity clause is removed then only one of two results is possible. The entire contract may be held void, on the basis that the other terms agreed were dependent on exclusivity, and this will lead to confusion regarding orders, deliveries and

---

[41] Case 127/73 *BRT v SABAM No 1* [1974] ECR 313, [1974] 2 CMLR 238.
[42] Case 22/71 *Beguelin Import Co v GL Import-Export SA* [1971] ECR 949, [1972] CMLR 81.
[43] eg *British Leyland v TI Silencers* [1981] 2 CMLR 75 (UK Court of Appeal).
[44] Case 56/65 *La Technique Minière v Maschinenbau Ulm GmbH* [1966] ECR 234, [1966] CMLR 357.
[45] Case 319/82 *Société de Vente de Ciments et Betons de l'Est SA v Kerpen & Kerpen GmbH & Co KG* [1983] ECR 4173, [1985] 1 CMLR 511.
[46] [1978] 3 CMLR 514 at 519 (Saskatchewan Court of Appeal).

obligations already incurred in application of the agreement. Alternatively, the contract may remain valid, but with the exclusivity clause removed. However, since the Court has no power to adapt the contract terms to take account of the lack of exclusivity, the remaining terms may now be commercially unjust or unacceptable to one or other party.

In some other legal systems it may be possible for the Court to rewrite the contract to some extent, so as to remove the exclusivity clause or in some way to adapt it. For example, a term providing for absolute exclusivity could be rewritten to provide only for a ban on active sales outside the distributor's territory. Depending on the circumstances, this might have the effect of bringing the contract within the scope of exemption through Article 81(3) or a block exemption, making it legal and enforceable, at least for the future.

2.4 ARTICLE 81(3)

The widely drawn prohibition contained in Article 81(1) is tempered by Article 81(3), which provides that an arrangement infringing that prohibition may benefit from exemption if it:

> contributes to improving the production or distribution of goods or to promoting technical or economic progress, while allowing consumers a fair share of the resulting benefit, and which does not:
>
> (a) impose on the undertakings concerned restrictions which are not indispensable to the attainment of these objectives;
> (b) afford such undertakings the possibility of eliminating competition in respect of a substantial part of the products in question.

This clause contains four separate requirements, all discussed in detail in the Commission's Guidelines on the application of Article 81(3).[47]

(1) Improving Production or Distribution or Promoting Technical or Economic Progress

The restriction may contribute to improving distribution, for example, because it effects a rationalisation which reduces costs, or provides sufficient incentive for resellers to join a network, or improves the speed or quality of the distribution service. Cost-related efficiencies must be able to be proved and quantified, and qualitative efficiencies explained in detail. They must be substantial and specifically brought about by the agreement.

Note that non-economic benefits, such as environmental protection and promotion of cultural diversity are not mentioned, suggesting that they should not be

---

[47] OJ 2004 C101/97.

considered. In the past such considerations have played a role in some cases, and this may be justified from a legal point of view by Treaty Articles which require them to be taken into account when applying other Treaty provisions.[48] However, in its very recent Guidelines on the application of Article 81(3) the Commission relies on ECJ and CFI cases to state that these should be taken into account only 'to the extent that they can be subsumed under the four conditions of Article 81(3)', which suggests that the Commission may be confining itself more strictly to consideration of economic benefits in the future.

(2) Consumers Receive Benefit

In the past this requirement was not often considered at length separately by the Commission, since the kind of improvements required under (1) were presumed to be passed onto consumers if there was a competitive market in the goods, as is required by Article 81(3)(b).[49] However, the Guidelines now require that the consumer (in the broad sense of the users of the product) benefit must be shown at least to compensate for any negative effects of the restrictions, so that the greater the restriction the greater the benefit that must be shown. This will be hard to prove in the case of qualitative benefits such as increased product variety or accessibility, and even in the case of price reductions it may be difficult to show precisely the impact of the restriction on price.

(3) No Indispensable Restrictions

If there is any less restrictive way of achieving the same improvement then exemption will not apply. The Commission's Guidelines require that the indispensability of the agreement be considered both with respect to the contract as a whole and its individual clauses.

(4) Competition not Substantially Eliminated

The agreement must not afford the undertakings the possibility of eliminating competition in respect of a substantial part of the products in question. In principle it is possible even for dominant firms to satisfy this requirement, since it refers

[48] eg Art151(4) TEU: 'the Community shall take cultural aspects into account in its actions under other provisions of this Treaty'.

[49] In some cases the benefit has not been economic, nor has it benefited individual purchasers: in *CECED* the Commission's exemption Decision referred to the reduction in environmentally harmful emissions which would be effected through the agreement, and said 'Such environmental results for society would adequately allow consumers a fair share of the benefits even if no benefits accrued to individual purchasers of machines', OJ 2000 L187/47, [2000] 5 CMLR 635. However, it may be that a more restrictive approach to this issue will be taken in the future.

to the effect of the agreement under consideration, and not to the market position of the parties. However, if the market affected by the distribution contract is not already subject to healthy competition, then in practice exemption is unlikely to apply, since even a slight further reduction in competition may cause the elimination of competition.

If these four substantive criteria are satisfied then the agreement benefits from exemption and does not infringe Article 81, and there is no need for any specific procedure to be followed. It is then fully legal and enforceable in a national court.[50] Note that exemption only applies as long as the four criteria are satisfied, so agreements and their market environment need to be kept under regular review. This means, for example, that a five-year non-compete clause which satisfied Article 81(3) at the outset of an arrangement but which two years later, because of the success of the product, is no longer 'indispensable', will cease to be enforceable. However, sunk costs and the need to recoup investment should be taken into account in making this assessment (Guidelines, para 44) and the Commission and national competition authorities would not normally accord priority to intervening in such cases.

The Commission's Guidelines make it clear that a party wishing to rely on Article 81(3) has a significant burden to discharge.[51] The stated aim of the Guidelines is to develop an economic methodology for applying Article 81(3), which must be applied 'in light of the circumstances specific to each case' and 'reasonably and flexibly', to establish whether an exemption is justified by economic efficiency gains. The detail given shows just how complex this may be, and the level of economic expertise that may need to be brought to bear. Particularly now that national courts and authorities, and the parties themselves, will more often than the Commission have to decide these issues, it may be that there will in the future be more focus on deciding whether or not Article 81(1) is infringed in the first place, and less discussion of Article 81(3), which appears so difficult to satisfy, particularly in the presence of high market shares. Some recent cases support this speculation (see p 80).

Although under the new procedural regime, applicable from 1 May 2004 and described below, assessment of arrangements under Articles 81(1) and 81(3) remains legally distinct, the procedural changes may lead in practice to their being examined together, particularly as much of the necessary economic analysis is relevant to both (though the burden of proof is different in each case).

Block exemptions

The Commission has the power to issue 'block exemption' Regulations which state that certain categories of agreement are treated as fulfilling the requirements of

---

[50] The application of Article 81(3) by arbitrators, as opposed to judges, raises several difficult issues. See eg Renato Nazzini, 'International Arbitration and Public Enforcement of Competition Law', [2004] ECLR 153.

[51] Art 2 of Reg 1/2003 states that the burden of proof is on that party.

Article 81(3).[52] If parties take care to draft an agreement so that it satisfies the requirements of a block exemption (in particular avoiding the inclusion of any of the forbidden or 'black-listed' clauses listed in the Regulation) then they enjoy the certainty that their arrangements are exempted, rather than having to rely on their own or their advisers' judgment on this issue. This is normally a much more attractive option than that of performing the economic and legal analysis necessary to establish that the agreement is outside the scope of Article 81(1), or to be reasonably certain that the substantive requirements of Article 81(3) are fulfilled.

At present two block exemptions exist for distribution agreements. One is applicable to all vertical agreements satisfying certain criteria, and the other applies only to distribution agreements concerning motor vehicles and their spare parts and after-sales services. They are mutually exclusive: motor vehicle distribution agreements are excluded from the scope of the block exemption Regulation on vertical restraints. Both will be analysed in detail in later chapters.

The fact that an agreement falls within the scope of a block exemption does not guarantee that it will not be found to infringe Article 82, which prohibits abuse of a dominant position.[53] This is stated explicitly in the Recitals to both the block exemption Regulation on vertical restraints and that on motor vehicle distribution.

Change of system on 1 May 2004

Before 1 May 2004 the procedural situation in respect of exemption under Article 81(3) was completely different. Only the Commission had the power to grant an exemption under Article 81(3). Thus, if a national court was called on to decide on the validity of a contract which had not been expressly exempted by the Commission, it had to confine itself to considering whether Article 81(1) was infringed, and, if so, whether a block exemption applied. Even if it seemed clear to the court that the Commission would have exempted the contract in question, that was irrelevant to the court's decision, unless the agreement had been notified to the Commission, in which case the court might stay proceedings to await the Decision of the Commission.

Under the new procedural regime, discussed in more detail later in this chapter, parties are spared the expense and time involved in approaching the Commission for an individual exemption, but they can no longer obtain the legal certainty that was available under this system.

---

[52] Block exemptions were first introduced at a time when exemption could only be granted by the Commission. Now that exemption is available automatically it might be more logical to replace the block exemptions with Guidelines, but block exemptions have been retained as they bind both the Commission and national courts and authorities and so provide more legal certainty than Guidelines.

[53] Case T-51/89 *TetraPak Rausing SA v Commission* [1990] ECR II-309, [1991] CMLR 334.

2.5 ARTICLE 82

This is the provision intended to deal with monopolies and undertakings with high levels of market power, and its application can lead to huge fines.[54] Whereas Article 81 covers arrangements involving co-operation between two or more businesses, Article 82 focuses on unilateral behaviour. Since the behaviour of a single company will only be of concern to competition law if it has a certain level of market power, Article 82 is only relevant to companies with a strong market position.

Before describing the way in which Article 82 has been applied until now, it is worth noting that there is a strong body of opinion in favour of a less formalistic and more economics-based approach to Article 82 cases than has characterised past Commission practice. The Commission's recent *Microsoft* Decision[55] goes in this direction, and it has indicated that it is seriously considering this general issue internally, with a view to issuing a Notice.[56] Such a Commission Notice cannot of course amend the wording of Article 82 or the related ECJ and CFI case law, but it can strongly influence policy choices as to which cases it pursues as a priority,[57] and this needs to be borne in mind when reading some of the older cases. However, the strength of this trend should not be exaggerated, particularly as the CFI recently upheld the Commission's *Michelin* Decision, which was based on a rigidly traditional approach.[58]

Article 82 states:

> Any abuse by one or more undertakings of a dominant position within the common market or in a substantial part of it shall be prohibited as incompatible with the common market in so far as it may affect trade between Member States.

The meaning of 'undertaking' and 'may affect trade between Member States' are the same as for Article 81 (see p 22 and p 24 respectively).

'Dominant Position'

First it is necessary to ascertain whether the undertaking is 'dominant': if it is in a position to take decisions without any real need to take into account the behaviour of other firms, then it has a dominant position:

---

[54] The largest competition law fine ever imposed on a single company was one of €497 million imposed on Microsoft for infringement of Article 82, 24 March 2004 (not yet officially reported, available on DG Comp's website); on appeal Case T-201/04, OJ 2004 C179/18.

[55] *Ibid.*

[56] See speeches by Director-General Philip Lowe and Commissioner Mario Monti at the Fordham Conference, October 2003 (available on DG Comp's website).

[57] However, private enforcement in national courts should continue on the basis of the case law of the CFI and ECJ, which does not yet show signs of change.

[58] Case T-203/01 *Michelin v Commission (No 2)* [2003] ECR II-4071, [2004] 4 CMLR 923.

Undertakings are in a dominant position when they have the power to behave independently, which puts them in a position to act without taking into account their competitors, purchasers or suppliers. That is the position when, because of their share of the market, or of their share of the market combined with the availability of technical knowledge, raw materials or capital, they have the power to determine prices or to control production or distribution for a significant part of the products in question. This power does not necessarily have to derive from an absolute domination permitting the undertakings which hold it to eliminate all will on the part of their economic partners, but it is enough that they be strong enough as a whole to ensure to those undertakings an overall independence of behaviour, even if there are differences in intensity in their influence on the different partial markets.[59]

If a company is not dominant on its own, it may be jointly dominant with other companies, even if its relationship with them is vertical. For example, in *Irish Sugar* the CFI held that the manufacturer Irish Sugar was jointly dominant with its distributor Sugar Distributors Ltd, because of its shareholding and board representation in the other company, certain policy-making structures and economic links in the form of various agreements, including an exclusive supply agreement.[60]

It is often hard to establish whether or not an undertaking has a 'dominant position'. Given that dominance refers to the possession of a certain degree of market strength, it is first crucial to define the geographic and product market (see p 23). The next step will be to quantify the company's market share, as this will assist in deciding whether Article 82 is potentially applicable.

Market Share Thresholds

Though levels of market power, and therefore dominance, do not directly equate with market shares, some rules of thumb based on market shares do exist and are a useful starting point.

If an undertaking has a very large market share in percentage terms then dominance will be assumed: a market share over 50 per cent, may, without more, create a presumption of dominance.[61] Between 50 per cent and 40 per cent, a variety of factors will be taken into account (see below). Below 40 per cent, a finding of dominance for the purposes of Article 82 is highly unlikely.[62]

Other Factors Relevant to Dominance

Market shares alone are not conclusive of dominance or its absence, and may indeed be misleading. Other relevant factors include the conduct of the allegedly

---

[59] *Continental Can* OJ 1972 L7/25, [1972] CMLR D11, para II-3.

[60] Case T-228/97 *Irish Sugar v Commission* [1999] ECR II-2969, [1999] 5 CMLR 1082.

[61] Case C-62/86 *AKZO Chemie v Commission* [1991] ECR I-3359, [1993] 5 CMLR 215.

[62] A rare exception to this is the Commission's Decision which was upheld by the CFI in *British Airways v Commission*, where BA had just under 40 per cent of the UK air travel agency services purchase market, Case T-219/99, 17 December 2003 (not yet officially reported), [2004] 4 CMLR 1008; on appeal Case C-95/04 OJ 2004 C106/22.

dominant firm, and the existence and importance of barriers to entry into the market.[63] If there are low barriers to entry in the industry, even a company with a 95 per cent market share may not be dominant, since it will probably have many potential competitors ready to enter the market immediately if prices are raised above a competitive level. Market structure, and in particular the number of competing undertakings and their respective market shares, is also important. For example, 45 per cent may well indicate dominance if the competitors in the market all have less than 5 per cent.

'The Common Market or . . . a Substantial Part of it'

Article 82 requires that the abuse of dominance cover at least a 'substantial part' of the common market, and this acts in some sense as a *de minimis* rule for Article 82. It refers both to the geographical area covered, and to the volume of trade as a proportion of the Community market. Both southern Germany and Belgium[64] have been held to be 'substantial' in relation to sugar production, as have individual facilities such as ports and airports.[65]

'Abuse'

It is not enjoyment of a dominant position that is prohibited as such, but only its 'abuse'. Whether particular conduct amounts to abuse may depend on many surrounding economic circumstances, including the extent to which the company is dominant: companies with extremely high market shares are sometimes referred to as 'super-dominant' and they may be found to have committed abuse when behaving in a way that would not been abuse by a less powerful company. In any case, a wide range of conduct may constitute abuse, and that conduct will frequently consist of practices that are standard in the industry, and perfectly legal if used by non-dominant companies. In *Van den Bergh Foods*[66] the CFI stated that the abusive conduct (freezer exclusivity):

> constitutes a standard practice on the relevant market. In the normal situation of a competitive market, those agreements are concluded in the interests of the two parties and cannot be prohibited as a matter of principle. However, those considerations, which are applicable in the normal situation of a competitive market, cannot be accepted without reservation in the case of a market on which, precisely because of the dominant position held by one of the traders, competition is already restricted.

---

[63] Case 85/76 *Hoffman-La Roche v Commission* [1979] ECR 461, [1979] 3 CMLR 211.

[64] *Suiker Unie*, above n 10, at para 864.

[65] eg Case C-179/90 *Porto di Genova* [1991] ECR I-5889, [1994] 4 CMLR 422; Case C-163/99 *Portugal v Commission* [2001] ECR I-2613, [2002] 2 CMLR 1319.

[66] Case T-65/98, [2003] ECR II-4653, [2004] 4 CMLR 14, para 159; appeal pending, Case C-552/03, OJ 2004 C59/13.

The fact that the use of certain business practices which are standard in the industry is denied to the most successful companies in the industry can be hard for businessmen to accept. Nor need any intention to harm competition be shown.[67]

Abusive practices are sometimes divided into the two categories of 'exploitative' conduct (making unfair use of market power) and 'exclusionary' conduct (using market power to eliminate, or weaken the position of, competitors), although many types of abusive conduct may have both exploitative and exclusionary effects. The abuse and effect generally occur in the market on which the dominant position is held, but behaviour or effects on a neighbouring market have been held to be within the scope of Article 82.[68]

Examples of abuse given in Article 82 itself are the following.

(a) directly or indirectly imposing unfair purchase or selling prices or other unfair trading conditions

This includes the notion of predatory pricing, in which a dominant undertaking prices its goods or services below the average marginal cost of production or, where there is evidence of an intention to eliminate a competitor from the market, below average total cost.[69]

(b) limiting production, markets or technical development to the prejudice of consumers

(c) applying dissimilar conditions to equivalent transactions with other trading parties, thereby placing them at a competitive disadvantage

Systems of discounts, bonuses or loyalty rebates offered by suppliers may constitute abuse where the effect of such behaviour is:

to apply dissimilar conditions to equivalent transactions with other trading parties in that two purchasers pay a different price for the same quantity of the same product depending on whether they obtain their supplies exclusively from the undertaking in a dominant position or have several sources of supply.[70]

Even if not discriminatory, such systems may constitute an exclusionary abuse if they foreclose smaller firms (which do not have the capacity to supply a large

---

[67] *Hoffman-La Roche*, above n 63.

[68] eg *Interbrew* (Annual Report on Competition Policy 1996), where the abusive behaviour in other Member States, where Interbrew was not dominant, was found to allow it better to exploit its dominance on the Belgian market, where it was dominant. See also Case C-333/94 *Tetrapak* [1996] ECR I-5951, [1997] 4 CMLR 662 where there was dominance in one product market and abuse and benefits in another, and *British Airways*, above n 62, where there was dominance and abuse in the market for purchase of travel agency services and a benefit in the air transport market.

[69] *AKZO Chemie*, above n 61. This leads to difficult questions in the context of e-commerce, since losses on sales on Internet sites are frequently recouped through means such as advertising, telecommunications charges and sale of customer databases.

[70] Case 85/76 *Hoffman-La Roche v Commission* [1979] ECR 461, [1979] 3 CMLR 211, para 90; Case 322/81 *Michelin (No 1)* [1983] ECR 3461, [1985] 1 CMLR 282; Case T-65/89 *BPB Industries Ltd and British Gypsum v Commission* [1993] ECR II-389, [1993] 5 CMLR 32 (appeal rejected in Case C-310/93). In *British Airways*, above n 62, a fine of €6.8 million for a system of loyalty rebates tying travel agents and discouraging them from selling tickets of other airlines was upheld by the CFI.

percentage of users' needs) from supplying part of those needs, by making these benefits dependent on the purchase of very large quantities or very large proportions of a user's total needs. However, if a discount or rebate is clearly attributable to, for example, costs saved by bulk production or delivery, then it should not be treated as abuse.

The case law on discounts and rebates has recently come under severe criticism for its formalism and failure to apply relevant economics, in that it is applied to some types of conduct regardless of whether there is any actual effect on the market.[71] The relevance of actual effect on the market is one of the points at issue in the *British Airways* appeal currently before the ECJ.

Discrimination as between football fans of different nationality was held to be abuse in a case in which the Commission fined the French World Cup organisers for the way in which ticket distribution was organised.[72]

(d) making the conclusion of contracts subject to acceptance by the other parties of supplementary obligations which, by their nature or according to commercial usage, have no connection with the subject of such contracts

Article 82 has frequently been applied to tying practices,[73] most recently as a basis for ordering Microsoft to unbundle its Windows operating system licence from its Windows-based media player. Market definition is crucial in such cases and may change quickly over time in new technology markets: if it had been decided in *Microsoft* that an operating system incorporating a media player was a single product then this practice would not have infringed Article 82.

Some other examples of conduct that have been characterised as abusive are as follows.

Refusal to Supply

Refusal to supply by a dominant firm may constitute abuse, in particular if the party to whom supplies have been refused was previously being supplied. Where a party is a regular customer then refusal to supply is likely to be regarded as abuse unless there are proved to be good reasons for termination of supply.[74] Therefore, it is advisable for firms in a strong market position to keep full records of any complaints and other correspondence with dealers leading up to termination.

It is currently uncertain in what circumstances, if any, a dominant supplier is entitled to refuse supplies so as to protect itself from losses to it caused by parallel exports of its products. We have seen earlier in this chapter that agreements aimed at discouraging parallel trade infringe Article 81, but it is uncertain to what extent

---

[71] See eg *Michelin v Commission (No 2)* and comment on it by RBB Economics in their Brief 13 of February 2004 (available at www.rbbecon.com).

[72] OJ 2000 L5/55, [2000] 4 CMLR 963.

[73] eg Case T-30/89 *Hilti Aktiengesellschaft v Commission* [1990] ECR II-163, [1992] 4 CMLR 16.

[74] *United Brands*, above n 18.

such conduct is subject to Article 82. The Commission has been actively considering the question, particularly since the *Bayer* judgment made it clear that Article
81 does not apply to all practices that restrict parallel trade. This issue is of great
importance in the pharmaceutical industry, given the high levels of parallel trade
in that sector (see p 20), and some clarification of the law is expected shortly as the
Greek Competition Commission has referred a number of questions to the ECJ on
this aspect of Article 82.[75]

Abusive Reliance on Intellectual and Industrial Property Rights

A particular type of refusal to supply involves intellectual property rights.
Although the refusal to grant a licence of an intellectual or industrial property
right is not *per se* characterised as abusive behaviour it may be so in certain exceptional circumstances, at least in respect of copyright.[76] In *Microsoft*, refusal to supply information which other companies needed in order to make their products
inter-operable with Microsoft's Windows systems, where it had supplied such
specifications in the past, was held to infringe Article 82.

As far as design rights are concerned, in *Volvo v Veng*[77] the ECJ held that the
right to prevent other parties producing an article protected by such a right by
refusing to grant a licence was 'the very subject-matter' of that right and therefore
could not constitute abuse. However, proceedings were later begun against Ford
following complaints from independent panel manufacturers that they were being
prevented from manufacturing and selling spare parts by Ford's reliance on intellectual property rights. The file was closed when Ford agreed to reduce considerably the term for which it exercised such rights.[78] Even in *Volvo*, it was stressed that
there could be abuse if the right-holder arbitrarily refused supplies of spare parts
to independent repairers, charged unfair prices or stopped producing spare parts
which were still in demand. It appears to be more risky to refuse supplies of goods
than to refuse a licence.

Enforcement of an intellectual property right so as to prevent imports from outside the EU into a Member State will only exceptionally constitute abuse.[79]

Refusal of Access to an Essential Facility

Only very rarely will refusal of access to a certain facility be held to be abuse of a
dominant position, and in the context of distribution no facility has ever been
held to be 'essential' in this sense. It was argued in *Bronner v Mediaprint* that the
refusal by a large newspaper publisher to allow a small newspaper publisher and

---

[75] Case C-53/03 *SIFAIT v Glaxosmithkline*, Advocate-General's opinion of 28 October 2004.
[76] Cases C-241/91 and C-242/91 *RTE/ITP v Commission* [1995] ECR I-743; Case C-418/01 *IMS
Health v NDC Health*, 29 April 2004 (not yet officially reported).
[77] Case 238/87 [1988] ECR 6211, [1989] 4 CMLR 122.
[78] Commission press release IP(90)4, 10 January 1990.
[79] Case T-198/98 *Micro Leader Business v Commission* [1999] ECR II-3989, [2000] 4 CMLR 886.

distributor access to its nationwide early morning home-delivery system, even in return for reasonable payment, was abuse of the former's dominant position. The smaller competitor argued that postal delivery would not take place until late morning, and that with its low number of subscribers it would be unprofitable for it to organise its own home-delivery system. The ECJ rejected this argument. It held that for there to be an abuse it was necessary:

> not only that the refusal of the service comprised in home-delivery be likely to eliminate all competition in the daily newspaper market from the person requesting the service and that such refusal be incapable of being objectively justified, but also that the service in itself be indispensable to carrying on that person's business, inasmuch as there is no actual or potential substitute in existence for that home-delivery scheme.[80]

It went on to say that newspapers could be distributed in many other ways, for example, through shops or by post, and moreover that it had not been established that the creation of a second home-delivery service could never be economically viable.

Freezer Exclusivity

The free loan of freezers by suppliers to distributors on condition that they only be used to stock the supplier's brand of ice cream was held to infringe Article 82 in *Van den Bergh Foods v Commission*, on the grounds that it foreclosed retail outlets to other suppliers.[81] However, the circumstances were very specific: ice cream (unlike other products such as soft drinks) can only be stocked in a freezer; the distributors were small 'corner shops' which did not have enough space for more than one freezer. A similar practice in respect of other products, or involving larger retailers or supermarkets, would not necessarily infringe Article 82. In addition a very high proportion of the market was covered by this and other similar networks.

Refusal to Honour Guarantee

In *Novo Nordisk*[82] the Commission held that refusal to honour a guarantee and disclaiming liability for malfunction of medical equipment on the grounds that the equipment had been used in conjunction with a competitor's components, despite the proven compatibility of those components, constituted abuse.

2.6   EXTRATERRITORIAL APPLICATION

The precise extraterritorial scope of the EU competition rules is not completely certain. It is established that an arrangement made outside Community territory

---

[80] Case C-7/97 [1998] ECR I-7791, [1999] 4 CMLR 112, para 41.
[81] The agreements were also held to have infringed Article 81.
[82] 1996 Annual Report on Competition Policy, para 62.

but at least partially implemented within the territory may fall within the scope of those rules, regardless of whether the undertakings concerned have any kind of establishment within the Community:

> If the applicability of prohibitions laid down under competition law were made to depend on the place where the agreement, decision or concerted practice was formed, the result would obviously be to give undertakings an easy means of evading those prohibitions. The decisive factor is therefore the place where it is implemented.
>
> The producers in this case implemented their pricing agreement within the Common Market. It is immaterial in that respect whether or not they had recourse to subsidiaries, agents, sub-agents or branches within the Community in order to make their contracts with purchasers within the Community.[83]

Fines may therefore be imposed on the firms concerned and termination of the agreement ordered, provided some implementing measures are taken on Community territory. For example, an American manufacturer or supplier could be fined for maintaining a network of independent distributors within the Community if the terms of the distribution agreements infringed Article 81(1). It would not be necessary for it to be shown that the American firm had a branch or subsidiary within the Community which had implemented the agreement. Whether and how the payment of such a fine could be enforced is a different question.

It is still uncertain what types of act constitute 'implementation'. Nor is it clear whether, in the absence of implementing measures, the Community has jurisdiction. For example, if a Japanese firm were to agree with an American firm not to supply certain products to the Community, could there be Community jurisdiction in such a case? It may be that a mere 'effect' in the Community and no actual act of implementation is sufficient to found jurisdiction. The Commission takes this latter, broader view of its jurisdiction, so non-Community enterprises could in principle have such behaviour challenged by the Commission, and have to argue the jurisdictional question on appeal to the CFI.

However, in the case of many third countries the problem is unlikely to arise in practice, thanks to provisions for cooperation in competition law enforcement included in international agreements, such as the European Economic Area Agreement (with Iceland, Liechtenstein and Norway), as well as to competition cooperation agreements in force with the United States, Canada and Japan.

2.7 COMMUNITY COMPETITION RULES VERSUS NATIONAL RULES

All Member States, including the 10 that joined on 1 May 2004, have competition laws which are very similar in substance to EU competition rules, and which apply only to anti-competitive behaviour affecting their national markets. But they frequently differ in their detail, and, even where the substantive law is identical,

---

[83] *Woodpulp* ECJ, above n11, at para 16.

procedural rules and sanctions vary.[84] It is therefore important to know when an alleged infringement is potentially subject only to national law (which is enforced only by national courts and authorities) or only to Articles 81 or 82 (which may be enforced either by the Commission or at national level) or to both. The separate question of how it is decided whether the Commission or one or more national authorities deals with a specific case is considered later in this chapter.

As already stated, the general principle is that Community law takes precedence over national law, and where there is a conflict between the two, a national court must apply the Community law rule (see p 13). Therefore, conduct that infringes Community law cannot be authorised by national law. The fact that national law or state measure permits, encourages or facilitates a particular practice is no defence to an allegation of infringement of Community law.[85]

In the area of competition law, there is a sharing of competence between the Community and the Member States. The requirement in Articles 81 and 82 that conduct have an effect on trade between Member States (see p 24) has been interpreted by the ECJ as creating and delimiting this division of competence: where an agreement has no appreciable effect on trade between Member States then it falls outside the scope of Community law and national law may be freely applied to the agreement.[86] However, although in cases where inter-Member State trade is not affected Community law does not apply, where such trade is affected, then both Community and national law may be applied, provided that the uniform application of Community law is not prejudiced.

For the Community institutions applying competition law the application of this principle is simple, since they only have the option of applying EU law provisions.[87] For national courts and competition authorities the question is more complicated, as they need to decide whether to apply EU law, national law, or both. The general principle clearly means that national law can never permit conduct which is prohibited by national law. However, until recently it was less clear whether, and if so when, this principle allowed national law to prohibit conduct which would not be prohibited by Article 81 or 82.

This aspect of the application of the general principles to Articles 81 and 82 is therefore expressly covered by the procedural Regulation 1/2003.[88] Article 3 provides that, whenever national bodies apply national competition law to an agreement or practice which affects trade between Member States, they must also apply Article 81. In such cases, application of national law must not lead to the

---

[84] For a description of the competition law enforcement regimes in each of the 25 Member States see David Broomhall and Joanna Goyder (eds), *Modernisation in Europe 2005* (Law Business Research, 2005).

[85] Case 123/83 *BNIC v Clair* [1985] ECR 392, [1985] 2 CMLR 430.

[86] *Consten & Grundig*, above n 6.

[87] However, if sanctions are imposed by both systems, the level of the Community fine will be set to take into account any national sanction imposed, Case 14/68 *Walt Wilhelm v Bundeskartellamt* [1969] ECR 1, [1969] CMLR 100. Whether the reverse is true depends on the relevant national law.

[88] Appendix 2. This replaced Regulation 17/62 as from 1 May 2004.

prohibition of agreements which do not infringe Article 81(1), or which fulfil the criteria of Article 81(3), or fall within the scope of a block exemption.

When national bodies apply national law to an abuse prohibited by Article 82, they must also apply Article 82. However, in this case national law may impose stricter national rules prohibiting unilateral conduct.

Article 3(3) states that these rules do not limit the application of national laws with other objectives. These would presumably include rules on consumer protection and protection of agents or franchisees, and sanctions for criminal cartel activity.

2.8 PROCEDURAL ASPECTS OF ARTICLES 81 AND 82[89]

Introduction

Enforcement of Articles 81 and 82 is a complex subject, involving a large number of actors, including public authorities and private undertakings, courts and competition authorities, and national bodies as well as EU institutions.

The procedural enforcement rules relating to Articles 81 and 82 underwent radical reform (often referred to as 'modernisation') on 1 May 2004, with the entry into effect of Regulation 1/2003 (Appendix 2). The main impact of that change is to shift more responsibility for the assessment of agreements under Article 81 to parties and their advisers, and to increase the powers and responsibilities of national courts and national competition authorities (NCAs) for enforcement of both Articles 81 and 82.[90]

In the description that follows, the old rules will only be described to the extent that this is necessary in order to understand judgments, Decisions and other texts which predate the change, the substance of which in most cases remains good law. The previous edition of this book provides further detail on the old regime. Apart from references to Articles 81 and 82, all references to Articles below refer to Regulation 1/2003. Note that additional detailed rules on procedural issues, including the rights of parties under investigation and third parties, the handling of complaints, time limits and the conduct of investigations and oral hearings, appear in Commission Regulation 773/2004 (Appendix 6).

Institutional Framework

In this section the interrelating roles of the EU and national authorities and courts is briefly described,[91] and it is explained how cases are allocated between the

---

[89] For comprehensive treatment of this subject see C Kerse and N Khan, *EC Antitrust Procedure*, 5th edn (Sweet & Maxwell, 2005).

[90] The Commission is to report on the functioning of the Regulation by 1 May 2009 and decide whether to propose amendments.

[91] See also Chapter 1 for a general description of each of the main EU institutions.

various authorities. The specific powers and responsibilities of the European Commission, and the role of private enforcement, will be discussed in more detail in later sections.

Commission

A broad responsibility for enforcement of Community competition law has lain principally with the Commission since 1962. At that time it was given a number of powers and duties, which it has made enthusiastic use of ever since. It has the power to carry out investigations and inspections, and to adopt various enforcement Decisions including those imposing fines and, since 1 May 2004, structural remedies.

One of the aims of the recent procedural reforms was to decentralise the enforcement of Articles 81 and 82, giving national courts and NCAs a greater role, and freeing the Commission's resources to pursue serious infringements such as major cartels and abuses of dominance affecting a large part of the EU. While the Commission continues to welcome and act on complaints concerning serious competition law infringements, the intention is that many more cases should now be handled at national level.

It used to be possible to notify agreements to the Commission with a view to obtaining a Decision stating either that Article 81(1) was not infringed or that it was but a block exemption applied ('negative clearance'), or that the conditions of Article 81(3) were fulfilled ('individual exemption'). In practice such formal Decisions were rare, and instead many informal administrative 'comfort letters' were given every year. These provided a lesser degree of legal certainty than a formal Decision, but in many circumstances they were sufficient in practice for the parties' commercial purposes.[92] The Commission no longer plays this role.

Despite this change, the Commission remains very influential, as will be seen from its current wide range of powers, discussed below. Apart from powers to investigate and to inspect premises, it has the power to withdraw cases from NCAs, and to make submissions in national litigation involving Articles 81 and 82. It also has the power to adopt a range of Decisions. The many Commission Notices and Guidelines, listed at the beginning of this chapter, will also ensure that in practice its views will exert considerable influence on national courts and NCAs.

Court of First Instance and European Court of Justice

The CFI hears all appeals from private parties against Commission Decisions, whether they are parties to the conduct concerned or third parties directly and individually concerned by the Decision. It carries out a full review of the case and its judgment may be appealed, on points of law only, to the ECJ.

---

[92] This was particularly the case for distribution agreements as these are normally vertical agreements and so could be formally exempted retrospectively if this later became necessary, for example because a contractual dispute arose or a complaint was made.

When a question of interpretation of Community law arises a national court has the option of consulting the ECJ. It may, or in some cases must, put a preliminary question to the ECJ under the procedure provided in Article 234 of the EC Treaty. The question has been raised whether the ECJ has the resources to deal with the many more such references which might occur under the new regime, but in practice national courts are most likely to have difficulty applying the law to the facts, rather than interpreting the law itself, so there may not be a great increase in preliminary references.

National Competition Authorities

National authorities are required to have full powers to enforce Articles 81 and 82. These are the powers to require termination of an infringement, to take interim measures, to accept commitments and to impose fines and penalty payments (Article 5 of Regulation 1/2003). This is intended to contribute to decentralisation of enforcement, since it will allow NCAs to deal with some cases that would previously have been dealt with by the Commission. When doing so they must not take decisions that would run counter to any existing Commission Decision (Article 16 of Regulation 1/2003).

Most NCAs have (under their national law) powers of investigation and inspection, which they use to enforce both the EU competition rules and their national competition laws. There is considerable variation in these, and in the decision-making procedures, including the type and level of sanctions they can impose. For example, in some jurisdictions infringement decisions or decisions imposing fines may only be made by a court, with the authority having a purely investigative role. The scope of legal professional privilege also varies widely.

NCAs may ask one another for assistance in their investigations, and the Commission may request an NCA to carry out an investigation for it, in which case the officials remain subject to their national procedural rules.

The question of whether Article 234 of the EC Treaty allows NCAs to request a preliminary ruling has not yet been settled, and is complicated by the widely varying types of bodies that are classed as NCAs for the purposes of Regulation 1/2003.[93]

Case Allocation and Information Exchange Between the Commission and NCAs

In order to promote a timely and appropriate allocation of cases amongst the NCAs and the Commission in the more decentralised system, a European Competition Network (ECN), consisting of the Commission and the NCAs, has been created. Its function is to facilitate information exchange and co-operation between its members in the enforcement of Articles 81 and 82. Article 11 of

---

[93] This question should be answered, at least in respect of the Greek Competition Committee, in the pending Case C-53/03 *SIFAIT v Glaxosmithkline*, Advocate-General's opinion of 28 October 2004.

Regulation 1/2003 requires the Commission and NCAs to notify one another when carrying out investigations or when planning to take certain decisions, to enable co-ordination of enforcement if more than one authority has an interest in the case.

The Commission's Notice on co-operation within the network of competition authorities[94] provides guidance on how cases are to be allocated. In principle the authority receiving a complaint is in charge of a case unless those ECN members interested decide that it should be reallocated so that a 'well-placed' authority can deal it with. Any such reallocation should normally happen within two months. An authority is considered 'well placed if:

- there are substantial effects or implementation in the jurisdiction concerned; and
- the NCA can effectively put an end to and impose sanctions for the infringement; and
- the NCA can, possibly with assistance from other NCAs, gather the necessary evidence.

The Commission may withdraw a case from an NCA in order to deal with it itself (Article 11(6)). If it has not done this during the initial two month period then it will only do so if:

- ECN members envisage adopting conflicting decisions; or
- they envisage taking decisions conflicting with established case law; or
- they unduly prolong proceedings; or
- a Commission Decision is needed to develop EU competition policy.

Article 12 of Regulation 1/2003 provides for significant volumes of information, including much confidential information, to be exchanged between members of the ECN, which raises considerable confidentiality concerns for companies. The information so exchanged may only be used for the purposes of enforcing Articles 81 and 82 and similar domestic laws, and there are express—though not completely clear—rules intended to maintain high levels of protection of fundamental rights. In particular such information should not be used to fine or imprison a natural person.

There are particularly acute issues in the context of information supplied to the Commission or an NCA with a view to obtaining leniency or immunity from fines in return for assistance provided to the authority in a cartel case. When there is uncertainty as to which authority will ultimately deal with the case, companies will face complex and time-critical decisions, and difficult logistical questions, when making such applications.[95]

---

[94]   OJ 2004 C101/43.
[95]   The Commission attempts to give some guidance on this in its Notice on co-operation within the network of competition authorities OJ 2004 C101/43. This Notice has a special status as NCAs have expressly agreed to abide by its principles; see para 42 of the Notice and the list of NCAs on DG Comp's website.

Legal professional privilege rules vary considerably from one Member State to another, and these differences may be exploited by NCAs so as to use the information exchange mechanisms to obtain access to documents not available to them under their domestic rules.

National Courts

National courts are empowered, and required, to apply Articles 81 and 82 in full. They must do so even where the parties do not raise competition law arguments, since these Articles are fundamental rules of public policy.[96] They must apply them in accordance with the case law of the CFI and ECJ, which are the highest authority for the interpretation of EU law. In addition, they may not take decisions running counter to any Decision taken (even if its application has been suspended), or even 'contemplated' by the Commission. This may sometimes necessitate a stay of a national court case, and appropriate interim measures, pending the outcome of Commission proceedings. In such circumstances the national court may also want to request a preliminary ruling from the ECJ.[97]

Allegations of infringement of Article 81 or 82 most commonly arise in the form of a so-called 'Euro-defence' when a defendant, against whom proceedings for breach of contract are being brought, claims that the contract is void and unenforceable under Article 81(2) for infringement of Article 81(1). National courts may also grant an injunction on the basis of a breach or threatened breach of these Articles, or damages (see p 60). They also review decisions of their NCAs.

Proceedings in a national court will often have advantages over Commission administrative proceedings, though this will depend to some extent on the procedural provisions of the relevant national law. Injunctions and interim measures can normally be obtained more quickly, the winning party may recover costs and there is the opportunity to combine the claim under Community law with a damages claim, and any other claim available under national law.

However, there are limitations on the ability of some national courts to deal with such cases. Complex economic evaluation is often necessary, as is a full understanding of competition law principles; national judges are not normally trained in economics, and in a number of Member States competition law itself is a relatively new concept. The national court will confine itself to the specific dispute arising between the parties, and cannot investigate the industry concerned in general terms, even if the evidence suggests anti-competitive behaviour on a wide scale; similarly, it will look at past behaviour only rather than, as the Commission does, have regard to the way in which the market is likely to develop in the future. Also, it will not be easy for evidence from other Member States to be obtained, and a judgment will normally have effects only in the jurisdiction and as between the

---

[96] C-126/97 *Eco Swiss China Time v Benetton* [1999] ECR I-3055, [2000] 5 CMLR 816.
[97] Case C-344/98 *Masterfoods v HB Ice Cream* [2000] ECR I-11369, [2001] 4 CMLR 449 and Art 16 of Reg 1/2003.

parties concerned. In some cases, therefore, action by the Commission, or an NCA, will be more appropriate, and generally cheaper for the complainant.

The Commission has published a Notice on co-operation between the Commission and the courts of the EU Member States in the application of Articles 81 and 82 by which it seeks to encourage greater reliance on national courts for the enforcement of EU competition law.[98]

National courts, when dealing with matters involving Articles 81 and 82, may contact the Commission to request information: such information may be procedural (for example, whether the Commission has investigated a given distribution system), substantive (that is, questions of interpretation of Articles 81 or 82) or factual (such as statistics, market studies and economic analyses). They may also ask for an opinion 'on questions concerning the application of the Community competition rules' (Article 15 of Regulation 1/2003). The involvement of the Commission raises issues as to the protection of parties' rights, and these are governed by national procedural law.[99]

National courts are not members of the ECN as their independent judicial status makes this inappropriate, but Member States are required to notify the Commission of their national courts' judgments concerning Articles 81 and 82. The Commission has no power to take over a case from a national court, but Article 15 provides that it may, if it is aware of such proceedings, make written observations in national litigation, and intervene orally if the national court agrees. NCAs also have the right to make observations on cases in the courts of their jurisdiction.

European Commission Powers of Investigation and Inspection

The Commission may open an administrative procedure with a view to obtaining the termination of an illegal agreement and maybe also imposing fines. It may do this pursuant to a formal complaint (see p 58) or an anonymous tip-off received about a distribution arrangement alleged to infringe the Treaty rules, as a result of which it decides to take investigative action. However, although such procedures are often initiated on the basis of a complaint received, the Commission can and does commence proceedings on its own initiative. As a result of the recent reforms the Commission was given the power to investigate not only particular sectors of the economy, but also particular types of agreements, where it suspects a restriction or distortion of competition (Article 17 of Regulation 1/2003).

The Commission obtains the vast majority of its information in its investigations through complaints and information supplied by third parties and the voluntary co-operation of the parties involved. It is in a company's interests to appear

---

[98] OJ 2004 C101/54.
[99] Joined Cases C-174/98 and 198/98 *Netherlands v Van der Wal*, [2000] ECR I-1 deal with the question of whether disclosure of such guidance to a national court may be obtained by a third party.

co-operative and helpful towards the Commission. In particular, this lends credence to claims that any infringement found was not intentional, and this may mean that any fine imposed will be lower than it would be otherwise. In particular, fines may be substantially reduced where information implicating other companies is provided (see p 54).

The Commission has two main ways of actively obtaining information, which are requests for information and inspection of premises.

Request for Information

Article 18 of Regulation 1/2003 empowers the Commission in performing its enforcement duties to 'require undertakings and associations of undertakings to provide all necessary information'. Supply of incorrect or misleading information can lead to fines of up to 1 per cent of the company's worldwide annual turnover (Article 23).

A simple request for information under Article 18(2) cannot be enforced, though the supply intentionally or negligently of inaccurate information can result in fines for undertakings. If no response or an inadequate response is supplied, then the Commission may take a formal Decision under Article 18(3) requesting the information to be provided within a certain period. If that Decision is not complied with then fines, again up to 1 per cent of the company's annual turnover, or periodic penalty payments up to 5 per cent of turnover (Article 24), may be imposed. If information is requested by the Commission by a certain date, it must still be supplied, even if a settlement as between the parties has been reached in the meantime, and a company failing to do so may be fined.[100]

Inspections

The notorious 'dawn raids' during which Commission officials arrive at a company's premises unannounced, with a mandate to enter land, buildings and vehicles in order to obtain evidence, have become much more frequent in recent years. Companies should be aware of the possibility of such an investigation and need to be prepared to deal with such a situation should it arise. Since 1 May 2004 it has also been possible, subject to judicial authorisation, to inspect non-business premises, including private homes (Article 21).

Article 20 of Regulation 1/2003 provides two alternative types of inspection:

(1) The Commission may arrive at an undertaking's premises with a simple mandate for investigation. The undertaking is not obliged to allow the inspectors in, though it may be better to do so in order not to create the impression that there is something to hide. If they are admitted, they must be allowed to enter the premises, look at documents and other records, take copies of anything

---

[100] *Compagnie des Cristalleries Baccarat*, OJ 1991 L97/16.

relevant, affix temporary seals as necessary, and ask oral questions about facts and documents related to the investigation.

(2) On the other hand, inspectors may come unannounced with a Commission Decision making it obligatory for the undertaking to allow the inspectors in. Refusal to admit can lead to financial sanctions, but forced entry can only be made with the aid of the relevant national authorities.[101] Those national authorities are obliged to co-operate, but the Commission must observe national rules relating to the provision of this assistance, so that undertakings' fundamental rights are protected.[102]

The formal Decision must state clearly the subject matter and purpose of the investigation.[103] The undertaking has a right to have a lawyer present, if a lawyer can be summoned reasonably quickly. Again, once they have gained admission, inspectors are entitled to be shown all documents and other records, including computer-stored information and mobile phones, and to ask on-the-spot questions about the records inspected.

During an investigation, however it is initiated, the Commission may ask detailed questions. A company has no general right to stay silent, but may refuse to answer to the extent that it would otherwise be compelled to provide answers which might involve admission of an infringement. The Commission must confine itself to asking for factual data. It cannot even ask questions such as 'What was the object of the meeting?' or 'What occurred at the meeting?' or require production of documents related to the meeting, in circumstances in which it is clear that the Commission suspects that the object of the meeting was to restrict competition.[104]

At the end of this onsite investigation the undertaking will be asked to sign a copy of the inspectors' note of what has taken place. It is important to ensure that all of what has been recorded is accurate and that any pertinent observations relating to the documents inspected, any claims of legal privilege or confidentiality and any objections to the conduct of or questions posed by the inspectors, are recorded.

It is also important to ensure that a note is taken of the documents and other records inspected or copied during the visit so that it is known precisely what information the Commission has in its possession.

Power to Take Statements

Since 1 May 2004 the Commission has had the power to take statements from any consenting person at any stage in an investigation (Article 19 of Regulation 1/2003). This may be on the occasion of an inspection, or at a separate time.

---

[101] For example, by the grant of an *Anton Pillar* type injunction from the High Court in the UK.
[102] Joined Cases 46/87 and 227/88 *Hoechst AG v Commission* [1989] ECR 2859, [1991] CMLR 410.
[103] *Ibid.*
[104] Case 374/87 *Orkem v Commission* [1989] ECR 3283, [1991] 4 CMLR 502; Case T-112/98 *Mannesmannröhren-Werke v Commission* [2001] ECR II-729, [2001] 5 CMLR 54; Case T-236/01 *Graphite electrode cartel*, 29 April 2004 (not yet officially reported).

Confidentiality

Commission officials are bound by a general obligation of professional secrecy in their work, and this obligation is mentioned explicitly in Regulation 1/2003 (Article 28). Information regarded as confidential with regard to third parties (such as business secrets and technical knowhow) should be clearly indicated as such so that it is not inadvertently disclosed by the Commission to third parties at a later stage. The precise scope of professional secrecy is not certain, and, more importantly, it may be overridden in the interests of ensuring that another party is sufficiently well informed to be able to defend itself before the Commission: the Commission is required to balance the interests of one party's right to defend itself against the damage that may be done to another party's business interests.[105]

Information obtained by the Commission during an inspection cannot be used for a purpose other than that stated in the inspection mandate (Article 28), but the Commission does have the right to start a second investigation in order to verify information found on a first investigation if that information leads to evidence of conduct contrary to the competition rules.[106]

Legal Professional Privilege

Legal professional privilege is recognised, and so communications between a party and its independent legal adviser need not be disclosed.[107] This privilege extends to protect documents which essentially reproduce the text or contents of the advice and are circulated internally within the firm, but not to documents evidencing legal advice provided internally, by in-house counsel, for example.[108]

There has for some time been considerable pressure for change of the rule which excludes in-house counsel from the benefit of legal privilege in proceedings before the Commission, especially as in some Member States they are now subject to similar professional disciplines as apply to independent practitioners. A recent interim Order by the CFI President suggests that the scope of privilege may be so extended but this will not be decided until final judgment is given.[109]

Access to the File

The law relating to the rights of complainants, those suspected of infringements of the competition rules and other third parties to see the information in possession

---

[105] *Hilti*, above n 73.
[106] Case 85/87 *Dow Benelux v Commission* [1989] ECR 3137, [1991] CMLR 410.
[107] Case 155/79 *AM&S v Commission* [1982] ECR 1575, [1982] 2 CMLR 264.
[108] *Hilti*, above n 73..
[109] Case T-125/03 *Akzo Nobel v Commission*, Order of 30 October 2003 (not yet officially reported), [2004] 4 CMLR 744, partially annulled in Case C-7/04 of 27 September 2004.

of the Commission is now codified in Regulations 1/2003 and 773/2004.[110] It extends to all relevant information held by the Commission, subject to the confidentiality rules (see above): there is a right to access to all documents unless they contain business secrets, or are internal Commission or NCA documents, or correspondence between ECN members, or are confidential for some other reason.

If the Commission refuses access to a document, this refusal cannot be formally challenged until the Commission has adopted a decision on the substance of the case, though it may be possible to reach an informal solution through the Hearing Officer.

Complainants are entitled to see relevant documents, though the Commission is well aware that the making of a complaint may be exploited by a company so as to obtain information about a competitor.

Hearings

In the course of an investigation the Commission will invite the parties concerned to an oral hearing of the case, and they often accept. The Commission considers an oral hearing to be an opportunity 'to clarify certain matters which have not been settled during the written procedure and to emphasise the main lines of a case'.[111]

It is not supposed to be adversarial, nor in itself to result in any specific decision or finding. The hearing, which will normally last no longer than a day, except in a complicated case involving many parties, is presided over by a Hearing Officer[112] and is tape-recorded. Undertakings suspected of infringement of the competition rules are entitled to be heard, and other persons such as third parties with a 'sufficient interest', such as the complainant or a competitor, may be heard if the Commission considers it necessary. It is usual for them to be represented by a lawyer. The Member States themselves are also entitled to be represented there. The Hearing Officer will then make a report to the Director General of DG Comp.

European Commission Decisions

Proceedings involving the Commission are often very informal at the outset. There may be meetings between the parties concerned and the Commission officials dealing with the case. Unless the Commission decides early on to close the file informally, it will give the company concerned its 'Statement of Objections' which formally outlines the allegations the Commission is making. All parties to

---

[110] Appendix 6. A Commission Notice on the internal rules of procedure for processing requests for access to the file gives more detail on practical procedures and the extent of the right of access, OJ 1997 C23/3, [1997] 4 CMLR 490. It is currently under review, OJ 2004 C 259/8.

[111] 11th Annual Report on Competition Policy, para 26.

[112] See Commission Decision of 23 May 2001 on the terms of reference of hearing officers, OJ 2001 L162/21.

the agreement and interested third parties must be given the opportunity to put forward their arguments and views[113] and there may be an oral hearing (see above). The Advisory Committee on Restrictive Practices and Dominant Positions, composed of representatives of the NCAs, will be consulted. Though such proceedings frequently end at some point during this procedure with informal closure of the file, they may also end with the adoption of one of the types of legally binding Commission Decision described below.

Before adopting a Decision accepting commitments (Article 9 of Regulation 1/2003) or making a finding of inapplicability of Article 81 or 82 (Article 10) the Commission is obliged to publish a Notice in the Official Journal inviting comments from third parties (Article 27).

Infringement Decisions and Fines and Other Remedies (Article 7)

The Commission may order infringing conduct to be terminated, or make a finding of a past infringement. Enterprises found to be in breach of Article 81 or 82 may also be fined up to 10 per cent of their annual worldwide turnover (Article 23(2)),[114] though the Commission generally does not use this power to its maximum. The Commission may also impose behavioural remedies (such as an order to a dominant company to continue to supply) or structural remedies (such as divestment of part of a business) when necessary. Structural remedies may only be used where there is no equally effective behavioural remedy, or that would be more burdensome to the company. They are expected to be extremely rare.

Commission Guidelines[115] indicate that minor breaches, such as distribution agreements affecting only a limited part of the EU, will normally attract fines of between €1,000 and €1 million; serious restrictions, such as larger scale distribution systems and abuse of dominant position, including refusal to supply and discrimination, will lead to fines between €1 million and €20 million; major cartels will attract even higher fines. These basic amounts are then adjusted to reflect the size and economic capacity of the company, the duration of the infringement, and any aggravating or attenuating circumstances.

A fine will be higher if the illegal conduct was intentional or negligent. In this context ignorance of the law, or inaccurate legal advice,[116] does not prevent conduct from being intentional if the anti-competitive nature of the conduct is known. Other aggravating circumstances include repeated infringements, refusal to cooperate with the Commission, a leading or initiating role, measures taken against other firms to enforce the illegal practice and high profits made as a result of the practice.

---

[113] See eg Case 17/74 *Transocean Marine Paint Association v Commission* [1974] ECR 1063, [1974] 2 CMLR 459.

[114] There is no provision at EU level for criminal sanctions or for fines on individuals, but some Member States' national laws provide for the possibility of such sanctions for certain competition law offences.

[115] Guidelines on the method of setting fines, OJ 1998 C9/3, [1998] 4 CMLR 472.

[116] Case 279/87 *Tipp-ex v Commission* [1990] ECR I-261.

It will be lower for a company (usually a smaller company) which has been party to an agreement or practice as a result of pressure from another party.[117] Fines will also be reduced if a company has a satisfactory compliance programme in place[118] or has made reparation to injured parties.[119] Other attenuating circumstances are a passive role, only partial involvement in the illegal practice, and prompt termination of the behaviour once the Commission becomes involved.

It will also be lower where a company is generally co-operative.[120] In addition, substantial reductions in fines or even total immunity are now available to companies which provide significant assistance to the Commission in an investigation. There is only formal provision for this in horizontal cartel cases[121] but the same principles have been applied by analogy in a vertical distribution case on the basis of the Guidelines on the method of setting fines.[122]

The largest competition law fine ever imposed on a single company was one of €497.2 million imposed on Microsoft for infringements of Article 82 consisting of tying certain software products and refusing to supply competitors with interoperability specifications (see p 34).

At one time the highest fine ever on an individual company for infringement of Article 81 was the one of €102 million imposed on Volkswagen for using its distribution system to impose market-partitioning measures. Volkswagen had, over a period of 10 years, systematically required its Italian dealers to reject orders from foreign customers, mainly German and Austrian, who were seeking to take advantage of lower Italian car prices. They had also terminated dealership agreements with dealers who refused to co-operate in this policy.[123] There have since been many substantial fines imposed in respect of vertical distribution arrangements, one even higher than that imposed on Volkswagen.[124]

---

[117] BASF Lacke & Farben, OJ 1995 L272/16, [1996] 4 CMLR 811; Case T-66/92 Herlitz v Commission [1994] ECR II-531, [1995] 5 CMLR 458.

[118] Unusually, the existence of a compliance programme was an exacerbating factor in British Sugar, OJ 1999 L76/1, [1999] 4 CMLR 1316. But this was because there had been behaviour contrary to wording contained in a compliance programme which had been announced to the Commission and had been taken into account as a mitigating factor during separate proceedings against British Sugar in 1986.

[119] Nintendo OJ 2003 L255/33, [2004] 4 CMLR 421, para 440. An appeal regarding the level of the fine is pending, Case T-13/03, OJ 2003 C70/27.

[120] eg Case T-77/92 Parker Pen v Commission [1994] ECR II-549, [1995] 5 CMLR 435; in Systemform OJ 1997 L47/11 the Commission took into account the fact that Systemform had not disputed the Commission's findings in its Statement of Objections, and had started to amend its infringing contracts before it received the Statement of Objections.

[121] Commission Notice on immunity from fines and reduction of fines in cartel cases OJ 2002 C45/3, [2002] 4 CMLR 906.

[122] Nintendo. See also Competition Policy Newsletter Spring 2003.

[123] The fine was reduced to €90 million by the CFI, and the CFI's judgment was upheld in Case C-338/00 [2003] ECR I-9189, [2004] 4 CMLR 351. Currently the highest in respect of Article 81 is one of €462 imposed on Hoffman-La Roche for its part in a vitamins cartel.

[124] eg Opel Nederland (€43 million), upheld in Case T-368/00, [2003] ECR II-4491, [2004] 4 CMLR 1402, appeal pending, Case C-551/03, OJ 2004 C71/8; JCB (€39.6 million), upheld but fine reduced in Case T-67/01, 13 January 2004 (not yet officially reported), [2004] 4 CMLR 1346, on appeal Case C-167/04, OJ 2004 C156/3; DaimlerChrysler (€71.825 million) OJ 2002 L257/1, [2003] 4 CMLR 95, appeal pending, Case T-352/01, OJ 2002 C68/15; Nintendo (€149.128 million).

Fines and periodic penalty payments can be imposed not only for substantive infringements of the competition rules, but also for failure to respect certain procedural rules (Articles 23 and 24 of Regulation 1/2003).

All Commission Decisions are subject to review by the Court of First Instance, which may annul a Decision and substitute its own judgment. It may also review the size of any fine imposed. Decisions may be appealed by the parties to whom they are addressed or by any other person if the Decision is of 'direct and individual concern' to that person (Article 230 of the EC Treaty). Appeal on a point of law only then lies to the ECJ.

The limitation period for the imposition of fines by the Commission is five years for substantive infringements (Article 25). There are also limitation periods during which any appeal from such a Commission Decision must be brought. Failure to introduce an appeal in time will result in the appeal being declared inadmissible.[125]

Interim Measures (Article 8)

The Commission may take a long time, even years, to deal with a case before it. If the matter is urgent, the Commission may on its own initiative adopt interim measures. In such cases the time limit for parties subject to complaint, and complainants, to make their views known may be shortened to one week (normally not less than four weeks is allowed). Since the entry into force of Regulation 1/2003, private parties may not themselves apply for such measures. In any case, interim measures will not be put in place in less than a few weeks and it may therefore be preferable where possible to seek an injunction or other interim measure from a national court or NCA.

Before the Commission's power to grant interim measures was made explicit in Regulation 1/2003, the ECJ had held that it could do so:

> when the practice of certain undertakings in competition matters has the effect of injuring the interests of some Member States, causing damage to other undertakings, or of unacceptably jeopardising the Community's competition policy.[126]

It held that a prima facie case must be made out[127] and that it must be shown that interim measures were necessary either to prevent likely serious and irreparable damage or to prevent a situation which was 'intolerable to the public interest'.[128] The former might be the case, for example, when a distributor is refused supplies and this threatens the continued viability of his business. However, it would be rare for a distributorship agreement to have such grave effects as to make it 'intolerable in the public interest'.

Then a number of procedural safeguards must be observed, and it is these safeguards that mean that at least a few weeks are required before interim measures are

---

[125] Case T-125/89 *Filtrona Espanola v Commission* [1990] ECR II-393.
[126] Case 792/79 *Camera Care v Commission* [1981] ECR 119, [1980] 1 CMLR 334, para 14.
[127] *Boosey & Hawkes* above n 20
[128] *Camera Care*, above n 126, at para 19.

ordered. Measures adopted must be for a specified time (which may be extended) and aimed at preserving the situation as it was before the conduct complained of occurred. Fines or periodic penalty payments may be imposed for failure to comply with such a Decision. The Decision to impose such measures may be appealed to the ECJ.

Commitments (Article 9)

Article 9 provides that the Commission may, instead of adopting an infringement Decision, accept binding commitments from a company. Such a Decision does not take a position on whether or not there has been or is an infringement, and it does not preclude a national court from making an infringement finding, or an NCA from taking up the case.[129]

The Commission's power under Article 10 to make a finding of inapplicability of Article 81 or 82 is discussed below.

Formal and Informal Guidance for Parties

Parties frequently have genuine doubts as to the applicability of Article 81 or 82 to their conduct, and this may well occur in the case of distribution arrangements. Before 1 May 2004 firms had the option of notifying the Commission, which would provide an answer through a formal Decision or, much more often, an informal 'comfort letter'.

Regulation 1/2003 changed this. In line with the policy of freeing up Commission resources and placing more assessment responsibility on companies themselves, the Commission will now respond to requests for guidance only in narrowly defined circumstances, and it will focus on cases in which the law is uncertain. Since the difficulties in applying competition law very often arise rather from the application of the law to the specific facts of a case, these procedures will only be available in a narrow range of cases.

Guidance may be given either through a formal Article 10 Decision, or by issuing 'informal guidance'.

Article 10 Decisions

Where justified by the 'Community public interest' the Commission will take a formal Decision stating that Article 81 or 82 does not apply in a particular situation. This will probably be rare: Recital 14 refers to 'exceptional cases . . . with a view to clarifying the law . . . in particular with regard to new types of agreement or practices that have not been settled in the existing case law and administrative practice'.

---

[129] This new provision raises a number of issues as to how it will be applied and what will be the legal effects of such Decisions, many of which are discussed in John Temple Lang, 'Commitment Decisions under Regulation 1/2003: Legal Aspects of a New Kind of Competition Decision' [2003] ECLR 347.

Informal Guidance

Commission policy in this area is described in its Notice on informal guidance relating to novel questions concerning Articles 81 and 82.[130] The criteria which need to be fulfilled before the Commission will consider giving guidance appear very restrictive, so it will be much more difficult to obtain than were comfort letters. The criteria are that:

- an issue on which the law is undecided or unclear is involved; and
- guidance would be useful in the light of:
  —the economic importance of the case to consumers;
  —the extent to which the practice in question is widespread;
  —the scope of any investments in relation to the size of the parties involved, and
  —the involvement of a structural operation such as a joint venture; and
- the parties provide sufficient information.

In addition, guidance will not be given if the same or similar issues are before the CFI or ECJ, or if the case itself is pending before the Commission, a national court or an NCA. Nor will it be given in the case of hypothetical or past circumstances.

Guidance given will be fully reasoned and published in full on DG Comp's website.

In the past, certain comfort letters were treated as Decisions, meaning that they were challengeable in the ECJ, and could not be reopened in the absence of new evidence,[131] and national courts were required to regard them as a relevant element of fact.[132] The same should apply to informal guidance.

The decision whether or not to apply for formal or informal guidance, or not to draw the Commission's attention to the matter at all, is of course a commercial decision as much as a legal one. It may be that when all factors are weighed up, the commercial decision is taken to risk invalidity of the contract and the imposition of fines by the Commission. This may occur when the contract in all probability infringes Article 81(1) and would not qualify for exemption. However, it may also occur when there is considerable uncertainty as to the legality of the agreement because such arrangements have not been thoroughly considered before by the Commission: in such circumstances the inconvenience and risks attendant on being the subject of a test case may lead the parties to decide against notification. The publicity which would be given to the arrangements may also be a factor influencing this decision.

---

[130] OJ 2004 C101/78.
[131] Case T-241/97 *Stork v Commission* [2000] ECR II-309, [2000] 5 CMLR 31
[132] Joined Cases 253/78 and 1-3/79 *Procureur du Roi v Guerlain*, [1980] ECR 2327, [1981] 2 CMLR 99, paras 11–12.

Enforcement by Private Parties

The main opportunities for private parties to enforce Articles 81 and 82 are through complaints to the Commission and NCAs, or claims in national courts.

Complaints

The Commission does not deal with all alleged infringements of Articles 81 and 82 that come to its attention. It has limited resources and the ECJ has confirmed that, although it has a duty to consider every complaint, it has a broad discretion in deciding which cases should be given priority in the Community interest.[133] Factors which may come into play include the limited economic or geographic impact of the alleged infringement, the fact that the conduct complained of has ceased, and the availability of remedies from a national court or NCA. The Commission has published a Notice on the handling of complaints which describes the complaints procedure before the Commission and includes guidance on the types of case it is likely to take up.[134]

A formal complaint may be made by 'natural or legal persons who can show a legitimate interest' (Article 7(2) of Regulation 1/2003). This probably includes anyone actually or potentially suffering damage as a result of the alleged infringement, as well as consumer associations. Complaints may be made, for example, by a distributor or retailer who is denied supplies by a producer in a dominant position, or by a distributor prevented from selling outside a limited geographical territory, or by a seller refused supplies to dissuade him from fulfilling export orders.

A complaint may be made in any form, even orally or anonymously, but the following rules should be observed if the rights connected with the making of a formal complaint are to be obtained:

- The complaint should be made in writing in compliance with Form C,[135] and if it is made by a party's representative, such as an officer of the company or a lawyer, then formal proof of that representative's authority to act must be supplied to the Commission.

---

[133] Case T-24/90 *Automec v Commission (No 2)* [1992] ECR II-2223, [1992] 5 CMLR 431, para 86: 'To assess the Community interest in pursuing the examination of a matter, the Commission must take account of the circumstances of the particular case, particularly the legal and factual aspects set out in the complaint referred to it. It is for the Commission in particular to weigh up the importance of the alleged infringement for the functioning of the Common Market, the probability of being able to establish the existence of the infringement and the extent of the investigation measures necessary to fulfil successfully its task of securing compliance with Articles [81 and 82]'. See also in the context of distribution Case T-186/94 *Guerin Automobiles v Commission* [1995] ECR II-1753, [1996] 5 CMLR 685 and on appeal Case C-282/95 [1997] ECR I-503, [1997] 5 CMLR 447; Joined Cases T-185/96, T-189/96 and T-190/96 *Riviera Auto Service* [1999] ECR II-93.

[134] OJ 2004 C101/65.

[135] Annexed to Regulation 773/2004 (Appendix 6).

- As much relevant information as possible should be included, including explanation of why the complainant has a legitimate interest in making the complaint. The identity and address of the complainant and any other relevant parties should be given, together with copies of all correspondence and other relevant documents. Details should be given of any connected proceedings (for example, proceedings before a national court). In many cases it will also be essential to give technical information regarding the product in question, so that the relevant product market may be ascertained. A description of the market structure and the market shares of the major players in the market, together with any information showing trends in the market should also be supplied where possible.
- The complaint should then be sent together with three paper copies, and a non-confidential version, to DG Competition.[136]

Complaints may also generally be made to NCAs,[137] but their processes for dealing with complaints and the applicable procedural rules vary considerably. However, if the Commission is dealing with a case, NCAs are prohibited from doing so themselves. On the other hand, if the Commission decides not to pursue a case there is no obligation on any NCA to take it up instead.

Commission's Obligation to Follow Up Complaint

The Commission may not ignore a formal complaint. It has said it will normally decide within four months whether to reject the complaint or to make further investigation. During that time it may seek further information from and have informal discussions with the complainant. If it decides on rejection, it must inform the complainant of this and of the reasons, and then give him a fixed time (not less than four weeks, and an extension can be requested) within which to submit further comments before finally rejecting the complaint. The duty to give such information may be enforced by Article 232 proceedings.[138] If the complainant does not respond, the complaint is deemed to have been withdrawn.

All other cases proceed to a third stage at which the Commission either initiates proceedings against the allegedly infringing undertakings, or rejects the complaint by a formal Decision (which the complainant may appeal in the CFI and ultimately in the ECJ). A formal complainant is entitled to receive a non-confidential version of the Statement of Objections (a formal document sent to the undertakings concerned, setting out details of the allegations) and is entitled to comment on it within a fixed time limit. The complainant also has the right to speak at

---

[136] The precise formal requirements in the Commission's Notice on the handling of complaints and Reg 773/2004 are contradicted by 'Recommendations for the submission of complaints and antitrust correspondence' published on DG Comp's website. The Regulation is legally binding and the Recommendations are themselves due to be updated, so it will be safest to comply with the Regulation, at least until the Recommendations have been updated, when the two should agree.

[137] The Commission Notice on the handling of complaints (OJ 2004 C101/65) indicates when this may be more appropriate.

[138] Case T-28/90 *Asia Motors France v Commission* [1996] ECR II-961, [1992] 5 CMLR 431.

any oral hearing. If the complaint is ultimately rejected, which must be done by reasoned Decision, the complainant has the same rights as described above, including the rights to comment and to appeal the Decision.

Once a Decision rejecting a complaint has been taken a complainant cannot ask for the investigation to be reopened unless it puts forward significant new evidence. However, the Commission can decide to reopen a file, and an NCA or national court can take up a case which has been closed by the Commission.

Injunctions and Damages

Interim measures may be imposed by the Commission (see above) or an NCA or national court, but damages for loss caused by anti-competitive conduct are not available through the Commission or the ECJ or CFI.

Community law requires that damages be available through national courts on the basis of an infringement of Article 81 or 82. Even a party to an infringing agreement is entitled to claim damages if, as a result of his weak bargaining position, he cannot really be said to be responsible for it.[139]

In contrast to the situation in the United States, damages claims are not yet common in EU Member States,[140] and there are a number of reasons for this. The Commission is particularly keen to promote private enforcement through damages claims in national courts and it is expected to propose further procedural reforms to this end (see Chapter 7).

Involvement of Third Country Authorities

It is in the nature of restrictive practices and abuse of market power that their effects are not always restricted to the territory of the European Union. A number of international agreements of different kinds now provide for contacts between the Community competition authorities and those of certain third countries.

The European Economic Area (EEA) Agreement effectively extends the European 'Single Market' to Iceland, Liechtenstein and Norway.[141] It provides for a 'Surveillance Authority' which in those three countries has equivalent powers and similar functions to the Commission, and includes competition rules almost identical to the EU competition rules described in this book.

In the case of restrictive agreements and abuse of dominant position the rules provide that the Community authorities are responsible in all cases where there is

---

[139] Case C-453/99 *Courage v Crehan* [2001] ECR I-6297, [2001] 5 CMLR 1058.

[140] The first ever award of damages by a UK court was made by the Court of Appeal in *Crehan v Inntrepreneur* [2004] EWCA 637. The case involved a non-compete obligation imposed by a brewery on a pub tenant which infringed Article 81(1).

[141] When the EEA Agreement entered into force on 1 January 1994 it was of considerably greater importance than it is now, since Austria, Finland and Sweden were not then Member States of the European Union but were part of the EEA.

an effect on trade between its Member States, even if trade between the other EEA states is also affected; the Surveillance Authority deals with cases only affecting trade between Iceland, Liechtenstein and Norway. In other cases in which there is no appreciable effect on trade within the Community (for example, because trade is only affected between say Sweden and Norway) then the Surveillance Authority is competent if the companies concerned achieve at least 33 per cent of their EEA turnover on the territory of Iceland, Liechtenstein and Norway, and the Community is competent if more than 67 per cent of their EEA turnover is achieved in Community Member States.

When relevant, there is exchange of information and mutual co-operation on cases between these two authorities, and co-operation in investigations and in applying decisions taken. A 'one-stop shop' principle applies so that in any given case one authority will have responsibility for the procedure, although the other authority may be closely involved, and any decision taken by either authority is valid and enforceable throughout the EEA.

A different type of co-operation is that provided for by the EC–US Cooperation Agreement, which provides simply for administrative co-operation between the United States' competition authorities and those of the Community. The Agreement has been in force since 1991, and provides for mutual assistance and information exchange. A similar agreement entered into force with Canada in 1999, and with Japan in 2003. The authorities in these four jurisdictions plan to establish a network to enable them to work closely together, particularly on international cartels and mergers. However, such Cooperation Agreements do not permit the authorities to pass on confidential information without the consent of the company concerned.

In 1998 a Positive Comity Agreement was signed between the EC and the United States. This builds on the comity provisions of the 1991 Agreement, providing that a party adversely affected by anti-competitive behaviour occurring in the territory of the other party may request the other to take action. There is also a presumption that in certain circumstances a party will normally defer or suspend its own enforcement activities, in particular, where anti-competitive behaviour does not affect consumers in the territory of the requesting party, or the behaviour is occurring principally in and is directed principally towards the other party's territory. However, confidential information still cannot be exchanged by the authorities unless the parties grant an express waiver of their right to confidentiality.

At global level, the Commission has for some years been considering the need for international competition rules. A 1995 report[142] stated that bilateral competition agreements between countries and regional groupings, such as those described above, needed to be expanded and deepened, with the medium-term aim of creating various multilateral agreements, the ultimate goal being to establish a global competition code policed by a single, international authority.

---

[142] A report compiled by Commission officials and external experts on 'Competition policy in the new trade order: strengthening international co-operation and rules'.

Discussions on the interaction of trade and competition policy went on for some years in the WTO Working Group, but failed to achieve agreement on the need to start negotiations for such a multilateral agreement, partly because the United States was not in favour. It preferred instead the strengthening of bilateral co-operation and the provision of technical assistance to countries which need it, and working through the OECD, or a new independent body.

Just such a new independent body, the International Competition Network, was established in 2001. It is an international forum for dialogue, and in particular the exchange of best practice, amongst competition enforcement authorities. It has been extremely successful in attracting membership from authorities across the world and currently has members from around 70 jurisdictions, including the European Commission. It is an informal, virtual network, which works principally through its various working groups and an annual conference.

3

Distribution Agreements

KEY POINTS

- A distribution agreement will not infringe EU competition law if it has no appreciable effect on trade between Member States, though national competition law may apply.
- If an agreement has an effect on trade and includes fixed or minimum resale prices or an absolute export ban ('hard-core' restrictions) it will almost certainly be unenforceable and may attract fines from the Commission or national competition authorities.
- If it does not include hard-core restrictions and is not capable of appreciably affecting competition then it will not infringe EU competition law.
- If it does affect competition but does not include hard-core restrictions, a block exemption may provide a 'safe harbour' for it, provided that the relevant market share (usually that of the supplier) does not exceed 30 per cent.
- Where the market share is over 30 per cent, whether it infringes EU competition law rules depends on the nature of the restrictive clauses it contains and also on its economic effect on the relevant market.
- In addition, if the restrictions in the agreement can be justified in terms of economic efficiency, and the market is sufficiently competitive, then a potentially infringing agreement may benefit from exemption and so be legal and enforceable.
- Responsibility for assessing whether an agreement infringes EU competition rules, including whether it qualifies for exemption, falls primarily on the parties themselves, subject to the control of the courts and authorities in the event of a dispute or complaint.
- A company with a market share above 40 per cent may have a 'dominant position', and it should check that none of its distribution practices constitute an illegal 'abuse'.

EC Regulation

Commission Regulation (EC) 2790/99 on the application of Article 81(3) to vertical agreements (Appendix 4)

Notice

Commission Guidelines on vertical restraints (Appendix 7)

ECJ Judgments

Cases 56 and 58/64 *Consten & Grundig v Commission* [1966] ECR 299, [1966] CMLR 418

Case 23/67 *Brasserie de Haecht v Wilkin (No 1)* [1967] ECR 407, [1968] CMLR 26

Case C-234/89 *Delimitis v Henninger Brau* [1991] ECR I-935, [1992] 5 CMLR 210

Case T-7/93 *Langnese-Iglo v Commission* [1995] ECR II-1533 upheld in Case C-279/95 [1998] ECR I-5609.

Case T-9/93 *Schöller Lebensmittel v Commission* [1995] ECR II-1611

Case C-344/98 *Masterfoods v HB Ice Cream* [2000] ECR I-11369, [2001] 4 CMLR 449

Bayer cases, Cases T-41/96 [2000] ECR II-381, [2001] 4 CMLR 126 and C-3/01, 6 January 2004 (not yet officially reported), [2004] 4 CMLR 653.

An understanding of the basic substantive and procedural rules of EU competition law is essential background to this chapter and those that follow. Readers not familiar with these are recommended to start by reading Chapter 2.

3.1 INTRODUCTION

Choice of a distribution method depends on many factors other than competition law. These may include matters relating to other areas of European Community or domestic law such as intellectual property law and consumer protection legislation, as well as all the non-legal considerations such as tax rules and the producer's level of familiarity with local markets. As for EU competition law, the landscape has been changing in recent years, as a result of a revolution in the European Commission's approach. The old approach had been widely criticised as too rigid and formalistic and it has been replaced by a more economics-based approach under which firms without market power have much more freedom than before.

When planning a distribution system, it is important to establish broadly the most important elements of the agreement. For example, is it important to retain control over resale prices? Is there a particular corporate image to be developed or promoted? Is it intended to grant distributors some degree of exclusivity within their sales area?

In some situations it may be possible and desirable to integrate vertically, so that goods are distributed by subsidiaries or other connected companies. (This may raise issues of control of mergers and acquisitions which are outside the scope of this book.) Once the entities charged with distribution are in fact under the control of the supplying company, EU competition law will not apply to agreements between them and terms and conditions under which the goods are required to be distributed, because companies may make such internal decisions freely. Only if a company occupies a dominant position on the market may it be necessary to consider whether its unilaterally imposed pricing and other policies are permissible under Community law.

If vertical integration is not the option chosen, it will be necessary to consider whether the type of distribution agreement envisaged is likely to infringe EU competition law. If the relevant market share is no more than 30 per cent, the arrangement may fit, or may be adapted so as to fit, into the framework of the vertical restraints block exemption Regulation. Where the agreement concerns motor vehicle distribution, it may benefit from the relevant sector-specific block exemption, provided it satisfies the relevant market share criteria. Although it is not mandatory to conform to a block exemption, if this can be done it will avoid the necessity to analyse the agreement and any restrictive clauses individually. This can often be convenient, as the concept of a clause restrictive of competition has been interpreted very widely.

In many cases the choice will lie between agency and exclusive distribution, and it will be necessary to weigh up the advantages and disadvantages of these two systems. The tightest control can be exercised over agents: agents may be instructed to charge particular prices, to deal only on particular terms and conditions or with limited categories of customers, and not to compete in any way with the principal. However, it is important to ensure that the actual agency relationship is the kind of relationship which will be regarded as agency under Community law. This is difficult at present, as the Commission Guidelines on vertical restraints in some respects contradict the case law of the European Court of Justice, but generally agents bearing no financial risk in respect of contracts entered into on behalf of their principal so qualify. Note that agents are often entitled to compensation on termination of the agency (see Chapter 6).

Exclusive distribution involves allotting an exclusive sales area or customer group to each distributor. It will not usually be possible to guarantee each distributor absolute protection within his area or group: other dealers must be permitted to fulfil unsolicited orders coming from purchasers outside their territory or group. Nor can the supplier restrict his distributors from supplying other resellers or dictate to the reseller the conditions on which he may resell. Exemption is usually available under the vertical restraints block exemption for exclusive distribution agreements where the supplier's (or buyer's, where the exclusive territory covers the whole of the EU) market share does not exceed 30 per cent; otherwise the four substantive conditions of Article 81(3), and in particular improvements in economic efficiency, will have to be satisfied if exemption is to apply.

Similarly, an exclusive purchasing requirement, meaning a requirement that all contract goods have to be sourced from the supplier, or a non-compete agreement limited to a maximum term of five years, will be exempted by the block exemption where the supplier's market share does not exceed 30 per cent; otherwise economic efficiencies will have to be present if exemption is to apply.

Franchising arrangements, provided franchisees are not granted any territorial protection, often do not infringe EU competition rules at all. Where there is territorial protection and the supplier's market share does not exceed 30 per cent the block exemption will normally apply; otherwise economic efficiencies will have to be present, as for exclusive distribution or exclusive purchasing.

Selective distribution is the only method apart from agency which can allow a supplier to control the channels through which the goods may eventually be sold right through until they reach the final user. Again, where the supplier's market share does not exceed 30 per cent the block exemption will apply, provided there are no restrictions on cross supplies between distributors or on the end-users whom retailers may supply. Even if selective distribution is used, resellers must remain free to fix their own resale prices, as indeed must any type of distributors apart from agents or subsidiaries.

3.2 HOW DOES EU COMPETITION LAW TREAT DISTRIBUTION AGREEMENTS?

Distribution agreements are usually 'vertical' agreements because they are made between parties operating, at least for the purposes of the agreement, at different levels in the supply chain. Most vertical agreements are viewed as relatively benign from the point of view of competition law. Horizontal agreements—which occur between competing firms—are treated much more strictly.[1]

In recent years there has been a fundamental shift in the Commission's approach to vertical restraints. As compared with its previous approach, there is now greater focus on the economic effects of restraints rather than on their contractual form. From an economic point of view, all types of vertical restraints are capable of being either pro-competitive or anti-competitive, depending on the surrounding circumstances. Ideally therefore, each agreement would be evaluated individually on its merits. But while theoretically attractive, such an approach would demand vast resources and create severe uncertainty for companies needing to know whether their arrangements are legal and enforceable.

Because a case-by-case investigation is not practicable, the European Commission has sought to make some generalisations about certain types of restraints (eg price-fixing, non-compete clauses) and certain types of situations (eg a market share not exceeding 30 per cent) in order to state some general rules, both in order to give legal certainty to companies and to relieve them, and the Commission and national courts and authorities, of the burden of carrying out an individual economic analysis of the benefits and anti-competitive effects of every agreement.

Restrictions in distribution agreements are frequently considered economically beneficial, provided that competition between competing brands (inter-brand competition) is strong.[2] Such restrictions often increase inter-brand competition and further market integration, for example, where a franchising system enables a franchiser's investment in developing an original business method to be used across a wide area by many independent businesses. They can help suppliers enter new markets by providing retailer incentives, and contribute to streamlining distribution logistics, reducing costs and improving quality.

The Commission's current approach is based on the belief that the main negative effects of vertical restraints are:

(i)   foreclosure of other suppliers or other buyers by raising barriers to entry;
(ii) reduction of inter-brand competition between the companies operating on the market, including facilitation of collusion amongst suppliers or buyers;
(iii) reduction of intra-brand competition between distributors of the same brand;
(iv) the creation of obstacles to market integration, including, above all, limitations on the freedom of consumers to purchase goods or services in any Member State they choose.[3]

---

[1] See the Commission Guidelines (Appendix 7), para 26 and other works on EU competition law generally (see p 199).

[2] Guidelines, paras 6 and 119/1.

[3] *Ibid*, para 103. The fact that EU competition law is used to pursue not only the economic aim of protecting competition but also the political aim of market integration accounts for a treatment of territorial restrictions that would seem very severe viewed from a purely economic standpoint. See also Guidelines, para 7.

The Commission therefore tries to apply Article 81(1) so as to prohibit only those restraints which may have significant negative effects. With a few major exceptions including price-fixing and absolute export prohibitions, clauses are not viewed as per se positive or negative, the analysis depending largely on the economic context in which they operate. The market context of the agreement is much more important than the precise form of words used. Competition law issues arise mainly in situations in which the business in question has significant market power, and where competition from competing brands is weak.

Also, restrictions on inter-brand competition, such as non-compete clauses, are generally viewed as more likely to raise competition problems than restrictions on competition within the same brand (intra-brand competition), such as exclusive distribution clauses. Other relevant circumstances include market shares and market structure, product differentiation, barriers to entry, potential competition, possible oligopolistic interaction or collusion between competing firms, the cumulative effects of several distribution networks, and buyer power.

There is now a general presumption, embodied in the vertical restraints block exemption, that most restrictions other than price-fixing and absolute export bans are not problematic where they occur in the context of a relevant market share not exceeding 30 per cent. Market share is used here as an indicator of market power. Although perhaps the best single indicator available, it remains a crude one. It inevitably denies the protection of the block exemption to some harmless agreements and provides a degree of immunity to some anti-competitive agreements. It also means that some companies will need to monitor their own and their competitors' market positions and regularly revisit the question of whether they still benefit from the block exemption.

The main burden of the current policy falls on firms with substantial market shares, which are required to perform detailed market analysis. They have to undertake the complex task of establishing both the relevant geographic and product markets, and then of assessing their share of that market. This will be particularly difficult in fast developing markets where market shares are volatile.

Even where it seems fairly clear that the relevant market share is above 30 per cent, there is no presumption that the agreement is illegal. The Commission has recently cleared agreements where suppliers had high market shares.[4] However, in such cases in practice a firm will want to be in a position to show the absence of significant anti-competitive effects, or the efficiency benefits, of any restraints, so as to be well placed to defend the legality of the agreement in the event that it is challenged either by the Commission or a national competition authority, or by another party before a national court.

In establishing the rules applicable it should be remembered that the highest legal authority is that of the case law of the European Court of Justice (ECJ), and, below that, the Court of First Instance (CFI). Next in the hierarchy of authority are

---

[4] De Beers' rough diamond supply agreements were cleared where its relevant market share was 60–65 per cent, with the rest of the market very fragmented, Commission Press Release IP/03/64, 16 January 2003. See also the beer supply cases cited below, note 53.

Council Regulations, and then the Commission's practice, as shown both in its individual Regulations and Decisions and in the various informal Communications, Guidelines and Notices in which it sets out its policy.

The current policy is embodied in a general block exemption Regulation on vertical restraints adopted by the Commission, replacing the three earlier, separate, and more formalistic, block exemptions covering exclusive distribution, exclusive purchasing and franchising respectively.[5] It is accompanied by extremely detailed Guidelines on vertical restraints[6] in which it sets out its policy towards many types of vertical distribution agreements.

The Guidelines represent the Commission's attempt to provide a degree of legal certainty in the context of its economics-based approach, and they provide a very valuable guide to its thinking. However, the interpretation given to the Regulation by the Commission in the Guidelines is in some instances debatable, and it is not necessarily the same as the interpretation which might be given either by the ECJ or CFI or by national courts or authorities: both the Regulation and the Guidelines are without prejudice to the views of the ECJ and CFI, as it may be expressed in both past and future judgments.

But in practice the Guidelines are very important. It is useful to understand as clearly as possible the way in which the Commission is likely to apply Article 81 to distribution agreements and in particular to interpret the Regulation, and the Court has been known to refrain from imposing a fine in a case in which an undertaking might have been misled by a Commission Notice into thinking its conduct was legal.[7] Moreover, there has been very little guidance from the ECJ and CFI on the new rules on vertical restraints since they entered into force in 2000, so the Commission's views as set out in its Guidelines remain extremely influential. They are likely to be relied on by national courts and competition authorities of the Member States when they are applying Articles 81 and 82. Though they are not legally bound by them, they are likely to treat the Guidelines as of at least high persuasive value.

In assessing how EU competition rules may apply to a distribution agreement, the first task is to assess whether it includes provisions infringing Article 81(1) of the EC Treaty.

3.3 DOES THE AGREEMENT INFRINGE ARTICLE 81(1)?

Below is discussed the way in which Article 81(1) applies to various types of clause frequently found in vertical distribution agreements. Horizontal agreements, and horizontal aspects of mixed agreements, are subject to a different set of rules (see p 103). Note that only the infringing clause, and not necessarily the whole agreement, risks being held void under Article 81(2) (see p 29).

---

[5] Commission Regs 1983/83, 1984/83 and 4087/88.
[6] Appendix 7. The Guidelines were due to be revised in 2004 to take into account the Commission's experience, in particular in applying the block exemption Reg 2790/1999: Commission Press Release IP/00/520, 24 May 2000. This exercise has been postponed.

Also, where a distribution system affects only small operators or for some other reason has no appreciable cross-border effect, Article 81 will not apply (see p 24). Similarly, if the relevant market shares are low, so that the agreement is not capable of appreciably affecting competition, EU competition rules are not infringed, unless the agreement contains hard-core restrictions such as price-fixing or absolute territorial protection (see p 26).

Below, different types of restrictions which may infringe Article 81(1), and in particular exclusive distribution and exclusive purchasing, are discussed.[8] Selective distribution, franchising and agency will be covered to some extent here, as they are largely subject to the same general rules that apply to all distribution agreements. However, later chapters also focus on each of these distribution methods separately, as each raises particular issues.

Exclusive Distribution and Territorial Protection

Exclusive distribution agreements provide for a dealer to be the only dealer for particular goods in a defined territory. The territory may be as small as a single town or as large as a whole country or continent, but the dealer appointed to that territory has the assurance that the manufacturer or supplier is not supplying any of the dealer's competitors in that territory. Such agreements do not usually exist in isolation: typically a manufacturer or supplier will distribute his goods through a network of such relationships, each one relating to a different territory. The allocation of exclusive territories is usually accompanied by provisions giving some degree of protection to the distributors' territories from exports from other territories.

It will be seen that the choice of exclusive distribution rather than, say, selective distribution or franchising, limits the supplier in the control that he may exercise on the way in which the goods are marketed. An even greater degree of control is permitted by the use of agents, since then prices and terms and conditions of resale may be set (see Chapter 6), but the Community law definition of an 'agent' is narrow, and there may often in practice be no alternative to an exclusive distribution network. The Commission's main concerns about such agreements are that they can reduce competition between distributors of the same brand (intra-brand competition) and that they contribute to market partitioning.

It was established very early on that exclusive distribution agreements which affect trade flows between Member States of the Community normally infringe Article 81(1). Until the case of *Consten and Grundig v Commission*,[9] it had not been certain whether such vertical agreements could infringe Article 81(1). In *Consten and Grundig*, the Court confirmed that Article 81 did indeed apply to vertical distribution agreements.

---

[7] Cases 40 etc/73 *Suiker Unie and others v Commission* [1975] ECR 1663, [1976] 1 CMLR 555.
[8] See also Guidelines, paras 121–33.
[9] Cases 56 and 58/64 *Consten and Grundig v Commission* [1966] ECR 299, [1966] CMLR 418.

In that case, Grundig, a German manufacturer of televisions, radios and other electrical equipment, had appointed Consten to be the exclusive distributor for its products in France. Consten undertook not to supply directly or indirectly anyone outside France. Grundig not only undertook not to deliver the contract goods to anyone in France, but provided additional territorial protection by imposing similar restrictions on its German wholesalers and on its distributors in other Member States. There was also an arrangement under which Consten had the exclusive right to use the trademark 'GINT'.

The case came to the ECJ on appeal from the Commission's Decision that the agreement was contrary to Article 81(1) and therefore unenforceable. Consten had brought an action in the French courts to try to prevent a rival dealer from selling parallel imports of Grundig products that the dealer had obtained outside France. This was a profitable operation for the dealer because Grundig products were available at an appreciably lower price in some other Member States than in France.

Consten was thus seeking protection for an arrangement which allowed it to be the only source of Grundig goods for customers in France. Within France its only competition could come from dealers selling the products of manufacturers and suppliers other than Grundig: it was subject to no competition at all in respect of Grundig products themselves, in which it enjoyed a monopoly. Its conduct was the subject of a complaint to the Commission, which found an infringement.

In *Consten and Grundig* the ECJ upheld the Commission's Decision to the extent that it condemned under Article 81(1) the clauses of the agreement granting absolute territorial protection to Consten. Further, the trademark agreement was also condemned to the extent that the exclusive right to the trademark was used to impede parallel imports.

It was argued unsuccessfully before the ECJ that in fact the effect of the clauses conferring territorial exclusivity on the French dealer was to increase the flow of trade, and that it enabled more goods to be sold than otherwise would have been the case. Thus, it was argued, such clauses were in fact pro-competitive. But the Court held that if trade flows were disturbed from the course that they would otherwise have taken in the absence of the restriction, then this was sufficient to infringe Article 81(1), whether or not the flow of trade affected in fact increased or decreased. However, the ECJ stated that the Commission had not given sufficient reasons to justify condemning certain other parts of the agreement that were not directly obstructive of parallel imports.

Thus, in that case the question was left open as to whether an agreement by a supplier simply to supply only one dealer in the contract territory, as opposed to a total ban on parallel imports and exports, infringed Article 81(1). In *Société Technique Minière v Maschinebau Ulm*,[10] the Court held that agreements for exclusive distributorship did not necessarily infringe Article 81(1) in the absence of absolute territorial protection or export and import bans: whether they did depended on the factual situation and the degree of protection provided by the

---

[10] Case 56/65 [1966] ECR 235, [1966] CMLR 357.

precise contract terms. The Court said that exclusivity might be justified in particular if it was necessary in order to penetrate a new market. Relevant factors were said to include:

(1) the nature of the product;
(2) whether the agreement is for supply of unlimited amounts or is limited to certain amounts;
(3) the share that each party has of the market in which he does business;
(4) whether the agreement is one of a number of similar agreements forming a distribution network for the goods;
(5) the strength of territorial protection provided to the distributor and the possibility of parallel imports.

The factors listed above seem to suggest that where the parties hold relatively small market shares or where there are not too many other similar agreements, exclusive distribution arrangements should fall outside the scope of Article 81(1). However, in practice exclusive distribution agreements have been treated by the Commission as infringing Article 81(1) and the above factors only taken into account when deciding whether or not exemption under Article 81(3) is available.

The factors listed in *La Technique Minière* also suggest that the most minimal form of territorial protection, which is an assurance that the supplier will supply no other reseller within the contract territory, would not necessarily infringe Article 81(1). However, the Commission has in the past issued a block exemption covering agreements incorporating even this limited degree of territorial protection, and has tended to assume that any form of territorial exclusivity requires exemption. Although this question is not in practice important in the many cases in which a block exemption clearly applies, it may be of relevance to agreements which fall outside the scope of the block exemption, since the burden of proof in respect of Article 81(3) falls on the party claiming its benefit, whereas the burden of proof that Article 81(1) applies is on the party alleging an infringement (Article 2 of Regulation 1/2003).

There are also more recent ECJ judgments which suggest that in some circumstances a limited form of territorial exclusivity may fall outside the terms of Article 81(1).[11] But these are limited to the field of new technologies, in particular licences of plant breeders' rights. It does not seem that the Commission or Court is ready to extend this line of thinking to agreements for distribution of established goods, whatever the market nature and structure.

So in practice, unless an agreement has only very limited effects, exclusivity, whether or not accompanied by any additional form of territorial protection, will probably bring it within the scope of Article 81(1) as far as the Commission is concerned. Furthermore, the Commission has held that such arrangements made between parties in a single Member State can infringe Article 81(1), so that even

---

[11] Case 258/78 *Nungesser v Commission* [1981] ECR 45, [1983] 1 CMLR 278; Case 27/87 *Erauw-Jacquery v La Hesbignonne* [1988] ECR 1919, [1988] 4 CMLR 576.

national exclusive distribution networks may fall within the prohibition laid down in that Article.[12]

Export Restrictions and Other Means of Market Division

Clauses prohibiting exports, whether in the context of exclusive distribution (see above) or not are automatically infringements of Article 81(1) and therefore prohibited. The per se nature of this rule has been emphasised by a number of Court judgments:[13] it is not even necessary that the clause be applied.[14]

The aim of market integration (that is, the establishment of a single market without frontiers throughout Community territory) has had a strong influence on competition policy and explains why export bans and other restrictions which tend to divide up markets, in particular along national lines, are treated severely. In *Miller*[15] the Court held that:

> by its very nature, a clause prohibiting exports constitutes a restriction on competition, whether it is adopted at the instigation of the supplier or of the customer, since the agreed purpose of the contracting parties is the endeavour to isolate a part of the market.

So market sharing is virtually always held to fall within the scope of Article 81(1), almost regardless of the market situation. The restriction may occur in the form of an express clause in a distribution agreement, a verbal agreement,[16] or a clause in the terms and conditions of sale,[17] and the fact that the export restriction in an agreement is not enforced is no defence to an allegation that the agreement infringes Article 81(1).[18]

At one time the highest fine ever on an individual company for infringement of Article 81 was one of €102 million imposed on Volkswagen for using its distribution system to impose market partitioning measures. Volkswagen had, over a period of 10 years, systematically required its Italian dealers to reject orders from foreign customers, mainly German and Austrian, who were seeking to take advantage of lower Italian car prices. They had also terminated dealership agreements with dealers who refused to co-operate in this policy.[19]

The highest fine ever imposed on a company in respect of a vertical agreement infringing Article 81 is now one of over €149 million imposed on Nintendo[20] for acting as the driving force behind a series of collusive practices with its

---

[12] *Gerofabriek* OJ 1977 L16/8, [1977] 1 CMLR D35. See also cases cited at p 25.

[13] eg Case T-77/92 *Parker Pen Ltd v Commission* [1994] ECR II-549, [1995] 5 CMLR 435; Case T-43/92 *Dunlop Slazenger International v Commission* [1994] ECR II-441.

[14] Case T-66/92 *Herlitz v Commission* [1994] ECR II-531, [1995] 5 CMLR 458.

[15] Case 19/77 *Miller International v Commission* [1978] ECR 131, [1978] 2 CMLR 334, para 7.

[16] Case 28/77 *Tepea v Commission* [1978] ECR 1391, [1978] 3 CMLR 392.

[17] Case 30/78 *Distillers v Commission* [1980] ECR 2999, [1980] 3 CMLR 121.

[18] *Miller International v Commission*, above n 15.

[19] Upheld on appeal to the CFI and ECJ, but the fine reduced to €90 million, Case C-338/00 *Volkswagen v Commission*, [2003] ECR I-9189, [2004] 4 CMLR 351.

[20] OJ 2003 L255/33, [2004] 4 CMLR 421. An appeal regarding the level of the fine is pending, Case T-13/03, OJ 2003 C70/27. See also the cases cited at note 124, p 54.

distributors, designed to prevent exports of its game consoles and cartridges from high-price to low-price[21] Member States. Not only did the formal agreements restrict parallel imports, but the distributors actively co-operated with Nintendo to identify exporting firms, on whom sanctions were imposed. The distributors themselves were therefore also fined substantial amounts, whereas more often in the case of distribution infringements it is the supplier only who is fined.[22]

Not only straightforward export prohibitions or restrictions, but also indirect restrictions on export, infringe Article 81(1). A number of types of clauses and practices have been treated as indirect restrictions on export, such as granting of bonuses in respect of domestic sales only.[23] Another example is a term requiring distributors to resell to third parties only unopened packages of goods, which was held to infringe Article 81(1) since it discouraged the repackaging of goods for different markets and thus indirectly restricted exports.[24] Trademark rights may also be used to restrict exports, as in *Consten and Grundig*. Other methods of market division include refusal of supplies, restrictions on the use to which the goods supplied may be put, restrictions on advertising outside a specified area, and an obligation on the distributor to sell to end-users only.

Another type of indirect export restriction is refusal to provide warranty or after-sales services in respect of products not bought from an authorised distributor: where a manufacturer offers a guarantee for products bearing his trademark, he has to ensure that that guarantee can be invoked throughout the whole of his EU distribution network.[25] It is permissible, however, for an individual distributor to offer a guarantee to his own customers only, in the absence of a manufacturer's guarantee, or to offer his own customers better terms than those included in the manufacturer's guarantee.[26]

Another example of an indirect export ban appears in *Accinauto v Commission*,[27] where the CFI upheld a fine for infringement of Article 81(1). In this case market partitioning was effected by means of a requirement on distributors to refer any customer enquiries coming from outside the distributor's territory to the manufacturer. The Court held that this requirement was intended to serve as a disguised prohibition on making passive exports without the manufacturer's prior authorisation.

---

[21] In early 1996 prices in the UK were up to 65 per cent cheaper than in Germany and the Netherlands.

[22] Some distributors are appealing against their fines: Case T-12/03, OJ 2003 C55/41 (*Itochu*); Case T-398/02, OJ 2003 C44/43 (*Linea Gig*). Similar practices by Topps in the market for Pokémon stickers and cards, where there were price differences of up to 243 per cent between EU Member States, resulted in a much smaller fine of €1.59 million, Commission Press Release IP/04/682, 26 May 2004. This was because the infringement was of short duration and stopped as soon as Topps had been warned by the Commission.

[23] *Opel Nederland* (€43 million), upheld in Case T-368/00, [2003] ECR II-4491, [2004] 4 CMLR 1302, appeal pending, Case C-551/03, OJ 2004 C71/8.

[24] *Bayer Dental* OJ 1990 L351/46.

[25] Case 31/85 *ETA Fabriques d'Ebauches v DK Investment* [1985] ECR 3933, [1986] 2 CMLR 674. See also *Saeco*, Commission Press Release IP/00/684, 29 June 2000. But in the case of selective distribution this rule applies only to goods purchased through an authorised distributor (see p 118).

[26] Case 86/82 *Hasselblad v Commission* [1984] ECR 883, [1984] 1 CMLR 559.

[27] Case T-176/95 [1999] ECR II-1635, [2000] 4 CMLR 33.

In *Dunlop*, the tennis ball producer was fined not only for the ban on exports of tennis balls, but also for other measures including refusal to supply, pricing measures, marking and follow-up of exported products, buy-back of exported products and the discriminatory use of official labels, all intended to ensure enforcement of the export ban.

In *Distillers*,[28] different prices were charged to UK whisky dealers according to whether they were buying the whisky for export or for sale within the United Kingdom. Although there was strong economic justification in the circumstances for treating the home market differently from the Continental European market in this case, the Commission found that such discriminatory pricing fell within the scope of Article 81(1).[29] In another Decision the Commission imposed a fine on Martell and its French distributor for an arrangement under which the distributor refused to grant rebates to a wholesaler who made parallel exports to Italy;[30] this was despite the fact that this practice did not prevent the parallel trading from being financially viable, although it did reduce the profits to be made. A publishing house has also been persuaded to end its practice of charging different prices for its journals depending on the subscriber's place of residence on the grounds that it was infringing Community competition rules.[31]

However, not all distribution policies aimed at preventing parallel trade infringe Article 81(1). Parallel imports are a major concern in the pharmaceutical sector, and the *Bayer* case is an example of an arrangement which, though it was intended to limit parallel trade and was held by the Commission to infringe Article 81, was ultimately said by the European Court of Justice to fall outside its scope, though on the narrow ground that only a unilateral policy, and no 'agreement', had been shown (see p. 20). Another example of an attempt to reduce parallel trade while avoiding the application of Article 81 was where Glaxo charged Spanish wholesalers different prices according to whether the goods were intended for domestic consumption or for export. Glaxo argued that it was setting only one price, but that Spanish pricing regulations imposed a second, artificially low price in the case of products for domestic consumption. The Commission rejected this argument, but Glaxo is hoping that the CFI will take a different view.[32]

One can imagine other means of market division made possible by the Internet and electronic commerce. For example, a supplier might require distributors' Internet sites to be accessible only via the supplier's own site, in such a way that the supplier could forward orders to the appropriate local distributor. Such an arrangement would infringe Article 81(1).

However, more sympathetic treatment is now available to most territorial restrictions, including even passive sales bans, imposed in the context of the

---

28 OJ 1978 L50/16, [1978] 1 CMLR 400.
29 The same result would probably be reached today even under the Commission's new economics-based policy, so strong is the market integration imperative.
30 *Gosme/Martell* OJ 1991 L185/28.
31 *Pergamon Press*, Commission Press Release IP(90)804.
32 *Glaxo SmithKline* OJ 2001 L302/1, [2002] 4 CMLR 335, appeal pending, Case T-168/01, OJ 2001 C275/17.

launch of new products, or entry into a new geographical market. In its most recent statement of policy the Commission says that:

> vertical restraints linked to opening up new product or geographic markets in general do not restrict competition. This rule holds, irrespective of the market share of the company, for two years after the first putting on the market of the product. It applies to all non-hardcore vertical restraints and, in the case of a new geographic market, to restrictions on active and passive sales imposed on the direct buyers of the supplier located in other markets to intermediaries in the new market. In the case of genuine testing of a new product in a limited territory or with a limited customer group, the distributors appointed to sell the new product on the test market can be restricted in their active selling outside the test market for a maximum period of one year without being caught by Article 81(1) (Guidelines, para 119/10).

This may be very useful in enabling suppliers launching products in a new territory to offer distributors in that new territory sufficient incentives to invest in marketing the product, especially in product markets where Internet sales channels are well established.

A clause prohibiting export to or from non-Community countries will only infringe Article 81(1) if there would otherwise be a reasonable likelihood of re-imports back into the Community.[33] For many goods and third countries the costs of transport and customs duties mean that this would not be economically worthwhile, though as the EU becomes larger and concludes more free trade agreements, this will apply to fewer countries.

Customer Restrictions

Care should be taken by a supplier when imposing any restrictions on the customers to whom a distributor may resell. A requirement that goods purchased be supplied only to a particular type of customer, such as end-users or specialist retailers, will often infringe Article 81(1). So will a clause by which the buyer agrees only to buy quantities needed to supply his own end-user customers, thus prohibiting him from reselling the goods to other distributors.[34]

In the context of selective distribution it is acceptable in certain circumstances to impose certain limitations on the type of dealers to whom supplies may be sold. Furthermore, in the context of selective distribution it is legitimate to require wholesalers not to supply end-users (see Chapter 4).

Resale price-fixing

Resale[35] price-fixing or setting of minimum resale prices is not only expressly prohibited by Article 81(1)(a) but it is also hardly ever exempted (see p 98). It attracts

---

[33] Case C-306/96 *Javico v Yves St Laurent* [1998] ECR I-1983, [1998] 5 CMLR 172; Cases 51 etc/75 *EMI v CBS* [1976] ECR 811, [1976] 2 CMLR 235. See also note 31, p 26.

[34] Guidelines, paras 178ff.

[35] It is of course *resale* price-fixing that is prohibited, and not price-fixing itself. This may sound obvious, but is important when analysing practices such as 'indirect fulfilment', where a large customer

heavy fines.[36] Maximum prices are acceptable, but not if they combine with other factors so as to impose a fixed resale price range.[37]

Even where the parties to the agreement or the relevant market share are very small any attempt to fix retail prices or minimum resale prices will fall foul of Article 81(1),[38] unless there is no effect on trade between Member States. For example, the Commission has taken the view that a resale price maintenance agreement for books within Germany ('*Sammelrevers*') had no effect on trade between Member States and therefore did not infringe Article 81(1).[39] But even retail price maintenance at a purely national level may fall within the scope of Article 81(1) if it is considered to have the effect of deflecting trade flows away from the channels in which they would naturally run if prices were fixed freely.[40]

Vertical price *recommendation*, on the other hand, has always been acceptable in the context of franchising[41] and this was said in *JCB* to apply also to 'a distribution system which is hybrid but very similar to a selective distribution system'.[42] The Commission in its Guidelines now accepts it in the case of other types of distribution agreement, provided that there is genuinely only a recommendation and no kind of pressure is put on distributors to sell at the recommended price. However, the Commission has said that it regards the provision of recommended or maximum resale prices with suspicion when the relevant market share is over 30 per cent because of the risk of it being followed by all or most distributors, and because it may facilitate collusion between them. It suggests that such clauses will infringe Article 81(1) where the supplier has a strong market position or where the market is a 'narrow oligopoly', and that exemption will not be available in such circumstances (paras 225–228).

concludes a purchase directly with a producer, and the producer sub-contracts fulfilment of the contract to one of its distributors. There is no official guidance on the point, but such practices should not infringe Article 81, provided there is only a direct sale to the customer and no purchase and resale by the distributor.

[36] eg *Volkswagen* (€30.96 million), annulled in Case T-208/01, 3 December 2003 (not yet officially reported), [2004] 4 CMLR 727, because no 'agreement' proved, appeal pending, Case C-74/04, OJ 2004 C94/24.

[37] *Nathan-Bricolux* OJ 2001 L54/1, [2001] 4 CMLR 1122. See also Commission Notice *Repsol CPP*, OJ 2004 C258/7.

[38] The Commission stated in Press Release IP/02/916, 24 June 2002 that minimum retail price-fixing in the form of a prohibition on the use of B&W loudspeakers as loss-leaders infringed Article 81(1).

[39] Commission Press Release IP/02/461, 22 March 2002. The agreement applies to exported and reimported goods only where they have been exported solely for the purpose of avoiding the resale price maintenance arrangements. See also Case C-360/92 *Publishers Association v Commission (No 2)* [1995] ECR I-23, [1995] 5 CMLR 33. Price-fixing for books often involves horizontal agreements between publishers: see p 104.

[40] Case 8/72 *Cement Dealers v Commission* [1972] ECR 977, [1973] CMLR 7.

[41] Case 161/84 *Pronuptia de Paris v Schillgalis* [1986] ECR 353, [1986] 1 CMLR 414.

[42] Case T-67/01, 13 January 2004 (not yet officially reported), [2004] 4 CMLR 1346, para 132, on appeal Case C-167/04, OJ 2004 C156/3.

Non-compete and Exclusive Purchase Obligations

Suppliers often choose to conclude agreements with their distributors which limit the extent to which the distributors may obtain goods from sources other than the supplier. The limitation may apply to all supplies of the contract goods (say, Bally shoes) or to all supplies of a particular generic product (say, all shoe requirements). The former does not prevent the buyer from obtaining and distributing competing goods, but the latter does. A supplier may want to impose either or both.

The terminology used to refer to such clauses has not always been clear, with 'exclusive purchase' and 'non-compete' sometimes being used interchangeably, and without specifying which of the two types of restriction is meant. It will be seen in some of the extracts quoted below that in past cases the Commission itself has not been consistent in its use of these terms. The usage adopted here, as in the Commission's Regulation and Guidelines, is as follows. The term 'exclusive purchasing' is used to denote the first type of clause, by which a supplier requires a buyer to obtain all or most his supplies of contract goods directly from the supplier, but leaves him free to buy and sell competing brands. A 'non-compete clause' refers to the second type of clause: it requires a distributor to obtain all or most of his requirements on a particular market from that supplier, though he may be permitted to obtain them either directly from the supplier or through other channels.

Non-compete Clauses

An obligation on the reseller not to manufacture or sell competing goods may fall under Article 81(1).[43]

The Commission described non-compete clauses (which it referred to as 'exclusive purchasing agreements') and their benefits in its Seventh Report on Competition Policy as follows:

> These are agreements under which the purchaser accepts an obligation to purchase particular goods from a single supplier only, over a relatively long period. They have an important business function in that they give a guarantee of ensured sales to one party and a guarantee of continuous supplies to the other. Exclusive purchasing agreements are consequently normal in almost all branches of the economy, as a rule in very large numbers; they are particularly common . . . between manufacturers and dealers . . . the purchaser is frequently given special privileges of the most varied kind, ranging from priority for deliveries and the assurance of technical assistance, through special forces, discounts, bonuses, premiums and fidelity rebates, and the guarantee of a specified margin, to long-term loans' (para 9).

This definition deals only with arrangements providing for absolute exclusivity. An agreement may fall under Article 81(1) even if a purchaser is not required to

---

[43] *Goodyear Italiana*, OJ 1975 L38/10, [1975] 1 CMLR D31.

take all, but only a major part of, his requirements from the supplier. Nor is it necessary that there be any legal or even moral obligation on him to do so. It is sufficient that in practice the agreement has a tendency to produce these effects.[44] It will apply to practices such as quantity forcing, where a buyer is required to purchase minimum volumes or a minimum percentage of his requirements, where this produces similar effects to a non-compete provision, or to a threat to stop supplies if a distributor deals in competing products.[45]

Other restrictions which have the effect of dissuading buyers from purchasing competing goods, such as an obligation to stock complete ranges of goods,[46] quantity discounts, non-linear pricing (for example, an initial lump sum plus a price per unit, meaning that the more the buyer buys, the lower the average cost of a unit) and other forms of quantity forcing will be analysed on the same basis as non-compete clauses. The same would be true of 'share of shelf' agreements by which retailers agree to reserve a specific proportion of shelf space, perhaps in a specified position, for the supplier's goods. Such clauses may well infringe Article 81(1) and require exemption if they are to be valid.

The Commission went on to state that:

> Exclusive purchasing agreements may endanger competition, because they limit the purchaser's freedom of choice and therefore at least potentially restrict the sales outlets open to other suppliers.[47]

In *BP Kemi*[48] it explained that when concluded for a long term, such contracts freeze the competitive process. It is true that at the time the agreement is made, the purchaser may choose the supplier offering the best terms available. However, during the whole duration of the contract, he is unable to switch to taking his supplies either from a new market entrant or from a competing supplier who has meanwhile become more competitive. These other potential suppliers are thus excluded from competing for a considerable length of time.

As in the context of many other types of agreement, the Commission and Court of Justice have stressed that non-compete obligations do not automatically fall within the scope of Article 81(1). They will infringe Article 81(1) only if they both affect trade between Member States and prevent, restrict or distort competition.[49] A number of factors are relevant in deciding whether these conditions are fulfilled:

In *BP Kemi* the Commission stressed the importance of taking into account the economic circumstances surrounding the agreement:

> depending, inter alia, on the length of the period and on the economic context, including the market shares and positions of the purchaser and seller, such a purchasing obligation may constitute a restriction on competition within the meaning of Article [81] (para 59)

[44] Twelfth Commission Report on Competition Policy, para 12.
[45] See Commission Press Release IP/02/521, 9 April 2002 on Check Point's software distribution practices.
[46] eg *SABA (No 1)* OJ 1976 L28/19, [1976] 1 CMLR D61.
[47] Seventh Commission Report on Competition Policy, para 9.
[48] OJ 1979 L286/32, [1979] 3 CMLR 684.
[49] Case 23/67 *SA Brasserie de Haecht v Wilkin (No 1)* [1967] ECR 407, [1968] CMLR 26.

When on such a market, which already displays a weak competitive structure, one of the most important suppliers enters into long-term contracts with one of the most important purchasers, which induce the purchaser to take all his requirements or the major part of his requirements from the same supplier, there exists an appreciable disadvantage for the supplier's competitors and for purchasers, and there is then a restriction of competition for the purposes of Article [81(1)]. (para 68)

In this case not only was the market itself characterised by weak competition, but also the parties involved happened to be very strong. Both these factors, amongst others, contributed to the finding that the agreement infringed Article 81(1).

In *Delimitis v Henninger Brau AG*[50] the Court said that a non-compete agreement for beer would not infringe Article 81(1) unless two conditions were satisfied. First, taking into account the economic and legal context, the national market for distribution of beer by retail drinks outlets must be subject to substantial barriers to entry or for other reasons be foreclosed to competitors who might establish themselves on that market or increase their share of that market. Secondly, the supplier's agreements must make a substantial contribution to that foreclosure.[51]

Delimitis was later applied by the Commission so as to grant informal negative clearance to Greene King's tied pub agreements.[52] It held that the UK beer 'on-trade' (sale in pubs and restaurants) market was foreclosed as the result of the existence of a number of networks but that Greene King, which had only 1.3 per cent of this market, could not be said to contribute substantially to this foreclosure.

In that case the Commission contrasted the situation of Greene King with that of bigger brewers such as Whitbread which held over 5 per cent of the market. However, more recently the brewer Interbrew was granted informal negative clearance for its amended beer supply agreements, including non-compete obligations, on the basis of economic analysis showing no foreclosure effects, where it had about 56 per cent of the relevant market. This is evidence that the new, more economics-based approach is being applied in this area.[53]

---

[50] Case C-234/89 [1991] ECR I-935, [1992] 5 CMLR 210.

[51] Where a supplier concludes different types of agreement the contribution of each type may exceptionally need to be considered separately, Case C-214/99 *Neste Markkinointi Oy* [2000] I ECR I-11121, [2001] 4 CMLR 993. However, the CFI rejected such an argument in Case T-65/98 *Van den Bergh Foods v Commission*, [2003] ECR II-4653, [2004] 4 CMLR, para 159; appeal pending, Case C-552/03, OJ 2004 C59/13.

[52] Upheld in Case T-25/99 *Roberts v Commission* [2001] ECR II-1881, [2001] 5 CMLR 828.

[53] Commission Press Release IP/03/545, 15 April 2003. The result in this case bears a striking resemblance to that in the Dutch competition authority's 2002 ruling that Heineken's beer distribution agreements, representing a market share of around 50 per cent, did not infringe the Dutch national equivalent of Article 81(1). DG Comp's Competition Policy Newsletter Summer 2003 refers to the fact that it worked closely with the Belgian and Dutch competition authorities on these cases and to 'the fruits borne by intensified contacts with NCAs'. See also the comment on the Dutch case in RBB Economics Brief 04, 'Pro-competitive Exclusive Supply Agreements: How Refreshing!' August 2002 (available at www.rbbecon.com).

In the *Ice Cream* cases,[54] the Court of First Instance followed *Delimitis* and approved the fact that the Commission had taken into account not only the proportion of sales outlets tied to producers (about 30 per cent) and the quantities to which those commitments related, but also the barriers to entry created by the practice of 'freezer exclusivity' (a system under which freezer cabinets are lent to retailers on condition that they do not use them to store competing goods).

The duration of a non-compete agreement is a crucial factor. Such an agreement imposed only for a short period, such as one year, might not infringe Article 81(1).[55] However, in practice suppliers are usually interested in longer periods, which make it likely that the contract infringes Article 81(1).

In *Liebig Spices*,[56] a manufacturer of spices concluded non-compete contracts with three large supermarket chains. This was another case in which both the supplier and the purchasers had very strong market positions, and the agreements together tied up a substantial part of the market, making it very difficult for other spice manufacturers to find large outlets through which to distribute their products. The agreements were found by the Commission to account for 35 per cent of the total retail spice market. Not only was Article 81(1) infringed but exemption was refused.

Not just the market share of the company in question but also the structure of the market is very important: if a number of strong competitors each has a substantial market share, there may be no infringement of Article 81(1), because competition may not be sufficiently affected.

Therefore in practice, unless it is only for a very short period, any agreement by a wholesaler or retailer with a strong market position to obtain his supplies of a specific product or service from one source only will almost certainly be characterised as violating Article 81(1) and will need to benefit from exemption either through a block exemption or under Article 81(3) if it is not to be void and unenforceable.

Exclusive Purchasing Clause

Such clauses raise not foreclosure concerns but rather market partitioning concerns. Whether they infringe Article 81(1) will depend on all the surrounding market circumstances, except in the case of selective distribution where they are treated as per se infringements.

'English Clause'

An English clause is one which permits the purchaser to obtain supplies elsewhere only if he can obtain them more cheaply than from his supplier, and is similar in

[54] Case T-7/93 *Langnese-Iglo v Commission* [1995] II ECR 1533 upheld in Case C-279/95 [1998] ECR I-5609 and Case T-9/93 *Schöller Lebensmittel v Commission* [1995] ECR II-1611. See also *Van den Bergh Foods*, above n 51 Athough in this latter case there was only freezer exclusivity and not a non-compete obligation, it was held that Art 81(1) was infringed and exemption was refused.

[55] But contracts of around one year's duration were found to infringe Art 81(1) in *Schöller Lebensmittel*, above n 54.

[56] OJ 1978 L53/20, [1978] 2 CMLR 116.

its effects to a non-compete clause. The exercise of the right to buy elsewhere is normally subject to a number of conditions. For example, it may apply only if the alternative supplier is offering a certain minimum quantity, or the purchaser may be required to give his supplier the opportunity to match or better the alternative offer.

In the *BP Kemi* case, the agreement included an English clause. The parties argued that this prevented the agreement from having the alleged restrictive effects on competition. However, the Commission considered that the conditions in which the clause could be invoked were so narrowly circumscribed that the clause did not significantly lessen the restrictive effects of the agreement.

Further, the Commission even commented adversely on English clauses, saying that they could act as a mechanism for the exchange of information on prices and conditions between competitors. Such exchange of information is viewed extremely suspiciously by the Commission. So even a straightforward English clause not hedged about with strict conditions may not be sufficient to take a non-compete agreement outside the scope of Article 81(1).

Tying

Article 81(1)(e) states that 'tying' or the obligation to buy, together with the product actually wanted, a second product or service which, by its nature or according to commercial usage, has no connection with the subject of the contract, infringes Article 81(1) (see also p 102). However, in practice the Commission has tended to raise concerns about tying only under Article 82, in situations where firms have a high degree of market power.

Intellectual Property Rights

Intellectual property rights can be used to impede parallel imports, for example, by using different trademarks for the same product in different territories, and an agreement to use such rights in this way will infringe Article 81(1).[57]

However, the use of intellectual property rights to partition Community territory frequently occurs through the unilateral action of the right-holder and in the absence of any agreement, and so is more often dealt with under Article 82 (see p 39) or under Articles 28 to 30 of the EC Treaty, which provide for free movement of goods.

A clause requiring the distributor to use the supplier's trademark does not infringe Article 81.[58]

---

[57] Cases 56 and 58/64 *Consten and Grundig v Commission*, above n 9.
[58] *BMW* OJ 1975 L29/1, [1975] 1 CMLR D44, para 32.

Other Acceptable Restrictions

Other clauses which do not usually infringe Article 81(1) include obligations to advertise[59] and to provide after-sales and guarantee services.[60] Similarly, restrictions which are necessary, for example, for health and safety reasons, such as a prohibition on selling medicines to children, do not infringe Article 81(1).[61]

3.4 NETWORK EFFECT

In order to decide whether trade between Member States is affected, it may be necessary to take into account not only the agreement in question but also any similar agreements making up part of the same network,[62] and if that single network does not affect trade sufficiently to infringe Article 81(1), other similar networks in the market (see also p 80).

The fact that a distribution system is one of several in the same market is one of the factors that must be taken into account in deciding whether Article 81(1) is infringed. However, the supplier's agreements must in themselves be of sufficient economic importance (in terms of the market positions of the parties and the duration of the contract) to contribute to making it difficult for competing suppliers to enter the market.[63] In other words, if a distribution system is of minor importance and has no significant effect on the competitive situation then the mere fact that it is one of a group of similar networks does not mean that it infringes Article 81(1).

The Court of First Instance held in the *Ice Cream* cases that, following *Delimitis*, it is necessary:

> to consider whether, taken together, all the similar agreements entered into in the relevant market and the other features of the economic and legal context of the agreements at issue show that those agreements cumulatively have the effect of denying access to that market for new domestic and foreign competitors. If, on examination, that is found not to be the case, the individual agreements making up the bundle of agreements as a whole cannot undermine competition within the meaning of Article [81(1)] of the Treaty. If, on the other hand, such examination reveals that it is difficult to gain access to the market, it is necessary to assess the extent to which the contested agreements contribute to the cumulative effect produced, on the basis that only agreements which make a significant contribution to any partitioning of the market are prohibited.[64]

Network effect is of particular concern to brewers who all tend to use similar types of exclusive purchasing and non-compete networks to distribute their beers (see p 80).

[59] *Ibid*, para 30.
[60] *IBM* OJ 1984 L118/24, [1984] 2 CMLR 341.
[61] *Kathon Biocide* OJ 1984 C59, [1984] 1 CMLR 476. See also Guidelines, para 49.
[62] *Brasserie de Haecht*, above n 49 *Delimitis*, above n 50.
[63] *Delimitis*, above n 50 and *Ice Cream* cases, above n 54.
[64] *Schöller Lebensmittel*, above n 54, para 76.

3.5 DOES THE BLOCK EXEMPTION REGULATION APPLY?

If an agreement falls within the scope of Article 81(1) then it requires exemption as provided for under Article 81(3) if it is to be legal and enforceable. The two types of exemption available are (1) through a 'block exemption' (see p 32) or (2) by satisfying the four substantive criteria of Article 81(3).

Block exemption will be available if the requirements of the block exemption Regulation 2790/1999 on vertical restraints (Appendix 4) are met (or, in the case of motor vehicles, if the requirements of the sector-specific block exemption discussed in Chapter 4 are met). Many distribution agreements which infringe Article 81(1) are automatically valid and enforceable, and incur no risk of fines, through the operation of this block exemption.

Regulation 2790/1999 entered into force on 1 June 2000, replacing three block exemptions covering exclusive distribution, exclusive purchasing and franchising respectively. In contrast with the three earlier block exemptions, Regulation 2790/1999 creates a broadly drawn, non-sectoral, economic effects-based exemption regime. However, its relatively liberal approach is balanced by a market-share cap of 30 per cent, above which it is not available. It therefore provides a zone of legal certainty for most firms, provided no prohibited clauses are included, but leaves considerable uncertainty for the most successful firms. Unless otherwise stated, all references to Articles in this Chapter (except for Articles 81 and 82 of the EC Treaty) refer to this Regulation.

Scope

The block exemption Regulation on vertical agreements is of general scope and is intended to cover purchasing and distribution agreements. It therefore covers a wide range of 'vertical agreements'. A very important characteristic of the Regulation is that it exempts all vertical agreements as defined. Unlike older block exemptions, it does not limit exemption to an exhaustive list of clauses contained in the Regulation. This means that any vertical restraint not expressly prohibited is exempted, and it leaves firms relatively free to draft their distributorship agreements as they think best from a commercial point of view.

Vertical agreements are defined as:

> agreements or concerted practices entered into between two or more undertakings each of which operates, for the purposes of the agreement, at a different level of the production or distribution chain, and relating to the conditions under which the parties may purchase, sell or resell certain goods or services. (Article 2(1)).

The Regulation applies only to 'vertical' agreements, meaning those between operators at different levels of the production or distribution chain. It covers agreements for purchase, sale and resale of goods or services. It extends to both intermediate and final goods and services, and to all levels of trade. Supply of goods for renting or leasing is covered, but not the contracts of rent or lease them-selves (Guidelines, para 25). The Regulation therefore covers wholesale, retail, OEM,[65] industrial supply and bottling agreements but not, for example, produc-tion or research and development agreements.

It is not limited to agreements referring to EU territory, and so can provide legal security to companies whose agreements concern distribution in third countries, but where there is a risk that EU competition rules apply because there is an effect on trade between EU Member States.

Distribution agreements concerning motor vehicles, and their spare parts and after-sales services, are excluded from the benefit of the exemption, meaning that only the sector-specific motor vehicle distribution Regulation (see Chapter 4) is available for such agreements. Also excluded are agreements covered by the technology transfer Regulation or the Regulations covering horizontal co-operation agreements (Article 2(5) and Guidelines, para 45).

The application of the Regulation is limited to situations in which the relevant market share (see below) does not exceed 30 per cent.

Market Share Threshold

Where a company has a market share over 30 per cent this is presumed to reflect a degree of market power which makes it undesirable that it benefit from auto-matic exemption, and so the block exemption does not apply (Article 3).

In the usual case, where the supplier's market share is relevant, it is the market 'on which it sells the contract goods or services' (Article 3(1)) which must be con-sidered. The relevant market share is that of the supplier unless exclusive supply is involved, in which case it is the buyer's share of the market 'on which it purchases the contract goods or services' which must be considered (Article 3(2)). For the purposes of this rule 'exclusive supply' is narrowly defined as 'any direct or indi-rect obligation causing the supplier to sell the goods or services specified in the agreement only to one buyer inside the Community for the purposes of a specific use or for resale'. This only applies where EU-wide exclusivity has been granted. Where national exclusive territories are granted, it is still the supplier's market share that is relevant. The reason for this rule is that where EU-wide exclusivity is granted it is seen as being imposed by a strong buyer rather than by the supplier.

Both the relevant product and geographic markets, and then the market share, need to be established. Note that Article 11 requires the market share of the whole of the supplier's corporate group to be taken into account. Market shares will fre-quently be very difficult to assess, even with the aid of Articles 9 and 11 of the Regulation, the Commission's Guidelines on vertical restraints (paras 88–99), and the Commission's Notice on calculation of market share (see further p 23). And even where the market definition is clear enough, companies do not generally keep

---

[65] OEM stands for 'original equipment manufacturers', who supply parts for incorporation into a new product, in contrast to manufacturers who supply replacement parts.

statistics and information in the form needed for ascertaining the necessary market share figures.

The relevant product market comprises 'any goods or services which are regarded by the buyer as interchangeable, by reason of their characteristics, prices and intended use' (Guidelines, para 90). Interchangeability will be especially difficult to assess in new technology markets: market definitions and shares shift rapidly with each technological development, and the phenomenon of 'convergence' means that distinct types of product quickly become combined with each other to form a new single product. In the case of intermediate goods or services which are not recognisable in the final product the market is normally defined on the basis of the direct buyers' views, whereas in the case of pure resale the preferences of the final consumers are more relevant (para 91).

Markets are not generally defined by the form of retail distribution used, as different distribution formats (eg supermarkets, smaller shops, mail order, Internet) usually compete (para 91). However, if different distribution channels clearly serve different purposes then they may represent separate markets.[66]

The question whether spare parts are a separate market from the original equipment is discussed by the Guidelines, which state that they can be, depending on factors such as the effects of the restrictions involved, the lifetime of the equipment and the level of repair and replacement costs (paras 94 and 96).

The relevant geographic market comprises:

the area in which the undertakings concerned are involved in the supply and demand of relevant goods or services, in which the conditions of competition are sufficiently homogeneous, and which can be distinguished from neighbouring geographic areas because, in particular, conditions of competition are appreciably different in those areas. (para 90).

The development of Internet distribution may broaden geographic market definition, particularly in the case of goods whose transport is easy and relatively cheap.

The 30 per cent threshold applies not only at the outset of the agreement, but is relevant throughout its term. It will therefore be important to make regular checks to ensure that an agreement which originally fell within the scope of the block exemption still satisfies the market share requirement, though Article 9 does give some flexibility in this respect.

Intellectual Property Rights

Restrictions concerning intellectual property rights[67] are within the scope of the Regulation only if they are 'directly related to the use, sale or resale' of the goods or services being supplied to the buyer and are not the 'primary object' of the agreement (Article 2(3)).[68]

---

[66] This possibility is acknowledged in merger cases such as M.2951, 27 September 2002 (health and beauty products) and M.3108, 23 May 2003 (office supplies).

[67] Article 2(3) is discussed in more detail in Chapter 5.

[68] Commission Regulation (EC) 772/2004 on the application of Article 81(3) of the EC Treaty to

Some situations, such as the exclusive licensing of a trademark to be used in the course of the sale of goods by an exclusive distributor, or marketing knowhow where goods are supplied to a franchisee, are clearly covered, but in others the assessment will be more difficult. For example, a complex manufacturing licence granted to the purchaser of a component would probably not be covered, because of the lack of a direct link to the component, but it might be if the degree of processing of the component were more limited.[69]

Note that the intellectual property (IP) right licence only falls within Article 2(3) of the block exemption if it is granted by the supplier to the buyer: so the type of sub-contracting agreement under which the buyer licenses a manufacturer to produce items using the buyer's IP right probably would not be covered by the Regulation.

Nor may the IP right be used in such a way as to circumvent the blacklisted obligations in the block exemption (see below), for example, by dividing up territories by prohibiting even passive sales of the goods sold under the licensed trademark outside a given territory.

Software may be supplied to distributors either by delivery of multiple diskettes for resale or through the supply of a single diskette together with the grant of a licence to copy the software onto blank diskettes for resale. The former is clearly supply of goods for resale (Guidelines, para 40). In the latter case it is hard to say whether the diskette or the licence is 'ancillary' since neither is any use without the other; the Commission considers that such a contract falls outside the block exemption (Guidelines, para 32).[70]

Where a copyright holder obliges resellers to resell books or software on condition that any buyer does not infringe the copyright, such an obligation, if it infringes Article 81(1), is covered by the block exemption. The same is true of any obligation on the buyer himself not to infringe the holder's copyright (paras 39 and 41).

Agreements Between Competitors

Most vertical agreements between competitors, whether actual or potential (defined in para 26), cannot benefit from the block exemption. In this context it is the product market which is relevant, and not the geographic market (para 26): a camera supplier active only in France may for these purposes be a competitor of a camera supplier only active in Italy (Articles 1(a) and 2(4)),[71] regardless of their potential to enter each other's markets.

categories of technology transfer agreements ('technology transfer block exemption') OJ 2004 L123/11, may apply to a licensing agreement excluded from the benefit of exemption by Article 2(3).

[69] The Commission considers that the dilution and bottling of a drink concentrate would be covered (Guidelines, para 35).

[70] Since the entry into force of the technology transfer block exemption Regulation on 1 May 2004 (see above n 68), software copyright licensing agreements have been covered by this Regulation, so this issue should not cause any further difficulty in practice. Para 32 also mentions that broadcasting contracts are not covered, and this interpretation was applied in *Telenor/Canal+/Canal Digital*, 29 December 2003 (not yet officially reported but available on DG Comp's website).

[71] Agreements between competitors are covered by the rules on horizontal co-operation (see p 103).

The exclusion of agreements between potential competitors from the scope of the Regulation may cause considerable difficulties, particularly where barriers to market entry are low. Also, assessment by the parties of whether this is the case may require knowledge of the business plans and current research projects of competitors. Not only may parties be reluctant to disclose information of this sort, but if they did the Commission might well consider such information exchange itself to be anti-competitive.

The exclusion from the scope of the Regulation of *reciprocal* agreements between competitors is absolute. Some *non-reciprocal* agreements between competitors do fall within the Regulation:

(1) if the buyer is a small firm, with an annual turnover not exceeding €100 million (Article 2(4)(a)); or

(2) if the parties compete only at the level of distribution of goods[72] (Article 2(4)(b)); or

(3) the parties compete in the provision of services but the buyer does not provide competing services at the level at which it purchases services from the supplier (Article 2(4)(c)).

Rules for the calculation of annual turnover for the purposes of these rules are given in Articles 10 and 11 of the Regulation.

Associations of Goods Retailers

Vertical agreements between members of a goods retailers' association and the association, or between the association and its suppliers, are exempted, provided no member, together with its 'connected undertakings' has an annual turnover above €50 million (Article 2(2)). The Commission has said that it will be flexible in the application of the €50 million rule (Guidelines, para 28). The calculation of annual turnover for the purposes of this rule is covered in Articles 10 and 11 of the block exemption Regulation.

This appears to mean that, for some small companies, joint purchasing agreements are exempted, despite the fact that they could be seen as horizontal rather than vertical in their effects. However, the usefulness of this Article is in practice limited. If, as will often be the case, there are horizontal[73] as well as vertical restrictions, the Regulation does not apply to the vertical aspects unless any horizontal restrictions are acceptable under Article 81 (para 29).

Also, where the members have significant market power, for example through the use of an exclusive label or their combined negotiating power, the Commission has the option of withdrawal of the benefit of the block exemption (see p 94).

---

[72] It is not clear whether the fact that the distributor is a potential competitor at manufacturing level is relevant, though logically it should be: otherwise a manufacturer who is also a distributor will more easily be able to make a distribution agreement with a potential competitor than will a manufacturer who does not distribute and who therefore cannot benefit from Art 2(4).

[73] eg a decision of the association to require members to purchase from the association, or to allocate exclusive territories to members.

Blacklist: Prohibited Clauses

Even companies falling under the 30 per cent market threshold cannot benefit from the Regulation if their agreements have any of the following 'blacklisted' or 'hard-core' objects. Such provisions are non-severable (Guidelines, para 66), so their inclusion results in the whole agreement falling outside the Regulation.

Article 4 begins: 'The exemption . . . shall not apply to vertical agreements which, *directly or indirectly, in isolation or in combination with other factors under the control of the parties,* have as their object . . .' (emphasis added). Therefore if any such restrictions are present, either in the terms of the contract or in the way in which it is applied, the Regulation does not apply and the agreement does not benefit from the block exemption.

(1) Fixed or Minimum Resale Prices, Whether Directly or Indirectly Enforced (Article 4(a))

Recommended prices, and probably advertising citing the recommended prices, is acceptable, as are maximum prices, provided there is no pressure or incentive on the buyer to abide by them. In some circumstances, for example, the pre-printing of recommended prices on the packaging of goods could mean that they functioned as resale price maintenance (Guidelines, para 47).

(2) Restrictions on the Buyer as to Where or to Whom He May Sell (Article 4(b))[74]

As a broad rule the Commission does not like such restrictions but it accepts that they can sometimes be beneficial. The following categories are therefore exempted.

(i) *A prohibition on active sales into an exclusive territory allocated to another buyer or exclusively reserved to the supplier.* Provided the other criteria of the Regulation are satisfied, it exempts a prohibition on the buyer on actively reselling into exclusively allocated territories or territories reserved to the supplier himself. Also, a supplier can agree with a distributor to impose prohibitions on active sales on its other exclusive distributors. But the Regulation does not exempt a prohibition on active sales into non-exclusively allocated territories.

This means that, if other exclusively allocated or reserved territories are listed in the distribution contract, the contract will have to be updated where territories become or cease to be exclusively allocated or reserved. Alternatively, the contract may simply refer to such territories generically, but a way will have to be found of keeping resellers informed about such changes.

---

[74] Article 4(b). The Guidelines provide many examples of direct and indirect measures covered by this prohibition. But a restriction on selling to certain end-users is not blacklisted to the extent that there is an objective justification, for example for health and safety reasons, for such a ban (para 49).

Such an active sales ban can be imposed on a non-exclusive distributor, so as simply to create an area of primary responsibility where the distributor will focus his marketing efforts. But this would only work provided that the other territories (to which the ban applies) are exclusively allocated. If the whole network is made up of non-exclusive dealers then active sales bans will need to satisfy the Article 81(3) conditions.

Active sales bans cannot be combined with selective distribution, since in this case active selling into other territories must be permitted (see p 119 and Guidelines, para 162). However, exclusivity in the sense that the supplier agrees not to appoint any other distributor for the territory is not blacklisted and so can be combined with selective distribution.

A territory may be reserved by the supplier for himself without the supplier yet being active in that territory. The reason for this rule is to combat free-riding: a supplier may for commercial planning reasons not want to roll out his distribution system to all EU Member States at the same time.

This means that the whole of the EU territory must be covered by exclusive distribution territories or reserved to the supplier if all active sales outside a distributor's territory are to be prevented. If, for example, selective distribution is used in another territory, or if a territory has two or more exclusive distributors for a single territory (unless separate customer groups are allocated to them), active sales into that territory may not be prevented. Partial exclusivity, where exclusivity in a given territory is shared between two or more distributors, is therefore not covered by the Regulation unless no such territorial protection is given. If such protection is to be given, individual exemption will be necessary. Suppliers may therefore prefer to allocate several small, exclusive territories, rather than larger territories each with several distributors.

An active sales ban may not be imposed further down the distribution chain: a distributor subject to an active sales ban must remain free to decide whether or not he imposes such a restriction when he resells the goods.

The concepts of 'active' and 'passive' sales are explained in the Guidelines (para 50). They refer essentially to actively approaching customers as compared to responding to unsolicited requests.

The advent of the Internet has changed the market environment in many sectors, as it means that consumers can easily compare prices and other conditions, and make purchases, over a far wider area than was previously possible. This means that parallel imports or 'grey goods' (legitimate goods imported into country A from country B, where they are available more cheaply than in country A) are becoming a much greater problem for manufacturers and suppliers than before. Traditional prohibitions on active selling outside a distributor's territory no longer provide an effective means of protection in these markets.

Internet sales are normally regarded by the Commission as passive sales, and a supplier may not reserve Internet sales to himself. The language(s) of an Internet site is considered irrelevant by the Commission: the fact that a French distributor has an Internet site offering French and English, it says, is the equivalent of there being an English-speaking assistant in the French shop, and not of opening a shop in England. However, it might be argued that, say, an Irish site including German language versions of its text is necessarily aiming its message outside Ireland. The Guidelines imply that this would have to be permitted if there were at least some German-language non-exclusively allocated territories (para 51).

The Internet can also be used actively: a sale initiated through an unsolicited e-mail addressed to someone outside the territory will be regarded as an active sale.

(ii) A prohibition on active sales to particular categories of customer. Similar considerations apply to the granting of exclusive customer groups. For example, a supplier of medicines may allow his distributor to supply chemists, but not hospitals, which he might either allocate to another buyer or reserve to himself. Such a customer group restriction can be combined with an exclusively allocated territory and territorial protection (Guidelines, paras 50–51).

It is not permissible, however, for a supplier to reserve all Internet sales to himself (or, presumably, to another distributor).

(iii) A prohibition on wholesalers supplying end-users

(iv) A prohibition on members of a selective distribution system selling to unauthorised distributors. This is not surprising, as it is inherent in selective distribution that the distributors are 'selected' *but* in this case active *and* passive sales by *retailers* to any end-users must be permitted (Article 4(c)).

In selective distribution, as in other types of distribution, it is permissible under the Regulation for a supplier to limit the number of appointed resellers in any territory.

(v) A prohibition on the buyer reselling components, which have been sold to it for incorporation into another product, to competing manufacturers. This exception is very limited, as it does not permit the supplier to prohibit resale to another reseller, who may himself resell to a competing manufacturer. In practice this means that OEM suppliers cannot keep their OEM and other distribution channels separate, and as a result the price of the OEM goods is less likely than it might otherwise be to be discounted.

Note that this situation is different from the blacklisted clause described below at (5), because it concerns resale by the buyer and not the supplier.

(3) A Prohibition on Selective Distribution Retailers Making Active or Passive Sales to any End-users (Article 4(c))

Where selective distribution is used there can be no exclusive territorial or customer allocation. The only territorial protection that can be given is the imposition of a location clause, requiring the supplier's approval before any additional sales outlet is opened by the distributor. Such a clause is apparently permitted in respect of both wholesalers and retailers.

*(4) A Prohibition on Cross-supplies Between Members of a Selective Distribution
Network, at Whatever Level of Trade They Operate (Article 4(d))*

When using selective distribution, no exclusive purchasing (in the sense of an obligation to purchase all the contract goods from the supplier) may be imposed, and cross-supplies between members of the network, whatever their level in the distribution chain, must be permitted.

*(5) Restrictions on the Sale of Parts to End-users and Independent Repairers by
Suppliers to OEM Manufacturers (Article 4(e))*

(In the English version of this Article 'to' needs to be read as 'from' for it to make sense. The French version reads correctly.) This is the only restriction on the supplier which is blacklisted, and it is helpful to independent repairers and consumers who might otherwise find it hard to obtain spare parts. Restrictions may be direct or indirect, as where the supplier of the spare parts is restricted in supplying technical information and special equipment which are necessary for the use of spare parts by independent third parties.

The Commission interprets the Regulation as allowing a restriction on the supplier from selling to the buyer's own network of repairers and service providers (Guidelines, para 56).

It is possible that the blacklisting of such restrictions encourages companies to reduce their reliance on sub-contracting, for example, by integrating vertically so as to take over their sub-contractors.

Where the specifications supplied by the buyer include the grant of an intellectual property right, the agreement will fall outside the block exemption anyway (see p 86).

Non-compete Obligations (Article 5)

Certain non-compete clauses, although not blacklisted (as are the clauses listed in Article 4), are prohibited. This means that their inclusion does not entail nullity of the entire agreement. Rather, if they are severable according to the applicable national law, they are excluded from the benefit of the Regulation, while the rest of the agreement may remain valid and enforceable under the Regulation (Guidelines, paras 57 and 67). The severed clause will need to be assessed separately under Article 81(1) and (3), and may turn out to be enforceable or unenforceable.

'Non-compete' is widely defined, and may include practices such as rebate schemes and ties which indirectly have the practical effect of preventing a distributor from sourcing goods and services elsewhere. It covers both:

• any direct or indirect obligation on the buyer not to purchase, sell or resell competing goods; and

- any direct or indirect obligation on the buyer to purchase more than 80 per cent (calculated on the basis of the value of its purchases in the preceding calendar year, or on the buyer's best estimate)[75] of its requirements of the contract goods and their substitutes from the supplier or a designated source (Article 1(b)).

Article 5 does not cover an exclusive purchase obligation relating to the contract goods themselves, even if it is of 100 per cent. Exclusive purchase in this sense is exempted by the block exemption, regardless of its duration,[76] except in the context of selective distribution. Similarly, clauses prohibiting distributors from dealing in other types of (non-competing) products are not mentioned in the Regulation and are therefore exempted.

Non-compete Obligations During the Term of the Agreement

A non-compete term applicable during the term of the agreement falls outside the Regulation if it is of indefinite duration or exceeds five years in duration. But if the buyer operates from premises owned or leased by the supplier a longer period is permitted, provided the duration of the non-compete clause does not exceed the period of occupancy.

This may encourage suppliers such as breweries to lease premises rather than providing the tenant with a loan to enable him to purchase the premises, since in the latter case the supplier will not be able to rely on the block exemption so as to enforce a non-compete clause lasting more than five years.

Post-term Non-compete Obligations

A post-term non-compete obligation covering manufacture, purchase, sale and resale is covered by the Regulation for a maximum period of one year after the contract has ended, provided that the obligation:

- is limited to goods or services that compete with the contract goods or services (apparently the buyer may continue to deal in the contract goods themselves if he can obtain supplies);
- is limited to the land and premises from which the buyer has operated during the agreement; and
- is indispensable to protect knowhow (as defined in Article 1(f)) transferred by the supplier to the buyer.

This exception is only likely to be of relevance in the case of franchising and technically innovative products and services.

The one-year maximum does not apply where the clause is necessary to protect know-how which has not entered the public domain.

---

[75] Guidelines, para 58.
[76] Because it is not blacklisted and all restraints not expressly prohibited are exempted.

Non-compete Obligations and Selective Distribution

In the case of selective distribution, members of the network may not be prevented from selling the brands of particular competitors—but an absolute non-compete ban of up to five years is permissible, as it is for other forms of distribution. This is because the Commission is concerned to avoid the risk of collusion between manufacturers to foreclose specific competitors (Guidelines, para 61).

Time Limits for Non-compete Obligations

The time limits in Article 5 are interpreted strictly by the Commission: a 10-year contract including a clause providing for non-compete will be treated as a 10-year non-compete clause, even if the agreement is terminable at any time by either party on three months' notice. Similarly, a one-year non-compete clause tacitly renewable will be treated as of indefinite duration and as not satisfying the one-year or five-year requirements. Parties may therefore choose to conclude five-year agreements, with a new agreement then being concluded after these five years have elapsed. Alternatively, if the rest of the agreement is for a duration longer than five years, it should be clearly stated that the non-compete clause expires after five years.

As a transitional measure, where non-compete clauses imposed before 1 January 2002 had no more than five years to run on that date, then they are exempted until the end of their term (Guidelines, para 70).

The Regulation contains no restriction on any limits that the supplier may wish to impose in respect of the sale of non-competing goods.

Tying

Tying, where it infringes Article 81(1), is exempted by the Regulation, as it clearly falls within the definition of 'vertical restraints' and is not blacklisted.

Duration

The duration of the agreement is irrelevant for the purposes of the block exemption, except where non-compete clauses are concerned. However, the block exemption itself expires in 2010, and it is impossible to say whether it will then be renewed in its existing form, or in what respects any successor Regulation may differ.

Withdrawal and Disapplication

In the case of agreements which fall within the scope of the block exemption but which the Commission nevertheless considers do not fulfil the criteria for exemption under Article 81(3) the exemption applies until the Commission or competent national authorities take a formal Decision removing the benefit of the Regulation. Such removal may occur even in the case of a company with a low market share, and it may happen in one of two ways.

Withdrawal in respect of an individual agreement

The benefit of the block exemption can be withdrawn either by the Commission (Article 6) or by the relevant national authorities (Article 7). Member State authorities can only withdraw in respect of that Member State or part of it, and provided that the area forms a 'distinct geographic market'.[77] If the Commission disagrees with a Member State's intention to withdraw it can open proceedings and grant an individual exemption itself (Guidelines, para 77), though clearly it would hope to avoid this type of conflict.

The Commission appears to envisage the principal importance of this clause as being in its use in dealing with cumulative network effects, and in particular in oligopolistic markets dominated by a few powerful firms. In such cases it will take into account not only the individual supplier's agreements, but also the cumulative effects of 'similar vertical restraints' implemented by competitors, though in any given case the agreements in question must contribute significantly to the overall anti-competitive effect (para 74). It is most likely to be used in the context of agreements at retail level (para 71).

Withdrawal may also be useful in dealing with issues of buyer power, as the existing rules have developed against the traditional background of powerful suppliers and manufacturers and weaker distributors. The balance of power in some markets is now shifting from supplier to retailer: for example, a supermarket is generally in a stronger position to decide no longer to stock a particular supplier's product than is the supplier to decide no longer to make or supply the product. The Commission's Guidelines mention the possibility of withdrawal when the buyer 'has significant market power in the relevant downstream market where it resells the goods or provides the service' (para 73) but does not refer to upstream 'buyer power' (that is, power on its purchasing market).

Withdrawal takes effect only from the date of a formal Decision of the Commission, and does not have retrospective effect (para 75). The onus is on the Commission to prove both an infringement of Article 81(1) and the non-fulfilment of the criteria for exemption under Article 81(3) (para 72).

The Commission's Guidelines mention many types of situation in which withdrawal may be appropriate, but it remains to be seen whether it will use this possibility more frequently in the future. So far it has been used extremely

---

[77] See Guidelines, paras 76–79. It will be possible therefore for a specific franchise agreement, for example, to be legal at EU level and in France, but not in the UK. It is not clear how Member States are expected to 'ensure that the exercise of this power of withdrawal does not prejudice the uniform application throughout the common market of the Community competition rules or the full effect of the measures adopted in implementation of those rules' (Recital 14 of the Regulation).

rarely,[78] despite the fact that a number of block exemptions have for some years now provided for withdrawal.

Disapplication to Particular Market

The Commission also has the power to disapply the benefit of the exemption with respect to particular markets, or to specific restraints within a market, where similar vertical restraints cover over 50 per cent of the market.[79] No such Decision has yet been taken.

This might be used to combat over-use of selective distribution in a particular sector, especially where the type of goods being marketed did not justify the use of selective distribution.

Such a Decision would sometimes create a sort of *de facto* sector-specific block exemption Regulation. It would become applicable no earlier than six months after its adoption (Article 8(2)). The exempted status of agreements affected by the disapplication during the period before it occurred would not be affected (Guidelines, para 87).

3.6 DOES INDIVIDUAL EXEMPTION UNDER ARTICLE 81(3) APPLY?

A distribution agreement that does not satisfy the block exemption does not necessarily infringe Article 81(1), as it may benefit from exemption under Article 81(3). In the past this was only possible by notifying the agreement to the Commission but as from 1 May 2004 the option of notification no longer exists, and instead it is for the parties themselves to assess whether they satisfy the four substantive conditions laid down in Article 81(3) (see p 33).

The burden of proof of an infringement of Article 81(1) lies on the authority or party alleging the infringement but the burden in respect of Article 81(3) is on the party claiming the benefit of exemption.[80] This means that a party relying on such exemption needs to be prepared, in the event of a complaint or dispute, to adduce evidence to the effect that the four conditions are satisfied.

Given the increasing importance of market analysis in applying Article 81, this burden is a considerable one (see p 30). The Commission has published a Notice 'on the application of Article 81(3)' which in fact makes detailed comment on both Article 81(1) and (3).

---

[78] An example is a Decision concerning ice cream distribution: *Langnese-Iglo* OJ 1993 L183/19, [1994] 4 CMLR 51.

[79] Article 8 and Guidelines, paras 80–87. This provision seeks to deal with a problem that has arisen in the past, which was that the Commission could withdraw the benefit of the Regulation in respect of a specific agreement, but could not prohibit the supplier in question from entering into similar agreements in the future. See *Langnese-Iglo*, above n78.

[80] This rule is included explicitly in Reg 1/2003 (Art 2). The burden and standard of proof are points of appeal in the pending Case C-552/03 *Van den Bergh Foods v Commission* OJ 2004 C59/14.

Below is discussed the likelihood that exemption applies to agreements containing certain terms commonly occurring in distribution agreements. Guidance in this area is available through consideration of terms granted automatic exemption in the block exemption, but since the block exemption grants automatic exemption it errs on the side of caution. It is always possible that a term is too restrictive to be permitted by the block exemption, but that individual consideration of the specific situation will lead to the conclusion that Article 81(3) applies.

Exemption under Article 81(3) only applies if its four criteria are satisfied. In particular, the agreement must be shown to contribute to 'improving the production or distribution of goods or to promoting technical or economic progress', or, in other words, improving economic efficiency. It will be important to gather as much evidence as possible that this is the case.

As already discussed, in assessing whether the agreement infringes Article 81(1), much will turn on market definition and structure: this means looking at factors such as the market shares of the parties and their competitors, the extent to which the market is covered by tied outlets, the existence of buyer power and barriers to entry, and competitive advantages held by the parties or their competitors. Whether the market is new or mature, and static or dynamic, is also relevant.

Similar considerations relating to the nature of the market will also be relevant in substantiating arguments that Article 81(3) applies. In particular, if there is strong inter-brand competition from suppliers and distributors of competing products then there will be a realistic possibility of individual exemption: conversely, exemption is unlikely in the context of an oligopolistic market dominated by a few powerful companies. Evidence will be needed when it is argued that, for example, restrictions are necessary to prevent free-riding by competing distributors, to protect investments and knowhow, or to create incentives for market opening: it will not be sufficient simply to state without more that a contractual restriction is necessary.

Exemption would appear most likely to apply where the relevant market share is between 30 per cent and 40 per cent. Below 30 per cent the block exemption will usually apply, and above 40 per cent a company risks being considered dominant, in which case the Commission has said there will not normally be grounds for exemption under Article 81(3) (Guidelines, para 135). This is despite the fact that the same economic efficiency arguments that apply in the case of non-dominant companies may well apply in the case of dominant companies, and it would not seem right that companies should be deprived of the chance to use efficient distribution methods on the basis of a high market share alone. However, recent beer supply cases suggest that competition authorities may feel more comfortable narrowing the scope of Article 81(1) than applying Article 81(3) in the presence of high market shares.[81]

---

[81] See the discussion of these and the *De Beers* case at p. 68. It is noteworthy that no individual exemptions of any kind of distribution agreement were granted by the Commission between the entry into force of the vertical restraints block exemption Regulation and accompanying Guidelines in 2000 and the abolition of individual exemption Decisions in 2004.

Similarly, the Guidelines say that a clause which is prohibited ('blacklisted') in the block exemption Regulation is unlikely to be exempted (para 46).

Over half of the Commission's lengthy Guidelines on vertical restraints are devoted to explaining its approach to individual examination of vertical restraints, and they provide detailed guidance in this area. Only the main points of this guidance are included in the summary of the rules given below.

Market Definition

As already discussed, ascertaining the relevant market, both geographic and product, is often a crucial step in assessing the status of an agreement under EU competition rules, because it can determine whether or not the agreement benefits from the block exemption on vertical restraints. The block exemption works on an intentionally simplified basis (Guidelines, para 22), taking into consideration only the supplier's share of the market onto which he sells the contract goods or services, or, in certain limited circumstances, the buyer's share of the market where he purchases the contract goods or services. When considering agreements on an individual basis other markets may be relevant too.

In the case of final products the market on which the buyer sells the products, as well as that between supplier and buyer, especially where the buyer is a retailer, is likely to be relevant. In the case of intermediate goods or services, on the other hand, the buyer's downstream markets are not likely to be relevant unless the buyer is the exclusive distributor for the whole of the EU (para 96).

Also, the growth of buyer power, in food retailing, for example, means that many retail distribution chains such as supermarkets exercise considerable power, and the issue of buyer or retailer power is one that has assumed increasing importance in recent years. Much of EU competition law as applied to distribution systems proceeds on the implied assumption that buyers and retailers are the weaker party in the distribution relationship. But in fact they may charge suppliers for shelf space or threaten not to stock products if suppliers do not accept certain restrictions. It will sometimes be possible to justify restrictive clauses imposed by a supplier partly on the basis that the buyer has sufficient countervailing power to resist the imposition of clauses that are not to its benefit.

For companies producing innovative products the market share situation is, at best, unclear, though the Commission's lenient attitude towards certain vertical restraints on such markets (see p 75) may mean that market definition problems do not often arise in practice.

Resale Price Maintenance, or the Imposition of Recommended, Maximum or Minimum Prices

Even where a distribution agreement is *de minimis* (that is, the parties are small or the relevant market share is no more than 10 per cent) any attempt to fix retail prices or minimum resale prices will fall foul of Article 81(1), unless there is no effect on trade between Member States. Nor will such a clause normally be exempted under Article 81(3).[82] There are only very limited exceptions to this rule, where products with special characteristics make resale price maintenance justifiable under Article 81(3): examples are newspapers[83] and, possibly, books (see p 104).

In the case of other products, the provision even of recommended or maximum resale prices (which is exempted by the block exemption where the 30 per cent market share threshold is not exceeded) when the relevant market share is over 30 per cent is regarded with suspicion by the Commission because of the risk of it being followed by all or most distributors, and because it may facilitate collusion between them. The Commission's Guidelines suggest that such practices infringe Article 81(1) where the supplier has a strong market position or where the market is a 'narrow oligopoly', and that exemption will not be available (paras 225–28).

Exclusive Distribution and Territorial Protection

Exclusive distribution together with territorial protection concerns the Commission mainly because of its tendency to partition markets and to reduce intra-brand competition.

As already discussed, absolute territorial protection will almost always infringe Article 81(1), even in the context of a highly competitive market and it will not normally be individually exempted (Guidelines, para 46). This rule applies not only to explicit bans on parallel imports and exports but also to indirect forms of territorial segregation.[84]

In *Zanussi*,[85] the original distributorship arrangement provided that the manufacturer's guarantee would be honoured only by the company's importing subsidiary which had directly imported the electrical goods from Zanussi into the Member State where the subsidiary operated. Thus, if parallel imports had subsequently been taken into another Member State, purchasers would not have been able to benefit from the guarantee by applying to the Zanussi subsidiary in that other Member State. Not only did such a clause infringe Article 81(1), but it did not qualify for exemption under Article 81(3). The Commission required that this rule be changed to require each local subsidiary to fulfil the terms of the manufacturer's guarantee for any appliance used in the Member State where it operated: only then did it grant an exemption under Article 81(3).[86]

---

[82] *Hennessy-Henkel* OJ 1980 L383/11, [1981] 1 CMLR 601 which also involved exclusive distribution, exclusive purchase and non-compete.

[83] Case 243/83 *Binon v AMP* [1985] ECR 2015, [1985] 3 CMLR 800.

[84] For a case in which it is argued that exemption should be granted to a dual-pricing system aimed at limiting parallel trade on the grounds that it enhances R&D capacity, see *Glaxo SmithKline*, above n 32.

[85] 1977 Commission Report on Competition Policy, para 20.

[86] This approach was approved by the ECJ in Case 31/85 *ETA Fabriques d'Ebauches*, above n 25. See also *Grundig* OJ 1994 L20/15.

Exemption is unlikely where the supplier has a strong market position and there is not sufficient competition from other suppliers. Also, markets where there are several exclusive distribution networks will arouse concerns as to the risk of collusion between competing producers or contributing with other networks to a cumulative effect.

However, the Commission recognises a number of efficiencies that can be brought about by exclusive distribution and which may justify exemption (paras 161–77). These include solving a problem of 'free-riding' by distributors, in particular, in order to provide distributor incentives when entering new markets. Exclusive distribution is viewed as particularly appropriate when the distributor is making significant relationship-specific investments (Guidelines, para 116). In any case, real efficiencies will need to be proved, whether these take the form of providing incentives for distributor investment, economies of scale in transport, or other benefits.

Territorial protection in respect of active sales normally falls within the block exemption, but not where it is combined with selective distribution. In such circumstances, or where exclusive distribution is combined with exclusive purchasing (a requirement to purchase all contract goods from the supplier), exemption where the relevant market share is over 30 per cent is unlikely, unless there are very clear and substantial efficiencies.[87] On the other hand, the combination of exclusive distribution with a non-compete clause, in the absence of foreclosure, will often be exempted for the whole duration of the agreement (which may be more than five years) because it increases the incentive for the exclusive distributor to focus its efforts on the particular brand, particularly at wholesale level (paras 119/6 and 171).

Exclusivity granted to a wholesaler is more likely to be exempted if there are no limitations on resale to retailers, always assuming the producer is not dominant. Generally speaking, exclusivity at wholesale level is regarded as less harmful than at retail level (paras 170 and 209).

In its Guidelines the Commission gives an example of a scenario involving exclusive distribution at wholesale level where exemption would probably be granted (para 213). It also describes a scenario involving multiple exclusive dealerships in an oligopolistic market, in which the benefit of the block exemption might be withdrawn, and one of exclusive distribution combined with exclusive purchasing, where exemption would probably not apply (paras 175–77).

Exclusive Supply

Exclusivity granted to a single distributor and extending to the whole EU (termed 'exclusive supply' by the Commission) is an extreme form of exclusive distribu-

---

[87] Para 172. In an earlier draft of the block exemption, a combination of exclusive distribution and exclusive purchasing was blacklisted.

tion. It concerns the Commission mainly because of the risk of foreclosure of other distributors (paras 202–14).

If it falls outside the block exemption, whether or not because the buyer has over 30 per cent of the supply market, then exemption is unlikely if it also has over 30 per cent of the resale market (para 204). Similarly, exemption is unlikely if the restriction will last over five years (para 205), or if the buyer is dominant (para 211).

In its Guidelines the Commission gives an example of a situation involving an exclusive supply agreement and substantial investment by the buyer which would probably merit exemption (para 213).

Exclusive Customer Allocation

Where a supplier supplies only one distributor for resale to a particular class of customers many of the same concerns arise as in the case of exclusive distribution (paras 178–83).

Such a provision is most likely to be exempted where distributors are required to invest in specific equipment, skills or knowhow so as to be able to fulfil the requirements of their customer group, and where the restriction lasts only as long as is reasonable to allow depreciation of such investment (para 182). In its Guidelines, the Commission gives an example of an exclusive customer allocation agreement, involving substantial investment by the buyer, which would probably qualify for exemption (para 183).

As in the case of exclusive distribution, exclusive customer allocation is unlikely to be exempted when combined with selective distribution (para 179).

Non-compete and Exclusive Purchase Obligations

An obligation on the reseller not to manufacture, purchase, sell or resell competing goods is exempted by the block exemption Regulation for up to five years. If it falls outside the block exemption because it lasts longer than five years, or because the 30 per cent market share threshold is exceeded, it may be eligible for individual exemption (paras 138–60).

The Commission's concerns focus on possible foreclosure, facilitation of collusion and loss of in-store inter-brand competition (para 138). However, it recognises that such clauses can be useful in overcoming free-riding between suppliers (para 116/1) or providing incentives for relationship-specific investment by the supplier (para 116/4): where such investment is substantial, exemption for more than five years may be justified (para 155).

The Commission will look mainly at the supplier's market position and that of its competitors, the extent and duration of the non-compete clause (if between one and five years it may be exempted, but this is much less likely if it exceeds five years, unless there is a high level of market-specific investment by the supplier), entry barriers and countervailing buyer power. Exemption will more readily be given in the case of intermediate products (para 146) or wholesale distribution (para 147).

Non-compete restrictions are common in beer distribution. Brewers often lease or sell pubs to their tenants on condition that they limit the extent to which they stock competing beers. Where the breweries are small, Article 81 probably will not be infringed at all, but where the brewery has a significant market share, and for some reason cannot benefit from the block exemption, an individual exemption may be granted, as the benefits of such agreements are well recognised by the Commission.[88] However, it will be important to avoid structuring such agreements in a way which contributes to foreclosure, for example, by providing for repayment of loans in increasing instalments (para 156), or imposing penalties for early repayment, or in any other way making it difficult for a tenant to break off an agreement after a reasonable period. Exemption will in any case be unusual where the brewer's market share exceeds 30 per cent, so such brewers may well have to untie or divest some of their pubs.

Quantity forcing, where the buyer has to purchase minimum quantities, or benefits from quantity rebates, and English clauses, where the buyer may only purchase elsewhere if his supplier refuses to match a cheaper price he has been offered elsewhere, can have similar, but usually reduced, effects to those of non-compete clauses, and so receive similar treatment.

Exclusive purchase obligations, where the supplier has a market share over 30 per cent, if combined with exclusive distribution, will probably infringe Article 81(1) and not be exempted (Guidelines, para 172).

In its Guidelines the Commission gives examples of two scenarios in which non-compete and quantity forcing agreements respectively would probably be exempted (paras 159–60).

Tying

Tying occurs when the purchase of one product is made conditional on the purchase of a separate product. The Commission's main concern is possible foreclosure on the market for the tied product, especially where the tying is combined with a non-compete clause in respect of the tied product (paras 215–24). Tying may also lead to higher prices for consumers and increased barriers for potential market entrants.

When tying occurs as a vertical restraint it may require individual exemption where the supplier's market share for either product exceeds 30 per cent. Factors considered relevant by the Commission in deciding whether individual exemption

---

[88] Individual exemptions for 20 years (about half of this period was accounted for by retrospective exemption) were granted to *Whitbread* OJ 1999 L88/26, upheld in Case T-131/99 [2002] ECR II-2023, [2002] 5 CMLR 81; *Bass* OJ 1999 L186/1, ultimately upheld in Case C-204/02, 10 December 2003 (not yet officially reported) and *Scottish & Newcastle* OJ 1999 L186/19.

is appropriate include the relative strength of the supplier's and buyer's market positions, and the presence of efficiencies such as joint production or joint distribution of the two products, bulk purchase of the tied product by the supplier and the maintenance of certain quality standards.

3.7 HORIZONTAL DISTRIBUTION AGREEMENTS

Although distribution agreements are typically vertical, they may be entered into by competitors, for example where one supplier agrees to distribute another's goods or services. In this case they are still vertical agreements, but the vertical restraints block exemption only applies to such arrangements in limited circumstances (see p 87). Any Article 81 analysis will have to take into account the possible horizontal as well as the vertical impact on competition.

Competing firms may also enter into joint distribution arrangements with each other, which will be pure horizontal agreements, perhaps even cartels, subject to the general principles of Article 81.[89] The Commission has published Guidelines on the applicability of Article 81 of the EC Treaty to horizontal co-operation agreements[90] and these may be relevant whenever distribution arrangements involve competing companies.

The Guidelines discuss 'commercialisation agreements', meaning co-operation in selling, distribution or promotion of products. They say that joint selling, even if non-exclusive, normally infringes Article 81(1), in particular because it involves co-ordination of pricing policy. Even in the absence of joint selling, Article 81(1) may well be infringed if the co-operation in distribution allows the exchange of sensitive commercial information,[91] or where it has a significant impact on the parties' costs. Similarly, agreements between suppliers in different geographic markets will lead to market partitioning and may infringe Article 81(1) unless the arrangement is objectively necessary to allow entry into another market. In all such cases there is a concern that actual or potential competition between the parties will be reduced.

Article 81(3) will apply if its four conditions are fulfilled. In practice it is more likely to be possible to show economic benefits of commercialisation agreements in the case of widely distributed consumer goods than for industrial products bought only by a limited number of users. An example of an Article 81(3) exemption is joint distribution by UIP of films for screening in cinemas, which was first exempted in 1989. The exemption has since been renewed twice.[92] The arrangements are

---

[89] eg *Dutch Electrotechnical Equipment* OJ 2000 L39/1, [2000] 4 CMLR 1208, upheld in Cases T-5/00 and 6/00, 16 December 2003 (not yet officially reported), on appeal Joined Cases C-105 and C-113/04 OJ 2004 C106/25 and 28.

[90] OJ 2001 C3/2.

[91] The Commission issued a negative clearance type 'comfort letter' in respect of the Opodo online travel agency joint venture after it put in place safeguards against the exchange of commercially sensitive information, and against market foreclosure, Competition Policy Newsletter, Spring 2003.

[92] OJ 1989 L226/25 and Commission Press Release IP/99/681, 14 September 1999.

considered to be administratively efficient, but each time the Commission has considered them it has required undertakings or contractual modifications aimed at ensuring that the parties retain a high degree of autonomy on the market, and it has checked that competition on the market is not unduly restricted.

Joint production agreements, which are generally viewed favourably under Article 81 are likely to infringe Article 81(1) if they 'fix the prices for market supplies of the parties, limit output or share markets or customer groups', though there is an exception for price-fixing in the case of joint ventures which carry out distribution as well as production.

Books

In a number of Member States retail book prices are frequently fixed through horizontal agreements between publishers,[93] which distributors agree to adhere to. Such agreements are likely to infringe Article 81(1) and have generally been held not to qualify for Article 81(3) exemption. They will only not infringe Article 81(1) if they are restricted in application to a single national territory or region. However, such national systems may not limit cross-border sales, except in respect of imports the sole purpose of which is to circumvent the national price-fixing system.[94]

The increasing success of Internet retailers in this sector means that the usefulness of such national systems is rapidly diminishing. The European Parliament has expressed its concern at this situation on a number of occasions and has drafted a proposed Directive which would allow significant limitations on cross-border sales in the interests of cultural policy objectives.[95] Though unlikely to be adopted as drafted, it demonstrates the strength of concern about this issue in some quarters.

3.8 ARTICLE 82

Until now this chapter has discussed only Article 81 of the EC Treaty, but it should not be forgotten that Article 82, which prohibits abuse of a dominant position and was discussed in Chapter 2, can also apply to the distribution arrangements of dominant companies. Practices that may constitute abuse include discriminatory or predatory pricing, refusal to supply, the granting of fidelity rebates or use of English clauses, imposition of non-compete obligations and tying.

---

[93] Where they are fixed by national law or government authority the EC Treaty rules on free movement of goods may be relevant.

[94] Joined Cases 43 and 63/82 *VBVB v Commission* [1984] ECR 19, [1985] 1 CMLR 27 and, more recently, *Sammelrevers*, Commission Press Release IP/02/461, 22 March 2002.

[95] European Parliament Committee on Legal Affairs and the Internal Market, *Report with Recommendations to the Commission on the Drawing up of a Directive of the European Parliament and of the Council on the Fixing of Book Prices* 2001/2061(INI), 21 February 2002, adopted by the European Parliament on 16 May 2002.

4

Selective Distribution

KEY POINTS

- Selective distribution is a system under which all dealers admitted to the supplier's network agree not to resell goods to other dealers outside the network.
- The legality of contracts making up a selective distribution system depends on the terms of the contracts and on the market environment in which the system operates.
- A selective distribution system to which dealers are admitted on the basis of objective and qualitative criteria will usually be legal, unless there are many such systems in the market.
- If there are many such systems, or if the system is not based on objective and qualitative criteria, the selective distribution system may be illegal and unenforceable, unless it is exempted.
- If the contracts contain no 'hard-core' restrictions and the relevant market share does not exceed 30 per cent, a general block exemption may apply so as to exempt the agreements. This is possible even if the system is based on non-objective criteria or fixed quotas, or if it is applied to goods for which it is not objectively necessary.
- Similarly, selective or exclusive distribution systems for motor vehicles and their spare parts and repair and maintenance services may be exempted by a sector-specific block exemption.
- Even if no block exemption applies, exemption will still be available if the system satisfies the four substantive criteria for exemption. In particular, it will be necessary to justify any non-qualitative selection criteria on the basis of marketing requirements or other efficiency gains relating to the specific type of goods concerned.

EC Regulations

Commission Regulation (EC) 2790/1999 on the application of Article 81(3) of the
  Treaty to categories of vertical agreements and concerted practices (Appendix 4)
Commission Regulation (EC) 1400/2002 on the application of Article 81(3) of the
  Treaty to categories of vertical agreements and concerted practices in the motor
  vehicle sector (Appendix 5)

EC Notices

Commission Guidelines on vertical restraints (Appendix 7)
Distribution and Servicing of Motor Vehicles in the European Union
  (Explanatory Brochure or 'EB')
www.europa.eu.int/comm/competition/car_sector/explanatory_brochure_en.pdf

ECJ Judgments

Case 26/76 *Metro v Commission (No 1)* [1977] ECR 1875, [1978] 2 CMLR 1
Cases 32/78 etc *BMW v Commission* [1979] ECR 2435, [1980] 1 CMLR 370
Case 107/82 *AEG-Telefunken v Commission* [1983] ECR 3151, [1984] 3 CMLR 325
Case 75/84 *Metro v Commission (II)* [1986] ECR 3021, [1987] 1 CMLR 118
Case C-376/92 *Metro v Cartier* [1994] *No 2* ECR I-15, [1994] 5 CMLR 331

Commission Decisions

BMW (No 1) OJ 1975 L29/1, [1975] 1 CMLR D44
Villeroy & Boch OJ 1985 L376/15, [1988] 4 CMLR 461
IBM PC OJ 1984 L118/24, [1984] 2 CMLR 342
Yves Saint Laurent Parfums OJ 1992 L12/24, [1993] 4 CMLR 120
Parfums Givenchy OJ 1992 L236/11, [1993] 5 CMLR 579

It is essential that this chapter be read in conjunction with Chapter 3 for a full under-standing of the treatment of selective distribution agreements.

4.1 DO SELECTIVE DISTRIBUTION AGREEMENTS INFRINGE ARTICLE 81(1)?

Selective distribution involves a distribution network made up of dealers selected at the wholesale or retail level (often both) on the basis of specific criteria decided on by the manufacturer or producer of the goods or services concerned.

Whatever criteria are imposed, it will be necessary in some way to prevent non-approved dealers obtaining supplies of the goods through members of the net-work, and it is this aspect of the arrangement which prevents such a distribution policy being purely unilateral behaviour (in which case it could not infringe Article 81(1)). Those dealers admitted to the system normally agree not to resell goods to other dealers unless these other dealers have also been approved by the manufac-turer or producer. It is essentially this restriction on resale that potentially infringes Article 81(1).

The selection criteria may be based on a variety of factors, including qualifications possessed by the dealer and his staff, the situation and appearance of the sales outlet, capacity to achieve a certain minimum level of turnover, capacity to perform certain after-sales services and repairs, and willingness to engage in particular promotional activities.

Suppliers may also want to apply quantitative criteria. In this case, in order to join the sales network it is not sufficient that a dealer can demonstrate that he fulfils the qualitative kind of criteria listed above: if the quota for the area in which he would operate is full, then he will not be admitted to the distribution network.

Typically, selective distribution is used to distribute luxury goods of high value such as expensive perfumes, and also the type of complex goods which require or benefit from the availability of repair, maintenance and other forms of after-sales service. It is therefore commonly applied by manufacturers of electrical and elec-tronic goods, and cars, for example. In fact it is so common in the car industry that there is a specific block exemption Regulation[1] automatically exempting certain agreements for selective distribution of motor vehicles and their spare parts and after-sales services from the application of Article 81(1).

Selective distribution, like other types of distribution, has been given a specific treatment by the Commission and the European Court of Justice (ECJ), which have frequently reiterated their opinion that selective distribution is a desirable form of marketing for goods of a kind requiring or benefiting from specialised knowledge at the point of sale or from after-sales service.

Selective distribution systems will often fall outside Article 81(1) altogether. The first time the ECJ gave judgment in a selective distribution case was in *Metro v Commission (No 1)*.[2] In its judgment it approved the approach taken up to then by

---

[1] Reg 1400/2002 (Appendix 5). See also p 129.
[2] Case 26/76 *Metro v Commission (No 1)* [1976] ECR 1875, [1978] 2 CMLR 1.

the Commission in *Omega*[3] and the other selective distribution Decisions it had made. The Court stated that selective distribution agreements, provided that they operate on the basis of objective and qualitative criteria which are applied uniformly and in a non-discriminatory way[4] to all potential dealers, do not generally infringe Article 81(1). That approach has been frequently restated in subsequent cases.[5]

The types of clause which will generally not infringe Article 81(1) include, first of all, those following from the application of objective qualitative criteria. These include clauses restricting dealers to supplying only end-users or other authorised dealers within the network and those clauses stipulating that non-authorised dealers may not be supplied. Nor does the fact that a system is not 'impervious' (because unauthorised distributors are able somehow, legally, to obtain the goods, perhaps because non-selective distribution methods are used in some territories) mean that it automatically infringes Article 81(1).[6]

The Commission's main concerns in the context of selective distribution are the risk of a reduction in competition between competing brands of goods, possible foreclosure of distributors or suppliers from entering or remaining on the market, and a reduction in competition as a result of the cumulative effect of a number of selective distribution networks operating on the same market.

So other clauses, including those requiring dealers to satisfy additional criteria not falling within the Commission's category of objective qualitative criteria, may infringe Article 81(1) unless they are exempted under Article 81(3). Exemption, either through the operation of a block exemption Regulation or by satisfying the four criteria of Article 81(3), will be needed to avoid invalidity of the agreement under Article 81(2) and the risk of fines and liability in damages.

It will sometimes be possible for a selective distribution system which infringes Article 81(1) to benefit from a block exemption. The motor vehicle block exemption (see p 129) only applies to that sector, but the block exemption on vertical agreements (see Chapter 3) is generally available where its conditions, including a relevant market share of no more than 30 per cent, are fulfilled. In particular, to benefit from this exemption, the agreement must contain no ban on active or passive sales by retailers to end users outside their allotted territories, and no restriction on cross-supplies between approved distributors at any level in the network. Even a system based on purely quantitative selection criteria can benefit from the block exemption.

The Commission has in the past been ready to grant individual exemption, or even negative clearance, to systems in which additional criteria are applied.[7] The first time that a selective distribution system came before the Commission was in the case of *Omega*. In granting an Article 81(3) exemption to the distribution agreements making up the system the Commission mentioned the potential benefits

---

    [3] OJ 1970 L242/22, [1970] CMLR D49.
    [4] Case 243/83 *Binon v Agence et Messageries de la Presse* [1985] ECR 2015, [1985] 3 CMLR 800 includes an example of an allegation of discriminatory application of selection criteria.
    [5] eg Case 31/80 *L'Oréal v De Nieuwe AMCK* [1980] ECR 3775, [1981] 2 CMLR 235, para 15.
    [6] Case C-376/92 *Metro v Cartier* [1994] ECR I-15, [1994] 5 CMLR 331.
    [7] Though the system of individual exemption ceased to exist as of 1 May 2004 (see p 33) the old cases continue to provide guidance on the substantive application of Article 81.

of such a system. These included enabling more intensive exploitation, continuity of supplies (given the limited production facilities) and the offering of a sufficient choice of models. Other advantages mentioned were the rationalising of distribution and the possibility of offering an efficient repair and guarantee scheme.

Until 1 June 2000, when the block exemption on vertical agreements entered into force, there was no block exemption generally available for selective distribution agreements, and so individual exemption was the only type of exemption available. After that, and until the system of individual exemption was abolished on 1 May 2004, there was much less need for individual exemptions for such agreements. Because of this, and because most selective distribution systems falling outside the scope of the block exemption would have involved suppliers with over 30 per cent market share, no formal exemption of a selective distribution system was in fact granted during that period.

Agreements may infringe Article 81(1) 'either individually or together with others'.[8] It is therefore important, as is usual in Community competition law, to look not only at the clauses themselves but also at the wider economic circumstances in which they operate. For example, in the course of a Decision refusing exemption for a selective distribution system for cars the Commission noted that the restrictive effects of the agreement were:

> magnified by the existence of similar exclusive and selective distribution systems operated by other vehicle manufacturers.[9]

Systems based on purely quantitative criteria, in which suitable dealers are refused supplies simply on the basis that a fixed quota has been filled or that the territory concerned does not have enough (or wealthy enough) inhabitants to justify the appointment of another distributor, infringe Article 81(1) and have rarely been individually exempted under Article 81(3), though they are exempted by the vertical restraints block exemption where the relevant market share does not exceed 30 per cent.

As usual (see Chapter 3), any clauses prohibiting imports or exports within the common market or fixing resale prices will generally infringe Article 81(1) and not qualify for exemption.

Unilateral Conduct

There can be no infringement of Article 81(1) on the basis of purely unilateral conduct. Therefore, an independent decision by a supplier to supply certain dealers and not others cannot be a breach of that Article.

However, if dealers admitted to the network are required to agree not to pass on the goods to dealers outside the network, or if pressure is exerted on them in some other way to dissuade them from doing so, this will constitute an agreement or

---

[8] *L'Oréal,* above n 5, at para 21.
[9] *Peugeot* OJ 1986 L295/19, [1989] 4 CMLR 371.

concerted practice for the purposes of Article 81. The principle is fairly easy to state: an unwritten and even unvoiced basis on which dealings take place between two parties may infringe Article 81(1). The difficulty is in knowing what evidence will be sufficient to establish this type of understanding (see p 21).

The ECJ said in *AEG Telefunken v Commission*[10] that the understanding that certain dealers would not be supplied:

> forms part of the contractual relations between the undertaking and resellers. Indeed, in the case of the admission of a distributor, approval is based on the acceptance, tacit or express, by the contracting parties of the policy pursued by AEG which requires inter alia the exclusion from the network of all distributors who are qualified for admission but are not prepared to adhere to that policy.

Similarly, in *Ford v Commission*[11] Ford stopped supplying left-hand drive cars to its German distributor in order to stem the flow of parallel imports which were taking place from Germany to the United Kingdom, because of the higher prices prevailing in the United Kingdom. This restrictive distribution policy was characterised as part of an agreement or concerted practice between Ford and its dealers. Ford appealed against the Decision, essentially on the grounds that such unilateral action could not be prohibited by Article 81, which only applies to consensual conduct. The Court rejected the appeal, on the grounds that the refusal was not unilateral but rather formed part of the contractual relations between Ford and its dealers. This was explained on the basis that 'admission to the Ford AG dealer network implies acceptance by the contracting parties of the policy pursued by Ford with regard to the models to be supplied to the German market.'[12]

This reasoning has the practical advantage for the Commission that it saves them from being obliged to prove collusion between the supplier and its dealers, but it leads to the unsatisfactory conclusion that dealers can be put against their will into a position in which they are party to an illegal agreement. More recently in *Volkswagen*[13] the Court of First Instance (CFI) held that a unilateral instruction by a supplier to its selective distributors to maintain certain price levels did not infringe Article 81(1) as the distributors had not acquiesced in this pricing policy. The CFI refused to accept that members of a legal selective distribution system should be assumed, in the absence of evidence to this effect, to agree to illegal terms subsequently introduced by their supplier. Nevertheless, the ECJ in *Bayer*[14] did not take the opportunity to endorse the CFI's approach. In practice it may therefore be advisable for a distributor to make clear written objection to any such conduct on the part of his supplier.

---

[10] Case 107/82 [1983] ECR 3151, [1984] 3 CMLR 325, para 38.

[11] Joined Cases 25 and 26/84 [1985] ECR 2725, [1985] 3 CMLR 325.

[12] *Ibid*, para 21.

[13] Case T-208/01 *Volkswagen*, 3 December 2003 (not yet officially reported), [2004] 4 CMLR 727, appeal pending, Case C-74/04, OJ 2004 C94/24.

[14] Cases T-41/96 [2000] ECR II-381, [2001] 4 CMLR 126 and C-3/01, 6 January 2004 (not yet officially reported), [2004] 4 CMLR 653, discussed at p 20.

The Metro Judgments

SABA, a producer of electronic equipment for the leisure market, distributes its products through a network of selected distributors. The competition rules on selective distribution are well illustrated by a series of early Commission Decisions and ECJ judgments relating to this particular selective distribution system. It is useful to examine this series of cases, partly because it provided the first opportunity for the Court to state the principles to be applied to selective distribution agreements. In addition, in its second judgment the Court took the opportunity to clarify some statements it had made in its earlier judgment about the kind of market conditions that might render the application of even objective, qualitative criteria contrary to Article 81(1).

The cases involved SABA's selective distribution network for consumer electronic goods, such as radios, televisions, tape-recorders, and video and hi-fi equipment. The network consisted of contracts and agreements with sole distributors, wholesalers and appointed retailers.

The Commission had said in its first SABA Decision that some of the terms in the agreements did not infringe Article 81(1) at all, and it had exempted the additional restrictions pursuant to Article 81(3).[15] Metro, a wholesale trading company which distributed through 'cash and carry' outlets, had been refused supplies by SABA on the grounds that it did not fulfil the conditions for admission as a SABA wholesaler, and it had unsuccessfully argued against the granting of an exemption by the Commission. In particular, Metro claimed that the operation of such a selective distribution system was a means of excluding outlets such as Metro's, which operated in such a way as to reduce overheads and therefore to be able to offer consumers lower prices.

Metro objected to the Commission's exemption Decision and appealed to the ECJ, asking for the Decision to be annulled. The Court rejected the appeal and confirmed that:

> the Commission was justified in recognising that selective distribution systems constituted, together with others, an aspect of competition which accords with Article [81(1)], provided that resellers are chosen on the basis of objective criteria of a qualitative nature relating to the technical qualifications of the reseller and his staff and the suitability of his trading premises and that such conditions are laid down uniformly for all potential resellers and are not applied in a discriminatory fashion.[16]

The ECJ stated that price competition, though very important, was not the only kind of competition to be considered,[17] thus justifying a system which, though restrictive in one sense, created the conditions for competition in different areas

---

[15] *SABA (No 1)* OJ 1976 L28/19, [1976] 1 CMLR D61.

[16] *Metro v Commission (No 1)*, above n 2, at para 20.

[17] This statement was later seized on (unsuccessfully) by the appellant in Cases 209 etc/78 *FEDETAB v Commission* [1980] ECR 3125, [1981] 3 CMLR 193 in an attempt to justify a form of retail price-fixing.

such as the provision of high-standard pre-sales and after-sales services. It confirmed that 'price competition is so important that it can never be eliminated'. However, although recognising that in this case 'the price structure [was] somewhat rigid' it went on to say that this did not permit the conclusion 'that competition had been restricted or eliminated on the market'.

The Court held that selective distribution necessarily implies the obligation on authorised dealers not to sell to dealers outside the network, as well as a method of checking that this rule is kept. It is therefore acceptable for a supplier to insist that a dealer keep records of all non-consumer sales and of proof that such buyers are authorised members of the network. Provided that these restrictions and checks only serve the purpose of ensuring that objective, qualitative requirements, themselves not infringing Article 81, are satisfied, then the restrictions and checks imposed will not infringe Article 81(1). However, most obligations guaranteeing the respect of terms that go further than this will infringe Article 81(1).

Further, it held that a prohibition on wholesalers' supplying private consumers, including schools, hospitals and military establishments, did not fall within the scope of Article 81(1). Such a separation of functions of wholesaler and retailer was accepted by the Court on the grounds that:

> if such a separation did not obtain the former would enjoy an unjustified competitive advantage . . . competition would be distorted if wholesalers, whose costs are in general proportionally lighter precisely because of the marketing stage at which they operate, competed with retailers at the retail stage, in particular on supplies to private customers. (para 29)

The term requiring non-specialist shops to open a special department for selling consumer electronic goods also escaped Article 81(1) altogether.

On the other hand, requirements on the wholesalers to participate in the creation and consolidation of the sales network, to achieve a minimum turnover and to conclude six-monthly supply contracts, fell within Article 81(1) and required exemption under Article 81(3).

However, the Court did see fit to qualify its approval of this selective distribution system. It said that even such a system as this might infringe Article 81(1) and not qualify for an exemption if:

> in particular as the result of an increase in selective distribution networks of a nature similar to SABA's, self-service wholesale traders were in fact eliminated as distributors on the market in electronic equipment for leisure purposes. (para 50)

This concluding qualifying statement caused some consternation amongst the operators of selective distribution systems and their advisers, and at the same time gave some hope to Metro. The Commission's exemption Decision, as confirmed by the ECJ, had been of limited duration. Several years later, when the exemption was due to expire, SABA applied for an extension of the exemption. The terms of the agreements were almost unchanged, and the Commission granted the extension requested.[18] Again, Metro contested the Commission's Decision.

---

[18] *SABA (No 2)* OJ 1983 L376/41, [1984] 1 CMLR 676.

This time Metro claimed that market conditions had changed. It said that there were now many more selective distribution systems in the consumer electronics market and that consequently wholesale traders such as Metro could not obtain direct supplies from producers. The Court had laid down a significant qualification to the general rule that agreements making up selective distribution networks based on objective, qualitative criteria are not generally caught by Article 81(1) and that if they contain other criteria, these will often be exempted, and this was explained further by the Court in *Metro (No 2)*. The Court said that the presence on the market even of those systems based only on objective, qualitative criteria (sometimes referred to as 'simple' systems) had to be taken into account in examining Metro's claim that the market had changed:

> It must be borne in mind that, although the Court has held in previous decisions that 'simple' selective distribution systems are capable of constituting an aspect of competition compatible with Article [81(1)] of the Treaty, there may nevertheless be a restriction or elimination of competition where the existence of a certain number of such systems does not leave any room for other forms of distribution based on a different type of competition policy or results in a rigidity in price structure which is not counterbalanced by other aspects of competition between products of the same brand and by the existence of effective competition between different brands.
>
> Consequently, the existence of a large number of selective distribution systems for a particular product does not in itself permit the conclusion that competition is restricted or distorted. Nor is the existence of such systems decisive as regards the granting or refusal of an exemption under Article [81(3)], since the only factor to be taken into regard is the effect which such systems actually have on the competitive situation.[19]

And it limited the application of this rule as follows:

> an increase in the number of 'simple' selective distribution systems after an exemption has been granted must be taken into consideration, when an application for renewal of that exemption is being considered, only in the special situation in which the relevant market was already so rigid and structured that the element of competition inherent in 'simple' systems is not sufficient to maintain workable competition.

So, qualitative selection may infringe Article 81(1), but the existence of a large number of such systems is not sufficient on its own to allow the conclusion to be drawn that there is infringement. The decisive factor is the effect of those systems. In this particular case other forms of distribution continued to exist in the market, and wholesalers such as Metro could obtain the same type of products from producers other than SABA. Therefore, the Commission's exemption Decision was upheld.

The ECJ also stated that if a distribution system is identical in all practical respects to a system previously in operation that was the subject of an exemption Decision, the Commission may assume, in the absence of evidence to the contrary, that the new system also fulfils the conditions of Article 81(3). The Court therefore considers that the burden of proof of a change in market conditions lies on third parties wishing to see a further exemption refused.

[19] Case 75/84 *Metro (No 2)* [1986] ECR 3021, [1987] 1 CMLR 118, paras 40–41.

For What Type of Goods May Selective Distribution be Used?

In a number of cases it has been said that it is necessary also 'to consider whether the character of the product in question necessitates a selective distribution system in order to preserve its quality and ensure its proper use'.[20]

In the same case it was stated that it must be considered 'whether those objectives are not already satisfied by national rules governing admission to the re-sale trade or the conditions of sale of the product in question.' If they are, then further rules imposed contractually may not be justified. This might well be the case for goods such as medicines or firearms, for example.

The Commission and ECJ have between them accepted the necessity for selective distribution in marketing a very wide range of goods. These include professional electronic equipment,[21] televisions, radios and tape-recorders,[22] perfume,[23] photographic equipment,[24] high quality clocks and watches,[25] personal computers,[26] newspapers,[27] cars,[28] jewellery,[29] high quality china tableware and ornaments[30] and dental supplies including artificial teeth.[31]

In *Villeroy & Boch*, a case concerning china tableware, it was said that:

> some products or services, which are not simple products or services, possess certain characteristics which prevent them from being sold properly to the public without the intervention of specialist distributors. (para 22)

It was stated in *Binon*, a case on newspaper distribution, that a selective distribution system would not be prohibited under Article 81(1):

> given the special nature of those products as regards their distribution. As AMP rightly pointed out, newspapers and periodicals can, as a general rule, only be sold by retailers during an extremely limited period of time whereas the public expects each distributor to be able to offer a representative selection of press publications, in particular those of the national press. For their part, publishers undertake to take back unsold copies and this gives rise to a continuous exchange of those products between publishers and distributors.

---

[20] *L'Oréal*, above n 5, at para 16. See also Commission Guidelines on vertical restraints (Appendix 7), para 185.
[21] Commission Notice re *Sony España SA*, OJ 1993 C275/3.
[22] *Metro (No 1)*, above n 2.
[23] *L'Oréal*, above n 5.
[24] *Kodak* OJ 1970 L147/24, [1970] CMLR D19.
[25] *Omega*, above n 3; *Junghans* OJ 1977 L30/10, [1977] 1 CMLR D82.
[27] *Binon*, above n 4.
[26] *IBM*, OJ 1984 L118/24, [1984] 2 CMLR 342
[28] *BMW (No 1)*, OJ 1975 L29/1, [1975] 1 CMLR D44.
[29] *Murat* OJ 1983 L348/20, [1984] 1 CMLR 219.
[30] *Villeroy & Boch* OJ 1985 L376/15, [1988] 4 CMLR 461.
[31] *Ivoclar* OJ 1985 L369/1, [1988] 4 CMLR 781. Notice of the Commission's intention to renew this exemption was published at OJ 1993 C251/3.

However, exemption was refused in a case involving distribution of tobacco products,[32] partly on the grounds that the case was distinguishable from *Metro (No 1)* in that that Decision had involved the distribution of 'highly technical, durable consumer goods so that traders had to be selected on the basis of qualitative criteria'.

The Commission has also stated that plumbing fittings do not necessarily require any special form of distribution outlet, at least at wholesale level. The producers argued that the system, restricting wholesale supplies to plumbers, was justified on the grounds that:

> plumbing fittings were semi-finished products which because of their technical complexity and the need for them to be installed required competent advice and guidance and professional standards of workmanship in their installation.[33]

The Commission rejected this argument, saying:

> Since it is doubtful whether plumbing fittings can be considered as technically advanced products and since wholesalers do not generally sell directly to final consumers but to retailers, it is questionable, at least at wholesaler level, whether the characteristics of the product necessitate a selective distribution system in order to preserve their quality and ensure their proper use.

However, this should be seen in the context of a very restrictive system, the declared aim of which was to prevent the fittings coming into the hands of ironmongers, department stores and DIY enthusiasts and for them to be available only to professional plumbing contractors. The main thrust of the Decision concerned the very restrictive nature of the system, which probably influenced the outcome of the Commission's investigation more than did the nature of the goods.

In summary, the cases suggest that almost any product may validly be the subject of some kind of selective distribution system without infringing Article 81, but only to the extent that the restrictions envisaged do not go beyond what is necessary for that particular product. For example, although selective distribution may in principle be used for high quality cosmetics, it is not permissible to include in the selection criteria the requirement that dealers be dispensing chemists.[34]

Also, it is important to be consistent in arguing for the necessity for selective distribution: the argument will not be convincing if simple mail order,[35] or an Internet site (without any 'bricks and mortar' outlet), is used to distribute the same goods. However, the fact that the supplier does not exclusively use selective distribution systems to distribute its goods, and that the system is therefore not 'impervious', does not mean that it infringes Article 81.[36]

---

[32] *FEDETAB*, above n 17.

[33] *Grohe* OJ 1985 L19/17, [1988] 4 CMLR 612, para 6; *Ideal Standard* OJ 1985 L20/38, [1988] 4 CMLR 627, para 6.

[34] Case T-19/91 *Vichy v Commission* [1992] ECR II-415. Vichy's argument was not helped by the fact that it distributed through chemists in some countries but not in others.

[35] But in *Kenwood*, mail order was accepted in combination with selective distribution because advice was available at the collection point where goods were delivered, OJ 1993 C67/9, [1993] 4 CMLR 389.

[36] *Metro v Cartier*, above n 6; Case T-88/92 *Leclerc v Commission* [1996] ECR II-1961, para 115.

Where the relevant market share does not exceed 30 per cent, the block exemption on vertical restraints provides automatic exemption for certain categories of selective distribution agreements *regardless of the goods or services concerned.*

4.2 CLAUSES NOT VIOLATING ARTICLE 81(1)

It is not possible categorically to state that particular clauses will never infringe Article 81(1). As was made clear in the *Metro* cases, even clauses enforcing the application of objective, qualitative selection criteria may, in the presence of certain market conditions, fall within the scope of this prohibition. However, it is possible to make some useful generalisations about the type of clauses which usually fall outside the scope of Article 81(1). These include the clauses necessary to ensure that objective and qualitative selection criteria are enforced, and certain other clauses regarded as ancillary to the main agreement.

Objective and Qualitative Criteria

The rule given in *Metro*, that if a selective distribution system is not to infringe Article 81(1) then it must be based on objective and qualitative criteria, has been repeated in a number of ECJ judgments and Commission Decisions.

The Commission Guidelines on vertical restraints (Appendix 7) say that:

> purely qualitative selective distribution is in general considered to fall outside Article 81(1) for lack of anti-competitive effects, provided that three conditions are satisfied. First, the nature of the product in question must necessitate a selective distribution system, in the sense that such a system must be a legitimate requirement, having regard to the nature of the product concerned, to preserve its quality and ensure its proper use. Secondly, resellers must be chosen on the basis of objective criteria of a qualitative nature which are laid down uniformly for all potential resellers and are not applied in a discriminatory manner. Thirdly, the criteria laid down must not go beyond what is necessary. (para 185)

From past cases it can be concluded that 'objective criteria of a qualitative nature' include those:

(1)   relating to the technical or professional training or qualifications required of the dealer or of his staff;[37]

(2)   relating to the type of equipment and installations available on the premises of the sales outlet;[38]

(3)   stipulating minimum quality levels in respect of materials or equipment used in servicing or after-sales care, whether or not the materials or equipment are supplied by the manufacturer or supplier;[39]

---

[37]   *Metro v Commission (No 1)*, above n 2.
[38]   *Ibid.*
[39]   *D'Ieteren motor oils* OJ 1991 L20/42.

(4) requiring the goods to be sold in a specialised shop or at least in a specialised department of a larger shop, and requiring separate display in an attractive setting. This may extend to the obligation to display quality goods in such a way as to confer prestige on them, by providing them with an attractive individual setting and not placing them near goods of inferior quality.[40] But this probably does not extend to a clause going as far as to require that the sales outlet be situated near other shops selling luxury goods;[41]

(5) imposing an obligation to take minimum supplies, keep minimum stocks and display a certain range of goods;[42]

(6) requiring the sales outlets to have a certain appearance;[43]

(7) stipulating particular opening hours;[44]

(8) requiring the provision of after-sales service and repairs and the fulfilling of guarantees;[45]

(9) requiring potential dealers to furnish evidence of financial means;[46]

(10) imposing quality standards relating to Internet sales.

The Commission's Guidelines on vertical restraints state that selective distributors cannot be prohibited from also selling through an Internet site, unless there is 'an objective justification'. It is not clear how 'objective justification' will be interpreted, but it is presumably a hard test to satisfy. However, 'the supplier may require quality standards for the use of the Internet site to resell its goods, just as the supplier may require quality standards for a shop or for advertising and promotion in general' (Guidelines, para 51). Presumably this means that not only the layout and general presentation of the site may be controlled, but also that the supplier may, for example, stipulate the use of encryption for electronic payment.

It should always be remembered that the criteria must also be necessary or beneficial for the sale of the particular type of goods in question if the agreements are not to fall within the prohibition in Article 81(1).

What Other Obligations May be Imposed Without Infringing Article 81(1)?

If a distribution system is based on objective and qualitative criteria as described above, then the ECJ and Commission accept that the agreements making up the system may in addition contain certain 'ancillary' obligations necessary to

---

[40] *Villeroy & Boch*, above n 30: it should be noted that this was said in the context of a very competitive market and a system which encouraged retailers to sell competing goods and imposed no sales targets. Such clauses might be viewed more severely within less generous systems.

[41] *Baccarat*, Commission Press Release IP/91/603, 1 July 1991.

[42] *Villeroy & Boch*, above n 30; *Murat*, above n 29. But such clauses have sometimes been judged to require exemption under Art 81(3) (see p 124).

[43] *Junghans* OJ 1977 L30/10, [1977] 1 CMLR D82; *Yves Saint Laurent Parfums* OJ 1992 L12/24, [1993] 4 CMLR 120.

[44] Case 210/81 *Demo-Studio Schmidt v Commission* [1983] ECR 3045, [1984] 1 CMLR 63.

[45] *IBM* OJ 1984 L118/24, [1984] 2 CMLR 342.

[46] *Ibid*.

maintain the system and still not fall within the terms of Article 81(1). These include obligations connected with the objective and qualitative criteria already discussed such as:

(1) the obligation on dealers to provide trading information enabling the manufacturer to check that sales are not being made to unauthorised dealers, and also information regarding the trading position, sales trends, the market situation, stocks and expected demand;[47]

(2) other obligations allowing checks to be made on whether dealers are observing the restrictions regarding resale;

(3) the requirement that the manufacturer's guarantee be honoured only in the case of goods bought from authorised retailers;[48]

(4) certain requirements relating to advertising;[49]

(5) the requirement that the manufacturer or producer's consent be obtained by a dealer before participation in any kind of trade fair or exhibition;[50]

(6) the obligation to use the manufacturer's name[51] or trademarks[52] in a specified manner;

(7) obligations aimed at maintaining a distinction between the respective functions of wholesalers and retailers. These include terms prohibiting wholesalers from selling to end-users. This is because the Commission and ECJ consider that selective distribution systems involving two tiers of distribution could not function without such obligations: wholesalers might undercut retailers, since they do not have the same obligations regarding matters such as trained staff and appearance of premises.[53] In *Villeroy & Boch* the Commission explained that: 'competition would be distorted if wholesalers, whose costs are in general proportionately lower precisely because of the marketing stage at which they operate, competed with retailers at the retail stage, in particular on supplies to private customers'. (para 36). Similarly, in *BMW (No 1)* it was accepted that the supplier could legitimately agree that it would not itself sell to individual customers;

(8) customer restrictions where the type of goods being supplied to the different groups of customer are sufficiently different. It was accepted in *Villeroy & Boch* that the kind of china supplied (i) to individuals, (ii) to hotels and restaurants, and (iii) to trade customers for use as advertising material and publicity aids, were different enough for a distribution system based on segregation of responsibility and channels for these different kinds of customer not to infringe Article 81(1). However, it is significant that the Commission emphasised the keenly competitive and very fragmented nature of the market in this case;

---

[47] *BMW (No 1)*, above n 28.
[48] *Metro v Cartier*, above n 6.
[49] *BMW (No 1)*, above n 28, at para 30.
[50] *Ibid*, para 32.
[51] *Omega*, above n 3.
[52] In *BMW (No 1)*, above n 28, this was said to be part of the trademark right.
[53] eg Commission Notice *re Schott-Zwiesel-Glaswerke* OJ 1993 C111/4.

(9) the supplier's exclusive right to appoint dealers. In *Villeroy & Boch* this was judged not to infringe Article 81(1), but in *SABA (No 2)* the Commission said that such a condition was too likely to be abused and required wholesalers to be able to appoint further distributors to the network on their own initiative under certain conditions.

4.3 EXEMPTION UNDER ARTICLE 81(3)

If a selective distribution agreement includes clauses which infringe Article 81(1) then it will require exemption if it is not to be void and unenforceable under Article 81(2), and to incur the risk of fines and liability in damages.

Such an exemption may be available either through the operation of the vertical restraints block exemption Regulation, or where the agreement satisfies the four criteria laid down in Article 81(3). (If it concerns distribution of motor vehicles or their spare parts, or motor vehicle repair and maintenance services, then it may benefit from automatic exemption under the sector-specific block exemption Regulation for motor vehicle distribution, described later in this chapter.)

Exemption Under Block Exemption Regulation 2790/1999

The vertical restraints block exemption Regulation 2790/1999 (Appendix 4) guarantees the validity of any contract falling within its terms. There is no need for any further examination of the contract if it satisfies the Regulation: it is fully valid and can be enforced in a national court.

Chapter 3 describes the general requirements which an agreement must fulfil in order to benefit from the exemption, including a relevant market share no greater than 30 per cent, and the absence of any fixed or minimum resale price or absolute territorial protection. Only issues specific to selective distribution arrangements will be discussed in this Chapter.

The Regulation defines 'selective distribution system' as:

> a distribution system where the supplier undertakes to sell the contract goods or services, either directly or indirectly, only to distributors selected on the basis of specified criteria and where these distributors undertake not to sell such goods or services to unauthorised distributors. (Article 1(d))

The specified criteria are not required to be objective or qualitative; in particular, systems based on quantitative selection criteria are covered by the block exemption, which applies to any kinds of goods or services except motor vehicles and their repair and after-sales services.

The Regulation states expressly that it applies to such a system where sales to unauthorised distributors by members of the system are restricted (Article 4(b)). The Guidelines specify, however, that this is permitted only in respect of markets where such a selective distribution system is operated: resale must therefore be permitted to any distributors in areas where there is either a different distribution system, or none at all (para 52).

A selective distribution system will not be able to benefit from the block exemption if it includes either of the two following 'blacklisted' characteristics.

(1) Members of the system operating at retail level are restricted from making active or passive sales to end users, though they may be prohibited from operating out of an unauthorised outlet (Article 4(c)). This means that dealers cannot be restricted in the users or purchasing agents of users to whom they may sell; for example, they must be free to advertise and sell through the Internet. But the Commission considers it legitimate, particularly in the context of selective distribution, to prevent a distributor from operating exclusively by Internet, and not maintaining a physical outlet.[54] In addition, appropriate 'quality standards' may be imposed in respect of any website (Guidelines, para 51). This would clearly extend to the layout and appearance of the site, and presumably also to the use of a secure payments system, but it is unclear how much further a supplier can go, for example, by imposing the use of certain logos, or specifying links to other sites that may or may not be included.

Recent Decisions show that the Commission is taking an active interest in restrictions in selective distribution systems involving Internet trading. It has fined Yamaha €2.56 million for fixing resale prices and for market-partitioning measures including requiring its dealers to contact Yamaha before fulfilling Internet orders.[55] The Commission also closed an investigation into B&W's selective distribution system, confirming by comfort letter that the block exemption applied, after B&W agreed to delete various clauses from its agreements, including a prohibition on distance sales via the Internet.[56]

In its Guidelines the Commission interprets Article 4(c) as allowing selective distribution to be combined with exclusive distribution in the sense that the supplier may commit itself to supplying only one dealer or a limited number of dealers in a given territory, provided there is no restriction on active or passive selling anywhere (para 53).

Dealers can be prevented from running their business from different premises or from opening a new outlet in a different location. In the case of a mobile outlet, such as an ice cream van, the Commission interprets this as allowing the supplier to define an area outside which the mobile outlet may not be operated (para 54).

(2) Members of the system, including those operating at different levels of trade, are restricted from cross-supplying each other (Article 4(d)). According to the Guidelines, this means that any restriction aimed at forcing distributors to obtain the contract products exclusively from a given source, such as an exclusive purchasing clause, will take the agreement outside the scope of the block exemption (para 55).

---

[54] This is the implication of the Commission's informal clearance of Yves St Laurent's selective distribution system for perfume, Commission Press Release IP/01/713, 17 May 2001. There are similarities with the *Yves Saint Laurent* Decision, OJ 1992 L12/24, [1993] 4 CMLR 120, mainly upheld in *Leclerc*, above n 36, in which it was accepted that distributors be prohibited from operating solely by mail order.

[55] Commission Press Release IP/03/1028, 16 July 2003 (not yet officially reported but available on DG Comp's website).

[56] *B&W*, Commission Press Release IP/02/916, 24 June 2002.

A clause imposing directly or indirectly any obligation which causes the members of the system not to sell the brands of particular competing suppliers will not have the benefit of exemption under the Regulation (Article 5(c)). Note that a general non-compete clause, obliging dealers not to sell any competing brands, is exempted provided it is for no more than five years. The Commission's objection to the specifying of particular competing brands is that it could facilitate horizontal co-operation between competing suppliers using the same network of outlets, so as to exclude specific competitors from those outlets, thereby foreclosing them from the market (Guidelines, para 61).

However, the wording of Article 5 means that, unlike the blacklisted clauses, this type of non-compete clause will not prevent the rest of the agreement from benefiting from exemption under the Regulation.

It might be thought that selective distributors could escape from the various restrictions described above by not specifying their selection criteria, and thereby falling outside the Regulation's definition of selective distribution system, quoted above. However, they would then not be able to claim the benefit of the Regulation for any restriction of sales to unauthorised distributors, which would defeat the point of the selective distribution system.

The possibility of withdrawal of the benefit of the block exemption (see p 94) exists for all types of agreement, but the Regulation mentions that it may in particular happen in respect of the cumulative effect of several selective distribution networks in the same market (Recital 13). The Guidelines provide that where the share of the market covered by selective distribution is below 50 per cent, or where it exceeds 50 per cent but the aggregate market share of the five largest suppliers is below 50 per cent, there will not normally be any problem (para 189). They also give an example of the type of situation in which the Commission might well withdraw the benefit of the block exemption because of such a cumulative effect (para 198).

The block exemption applies regardless of the nature of the product concerned and the necessity for the use of selective distribution. However, the Guidelines mention that the Commission may withdraw the benefit of the exemption where a distribution system is not justified by the nature of the product, and so does not bring about sufficient efficiency gains to counterbalance a significant reduction in competition between brands (para 186).

The existence of several parallel selective distribution networks covering more than 50 per cent of a particular market may also lead to the adoption by the Commission of a Regulation disapplying the benefit of the block exemption in respect of specific restraints in distribution agreements in that market (see p 94).

Exemption Under Article 81(3)

A number of additional restrictions sometimes found in selective distribution agreements, though usually infringing Article 81(1) and not covered by the block exemption, in particular because the relevant market share exceeds 30 per cent, may benefit from exemption by satisfying the four substantive criteria of Article 81(3) (see p 30). However, exceptional economic efficiencies will need to be proved where the relevant market share is high.

The Commission's main competition concerns regarding selective distribution are:

(1) foreclosure of the purchase market, with certain resellers being unable to obtain supplies;
(2) facilitation of collusion between suppliers or distributors; and
(3) reduction or elimination of intra-brand competition, possibly leading to weakening of inter-brand competition (Guidelines, paras 110 and 185).

Generally, the stronger the market position of the supplier, and the more selective distribution systems there are present on the market, the less likely it is that exemption will be available (para 187). A mature market is another factor which will militate against exemption (para 194); also the Commission says in its Guidelines that exemption is unlikely where selective distribution is not necessary for the product in question: selective distribution systems involving new products, complex products, products which are difficult to judge before consumption ('experience products') and products difficult to judge even after consumption ('credence products') are most likely to merit exemption (paras 195 and 116(3)).

(a) Exclusivity and Territorial Protection

Exclusive territories and territorial protection are a common, though by no means inevitable, feature of selective distribution networks, in particular at the wholesale level, and generally infringe Article 81(1).[57] The Commission has said in its Guidelines that even 'open' territorial exclusivity (where passive sales are permitted outside the exclusive territory) combined with selective distribution generally infringes Article 81 where the supplier's market share exceeds 30 per cent or where there is a cumulative effect as a result of a number of networks.

Exemption will exceptionally be available, where exclusivity is shown to be indispensable to protect substantial and relationship-specific investments made by the authorised dealers.[58] Normally, it will be necessary that total territorial exclusivity is not conferred on wholesalers.[59]

In *Yves Saint Laurent Parfums* the Commission required removal of a term imposing an export ban, but allowed it to be replaced by a prohibition on active sales by authorised retailers in Member States where a new product had not yet

---

[57] *Omega*, above n 3. See also Guidelines, para 195.
[58] eg *Yves Saint Laurent Parfums*, above n 43; Commission Notice re *Schott-Zwiesel-Glaswerke*, above n 53. See also Guidelines, para 195.
[59] Guidelines, para 195. See also *Ivoclar*, above n31; in *Junghans*, above n 43, an exclusive territory for wholesalers combined with an obligation not to market actively outside that territory was exempted.

been launched, for one year from the first launch of the product in the European Union. This was justified on the basis that it was necessary so as not to jeopardise the official launch of the product in those retailers' territories.

(b) Non-competition Clauses

Dealers are sometimes restricted from selling competing goods, or there may be provision for the supplier's consent to be obtained before other goods are sold: in any case these will infringe Article 81(1) and exemption will be necessary.[60]

Where the vertical restraints block exemption does not apply, the Guidelines state that obligations causing authorised dealers not to sell the brands of particular competing suppliers are unlikely to qualify for exemption where the aggregate market share of the five largest suppliers is 50 per cent or above, unless none of the suppliers imposing such an obligation is among these top five. This is aimed at avoiding horizontal collusion between suppliers (para 192).

The Commission also believes that non-compete clauses combined with selective distribution may lead to significant foreclosure effects, effectively excluding competing suppliers from the market, in which case exemption is unlikely (para 193).

A prohibition on selling competing cars was exempted in *BMW (No 1)*, though the non-competition clause relating to spare parts was only allowed to be of narrow scope: dealers were still required to be permitted to sell competing spare parts and accessories of comparable quality to customers, and where the safety of the car was not affected, the dealer had to be permitted to sell any kind of competing spare parts or accessories at all.

(c) No Supply to Non-members of Network

The obligation on members of a network not to supply for resale outside the network,[61] if the criteria for membership are not objective and qualitative, generally infringes Article 81(1).

If the criteria themselves satisfy the four Article 81(3) criteria, then this restriction will also be exempted. However, when granting an exemption in *BMW (No 1)* to a selective distribution system for car parts, the Commission noted with approval that, despite the general rule against supply outside the network, dealers were free to supply spare parts to persons outside the network provided that these parts were to be used only for effecting repairs and not for resale. This requirement is also incorporated in the block exemption Regulation relating to motor vehicle distribution (see p 143).

---

[60] *Junghans*, above n 43.
[61] In *Metro v Commission (No 1)*, above n 2, this obligation was characterised not as a restriction but as an accessory to the principal obligation (para 27).

(d) Quantitative Selection Criteria

'Quantitative' criteria include limitations on the number of retail outlets with reference to a certain area or to a minimum number of inhabitants in the vicinity of an outlet and they restrict competition within the meaning of Article 81(1).[62]

The ECJ has stated that, although quantitative selection criteria are 'by definition' restrictive of competition, they may be exempted under Article 81(3).[63] However, the Commission has stressed that they will only be exempted in cases in which close co-operation between the supplier and his distributors is necessary and is not possible in the absence of such restrictions. Quantitative limitations on the number of distributors of dental equipment were exempted by the Commission in *Ivoclar*. Exemption was justified on the basis that it was necessary to keep the numbers manageable: 'supplying a much larger number of distributors would be detrimental to [Ivoclar's] objective of ensuring competent distribution of its products'.

In its Guidelines the Commission gives an example of a situation in which a quantitative selective distribution system falling outside the scope of the block exemption could benefit from exemption (para 197).

(e) Obligation to Promote Sales of the Supplier's Goods[64]

Such additional obligations as this, and those under (f) and (g), when combined with selective distribution, may lead to significant foreclosure effects, effectively excluding competing suppliers from the market, in which case exemption is unlikely to apply. But the Commission states in its Guidelines that this is unlikely to be a problem where less than 50 per cent of the market is covered by selective distribution and the five largest suppliers have an aggregate market share below 50 per cent (para 193).

(f) Obligation to Take Part in Setting Up a Network of Dealers[65]

(g) Requirements of a Minimum Scale of Business and Minimum Supplies to be Ordered and Stock to be Maintained,[66] Specified After-Sales or Guarantee Service to be Provided[67] and a Full Range of Goods to be Kept.[68]

However, in some cases such clauses have been held to fall outside the scope of Article 81(1) altogether.

---

[62] Case 86/82 *Hasselblad v Commission* [1984] ECR 883, [1984] 1 CMLR 559. It is possible for selection criteria to appear qualitative but in fact to be quantitative if national legislation sets quotas for certain types of retailers: *Vichy v Commission*, above n 34, involved dispensing chemists.

[63] *Binon*, above n 4, at para 29.

[64] *Villeroy & Boch*, above n 30: 'even if the obligation to promote sales of Villeroy & Boch goods cannot strictly be regarded as qualitative selection criteria compatible with Article [81(1)], they, are not to be considered *in this case* as giving rise to any appreciable restriction of competition' (para 30) (emphasis added).

[65] *Metro v Commission (No 1)*, above n 2.

[66] *BMW (No 1)*; above n 28 *Yves Saint Laurent Parfums*, above n 43.

[67] *BMW (No 1)*, above n 28.

[68] *Metro(No 2)*, above n 19.

(h) Customer Restrictions

A supplier may reserve for itself the right to supply specific types of customers: in *Peugeot* the supplier agreed not to sell to ordinary end-users but only to fleet buyers, government departments and certain Peugeot employees.

However, exemption will not apply where the supplier reserves to itself the exclusive right to supply models having different specifications to those normally required by local customers, since this affords a means of effectively eliminating competition and dividing markets. In *Grohe* and *Ideal Standard* customer restrictions were strongly condemned and the distribution system was refused exemption. In these systems, wholesalers were prohibited from supplying the supplier's plumbing fittings to anyone except plumbing contractors, other approved wholesalers and specialised industrial firms for their own installation. In other words, ordinary retailers, whether traditional ironmongers or modern department stores, and therefore individual consumers who wished to buy parts to fit themselves, were prevented from obtaining supplies of these fittings.

(i) Perfume and Luxury Cosmetics

Selective distribution in the perfume and luxury cosmetics sector was at one time treated particularly leniently by the Commission, which stated that because of the very competitive market structure in this sector, it could be more generous in evaluating whether certain criteria, even quantitative, infringed Article 81(1).[69]

However, it later changed its approach, bringing the treatment of perfume distribution systems into line with that in other sectors, despite the fact that the perfume sector remains highly competitive. For example, quantitative limits on admission to a selective distribution system were not permitted in *Yves Saint Laurent*, nor in *Parfums Givenchy*.[70] These decisions were appealed by distributors who had been refused authorisation, and the Court of First Instance upheld them, except in respect of a clause allowing Yves St Laurent to treat applicant retailers less favourably if perfumery represented a minority of their activity.[71]

4.4 CLAUSES UNLIKELY TO BENEFIT FROM EXEMPTION
UNDER ARTICLE 81(3)

Certain types of clause or practice are virtually certain never to satisfy the four exemption criteria in Article 81(3). They also provide an indication of the likelihood

---

[69] In its Fourth Annual Report on Competition Policy the Commission reported on its examination of the selective distribution systems operated by Dior and Lancôme after which it came to the conclusion that, after certain clauses had been removed, the agreements fell outside the scope of Art 81(1) and therefore did not require exemption under Art 81(3).

[70] OJ 1992 L236/11, [1993] 5 CMLR 579.

[71] Case T-19/92 [1996] ECR II-1851; *Leclerc*, above n 36; Case T-87/92 *Kruidvat BVBA v Commission* [1996] ECR II-1931, upheld in Case C-70/97 [1998] ECR I-7183.

of withdrawal of the benefit of the vertical restraints block exemption, in the event that they fall technically within the terms of the block exemption Regulation.

Absolute Territorial Restrictions

As in the case of other types of distribution contract, exemption will not be available for any term which tends to divide one area of the common market from another entirely. Thus, a term requiring a dealer not to supply end-users outside his territory will infringe Article 81(1) and not qualify for exemption.

In the past the Commission has frequently required the removal of an export ban from distribution agreements before granting exemption or negative clearance.[72] Territorial division is sometimes attempted by imposing a surcharge on goods ordered by customers resident in a different Member State or territory. Such action will always infringe Article 81(1) and will not be exempted. It may also lead to fines being imposed.

In *BMW (No 1)* the Commission exempted a selective distribution network through which BMW sold its cars, motorbikes and spare parts, and carried out repairs and other after-sales services in a number of Community countries. When the agreements making up the network had first been notified to the Commission, they had contained export bans on dealers. Exemption for these agreements was refused. It was only with respect to new agreements without such a prohibition that the Commission was prepared to grant an individual exemption to BMW under Article 81(3).

Later, the distribution system came before the ECJ, as a result of a complaint about a circular issued by BMW's main distributor in Belgium to discourage its dealers from exporting cars, in particular to the United Kingdom. The Court condemned this behaviour, saying that it was an essential characteristic of the exempted agreement that dealers be able freely to sell cars to other BMW concessionaires and to end-users and their intermediaries.

In *Ford* the finding that the car manufacturer had been acting so as to prevent parallel imports has been accepted by the ECJ as justifying the Commission's refusal even to consider the possibility of granting an exemption to that undertaking's selective distribution system:

> the Commission is not obliged to carry out a detailed examination of all the advantages and disadvantages likely to flow from a selective distribution system when it has good reason to believe that a manufacturer has used such a system to prevent parallel imports and thus artificially to partition the common market.

Several car manufacturers have been heavily fined for operating selective distribution systems so as to partition national markets. The practices concerned include bonuses limited to domestic sales,[73] instructions not to export, backed up by

---

[72] eg *Peugeot*, above n 9.
[73] *Opel Nederland* (€43 million), upheld in Case T-368/00, [2003] ECR II 4491, [2004] 4 CMLR 1402, appeal pending, Case C-551/03, OJ 2004 C71/8.

threats to reduce deliveries, and an obligation to require customers from outside the territory to pay a 15 per cent deposit when ordering,[74] and hindering of cross-sales between authorised selective distributors.[75]

Refusal to Supply or Expulsion from Network

As described above, the legality of a given selective distribution system depends partly on the existence of the possibility for dealers within the network to buy and sell the products in question from and to each other, and to supply end-users regardless of their place of residence. It is also dependent on the non-discriminatory application of objective and qualitative criteria in appointing distributors.

Therefore, if the exercise of this possibility of cross-supply is in practice discouraged in any way, the agreements will be illegal. This is the case, for example, if dealers are expelled or threatened with expulsion from the network if they supply dealers outside their own territory; it is also true if any kind of inducement is offered to dealers to discourage them from making such sales or purchases, or if contracts are in fact refused or terminated for reasons other than those to be found in the non-discriminatory application of legitimate selection criteria.

In *AEG* the Court said of a selective distribution system in which the above rules were not respected:

> Such a practice must be considered unlawful where the manufacturer, with a view to maintaining a high level of prices or to excluding certain modern channels of distribution, refuses to approve distributors who satisfy the qualitative criteria of the system (para 37).

It was argued that such refusal to appoint dealers was purely unilateral conduct which could not therefore be subject to the application of Article 81(1) because of the absence of an agreement or concerted practice. The Court rejected this argument. It considered that where a particular policy is being pursued (in this case the refusal to deal via the kind of outlets where low prices were likely to be charged), such refusals are:

> performed in the context of the contractual relations with authorised distributors inasmuch as their purpose is to guarantee observance of the agreements in restraint of competition which form the basis of contracts between manufacturers and approved distributors. (para 39)

The illegality of such conduct is dependent on its being systematic and not simply isolated instances of unjustified refusal to appoint. However, systematic conduct may be found on the basis of a relatively small number of occurrences.[76]

---

[74] *DaimlerChrysler* (€71.825 million) OJ 2002 L257/1, [2003] 4 CMLR 95, appeal pending, Case T-352/01, OJ 2002 C68/15.
[75] *JCB* (€39.6 million), upheld but fine reduced in Case T-67/01, 13 January 2004 (not yet officially reported), [2004] 4 CMLR 1346, appeal pending, Case C-167/04 OJ 2004, C156/3.
[76] See also p 109.

Under the old procedural rules, the Commission frequently imposed conditions when granting exemptions and comfort letters, in order to ensure that the freedom to appoint and terminate distributors was not abused. In *SABA (No 2)* the Commission agreed to renew the exemption it had granted to SABA's selective distribution system only on condition that certain changes were made to the procedure for admission to the network of specialist distributors. The system was a two-tier one, consisting of wholesalers and of specialist retailers. Originally, SABA itself had sole responsibility for deciding whether or not a specialist distributor fulfilled the criteria for admission. The revised system allowed the wholesalers to admit to the network and supply with goods any retailer satisfying those criteria.[77]

Similarly, the Commission made it a condition of a comfort letter that it granted to Sony that there be an independent arbitration and appeals procedure for dealers and wholesalers refused entry into the network. In addition, written justification in advance was to be given to authorised dealers who were refused supplies.[78] However, even if it finds that Article 81(1) has been infringed, the Commission has no power to order a supplier to supply a particular dealer, since this would interfere with the fundamental principle of freedom of contract.[79]

Exclusion of 'Certain Modern Forms of Distribution'

A system that excludes department stores even when they have suitable premises and staff will not be exempted. In *Villeroy & Boch* it was considered significant that the acceptance of, as well as specialist retailers, retail outlets having a specialised department, did not exclude 'certain modern forms of distribution' (para 25). By this were meant department stores or other large outlets whose scale of operation permits them to charge lower prices than are charged by small, specialist shops selling the same goods. Provided that a specialised department is available and meets the selection criteria, admission cannot be refused on the basis that the shop deals in many other kinds of goods as well.

This was explained in *AEG-Telefunken*: it was said that in many cases of selective distribution a certain amount of price rigidity is the inevitable price to be paid for the other types of competition (such as expert advice and after-sales service) that exist in consequence of the selective distribution system. This justification for price rigidity goes if new forms of distribution which enable lower prices to be charged—as well as the other forms of competition to be maintained—are excluded from the network.

The same principle would presumably apply if attempts were made to exclude distributors operating through the Internet, provided that the supplier's criteria

---

[77] See also the conditions imposed in *Yves Saint Laurent Parfums*, above n 43, and *Parfums Givenchy*, above n 70.

[78] *Sony*, Commission Press Release IP/95/736, 11 July 1995.

[79] Case T-24/90 *Automec v Commission (No 2)* [1992] ECR 2223, [1992] 5 CMLR 431.

for network membership, such as, say, expert advice being available to customers, were met.

The Commission's Guidelines mention its awareness that selective distribution is 'particularly well suited to avoid pressure by price discounters on the margins of the manufacturer, as well as on the margins of the authorised dealers' (para 188).

Price-fixing

Resale price-fixing in any form (see p 76) virtually always infringes Article 81(1). This includes not only the laying down by a manufacturer of precise retail prices, but also less restrictive forms of control such as agreement on the size of margins allowed.[80] Volkswagen was recently heavily fined for fixing the resale prices to be applied by its selective distributors.[81]

However, in the context of selective distribution it may be permissible to prevent resellers from using expressions such as 'cash-and-carry prices, self-service prices or takeaway prices': in *Grundig* the Commission considered that such a restriction was a necessary part of maintaining quality standards and therefore did not infringe Article 81(1).[82]

Abolition of Wholesale Level

Exemption or clearance is unlikely to be granted where a manufacturer, despite the fact that he wishes to distribute his goods in a number of different Member States, envisages eliminating the wholesaler distribution level. This is because the Commission considers that parallel trade is more likely to be restricted in such circumstances.[83] This indicates that selective distribution networks in which the supplier is vertically integrated as far as wholesale level, but not at retail level, are less likely to be legal than those which include independent wholesalers.

4.5 BLOCK EXEMPTION REGULATION FOR MOTOR VEHICLE DISTRIBUTION AGREEMENTS

From the start of its competition enforcement activity the Commission has considered selective distribution as generally justified in the context of distributing and servicing motor vehicles and their spare parts. Early on, it received several notifications of such agreements, resulting in a number of Decisions granting

---

[80] *FEDETAB*, above n 17.
[81] *Volkswagen* (€30.96 million), annulled in Case T-208/01, 3 December 2003 (not yet officially reported), [2004] 4 CMLR 727, because no 'agreement' proved, appeal pending, Case C-74/04, OJ 2004 C94/24.
[82] OJ 1994 L20/15, [1995] 4 CMLR 658, para 31.
[83] *Sony*, Commission Press Release IP/95/736, 11 July 1995.

individual exemptions. Following the ECJ's judgment in *BMW (No 1)* the Commission adopted Regulation 123/85, granting automatic exemption for certain categories of motor vehicle distribution and servicing agreements.[84] This was replaced in 1995 by Regulation 1475/95,[85] which was itself replaced in 2002 by Regulation 1400/2002 (Appendix 5).

The first such block exemption, Regulation 123/85, created a specially favourable regime for motor vehicle distribution, on the basis that motor vehicles were technologically complex products requiring regular expert maintenance and repair, so that their distribution justified manufacturers in imposing some very restrictive contractual arrangements that would not have been acceptable in other product markets. Since then the Commission's experience has caused it to change its stance radically, to the point where Regulation 1400/2002 is now considerably stricter in the limitations and obligations it imposes on vehicle manufacturers than both its predecessor in the motor vehicle sector and also the generally applicable block exemption Regulation on vertical restraints.[86]

The special arrangements permitted to the car industry under these Regulations have long been controversial. Manufacturers have argued that they were necessary in order to ensure proper safety standards and after-sales services, whereas others pointed to them as at least a contributing factor to limited competition in the sector and continuing wide price differentials from one Member State to another.

The Commission has frequently voiced its concern over these continued differentials, and its Notice published at the same time that it adopted Regulation 123/85 stated that if they exceeded certain specified thresholds then the benefit of the Regulation could be withdrawn. In fact withdrawal never happened, despite the fact that the twice-yearly reports on price differentials across the European Union continued to indicate that the situation was not improving. Manufacturers explained the situation on the basis of the different VAT and registration charges applicable in different Member States, and currency fluctuations, which meant that they had to adjust their pre-tax prices to take these into account.

In addition, a number of Commission Decisions and ECJ judgments have arisen out of complaints about practices of manufacturers, importers and dealers which make it difficult for Community citizens to buy cars where they are cheapest. One such Decision was taken against Ford for its decision no longer to supply right hand drive cars to German dealers, thus effectively preventing orders from UK citizens from being fulfilled in Germany, where the cars were cheaper than in the United Kingdom (see p 110).

As a result of these concerns, Regulation 1475/95 was slightly more favourable to dealers (and probably consumers) than its predecessor, but fell a long way short of the demands made by dealers' and consumers' organisations during the discussions leading up to its adoption.

---

[84] OJ 1985 L15/16.
[85] OJ 1995 L145/25.
[86] Motor vehicle distribution and servicing arrangements cannot benefit from the block exemption on vertical restraints: Reg 2790/1999(Appendix 4), Art 2(5).

By May 2000 Commissioner Monti was making reference to 'questionable' assumptions on which Regulation 1475/95 was based: these were that there was effective competition in the market, that after-sales services should always be provided by distributors, and that brand specialists are needed to carry out repairs. He also said that several objectives of the legislation were not being met, and in particular that dealers' independence had not been sufficiently strengthened; nor was there much parallel trade, despite the existence of significant price differences across borders, and supermarkets claimed that they had been unable to obtain supplies to enable them to enter the retail market.[87] Another factor referred to by Commissioner Monti and which clearly influenced his approach to the industry was that car manufacturers frequently flouted the generous regime accorded to them: Volkswagen had been heavily fined for its misconduct, as had Opel, and investigations into the practices of other manufacturers, including DaimlerChrysler, Renault and General Motors, were ongoing (see p 54).

The Commission (as required by the Regulation) carried out a survey of interested parties, resulting in the return of over 100 replies, commissioned a number of independent reports, and in November 2000 published an evaluation report[88] indicating that it was far from satisfied with the way in which the Regulation was working, and concluding baldly that:

> the block exemption has not achieved part of the aims stated by the Commission in 1995 when it renewed its permission to use selective distribution networks for the sale of motor cars. Consumers in particular do not seem to derive from this distribution system the fair share of the benefits of the creation of a European single market.[89]

The new Regulation 1400/2002 therefore introduced fairly radical change, intended to deal with perceived failures of the existing regime. When first proposed, it was the subject of fierce lobbying by manufacturers and some Member State governments such as France and Germany, with whom it was extremely unpopular. But it was eventually adopted substantially as proposed by the Commission, except for the postponement of one key rule change, a ban on 'location clauses', until 2005.

The Regulation as adopted:

- removed the possibility for manufacturers to combine exclusive with selective distribution (they must now choose between the two);
- severed the link between sales and after-sales services (in the past dealers were obliged also to provide such services);
- made it easier for dealers to be able to sell competing brands from a single outlet, and to open secondary outlets anywhere in the Community;
- loosened restrictions on intermediaries who purchase on behalf of consumers;

---

[87] Speech 00/177, 11 May 2000.
[88] Report on the evaluation of Regulation (EC) No 1475/95 on the application of Article [81(3)] of the Treaty to certain categories of motor vehicle distribution and servicing agreements COM(2000)743 of 15 November 2000.
[89] Commission Press Release IP/00/1306, 15 November 2000.

- required manufacturers to provide the necessary technical information to any-one wanting to provide repair or maintenance services;
- strengthened dealers' protection against wrongful termination;
- facilitated the transfer of their business by dealers and repairers;
- improved business opportunities for suppliers of after-sales services and spare parts, including allowing them to source spare parts from the original producer.

The Regulation, which is long and complex, is described below. Much useful detail is contained in the introductory Recitals which precede the main body of the Regulation.[90] As always with block exemptions, it is essential that the agreement fall strictly within the letter of the terms of the Regulation, or it will not apply.

It should always be borne in mind that Regulation 1400/2002 does not impose a legally obligatory framework. Rather it offers exemption from the application of Article 81(1) to agreements which fulfil its criteria. Manufacturers remain free, at least in theory, to work outside the block exemption, by ensuring either that they do not infringe Article 81(1), for example by appointing 'genuine' agents (see Chapter 6), or that they fulfil the four substantive criteria of Article 81(3). In some cases the arrangements may represent a small enough market share for them to benefit from the Commission's Notice on agreements of minor importance.[91]

Structure and Scope of Regulation 1400/2002

Regulation 1400/2002 applies to vertical agreements relating to the conditions under which the parties may purchase, sell or resell new[92] motor vehicles, or spare parts or repair and maintenance services for motor vehicles (Article 2(1)), and is similar in structure to the general block exemption Regulation on vertical restraints described in Chapter 3. Though it is stricter than that Regulation in a number of ways, it does offer a certain amount of flexibility, giving suppliers a number of options for organising their distribution structures.

'Motor vehicle' here means 'a self-propelled vehicle intended for use on public roads and having three or more road wheels' (Article 1(m)). The Commission considers agricultural machinery to fall outside the scope of this definition, since it is intended primarily for use on the land.[93]

---

[90] When Regulation 1400/2000 entered into force, DG Comp produced an 'explanatory brochure' (EB). This text was announced in Commission Press Release IP/02/1392, 30 September 2002 and is available at DG Comp's website. The Commission says that it 'deals with every aspect of the new regulation in a clear, user-friendly way'. This is complemented by a 'Frequently Asked Questions' document, also available on the website.

[91] An example is Porsche's dealer network, with a market share of less than 5 per cent in every Member State: Commission Press Release IP/04/585, 3 May 2004.

[92] 'New' is not defined. The Commission indicates that it is a question of trade usage, EB, Q39. In OJ 1988 L45 *ARG/Unipart* 34 an individual exemption was granted in respect of second-hand cars.

[93] Commission Press Release IP/90/917, 16 November 1990 (which concerned an earlier Regulation).

The Regulation will normally not apply if the parties concerned or their connected undertakings[94] are competitors, in particular where they are both manufacturers of motor vehicles (Article 2(3)). In such circumstances, there is too great a risk that the agreement is a means of reducing competition between the two manufacturers. However, the Regulation provides for some limited exceptions, in particular where the buyer's total annual turnover does not exceed €100 million.[95]

The Regulation is not restricted in its application to agreements for retail sale. Most manufacturers of motor vehicles operate at least a two-tier system, in which a different national distributor is responsible in each country for arranging distribution to local independent dealers in this territory. This Regulation can apply to agreements at these different levels. Examples of the kind of agreements potentially within the scope of the Regulation are those between:

- a vehicle manufacturer or its subsidiary, and independent importers or wholesalers who are entrusted with supplying and management of the manufacturer's distribution and repair network;
- a vehicle manufacturer or its subsidiary and individual members of its authorised network of distributors and repairers;
- a vehicle manufacturer, a main distributor and a sub-distributor or agent;
- a vehicle or spare parts manufacturer and an association of small authorised or independent dealers or repairers who jointly buy vehicles or spare parts;
- a supplier of spare parts and individual members of a network of independent or authorised repairers (EB, Q3).

Exemption under the Regulation applies to all such agreements, provided that certain market share thresholds are not exceeded and that no 'blacklisted' (or 'hardcore') restrictions are present, and certain other positive requirements are fulfilled. Unlike its predecessors, this Regulation contains no 'white list' of permitted clauses: any restriction not expressly prohibited is permitted. For this reason certain types of restriction which featured in earlier motor vehicle block exemptions are not discussed at all in Regulation 1400/2002.[96]

As under the vertical restraints block exemption there is also a category of restrictions, mainly types of non-compete clauses, which do not benefit from exemption under the Regulation but which do not necessarily prevent the rest of the agreement from so benefiting, provided they are severable under the relevant national law. Similarly, agreements including clauses relating to intellectual property rights can be covered, provided the provisions are ancillary to the main distribution arrangements.

---

[94] See Art 1(2) for the definition of 'connected undertakings': it essentially includes all members of the same corporate group.

[95] Art 2(3)(a). Guidance on calculation of turnover is given in Art 9.

[96] These include obligations relating to minimum standards of facilities, equipment, professional staff, repair and servicing, advertising, ancillary customer services such as storage and delivery, minimum stocks and sales targets and the stocking of demonstration vehicles, obligations to honour guarantees, appointment of sub-dealers and the activities of intermediaries who purchase on behalf of consumers.

Market Share Thresholds

As is now standard in block exemption Regulations, Regulation 1400/2002 applies only if certain market share thresholds are not exceeded. The basic rule here is that the supplier's market share must not exceed 30 per cent of the relevant market on which it sells the vehicles or services. However, in the case of the sale of new vehicles through quantitative selective distribution the threshold is 40 per cent, and no threshold applies to any qualitative selective distribution system.[97]

Article 8(2) provides some flexibility where the thresholds are exceeded for short periods.

Market Definition

Before it is possible to assess the level of the relevant market shares, and thus whether the relevant threshold is exceeded, it must be established what are the relevant geographic and product markets. Given that the applicability or otherwise of the Regulation may well turn on the relevant market share figures, market definition is key. As discussed in Chapter 3, guidance may be sought from various sources[98] but in addition to the general guidance available on market definition, some additional pointers are available in the context of motor vehicles. Still, there are few clear answers in this area.

Article 3(1) states that the market to be considered is (except in the unusual case of 'exclusive supply') 'the supplier's market share on the relevant market on which it sell', which means the wholesale rather than the retail market. A relevant market is one that includes all products or services which can be regarded as substitutable for each other. The Regulation requires substitutability to be looked at from the dealer or service provider's point of view. DG Comp suggests that, at least at retail level, what is substitutable from his point of view 'will normally be determined by the preferences of end-users',[99] but there are many circumstances in which the two will differ.[100]

As far as passenger cars are concerned, the Commission states that it has never defined the relevant market precisely in any of its Decisions.[101] The narrowest

---

[97] Where a supplier agrees to sell particular goods and services only to one buyer in the Community (a situation likely to be very rare), then the *buyer's* share of the market on which it purchases them must not exceed 30 per cent (Arts 3(2) and 1(1)(e)).

[98] In particular, the Commission Notice on the definition of relevant market, OJ 1997 C372/5, and EB, section 6.

[99] EB, 6.1.4.

[100] For examples, and for further comments on the market share rules, see Houthoff Buruma and Liedekerke Wolters Waelbrock Kirkpatrick 'Flawed Reform of the Competition Rules for the European Motor Vehicle Sector' [2003] *ECLR* 254.

[101] EB, 6.1. Guidance on market definition is available in some of the car distribution cases cited at p 54. See also a study on market definition in the passenger car market produced for the Commission by Frank Verboven, September 2002.

likely definition is by industry 'segment', but, at the other end of the spectrum, the effect of 'chains of substitution' (where, for example, certain cars in segment A are substitutable for some in segment B, and others in B are substitutable for some in C) could lead to the conclusion that there was one market for all passenger cars.

In the case of spare parts, parts produced by third parties may sometimes form part of the same market. They are likely to do so in the case of basic products such as batteries, but not in the case of brand-specific parts for which an alternative cannot easily be found. However, this assessment may vary according to whether retail or wholesale trade is being considered, with retail markets being more likely to be defined more narrowly, both as to product and geographically.

As for repair and maintenance services, the Commission tends to define the relevant market as brand-specific. This is questionable, particularly if supply-side substitutability (the possibility of repairers switching from repairing one brand to repairing another brand) is taken into account. On the basis of the Commission's view, in most cases the relevant market shares are over 30 per cent, making qualitative selective distribution the only available option under the Regulation.[102]

As to the relevant geographic market, this will normally be national for distribution of new vehicles, and national or smaller for after-sales services. It may be broader, even Community-wide, in the case of sale of components.[103]

Calculation of Market Share

Article 8 states some rules as to how market shares are to be calculated for the purposes of Regulation 1400/2002. These rules therefore prevail over other more general principles of market definition.

Distribution of New Vehicles

Market share is based on the *volume* of all contract goods and corresponding goods sold by the supplier, together with other goods sold by the supplier which are regarded as substitutable by a dealer (taking into account possible chains of substitution). It is surprising that the reference is to volume rather than to value. Elsewhere,[104] the Commission has required market shares to be calculated by reference to value, whereas here value data may only be used if volume data is not available.

---

[102] This is borne out by the first instances of Commission intervention on the basis of Regulation 1400/2002 which it has made public. See Commission Press Releases IP/03/80, 20 January 2003 (*Volkswagen* and *Opel*) and IP/04/585, 3 May 2004 (*Porsche*), both of which involved the use of qualitative selective distribution for after-sales service providers.

[103] EB, 6.1.

[104] Not only elsewhere in Art 8 of this Regulation, but also in the Commission's Notice on agreements of minor importance (Appendix 8). Two completely different sets of data may therefore be needed to check whether that Notice or Regulation 1400/2002 (Appendix 5) applies to a vehicle distribution agreement.

Distribution of Spare Parts

Market share is based on the *value* of all contract goods and other goods sold by the supplier, together with other goods sold by the supplier which are regarded as substitutable by the dealer.

Provision of Repair and Maintenance Services

Market share is based on the *value* of the contract services sold by the members of the supplier's distribution network, together with any other services sold by these members which are regarded as substitutable by customers. Authorised repairers are viewed by the Commission as being in a similar position to franchisees, and so it considers that the supplier's market share should be calculated both on the basis of the goods and services it provides to its network, and of the services the repairers provide at retail level.[105]

Note that the calculation of a company's market share must include any share attributable to its 'connected undertakings' (defined in Article 1(2)).

Choice of Distribution Mmethod

If they want to benefit from this block exemption, manufacturers have to choose between exclusive and selective distribution (though both can be used at different levels of the supply chain, or in different territories). Depending on the relevant market shares, the selective distribution may be qualitative, quantitative, or a combination of both, in which case it will count as quantitative for the purposes of the market share threshold rules. Unlike earlier Regulations in this sector, and unlike the vertical restraints block exemption, Regulation 1400/2002 does not provide exemption for distribution agreements which combine exclusive territories with selective distribution.

Though it is possible in principle for a vehicle manufacturer to use different systems in different territories, this will not normally be an attractive option. For example, if selective distribution is used in territory A, and exclusive distribution in territory B, dealers in A wanting to sell vehicles in B can be restricted to making passive[106] sales to end-users or dealers in B, meaning that the exclusivity rights of dealers in B remain protected. However, dealers in B must be free to sell actively to end-users and to dealers (authorised and unauthorised) in A, so that distribution cannot be kept within the authorised selective distribution network (Article 4(1)(b) and (d)).[107]

---

[105] Recital 7 and EB, 6.1.
[106] See p 90. and also EB, Q12.
[107] That this is the intention is confirmed in Recital 13.

In fact virtually all manufacturers have opted for selective distribution at retail level.[108] This is because it is the only means available under the Regulation to maintain control over who is reselling their vehicles. Qualitative selective systems have the advantage that there is no concern over market definition and the market share thresholds, since the Regulation exempts them regardless of market share, but in fact many manufacturers have chosen to use quantitative, or mixed, systems.

In the case of authorised repairer networks, manufacturers in fact have little choice of distribution method under the Regulation. The Commission's view of market definition, discussed above, results in high market shares for virtually all manufacturers' repair networks, so that qualitative selective distribution is generally the only available option.

Prohibited 'Hard-Core' Restrictions

Article 4(1) lists 12 types of restriction which prevent application of the block exemption. It begins: 'The exemption shall not apply to vertical agreements which, *directly or indirectly, in isolation or in combination with other factors under the control of the parties,* have as their object . . .' (emphasis added). Therefore, if any such restrictions are present, either in the terms of the contract or in the way in which it is applied, the Regulation does not apply and the agreement does not benefit from automatic exemption.

New Vehicles, Repair and Maintenance Services and Spare Parts

The first five apply to the sale of new vehicles as well as of repair and maintenance services and spare parts. They essentially mirror the hard-core restrictions listed in the vertical restraints block exemption, covering resale price-fixing, territorial and customer limitations and restrictions on cross-supply in selective distribution. The main impact of the differences is that exclusive and selective distribution cannot be combined for the same territory at the same level of trade, and use of a combination for different territories is rendered unattractive (see above). Otherwise, the comments about these black-listed clauses made in Chapter 3 apply here too.

Examples of blacklisted indirect restrictions of sales include making dealer remuneration or bonuses, or purchase price, dependent on the destination of vehicles or the place of residence of the end-user, supply quotas based on sales territories smaller than the EU, and discriminatory product supply (Recital 16). Similarly, authorised repairers within a supplier's network must be required to honour warranties, perform free servicing and carry out recall work for any vehicle of the relevant make sold anywhere in the EU (Recital 17).

---

[108] An exception is Suzuki, which is said to be using exclusive distribution.

Note that the blacklist refers to restrictions imposed by a supplier, but does not place limitations on the independent conduct of dealers. A dealer may independently offer more favourable guarantee or servicing terms to his customers: for example, a dealer might decide to try to attract custom by offering two free services to anyone purchasing a car from him during a specific promotional period, even though the manufacturer only required him to offer one free service. In such a case, the Regulation allows the more favourable terms to be fulfilled only in respect of customers purchasing from that individual distributor.

New Vehicles

The next two hard-core restrictions apply specifically to the sale of new vehicles. One relates to restriction of a dealer's ability to sell any vehicle 'which corresponds to a model within its contract range'. This is the so-called 'availability clause', intended in particular to allow customers in the United Kingdom and Ireland, where prices still tend to be higher than in other Member States, to purchase right-hand drive vehicles abroad. The prohibition includes 'discriminatory or objectively unjustified supply conditions, in particular those regarding delivery times and prices'.[109] The other ensures that dealers are not required themselves to provide repair and maintenance services: they must be free to contract these out to the manufacturer's authorised repairers.

Repair and Maintenance Services and Spare Parts

The remaining five 'blacklisted' clauses are specific to agreements for the sale of repair and maintenance services and of spare parts. They relate to authorised repairers' rights not also to sell vehicles, to the right of selective distributors of spare parts to sell these to independent repairers, to restrictions on resale imposed on manufacturers of spare parts, to restrictions on dealers or repairers as to the use of spare parts obtained elsewhere than from the vehicle manufacturer, and to the rights of independent component and spare parts suppliers to place their trade mark or logo on them.

Access to Technical Information

Independent operators, including manufacturers of repair equipment, distributors of spare parts, publishers of technical information, automobile clubs and roadside assistance operators, must be able to obtain access to any technical information, diagnostic and other equipment, tools, including relevant software, and any training they need to carry out their activities. Moreover, such access must be granted in a 'non-discriminatory, prompt and proportionate way' (Article 4(2)). This means in particular that there can be no discrimination between unauthorised and authorised operators.

---

[109] Recital 20 and see also EB, 5.1.1.

If certain items are protected by intellectual property rights or constitute 'knowhow' (defined in Article 1(1)(j)) then access may be withheld except to the extent that this would be an abuse within the meaning of Article 82 of the EC Treaty.[110]

Competing Goods and Services

Article 5(1) makes unenforceable a number of restrictions concerning a dealer or repairer's ability to deal in goods or services which compete with, or are similar to, those of his supplier. These include simple non-compete clauses, restrictions on providing after-sales services for vehicles from competing suppliers, and any other direct or indirect obligation causing members of a distribution system not to sell competing vehicles or spare parts of particular competing suppliers, or not to provide services in respect of other suppliers' vehicles. Also mentioned is any clause barring a dealer or repairer from working on the motor vehicle market after termination of the agreement.

The meaning of 'non-compete obligation' is specific to this Regulation: it includes not only an outright prohibition in dealing in competing products and services, but also any requirement that a buyer purchase more than 30 per cent of the value of his annual purchases[111] of that type of product or service from the supplier or someone designated by the supplier. This is meant to ensure that a dealer should always be in a position to be a dealer for at least three different manufacturers. If a 30 per cent (or lower) requirement is to be exempted, it must allow those purchases to be made not only directly from the manufacturer, but also from other network dealers or importers or suppliers.

It is also specified that an obligation that a dealer sell competing vehicles in separate areas of the showroom does not amount to a non-compete obligation. Nor does provision for brand-specific staff, provided the supplier pays the additional costs involved.[112]

All such restrictions are prohibited, in the sense that they are not exempted and are therefore unenforceable. However, they will not affect the application of the Regulation to the rest of the agreement, provided that the national law applicable to the contract allows their severance.

Leasing

Similarly, any contract term hindering a dealer from selling leasing services will be unenforceable (Article 5(2)(a)), unless, in the context of selective distribution, the

---

[110] See p 34 on Art 82 EC. See also EB, 5.5.1 on access to technical information.
[111] Art 1(1)(b). The equivalent figure in the vertical restraints block exemption Regulation is 80 per cent. See also EB, 4.5.1.
[112] *Ibid.* See also EB, Q14 and Q15 and 5.3.2.

leasing contracts used provide for a transfer of ownership or an option to purchase the vehicle prior to the expiry of the contract.[113]

Location of Premises

Where a supplier operates through selective distribution, providers of repair and maintenance services and sellers of spare parts are free to work from whatever location they choose, including additional outlets, and any contractual provision to the contrary will be unenforceable (Article 5(3)).

On the other hand, as far as the sale of new vehicles is concerned, until 1 October 2005 manufacturers may continue to control the location from which its selective distributors operate, and refuse to allow them to open a secondary outlet. As of this date, any restriction on such a dealer in passenger cars and light commercial vehicles 'which limits its ability to establish additional sales or delivery outlets at other locations within the common market where selective distribution is applied' will be unenforceable (Article 5(2)(b)).[114] However, even then, the supplier may continue to dictate the location of the primary establishment, and it will always be legitimate for a supplier to insist that the qualitative criteria for the area where the outlet is situated are satisfied by any additional outlet opened by a dealer or repairer.

This last rule was the part of the Regulation most bitterly opposed by car producers and those who supported them, which is why it proved necessary to postpone its implementation until 2005. The Commission and consumer groups hope that, when it enters into force, it will considerably increase competition between dealers and reduce barriers to cross-border trade. The car industry for its part has predicted that the final result will be that a small number of powerful dealer networks will predominate, forcing many small dealers out of the market, and leading to lower levels of choice and service for consumers.

Dealer Protection

Regulation 1400/2002 makes exemption conditional on the inclusion of a number of contractual provisions intended to strengthen dealers' and repairers' positions with respect to their supplier.

Any agreement between a supplier of new vehicles and a dealer or authorised repairer must apply for a term of at least five years and provide for a minimum of six months' notice by the supplier of its intention not to renew the agreement.[115]

---

[113] Recital 1(1)(w), and see EB, 5.3.1.2.

[114] Restrictions in respect of dealerships for other vehicles such as buses, coaches and lorries will remain valid even after 2005, except insofar as they limit the expansion of the dealer's business at the authorised location.

[115] The consequences of failure to do so are a matter of national law, according to DG Comp: EB, Q68. The same will be true of failure to fulfil other contractual terms on notice periods or the provision of reasons.

Alternatively, if the agreement is for an indefinite period, the notice period for 'regular' termination must be at least two years: this is reduced to one year if either the supplier is obliged by domestic law or by special agreement to pay 'appropriate' compensation on termination of the agreement, or if termination is necessary in order to reorganise the whole or a substantial part of the network (Article 3(5)).

These rules on notice periods only apply to the situation in which both parties have been fulfilling their obligations under the contract: they do not affect the possibility of more sudden termination for breach of contract where that is available under the applicable national law (EB, Q69). This does open up the possibility of abuse by manufacturers who may include clauses in the contract which allow them to terminate contracts with their dealers for very minor breaches, thereby making it relatively easy to find an excuse for terminating a contract when they choose. The Regulation therefore makes exemption of any agreement involving a dealer or repairer conditional on the agreement requiring written and fully reasoned notice of termination 'in order to prevent a supplier from ending a vertical agreement with a distributor or repairer because of practices which may not be restricted under this Regulation' (Article 3(4)).[116]

Dealers and authorised repairers must also be entitled to agree to transfer their rights and obligations to any other member of the network of their choice (Article 3(3)). Recital 10 specifies that this applies as between operators 'of the same type', meaning that a dealer who does not also provide after-sales service cannot insist on transfer of its contract to an authorised repairer who is not also a dealer.

The Regulation also requires that each of the parties to any agreement have the right to refer disputes over performance of contractual obligations to an independent expert or arbitrator. National court action is also always an option in such situations (Article 3(6)).

Sales Through Intermediaries

Dealers have the right to sell to intermediaries who buy on behalf of customers who have specifically authorised them to do so,[117] and this Regulation is more generous in respect of companies acting as intermediaries than were earlier Regulations.

Sales through intermediaries have caused particular problems in the past, because they have sometimes been suspected of being used as a means for unauthorised distributors to obtain supplies of vehicles which the manufacturer wants, legitimately, to distribute exclusively through his authorised selective distribution network. Though customer limitations are in principle blacklisted, Article 4(1)(b)(iii) allows, in the context of selective distribution, the restriction of supplies to unauthorised distributors.

---

[116] Examples of the kind of pro-competitive behaviour that suppliers might want to prevent are sales to foreign consumers, sale of competing brands and sub-contracting of after-sales services (Recital 9).
[117] Recital 14 and see also EB, 5.2.

Issues have arisen in the context of selective distribution systems for cars when customers have sought to obtain cars (usually in another country than their own in order to take advantage of lower prices) through an agent. In *Peugeot v Commission*[118] Peugeot argued (in the context of a previous block exemption) that a professional intermediary placing orders on a regular rather than an occasional basis was really acting as a reseller, and on this basis claimed to be entitled to order its distributors to refuse these intermediaries. The Commission argued, and its approach was ultimately upheld by the ECJ, that an agent does not cease to act as an agent simply because he does so on a regular basis: provided he is in possession of a specific order from a customer for each car, he is still acting as an agent.

DG Comp takes the view that a supplier can only require its dealers to ensure that an intermediary has a prior signed and dated authorisation from the consumer to purchase and/or collect a specified vehicle.[119]

The Regulation cannot be used to regulate the other activities of companies acting as intermediaries. Like any block exemption Regulation, its effect is only to define a category of relationships between a supplier and dealer which may benefit from exemption from the prohibition set out in Article 81. It does not set out an obligatory distribution system in this sector, and therefore cannot be invoked to restrict the freedom of action of third parties such as intermediaries or parallel importers. The ECJ confirmed this when it rejected the argument that the Regulation prohibited an independent (unauthorised) dealer from acting simultaneously as an intermediary, whom distributors, under the Regulation, may not be prohibited from supplying, and as an unauthorised distributor of parallel imports. It stated that an earlier block exemption could not be interpreted:

> as prohibiting a trader who is outside the official distribution network for a given make of motor vehicle and is not an authorised intermediary within the meaning of that Regulation from acquiring new vehicles of that make by way of parallel imports and independently carrying on the business of marketing such vehicles.[120]

Sale and use of spare parts

Suppliers of 'original spare parts' (those manufactured according to the vehicle manufacturer's specifications and production standards) and 'spare parts of matching quality' (those for which the parts manufacturer can certify that they match the quality of the components used in the original vehicle), as well as other relevant equipment, must remain free to supply authorised or independent operators or end-users, both within and outside the vehicle manufacturer's network

---

[118] Case C-322/93 [1994] ECR I-2727.

[119] EB, 5.2.

[120] Case C-309/94 *Nissan France* [1996] ECR I-677, [1996] 4 CMLR 778, para 20. See also Case C-128/95 *Fontaine v Aqueducs Automobiles* [1997] ECR I-967, [1997] 5 CMLR 39; Case C-226/94 *Grand Garage Albigeois* [1996] ECR I-651, [1996] 4 CMLR 778.

(Article 4(1)(j)).[121] The Commission considers this essential to foster competition from independent service providers.[122]

Even within a selective distribution system, there can be no prohibition on selling spare parts to independent repairers or making the necessary technical information available to them (such restrictions are blacklisted by Articles 4(1)(i) and 4(2)).

Dealers must be permitted to source original spare parts or parts of matching quality from third parties (except to the extent that the manufacturer takes advantage of the possibility of imposing a non-compete clause in respect of up to 30 per cent of the dealer's requirements, see p 139). The only exception to this is that vehicle manufacturers may require dealers to use original spare parts supplied by it for repairs carried out under warranty, free servicing and vehicle recall work (Article 4(1)(k)).

Sale Through Supermarkets and the Internet

One of the criticisms levelled at the functioning of the previous block exemption was that it did not provide for distribution via supermarkets. In fact, during the extensive public consultation that preceded the adoption of Regulation 1400/2002, little input was received from supermarkets, and nor did consumers appear enthused by this idea. The current Regulation therefore makes no specific mention of supermarkets, but a supermarket, like any other company, is entitled to become a car dealer if it satisfies the criteria applied by the vehicle supplier. It may also act as an intermediary for customers.

Pure Internet operators do not have any right under the Regulation to become part of a sales network (though they can and do act as intermediaries for consumers). However, Recital 15 confirms that the use of Internet, including Internet referral sites, may be combined with a traditional sales outlet, even where a dealer is restricted to making passive sales. The vehicle supplier may require that such sites meet given quality standards. E-mail may also be used, but it is treated as an active, rather than a passive, selling method.[123]

Withdrawal of Exemption

The following are mentioned in the Regulation as examples of circumstances which may lead to withdrawal of the benefit of the Regulation in a particular case,

---

[121] See also EB, QQ97–83.

[122] The Commission has proposed legislation on the intellectual property rights of manufacturers, intended to make it easier for independent producers to compete in producing visible vehicle spare parts such as doors, bumpers and windscreens, COM (2004) 582.

[123] See also EB, QQ44 and 45.

even in the event that all the formal requirements of the Regulation are met. There is an important difference between the conditions discussed above, breach of which leads either to the clause in question being unenforceable, or to the Regulation being completely inapplicable, and the situations discussed below. The latter do not affect the application of the Regulation until the Commission has taken a formal Decision to the effect that the benefit of exemption is withdrawn. Such a Decision must be accompanied by the usual procedural requirements such as the right of interested parties to be heard.

Examples given of situations that may lead to withdrawal are where:

(a) market access is significantly restricted by the cumulative effect of parallel networks of similar agreements (most likely when selective distribution is common); or

(b) competition is restricted on a market where one supplier is not exposed to effective competition from other suppliers; or

(c) prices or conditions of supply differ substantially between geographic markets; or

(d) discriminatory prices or sales conditions, or unjustifiably high supplements, such as those charged for right-hand drive vehicle, are applied within a geographic market.[124]

Previous versions of the Regulation also provided for withdrawal, but the Commission has never made use of this power, although arguably there have frequently been grounds for it.

Article 6(2) provides that where appropriate such withdrawal may be effected by a national competition authority in respect of the whole or part of its territory.

Non-Application of the Regulation

'Non-application' may be declared by the Commission in a Regulation, where parallel networks of similar vertical restraints cover more than 50 per cent of a relevant market. It is similar to withdrawal in that it requires a formal act by the Commission, but it applies not to the whole of one specific set of distribution arrangements, but to particular restrictions contained in any agreement relating to that specified market. Such a Regulation cannot enter into force earlier than one year[125] following its adoption (Article 7), so that companies concerned have time to adapt to the new situation.

---

[124] Art 6 and Recital 32.
[125] The equivalent period in the vertical restraints block exemption is six months.

Impact of Regulation 1400/2002

Regulation 1400/2002 represents the Commission's latest attempt to introduce more inter-brand and intra-brand competition, facilitate cross-border sales, and generally free up trading conditions for dealers, repairers and producers and sellers of spare parts, with the ultimate aim of benefiting consumers. It is still too early to say whether the new regime will achieve all this, particularly as, although the Regulation entered into force on 1 October 2002 and the transitional period ended one year later, the prohibition on 'location clauses' will only enter into force on 1 October 2005.

This block exemption is now commonly used by virtually all motor vehicle distribution networks in the Community.[126] Almost all manufacturers have opted to distribute their vehicles through selective distribution, in order to be able to prevent their vehicles being retailed outside the authorised network. Some have aligned their prices to some extent; others have bought dealerships in order to be free to operate outside the constraints of the Regulation. Meanwhile, some convergence in prices across the Community has already been recorded.[127]

Problems already brought to the Commission's attention include delays in supply of cars ordered abroad, the use of apparently qualitative criteria to impose quantitative limitations, and delays in the grant of access to technical information, and the Commission has pledged to clamp down on these and other illegal practices.[128] It has also been alleged that some manufacturers have made it difficult for dealers to sell more than one brand and to stock competing spare parts, and in other cases there have been complaints that bonuses are reduced or refused in respect of cars sold outside the dealer's territory.

The Commission is required to monitor the operation of the Regulation and to draw up an evaluation report by 31 May 2008. This is intended to allow proper debate on the future of this sector well before the Regulation expires on 31 May 2010.[129]

---

[126] In May 2000, Competition Commissioner Monti referred to the previous Regulation 1475/95 as being used by manufacturers 'as a *de facto* binding framework for their distribution system', Speech 00/177, 11 May 2000. The same is true of its successor.

[127] Commission Press Release IP/04/1003, 29 July 2004.

[128] Mario Monti,Car Retailing at a Crossroads', 03/59 6 February 2003; Commission Press Release IP/04/1235, 15 October 2004.

[129] This date was set so as to coincide with the expiry of the vertical restraints block exemption Regulation 2790/1999, allowing the Commission to review its vertical restraints policy as a whole.

5

Franchising

KEY POINTS

- The legality of a franchise contract depends on the particular clauses included in it and on the market environment in which it operates.
- Any clause (unless the contract involves only very small areas or parties) by which the franchisor seeks (i) to fix retail prices or (ii) to ban exports to or imports from other EU Member States will be void and fines may be imposed by the European Commission or national competition authorities. But it is permissible for the franchisor to indicate recommended prices to franchisees.
- Any clause necessary to prevent the franchisor's knowhow benefiting his competitors or potential competitors outside the franchise network is valid.
- Any clause necessary for the maintenance of the identity and reputation of the franchise network is valid.
- Other obligations such as provision for territorial or customer exclusivity may render the contract void and open to the risk of fines or damages claims unless an exemption applies.
- An exemption applies if either (i) the contract fulfils all the conditions laid down in the vertical restraints block exemption Regulation, including a relevant market share of no more than 30 per cent, or (ii) it satisfies the four criteria set out in Article 81(3) EC Treaty.

EC Regulation

Commission Regulation (EC) 2790/1999 on the application of Article 81(3) of the
Treaty to categories of vertical agreements and concerted practices (Appendix 4)

EC Notice

Commission Guidelines on vertical restraints (Appendix 7)

ECJ Judgment

Case 161/84 *Pronuptia de Paris GmbH v Pronuptia de Paris Irmgard Schillgalis*
[1986] ECR 353, [1986] 1 CMLR 414

Commission Decisions

Charles Jourdan OJ 1989 L35/31, [1989] 4 CMLR 591
Computerland OJ 1987 L222/12 [1989] 4 CMLR 259
Pronuptia OJ 1987 L13/39, [1989] 4 CMLR 355
Servicemaster OJ 1988 L332/38, [1989] 4 CMLR 581
Yves Rocher OJ 1987 L8/49, [1988] 4 CMLR 592

It is essential that this chapter be read in conjunction with Chapter 3 for a full under-standing of the treatment of franchising agreements.

5.1 INTRODUCTION

'Franchising' is not a technical legal term and has a number of different meanings commercially. In EU competition law, this expression has generally been used to refer to a means of distributing goods or services through a network of legally and financially independent retailers, but in such a way as to create an outward appearance of uniformity throughout the network. The uniformity may be manifested, for example, in the appearance of the retail outlet or the goods, or in the use of particular trademarks or sales methods, and usually through a combination of such factors. Although many people associate franchising with fast food and fashion outlets, in fact it is a marketing formula which has been applied to the retailing of a very wide variety of goods and services. Since its first appearance in Europe in the 1970s it has been used to sell everything from pet dogs to hot dogs, and has become extremely popular as a distribution method.

For the manufacturer or supplier ('the franchisor') it is often seen as an advantageous compromise between, on the one hand, the expense and risk of setting up many more sales outlets itself and, on the other hand, the loss of control involved in distributing its goods through completely independent distributors: it allows a network to be expanded very quickly without the substantial capital outlay that would otherwise be required. The retailer ('the franchisee') in its turn may be glad of the opportunity to take advantage of an already well-known name and image and the practical and technical help that the franchisor will give it in setting up and running its new business.

There is only one judgment from the European Court of Justice (ECJ) in the area of franchising. Nor are there many exemption Decisions of the Commission. The adoption in 1988 of a block exemption Regulation on franchise contracts (which has since expired) quickly obviated the need for notification in many cases and ensured that very many franchise networks either were already valid or could be easily adjusted so as to bring them within the terms of the Regulation. It probably also discouraged the use of clauses that might take a franchising system outside the terms of that Regulation. There were no individual exemption Decisions on franchising agreements between 1989, when the original franchising block exemption entered into force, and 2004, when the Commission lost the power to grant individual exemptions.

The franchising-specific Regulation was replaced in 2000 by a general block exemption Regulation on vertical restraints which covers a wide range of distribution arrangements, including many franchise agreements. Some of these would previously have been covered by the old Regulation, and some not. On the other hand, some arrangements which had previously been within the scope of the 1988 Regulation, and in particular any where the relevant market share exceeded 30 per cent, no longer enjoy the benefit of a block exemption.

There is a degree of inconsistency between the ECJ and the Commission on some issues concerning franchising, as described below. It is true that the Court's judgment is of higher legal authority than any Commission Decision, and that a Commission Decision, may be challenged in the European Courts. However, in practice it is the Commission (or national competition authority) rather than the Court which will make any infringement decision; appeal to the Court will often not be an attractive option, for the usual reasons that lead parties to avoid litigation. Where the two institutions conflict, therefore, it will generally be prudent to follow the Commission's interpretation of the rules if possible.

What is a Franchise?

The word 'franchise' is sometimes (particularly in the United States) used in a wide sense more or less synonymous with distributorship.[1] It is not a technical legal expression, but in Europe the word generally connotes something along the lines of the set-up described below.

It is a distribution method adopted by a manufacturer or supplier who has developed a well-known name and appearance for its product (usually including intellectual property rights). It may manufacture the goods itself, or it may simply select goods produced by a third party. In the latter case the franchise may be described as a 'business format' franchise, since it is essentially a business format that is being exploited. In either case, it will probably also have established an 'image' for its existing sales outlets, connected with the physical appearance of the outlets and the business methods applied. These names, trademarks and 'image' will be known by the public and attract customers who recognise these familiar signs. Service franchises, such as photocopy shops and hairdressing salons, are also a type of business format franchise.

In order to capitalise on this public recognition and on the package of intellectual property and business knowhow it has created, it may license another, completely independent, person to use the package. In return for the licence, it will demand royalties and maybe a lump sum.

The distributor will in return have the benefit of opening its outlet on the basis of a name and appearance readily recognisable to consumers, and the franchisor's business knowhow. Thus, a franchise is often attractive to an individual with little or no experience or reputation in the business, but with a small amount of capital (perhaps a redundancy payment) available with which to buy the franchise.

---

[1] This chapter will discuss distribution (goods and services) franchising only. However, note that the term 'franchise' is used in other legal and commercial contexts in an extended sense to cover also production franchising (where franchisees are licensed to produce a particular product), or to refer to distribution arrangements which EU competition law treats as agency.

European Commission and ECJ's Perception of Franchising

It was stated above that no general legal definition of franchising or a franchise agreement exists. It is not a technical legal expression in EU law: no consequences necessarily flow from classifying any given network as a franchise. The way in which the network is organised and, in particular, the terms of the agreements made between the franchisor and the franchisee, differ widely from one franchise network to another. The ECJ has made it clear that in principle the validity of any specific franchising contract will be decided on the basis of the individual terms included in that contract.[2]

In a number of respects the ECJ and the European Commission have tended to be more generous in their appraisal of a clause in the context of a franchise network than of the same clause in a different kind of distribution system. It is therefore necessary to know what they consider the essential characteristics of franchising, since this may indicate whether or not a particular contractual restriction is likely to be treated leniently.

The favourable treatment referred to above is due mainly to the conception that the Commission and the Court have of franchising as a system essentially advantageous to small business. It has been viewed as a means of allowing people who would not otherwise be able to set up in business independently to do so: they are enabled to do this through the use of the franchisor's established reputation and the continuing help and advice which it makes available to the franchisee. Considerable importance is attached to this concept in the application of the competition rules to franchising. The provision by the franchisor to the franchisee of substantial knowhow is therefore a crucial element in the definition of franchising.[3] In its *Charles Jourdan*[4] Decision the Commission listed the areas of knowhow and assistance provided as covering purchasing, decorating, stock, management, sale and advertising.[5]

It is therefore likely that, provided that a distribution agreement includes a sufficient degree of provision of knowhow and continuing help to the dealer, it will be treated with relative leniency. The Commission expressly confirms this in its Guidelines on vertical restraints (Appendix 7):

> In addition to the licence of [intellectual property rights], the franchisor usually provides the franchisee during the life of the agreement with commercial or technical assistance, such as procurement services, training, advice on real estate, financial planning etc. The licence and the assistance are integral components of the business method being

---

[2] Case 161/84 *Pronuptia de Paris GmbH v Pronuptia de Paris Irmgard Schillgalis ('Pronuptia ECJ')* [1986] ECR 353, [1986] CMLR 414.

[3] *Ibid*, para 15: 'the system gives traders who do not have the necessary experience access to methods which they could not have learned without considerable effort'. Also see *Yves Rocher* OJ 1987 L8/49, [1988] 4 CMLR 592, para 39: 'It . . . gives non-specialists access to the use of . . . proven trading methods'.

[4] OJ 1989 L35/31, [1989] 4 CMLR 591, para 11.

[5] The Commission said that the knowhow was primarily commercial although it also covered management aspects. It was 'substantial' and gave the trader 'a clear advantage over competitors'.

franchised (para 42) . . . The more the vertical restraint is linked to the transfer of know-how, the more reason there may be to expect efficiencies to arise and the more a vertical restraint may be necessary to protect the know-how transferred or the investment costs incurred'. (para 119)

On the other hand, an agreement designated as a franchise by the parties is not likely to be treated as such if it does not embody this kind of relationship. Furthermore, the favourable attitude taken to franchising is always subject to the economic context in which the network operates. In *Yves Rocher*, for example, the Commission prefaced its remarks with the explanation 'having regard to existing structures of production and supply in the relevant market' (para 39).

5.2 APPLICATION OF ARTICLE 81(1) TO FRANCHISING

Do Franchising Contracts Infringe Article 81(1)?

As far as the requirement in Article 81(1) that the agreement affect trade between Member States is concerned, the ECJ stated expressly in *Pronuptia* that even if the franchise agreement is concluded between two parties in the same Member State it will affect trade between Member States if the franchisor is prevented from establishing itself in another Member State.

Beyond this, the answer to this question depends on the precise terms of the contract in question. As in any other context, a term granting absolute territorial exclusivity to a franchisee or imposing on it fixed or minimum resale prices will certainly fall foul of Article 81(1). Very many franchising contracts contain clauses providing for some degree of territorial exclusivity, since in the absence of such exclusivity a potential franchisee would often not be prepared to make the necessary investment in setting up and equipping its outlet. Usually, the franchisee will be allotted a territory in which it is assured that no one else will be granted the right to exploit the franchise. For its part, the franchisee is required only to operate the franchise from the location specified in its contract so that it cannot either change location or open a second outlet.

The Court in *Pronuptia* said that a territorial exclusivity clause, when combined with a clause prohibiting the opening of a second outlet, might infringe Article 81(1). Because the Court referred to this combination of clauses, it might be argued that bare exclusive territoriality, without a 'second outlet' clause, may not infringe Article 81(1). But given the radical departure from previous rulings that this would imply, it is not an interpretation that could safely be relied on. In any case, such 'exclusivity' would give only limited protection to a franchisee, since it would protect it only from competition from the franchisor itself, and not from other franchisees.

The five Commission Decisions in the 1980s followed this approach, namely that the infringement of Article 81(1) arose out of a combination of the territorial exclusivity with the prohibition on opening a second outlet from which to exploit the franchise. In *Computerland* this was the case even though each territory was less than one kilometre in radius, and franchisees were free to sell to customers outside their territory (para 7). However, in all five cases exemption was granted under Article 81(3).

In *Pronuptia* the Court also qualified its statement that exclusive territoriality would infringe Article 81(1) with the words 'if it concerns a business symbol which is already well-known' (para 24). This requirement has not received much attention in individual Commission exemption Decisions. This may not now make that much difference in practice: most franchise agreements containing such a clause will be automatically exempted by the block exemption on vertical restraints provided the relevant market share does not exceed 30 per cent, and where it exceeds 30 per cent the franchise would presumably be 'well-known'.

Also, given that the Court[6] and the Commission[7] have accepted that sometimes territorial exclusivity is essential to the establishment of the network, it might be thought that a territorial exclusivity clause, like the many terms discussed below, could fall outside Article 81(1) on this basis. In fact, neither the Court nor the Commission has yet gone that far. The Commission has consistently held that territorial exclusivity clauses require exemption under Article 81(3), even in the context of very competitive markets.[8]

In the context of franchising, provision for exclusive territories will in practice be favourably treated. In particular, a degree of territorial exclusivity is automatically exempted by the vertical restraints block exemption (see p 89) where the franchisor's market share does not exceed 30 per cent.

Although there is no difference in practice between an agreement falling outside Article 81(1) and an exempted agreement, the point just discussed is not without significance. It could, of course, be crucial in a situation in which for some reason (such as too high a market share) the agreement falls outside the block exemption, and its validity is called into question.

In the Commission's published decisions on franchising, all taken over 15 years ago, it paid little more than lip service to the notion that the surrounding economic circumstances and structure of the market should be taken into account in deciding whether a clause in a franchising agreement has restrictive effect.[9] In every such Decision there has been a competitive market and yet clauses giving a degree of territorial exclusivity have apparently brought the agreement virtually automatically within the scope of Article 81(1).

For example, in *Computerland*, a franchise network for the sale of microcomputers was granted exemption, rather than negative clearance, chiefly because of the clauses granting territorial exclusivity. This was despite the fact that the

---

[6] *Pronuptia ECJ*, above n 2, at para 24.

[7] *Computerland* OJ 1987 L222/12, [1989] 4 CMLR 259, para 33: 'The restrictions . . . are indispensable to ensure the existence of the network: potential franchisees would not be willing to make the investments necessary . . . if they were not assured that no other Computerland outlets will be established in their near vicinity'; see also *Yves Rocher*, above n 3, at para 63 and *Charles Jourdan*, above n 4, at para 39.

[8] *Yves Rocher*, above n 3, at para 54. The ECJ took this approach in *Pronuptia ECJ*, above n 2, at para 24.

[9] *Pronuptia ECJ*, above n 2, at para 27(1).

Commission found that there were around 10,000 authorised microcomputer dealers (excluding non-specialised retailers who also dealt in these goods) in Western Europe, of which fewer than 1 per cent were Computerland outlets. Furthermore, these outlets accounted for about 3 per cent of total Community sales, and in no Member State was the Computerland market share much above 4 per cent.[10]

Similarly, in *Yves Rocher*, the Commission found the cosmetics market in question to be extremely competitive. Yves Rocher held 7.5 per cent of the French market, 6 per cent of the Belgian market and less than 5 per cent of the market in the other Member States in which it marketed cosmetics. Furthermore, the franchisor, though not permitted to open an outlet within the franchisee's protected territory, could sell into the area by other means including mail order.[11] Even so, negative clearance was refused and exemption granted instead.

However, the block exemption on vertical restraints and the accompanying Guidelines, which entered into force in 2000, are rooted in an approach giving much more prominence to economic analysis, so similar cases arising now might well be treated differently. So far, however, there have been no formal Commission Decisions or ECJ judgments applying these new rules to franchise agreements.

The *Pronuptia* Judgment

The only case in which the ECJ has discussed franchising is the 1986 case of *Pronuptia* in which a German court put a number of questions to the ECJ regarding the validity of a franchising contract in the light of EU competition law.

This case came before the ECJ in the form of a request for a preliminary ruling. The plaintiff before the German court was a German subsidiary of the French franchisor 'Pronuptia de Paris', a distributor of wedding dresses and other wedding clothes and accessories. This subsidiary, Pronuptia de Paris Gmbh, had granted a franchise to a German franchisee, Mrs Schillgalis, for three separate territories in the Federal Republic, and a dispute had subsequently arisen over unpaid royalties claimed by the franchisor. The franchisee was relying on the argument that the franchise contract was void and unenforceable for infringement of Article 81(1).[12]

The contract granted the franchisee the right to use the franchisor's trademark in defined territories and to receive continuing assistance and advice from the franchisor on many aspects of running the business. The franchisor also agreed not to open a shop itself or by any other means supply third parties, nor to grant a trademark licence to anyone else, in the territories.

The franchisee for her part promised:

• to pay a 10 per cent royalty on all sales made;

---

[10] *Computerland*, above n 7, at para 3.

[11] *Yves Rocher*, above n 3, at para 19.

[12] Such 'Eurodefences' are often regarded as the last resort of a scoundrel, put forward only in the absence of any more morally appealing defence. There may often be some justification for such a view, but awareness of this kind of risk should provide an incentive to parties and their legal advisers to ensure that they do not leave themselves open to such a challenge.

- to use the trade mark only in connection with the retail shops in the specified territories;
- to conduct business only from those specified retail shops, which were to conform to the specifications of the franchisor;
- to purchase at least 80 per cent of stocks from the franchisor and the balance only from approved suppliers;
- to co-operate over advertising, including that giving recommended prices;
- not to compete with the franchisor anywhere in West Germany for one year after the end of the contract; and
- not to assign the franchise without the franchisor's consent.

The Court first stressed that franchising contracts must be judged individually, according to the particular restrictive clauses present in them. It commented favourably on franchising as a legitimate way for the franchisor to exploit an asset which it had developed. It then went on to hold that most of the clauses in this, fairly typical, franchise contract, were inherent in the nature of franchising itself, which could not function without them. Therefore, in accordance with the principle of 'ancillary restraints' (see p 28), these clauses did not infringe Article 81(1):

> In a system of distribution franchises of that kind an undertaking which has established itself as a distributor on a given market and thus developed certain business methods grants independent traders, for a fee, the right to establish themselves in other markets using its business name and the business methods which have made it successful. Rather than a method of distribution, it is a way for an undertaking to derive financial benefit from its expertise without investing its own capital. Moreover, the system gives traders who do not have the necessary experience access to methods which they could not have learned without considerable effort and allows them to benefit from the reputation of the franchisor's business name . . . Such a system, which allows the franchisor to profit from his success, does not itself interfere with competition. In order for the system to work, two conditions must be met. (para 15)

The two conditions were then set out. They are that the franchisor's knowhow be protected, and that the identity and reputation of the network be maintained. Each one provides the justification for a set of clauses that ensure that these conditions are met. Because they are considered essential to the success of a franchising system (which would presumably not be able to exist or succeed without them), they are characterised as not infringing Article 81(1). The two groups of clauses associated with these two conditions were subsequently developed by the Commission through a number of Decisions and through the 1988 block exemption Regulation on franchise agreements, which has since expired.

Below will be considered three groups of clauses generally considered to fall outside the prohibition contained in Article 81(1), either because they are necessary to fulfil one of the two conditions stated to be essential to the working of a franchise network, or because they are irrelevant to competition. Next exemption, either through the application of the block exemption Regulation on vertical restraints or by operation of Article 81(3), will be discussed.

5.3 CLAUSES NOT VIOLATING ARTICLE 81(1)

Clauses Necessary for the Protection of the Franchisor's Know-how

> First, the franchisor must be able to communicate his know-how to the franchisees and
> provide them with the necessary assistance in order to enable them to apply its methods,
> without running the risk that that know-how and assistance might benefit competitors,
> even indirectly.[13]

The type of obligations undertaken by the franchisee and deemed necessary to fulfil this condition are as follows.:

(a) *Obligations of confidentiality.* A franchisor may oblige its franchisees to observe confidentiality towards confidential information and knowhow that it transmits to them. This may include the duty not to make disclosure to employees unless necessary, and to pass on to employees to whom it is disclosed the same obligations of confidentiality.[14]

(b) *Prohibition during the term of the contract on opening the same or a similar kind of shop in an area where it might compete with another franchisee, or generally on carrying on any kind of competing activities.*[15] In *Yves Rocher* it was noted that such a clause did not prohibit a franchisee from carrying on a non-competing business, provided the franchisee's personal commitment to the Yves Rocher franchise was ensured (para 49). In *Computerland,* the Commission required an absolute non-competition clause to be amended so as to allow franchisees to acquire financial interests in the capital of competing undertakings, although not to the extent that such participation would enable them to control those undertakings (para 22(ii)).

A clause stipulating that a franchisee's acquisition of a financial interest in a competing undertaking was permissible provided it did not involve the franchisee personally in taking part in competing activities was held not to infringe Article 81(1) in *Yves Rocher* (para 47).

Even a clause limiting acquisition of a financial interest in the capital of a public company to a maximum of 5 per cent was held to be essential to the protection of the franchisor's knowhow and therefore outside the terms of Article 81(1) in *Servicemaster.*[16] However, two points should be noted about this Decision:

- It concerns a service franchise, and the Commission stated in its Decision that the protection of know-how was even more important in the context of a service franchise than in a distribution franchise, even though the two kinds of franchise could basically be treated in the same way (para 6);
- The Commission stated that such a clause could infringe Article 81(1), but that it did not in the circumstances, because the franchisees tended to be small

---

[13] *Pronuptia ECJ*, above n 2, at para 16.
[14] *Computerland*, above n 7, at paras 5 and 22(i).
[15] *Pronuptia ECJ*, above n 7, at para 16.
[16] OJ 1988 L332/38, [1989] 4 CMLR 581.

undertakings for whom such a 5 per cent limit would not normally constitute a hindrance to business activity (para 10).

(c) *Prohibition for a reasonable time after the termination of the contract on opening the same or similar kind of shop in an area where it might compete with another franchisee*[17] Non-competition clauses lasting more than one year after the franchise contract comes to an end are unlikely to be considered necessary, or to be exempted under Article 81(3).

In *Computerland* a term of three years, with the restrictions on competing becoming gradually less strict over the three years, was considered excessive by the Commission, and was not exempted. It was replaced with a one-year ban on competing within a radius of 10 kilometres of the original outlet. However, it was implied that even this reduced term was allowed partly on the basis that the very limited territorial restrictions imposed on franchisees by the contract meant that they had the opportunity during the term of the agreement to build up goodwill and clientele beyond the area immediately surrounding their franchise outlet (para 22).

A one-year post-term ban on the franchisee's opening a retail cosmetics store within its previous exclusive territory was held to fall outside Article 81(1) in *Yves Rocher*. It was pointed out that an ex-franchisee thus had the possibility of immediately setting up a shop anywhere else, including within the exclusive territory of another franchisee (para 48).

However, in *Charles Jourdan* it was stated that a post-term competition ban would not have been justified 'as the know-how provided includes a large element of general commercial techniques, and second, as this type of franchise is primarily granted to retailers who are already experienced in selling shoes' (para 27). This suggests that the Commission did not consider the knowhow element of this franchise to be substantial enough to warrant generous treatment.

But it was also stated in *Computerland* and *Yves Rocher* that although such a post-term competition ban may not infringe Community law, this does not prevent franchisees from benefiting from any rights to which they may be entitled under applicable national law.[18] National law may be stricter in the kind of post-term competition bans it accepts. In such a case, the stricter, national law will apply, provided that it is seen as pursuing an objective other than the maintenance of competition, such as franchisee protection (see p 43).

(d) *Prohibitions on selling to a third party the sales outlet used to exploit the franchise,*[19] *without the prior consent of the franchisor.* In *Charles Jourdan* a clause requiring the franchisor to be given first offer when a franchise outlet was to be sold (with the franchisor being given a month to make up its mind) was cleared (para 27).

(e) *Prohibition on assigning in whole or in part the benefit of the franchise contract without the consent of the franchisor.*[20]

---

[17] *Pronuptia ECJ*, above n 2, at para 16.
[18] *Computerland*, above n 7, at para 22(iii); *Yves Rocher*, above n 3, at para 48.
[19] *Pronuptia ECJ*, above n 2, at para 16.
[20] *Yves Rocher*, above n 3, at para 47.

Clauses Necessary to Maintain the Identity and Reputation of the Network

Secondly, the franchisor must be able to take the measures necessary for maintaining the identity and reputation of the network bearing his business name or symbol.[21]

The types of clauses considered necessary to fulfil this condition are as follows.

(a) Freedom to select franchisees and their managers. Franchisees may be chosen freely by the franchisor.[22] Nor is it necessary that such choice be made on the basis of objective and qualitative criteria, as has been required in the context of selective distribution systems. In *Charles Jourdan* a clause requiring advance approval by the franchisor of any manager employed to run a shop was accepted (paras 8 and 27).

In the *Yves Rocher* system, franchisees were chosen on the basis of personality, aptitude for the cosmetics business and performance in a training programme. The absence of any stated selection criteria was justified on the basis that it was the franchisor which trained the franchisees itself:

> Yves Rocher itself trains franchisees during an induction course with a view to setting up new franchise shops. It is logically entitled to choose its partners freely and turn down applicants who do not, in its view, have the personal qualities and business qualifications which it requires for the application of the formula it has developed. (para 41)

Similarly, in *Computerland*, a like system was said to be a 'justified means of ensuring that every Computerland outlet is managed in keeping with the business standards developed by the franchisor'. (para 23)

It is hard to see any logical distinction between this situation and the selection of dealers being made by a manufacturer setting up a selective distribution network. It might seem that the considerations cited in *Yves Rocher* and *Computerland* could be satisfied by the application of objective, qualitative criteria of the sort a selective distributor is required to apply if it is to escape Article 81(1). The existence of a training programme seems to be important in the Commission's eyes: it demonstrates the extent to which the franchisor is genuinely assisting his franchisees to run their franchises successfully. As stated earlier (see p 150), the degree to which the franchisor acts as a trainer and advisor to its franchisee is likely to be crucial to obtaining this kind of generous treatment of any given distribution network.

However, if this right to appoint franchisees were to be seen to be used in order to achieve price-fixing, by rejecting applicants likely to charge low prices, then it would as in other contexts be an infringement of Article 81(1).

(b) An obligation on the franchisee to apply the business and trading methods developed by the franchisor and to use the knowhow and industrial property rights provided by the franchisor.[23]

(c) An obligation on the franchisee to use the franchisor's knowhow, trademarks, trade names or other industrial property rights in a manner in keeping with their subject matter.[24]

[21] *Pronuptia ECJ*, above n 2, at para 17.
[22] *Ibid*, para 20.
[23] *Pronuptia ECJ*, above n 2, at para 18; *Yves Rocher*, above n 3, at para 43.
[24] *Yves Rocher*, above n 3, at para 40.

(d) An obligation on the franchisee not to use the franchisor's trademarks, trade names or other identifying marks anywhere other than at the agreed franchise location and to stop using them after termination of the contract.[25] In *Computerland*, the Commission insisted that to this obligation be added the qualification that ex-franchisees be expressly entitled:

> to continue using innovations or improvements they have developed which are demonstrably separable from the Computerland system.

(e) An obligation on the franchisee to devote its best efforts to the operation of the franchise outlet and not to carry on activities incompatible with being a franchisee.[26]

(f) A term prohibiting the franchisee from carrying on any activity at the outlet apart from exploiting the franchise.[27] In the case of a 'franchise corner' situated in part of a larger shop, such a restriction must presumably be limited in application to the 'corner' only.

(g) An obligation on the franchisee to use for the sales outlet the layout and decor, both interior and exterior, required by the franchisor.[28]

(h) An obligation on the franchisee to exploit the franchise from a particular location and not to change that location without the franchisor's consent. A clause simply confining the franchisee to exploiting the franchise from a specified location was stated by the Court to be compatible with Article 81(1).[29]

In *Yves Rocher*, the Court stated:

> The franchisor must also be able to participate in determining the location of the Beauty Centre with the franchisee, in their mutual interest: a bad choice might cause the franchisee to fail in business and indirectly damage the network's reputation. In practice, Yves Rocher carries out a preliminary market and location survey, and proposes to the franchisee the most promising area. The exact location of the shop is determined by the franchisee with the franchisor's consent. In any event, the shop's location is agreed upon in the general interest of all members of the chain. (para 42)

In *Computerland*, the Commission pointed out that in fact the location of sites was decided on the basis of objective criteria, and said:

> The main objective in setting up these criteria for site approval is to ensure that the success of the outlet is not hampered because of a possibly unfavourable location.[30]

Again, the only feature distinguishing this scenario from that of selective distribution (where such a clause infringes Article 81(1)) is that the franchisor is seen as helping the franchisee to make a decision that is in the franchisees' collective best interest: in a selective distribution system the supplier is assumed to be making the decision in its own best interests. This too shows the importance of characterising the franchisor

---

[25] *Computerland*, above n 7, at para 23(ii).
[26] *Yves Rocher*, above n 3, at para 49; *Computerland*, above n 7, at para 23(iv).
[27] *Computerland*, above n 7, at para 23(iv).
[28] *Pronuptia ECJ*, above n 2, at para 19; *Computerland*, above n 7, at para 23(v); *Yves Rocher*, above n 3, at para 43.
[29] *Pronuptia ECJ*, above n 2, at para 19.
[30] *Computerland*, above n 7, at para 23(v).

as the franchisee's helper if the agreement is to be treated by a court or competition authority as a franchise contract, with the leniency which that implies.

This kind of obligation only escapes Article 81(1) to the extent that relocation may only be refused for reasons connected with maintaining the reputation of the franchise network.[31]

However, it should be noted that a restriction on opening a second shop when combined with an exclusive territory will generally violate Article 81(1) (see p 152). This is explained by the ECJ on the basis that this combination of restrictions divides up the market.

(i) Obligation on the franchisee not to sell competing goods. A franchisor may, on certain conditions, prohibit a franchisee from selling any goods apart from those supplied or selected by the franchisor.[32]

The Commission stresses in its Guidelines on vertical restraints that a non-compete obligation which is necessary to maintain the common identity and reputation of the franchised network does not infringe Article 81(1) and so does not require exemption. This is the case whatever the duration of the non-compete clause, provided it does not extend beyond the term of the franchise agreement itself (para 200). Also, a non-compete restriction for the whole duration of the contract may fall outside Article 81(1) on the basis that a supplier has made a substantial and irreversible transfer of knowhow and that the duration of the restriction corresponds to the time necessary to justify such an investment (paras 116/5, 119/9 and 157).

The ECJ suggests that such a clause will escape Article 81(1) to the extent either that it is impractical to lay down quality specifications or that it is too expensive to ensure that such specifications are observed. In any case, such a clause cannot be used to prevent franchisees from obtaining those products from other franchisees in the network. The example of goods for which it is impractical to lay down quality specifications given in *Pronuptia ECJ* was that of fashion items, and it may be that this is true of many of the types of goods likely to be sold through a franchise network.

In the context of a service franchise the Commission has accepted a clause in which it was provided that franchisees might obtain supplies of cleaning materials of equivalent quality from third parties rather than from the franchisor. Qualities such as safety, non-toxicity, biodegradability and effectiveness were mentioned.[33] Although these cannot all be measured in entirely objective terms, a clause which makes an attempt to introduce as much transparency and objectivity as possible into the situation is more likely to be looked on with favour by a court or authority.

Nor is it at all clear what 'too expensive' covers: it will always be more expensive to ensure observance of quality specifications than of a blanket prohibition on the sale of any goods not supplied by the franchisor or with his approval. In a Decision involving a computer distribution franchise, the Commission stated:

---

[31] *Yves Rocher*, above n 3, at para 42.
[32] *Pronuptia ECJ*, above n 2, at para 21. This type of clause is treated more strictly outside the context of franchising.
[33] *Servicemaster*, above n 16, at para 17.

given the wide product range (there are over 3,000 items on [the franchisor's] product list) and the very rapid technological evolution in this product market, it would be impracticable to ensure the necessary quality control by establishing objective quality specifications which franchisees could apply themselves. In fact, laying down objective standards could be detrimental to the franchisees' freedom to sell the most up-to-date products, unless the specifications were constantly updated, an overly burdensome if not impossible task.[34]

In that system, a requirement of prior approval by the franchisor was accepted by the Commission. However, the Commission probably took into account the fact that the clause allowed for flexibility in certain circumstances, and the fact that franchisees in practice had considerable influence in proposing products for approval.

In *Yves Rocher* it seems to have been accepted without question that the franchisee could be restricted to selling only goods bearing the Yves Rocher trademark (para 45). It was said that the sale of other goods would allow other producers to benefit unfairly from Yves Rocher's reputation and knowhow and would detract from the identity of the network. 'Accessories', shop furnishings and products for beauty treatments could be obtained from other sources, though sale of these was subject to the prior approval of the franchisor.

There is, of course, a distinction between the kind of system like that in *Yves Rocher*, in which the franchise is based on the sale of products through particular trademarks and symbols which are placed on the goods themselves, and a system such as that in *Computerland* in which the goods themselves bear no particular signs or marks connecting them with the franchise network. Stricter controls could be expected to be acceptable in the former type of franchise.[35]

It must be possible, though, for the franchisee to obtain goods not connected with the 'essential object' of the franchise from whomsoever it pleases. The franchisor may still control the quality of these ancillary goods and interfere if they would damage the reputation of the network.[36]

(j) An obligation on the franchisee to obtain the franchisor's approval for the nature of any advertising to be done by the franchisee.[37]   This is only acceptable provided it is not used to influence prices advertised or charged by franchisees. In *Yves Rocher* it was explained by the Commission that such a clause enabled Yves Rocher to ensure that 'the theme of natural beauty from plants, on which the network's image [was] based' was adhered to in all advertising material (para 44). It is also acceptable for an advertising and promotional levy to be collected from franchisees.[38]

---

[34] *Computerland*, above n 7, at para 23(vi).
[35] This difference is also evident in the Commission's Decision in *Pronuptia* OJ 1987 L13/39, [1988] 4 CMLR 259 ('*Pronuptia EC* '), para 12(b). The Commission insisted that Pronuptia insert a clause making it clear that franchisees had the right 'to purchase goods not connected with the essential object of the franchise business from suppliers of their choice, subject to *ex post* qualitative vetting by the franchisor'.
[36] *Pronuptia EC*, above n 35, at para 25.
[37] *Pronuptia ECJ*, above n 2, at para 22; *Computerland*, above n 7, at para 23(vi).
[38] *Pronuptia EC*, above n 357, at para 26.

(k)   An obligation on the franchisee to sell only to end-users or to other franchisees.
In certain types of franchise this type of restriction will not infringe Article 81(1).
This is the case when the goods, when passed on to other resellers, bear some mark
or name connecting them with the franchise.

Thus, in *Computerland* the Court said that:

> In certain franchise systems, for example where franchisees sell products bearing the
> franchisor's name and/or trade mark, the prohibition on resale by franchisees to resellers
> who do not belong to that franchise network is based on the legitimate concern that the
> name, trade mark or business format could be damaged if the contract products were
> sold by resellers who do not have access to the franchisor's know-how and are not bound
> by the obligations aimed at preserving the reputation and unity of the network and its
> identifying marks. (para 26)

An example of such a system appears in *Yves Rocher*. In other circumstances, such
as those of the Computerland system itself, such a restriction will violate Article
81(1) and require exemption if it is to be valid.

It should be noted that Article 81(1) will be infringed if franchisees are not
allowed to obtain supplies from other franchisees. In *Charles Jourdan* the
Commission requested that an express clause permitting such cross-supply be
inserted in the agreement used before exemption was granted (para 16).

(l)   An obligation on the franchisee to submit to inspections of the outlet,[39] *including checking of stock levels, accounts and balance sheets.*[40] In *Yves Rocher*, the
express warning was made that:

> the Commission reserves its right to intervene in case these controls would [sic] be used by
> the franchisor to affect the freedom of the franchisees to fix their selling prices. (para 50)

(m)   An obligation on the franchisee to supply regular reports and accounts.[41]

*(n)   Recognition by the franchisee of the validity and ownership of the franchisor's
trademarks and trade names.* In *Computerland*, such a term was not objected to:
however, it was pointed out that there was no restriction on the franchisee's right
to contest the franchisor's industrial property rights (para 5). Such a non-contest
clause would probably infringe Article 81(1).

(o)   To hold stocks and to make orders in advance according to a fixed timetable.[42]

(p)   Recommended prices. The practice of recommending retail prices in the
context of a franchising agreement does not infringe Article 81(1).[43] As in other
contexts, any attempt to enforce adherence to minimum prices that goes beyond
simply informing dealers of those prices will be a serious breach of Article 81(1).[44]
In *Pronuptia EC* the Commission required Pronuptia to remove a clause requiring
the franchisee not to harm the brand image of the franchisor by its pricing level

---

[39]   *Computerland*, above n 7, at para 23(viii).
[40]   *Yves Rocher*, above n 3, at para 50.
[41]   *Ibid*; *Charles Jourdan*, above n 4, at para 27.
[42]   *Ibid*, para 27.
[43]   *Pronuptia ECJ*, above n 2, at para 25.
[44]   *Yves Rocher*, above n 3, at para 51; see also *Charles Jourdan*, above n 4, at paras 18 and 29.

(para 12(c)). Such a clause was presumably considered to set some kind of implied minimum price rule.

Clauses Irrelevant to Competition and Therefore Excluded from the Scope of Article 81(1)

The following clauses may be included in franchising contracts without affecting their legality, since the Commission does not consider them relevant to competition. However, this does not prevent the application of any relevant rules of national law. The following enumeration is by no means exhaustive, and only reflects some clauses which have been the subject of comment by the Commission.

(a) *An obligation on the franchisee to pay royalties or advertising contributions.*[45] In *Computerland*, however, the Commission required it to be specified that royalties were not payable on sales between franchisees (para 24).

(b) *An obligation on the franchisee to form a corporation.*[46]

(c) *An obligation on the franchisee to indicate its independent status.* This was characterised in *Computerland* as a measure of consumer protection. It was said to be desirable in that it puts the public on notice that the franchise outlet is the sole responsibility of the franchisee.[47]

(d) *An obligation on the franchisee to indicate his name and address on the products he sells.*[48]

(e) *Provisions relating to the term and conditions of renewal of the franchise contract.*[49]

(f) *An obligation on a franchisee to take out insurance covering its civil liability and employers' liability during the term of the contract.* Such a clause was included in the *Yves Rocher* agreement (para 17) and was not objected to, probably because it was not relevant to competition.

5.4 EXEMPTION UNDER ARTICLE 81(3)

If a franchising agreement includes clauses which infringe Article 81(1) then it will be void and unenforceable under Article 81(2), and incur the risk of fines and damages claims, unless it is exempted. Exemption, where applicable, applies automatically. It may occur either through the operation of the vertical restraints block exemption Regulation, or by satisfying the four substantive criteria set out in Article 81(3).

---

[45] *Computerland*, above n 7, at para 24(i); *Pronuptia EC*, para 26.
[46] *Computerland*, above n 7, at para 24(ii).
[47] See also *Yves Rocher*, above n 37, at para 17.
[48] *Computerland*, above n 7, at para 24(iv).
[49] *Ibid*, para 24(v).

Vertical Restraints Block Exemption Regulation 2790/1999

This block exemption Regulation[50] grants automatic validity to any contract falling within its terms.[51] There is no need for any involvement of the Commission or any national authority if the contract satisfies the Regulation: the contract is fully valid and can be enforced in a national court without the need for any formality.

Regulation 2790/1999 provides a very broad definition of 'vertical restraints' to which it applies (see Chapter 3). Many franchising arrangements, including those based on agency and those incorporating selective distribution, fall within its scope, and thereby benefit from exemption.

In particular, the Regulation expressly includes arrangements involving the assignment or use of intellectual property rights,[52] provided that they are ancillary to the main agreement: the intellectual property provisions must not 'constitute the primary object' of the agreement (Article 2(3)). The idea is to cover agreements where the distribution of goods or services can be performed more effectively because such rights are assigned to or transferred for use by the buyer.[53] There is, therefore, no obstacle to its application where the franchisor, for example, licenses the use of his knowhow or of its trademark to assist a buyer in distributing goods or services. An agreement, on the other hand, which is essentially a trademark licence or a technology transfer agreement, will not be covered.[54]

The Commission Guidelines on vertical restraints (paras 30–44) show that distribution franchising, both for goods and services, is clearly considered by the Commission to be covered, but that industrial or production franchising is not. They set out in some detail the distinction between the kind of arrangements covered by the block exemption and those which fall outside its scope.

Paragraphs 30–36 state that the block exemption applies in the presence of intellectual property right (IPR) provisions where five conditions are fulfilled:

(1) The IPR provisions must be part of a vertical agreement, ie an agreement with conditions under which the parties may purchase, sell or resell certain goods or services: examples of agreements not covered include provision of a drink recipe combined with a licence to produce the drink, provision of a mould or master copy together with a licence to produce and distribute copies, a pure licence of a trademark or sign for merchandising purposes, sponsorship

---

[50] Commission Reg (EC) 2790/1999 on the application of Article 81(3) of the Treaty to categories of vertical agreements and concerted practices (Appendix 4).

[51] It applies to all product sectors except for motor vehicles and their spare parts, repair and maintenance which are covered by a sector specific Regulation (see Chapter 4 and Appendix 5).

[52] Defined as including 'industrial property rights, copyright and neighbouring rights'.

[53] Commission Guidelines on vertical restraints, para 31.

[54] Commission Regulation (EC) 772/2004 on the application of Article 81(3) of the Treaty to categories of technology transfer agreements ('technology transfer block exemption') OJ 2004 L123/11, may apply to such agreements.

contracts permitting a party to advertise itself as an official sponsor of an event, and copyright licensing such as broadcasting contracts.

(2) The IPRs must be assigned to or for use by the buyer: the Guidelines go on to say that there can therefore be no sub-contracting involving the transfer of knowhow to a sub-contractor, suggesting that in this context the notion of IPRs extends to know-how. However, the provision of specifications to the supplier, describing the goods or services to be supplied, is covered.

(3) The IPR provisions must not constitute the primary object of the agreement.

(4) The IPR provisions must be directly related to the use, sale or resale of goods or services by the buyer or its customers. In the case of franchising where marketing forms the object of the exploitation of the IPRs, the goods or services must be distributed by the master franchisee or the franchisees: the Guidelines state that the supply of a concentrated drink extract to be diluted before sale as a drink is permitted.

(5) The IPR provisions, in relation to the contract goods or services, must not contain restrictions of competition having the same object or effect as vertical restraints which are not exempted under the block exemption Regulation.

Whether specific franchising arrangements benefit from the Regulation will also depend on whether all the criteria laid down in the Regulation are satisfied: these are essentially that the franchisor's market share does not exceed 30 per cent and that no 'blacklisted' clauses (such as fixing of minimum resale prices or provision for absolute territorial or customer group protection) are present. Those generally applicable criteria are considered in detail in Chapter 3, and the focus in this chapter is on considerations specific to franchising.

Market Share

In order to establish whether the 30 per cent threshold is exceeded, the same general rules on market definition apply to franchising as they do to other forms of distribution. On a literal interpretation of the Regulation, the relevant market should be that on which the franchisor is active, and so would comprise all franchise systems regarded as substitutable by potential franchisees. However, the Guidelines comment specifically on the relevant market in respect of franchising, and provide a different interpretation. First, they deal with distribution franchises, where the franchisor directly or indirectly provides goods which the franchisee resells:

> Where the vertical agreement, in addition to the supply of contract goods, also contains IPR provisions—such as a provision concerning the use of the supplier's trade mark—which help the buyer to market the contract goods, the supplier's market share on the market where it sells the contract goods is decisive. (para 95)

Then they discuss the case of business format franchising:

> Where a franchisor does not supply goods to be resold but provides a bundle of services combined with IPR provisions which together form the business method being

franchised, the franchisor needs to take account of its market share as a provider of a business method. For that purpose, the franchisor needs to calculate its market share on the market where the business method is exploited, which is the market where the franchisees exploit the business method to provide goods or services to end users. The franchisor must base its market share on the value of the goods or services supplied by its franchisees on this market. On such a market the competitors may be other franchised business methods but also suppliers of substitutable goods or services not applying franchising.

They go on to show how this might apply to a fast food franchise, and how the market share calculation would differ according to whether or not the franchisor itself supplied certain ingredients (para 95).

The reason for this approach is that the Commission considers that competition problems are more likely to arise on the market for the franchised goods or services than on the market for the franchise itself. While the Regulation takes precedence over the Guidelines, in practice the Commission's views as expressed in the Guidelines will influence not only its own enforcement policy, but often that of national authorities and courts. Parties may well be advised to take the Commission's view into account, rather than relying on the possibility, probably inconvenient, of challenging this interpretation through the ECJ.

Non-compete Clauses

As described above, non-compete obligations contained in a franchise agreement will generally not infringe Article 81(1), provided they are necessary to maintain the common identity and reputation of the franchised network.

If they do infringe then, provided they fit within the definition of:

> any direct or indirect obligation causing the [franchisee] not to manufacture, purchase, sell or resell goods or services which compete with the contract goods or services, or any direct or indirect obligation on the [franchisee] to purchase from the [franchisor] or from another undertaking designated by the [franchisor] more than 80 per cent of the [franchisee's] total purchases of the contract goods or services and their substitutes . . . (Article 1(b))

then they can be imposed for up to five years, unless the franchisee operates from the franchisor's premises, in which case they may last as long as the occupancy of those premises.[55]

The Commission states that the following obligations are 'generally considered to be necessary to protect the franchisor's intellectual property rights' and so are exempted by the Regulation insofar as they infringe Article 81(1):

(a) an obligation on the franchisee not to engage, directly or indirectly, in any similar business;

---

[55] Art 5(a).

(b) an obligation on the franchisee not to acquire financial interests in the capital of a competing undertaking,[56] which would give the franchisee the power to influence the economic conduct of such undertaking. (Guidelines, para 44)

Post-termination Non-compete Clauses

These are treated more leniently in the context of agreements in which substantial knowhow is transferred, as opposed to other types of distribution arrangement, where the Regulation does not exempt them at all.

Franchise agreements are therefore effectively the only type of agreements in respect of which the Regulation exempts post-term non-compete clauses.[57] They are exempted by the Regulation provided that they:

- relate to goods or services which compete with the contract goods or services; and
- are limited to the premises and land from which the buyer has operated during the contract period; and
- are indispensable to protect knowhow transferred by the supplier to the buyer; and
- last no more than one year after termination of the agreement (Article 5(b)).

The Regulation makes it clear that it does not place any limit on the duration of a restriction on the use and disclosure of knowhow which has not entered the public domain.

Use of Knowhow

Knowhow is defined as:

a package of non-patented practical information, resulting from experience and testing by the supplier, which is secret, substantial and identified: . . .

'secret' means that the know-how, as a body or in the precise configuration and assembly of its components, is not generally known or easily accessible; . . .

'substantial' means that the know-how includes information which is indispensable to the buyer for the use, sale or resale of the contract goods or services; . . .

'identified' means that the know-how must be described in a sufficiently comprehensive manner so as to make it possible to verify that it fulfils the criteria of secrecy and substantiality. (Article 1(f))

---

[56] In this context, 'competing undertaking' should mean a business which competes on the market for the goods or services which are the subject of the franchise, regardless of whether or not this business is part of a franchise network. The context is different from that of Art 2(4) where it should be the upstream market that is relevant, though it is not clear whether this would be the market for franchises operating in any retail sector, or only franchises in the same business sector.

[57] Defined as 'any direct or indirect obligation causing the buyer, after termination of the agreement, not to manufacture, purchase, sell or resell goods or services'.

The information must be non-patented: if the knowhow being passed on is of sufficiently scientific or technical nature to be patented, then the arrangement does not fall within the Regulation definition of a franchise agreement. It may, however, benefit from the block exemption Regulation applicable to technology transfer.[58] It is, however, unlikely in the context of a distribution franchise that the knowhow would be patentable.

The amount of testing and experience that there must be behind the knowhow is not specified, but presumably it means that the franchisor must itself have for some period of time worked in the business in which its franchisees will be engaged in. Note that the experience and testing must be that of the franchisor and that it is not sufficient that it has been done by someone independently of the franchisor. However, presumably independent agents, management consultants and market researchers working for the franchisor would also be able to fulfil this requirement on behalf of the franchisor.

The requirement that the knowhow be indispensable to the franchisee is a personal one. In fact, potential franchisees generally tend to be new to the business in question, and to be looking for a 'safe' way to start up in business on their own. In such cases it should not be hard to satisfy this requirement. However, were the franchisee already experienced itself, it might be harder to establish that the knowhow (rather than only the intellectual property rights and 'image') was in fact indispensable to it.

The knowhow must be described: apart from a written document, a video-tape or a course in the form of programmed instruction that the franchisee could use on its personal computer should be acceptable.

The following obligations relating to knowhow are 'generally considered to be necessary to protect the franchisor's intellectual property rights' and so are exempted by the Regulation insofar as they infringe Article 81(1):

(c) an obligation on the franchisee not to disclose to third parties the know-how provided by the franchisor as long as this know-how has not fallen in the public domain;
(d) an obligation on the franchisee to communicate to the franchisor any experience gained in exploiting the franchise and to grant it, and other franchisees, a non-exclusive licence for the know-how resulting from that experience . . .
(f) an obligation on the franchisee not to use know-how licensed by the franchisor for purposes other than the exploitation of the franchise. (Guidelines, para 44)

It is not clear what would be the consequence of the know-how's ceasing to qualify as know-how (for example, because no longer 'secret') during the term of an agreement exempted under the Regulation at the time of its conclusion.

Intellectual Property Rights

Agreements involving intellectual property rights are covered by the Regulation providing that the rights are ancillary to the main agreement (see p 164).

---

[58] See above n 54.

Intellectual property rights are defined as including 'industrial property rights, copyright and neighbouring rights' (Article 1(e)).

The following obligation is 'generally considered to be necessary to protect the franchisor's intellectual property rights' and so is exempted insofar as it infringes Article 81(1):

(e) an obligation on the franchisee to inform the franchisor of infringements of licensed industrial or intellectual property rights, to take legal action against infringers or to assist the franchisor in any legal action against infringers.

Master Franchise Agreements

Master franchise agreements whereby the franchisor grants a master franchisee the right to exploit a franchise for the purposes of concluding franchise agreements with third party franchisees can benefit from the block exemption (Guidelines, para 43).

This type of delegation will be particularly important in the context of networks spread over a number of different countries throughout the European Union, since the markets and therefore the commercial or technical assistance required may vary considerably between one Member State and another, because of cultural, social and linguistic differences. This allows a franchisor to employ a resident and indigenous agent who is best equipped to take into account local conditions in doing the job in a particular country.

Selective Distribution

Franchises for the distribution of goods often operate through selective distribution, the franchisor appointing only franchisees which satisfy specified qualitative criteria, and prohibiting franchisees from reselling to distributors who are not authorised franchisees. As described above, in the absence of territorial exclusivity this will normally not infringe Article 81(1). However, if Article 81(1) is infringed such arrangements can benefit from the block exemption, provided that the specific rules laid down there for selective distribution are followed (see p 119). (Service franchises are unlikely to incorporate selective distribution because there are no goods to be resold and there is therefore no need to take measures to prevent unauthorised outlets obtaining the goods.)

Under the Regulation, if selective distribution is used, franchisees may not be prohibited from buying from and selling to other authorised franchisees, and they must remain free to make both active and passive sales to any consumer in any territory. An exclusive territory is permitted in the sense that the franchisor may agree only to supply a specified franchisee within that territory, but no other form of protection of that territory is allowed. A clause prohibiting the franchisee from selling the brands of particular competing suppliers does not preclude the block exemption from applying to the agreement, but that clause itself will not benefit from exemption and so will be void.

The Regulation allows a franchisor using selective distribution to benefit from exemption while imposing a location clause on franchisees, prohibiting them from operating out of an unauthorised outlet.[59] The Commission interprets this as meaning that they may be prevented both from running their business from different premises and from opening a new outlet in a different location. It also interprets it as meaning that if the dealer's outlet is a mobile one, such as an ice-cream van, an area may be defined outside which the mobile outlet cannot be operated. In the case of many types of goods and services—including ice-cream—this will in practice provide effective territorial protection. However, in the absence of territorial exclusivity, such clauses probably fall outside Article 81(1) altogether in the context of franchise agreements. So this aspect of the Regulation would only represent an advantage where a location clause is combined with the limited degree of territorial exclusivity covered by the Regulation in the context of selective distribution.

Franchisors wishing to benefit from the block exemption Regulation may therefore need to consider carefully whether to structure their franchises either so as to avoid falling within the definition of selective distribution, or else so as to benefit from the specific rules applicable to selective distribution. Usually it will be more advantageous under the Regulation to avoid characterisation of a franchise as selective distribution.

Assignment of Franchise

According to the Commission's Guidelines, the following obligation is 'generally considered to be necessary to protect the franchisor's intellectual property rights' and so is exempted by the Regulation insofar as it infringes Article 81(1):

> (g) an obligation on the franchisee not without the franchisor's consent to assign the rights and obligations under the franchise agreement. (para 44)

Withdrawal or Disapplication of the Benefit of the Regulation 2790/1999 (Articles 6 and 7)

The Commission, or national competition authorities, may in a specific case withdraw the benefit of the Regulation where they find that it has effects incompatible with the conditions laid down in Article 81(3) (see p 94) and:

> . . . in particular where access to the relevant market or competition therein is significantly restricted by the cumulative effect of parallel networks of similar vertical restraints implemented by competing suppliers or buyers.

However, such withdrawal would have to be made following the full Commission Decision (or relevant national) procedures, and could not be retrospective.

---

[59] Art 4(d); Guidelines, para 54.

There is also provision for the benefit of the Regulation to be disapplied in respect of certain types of agreement where parallel networks of similar vertical restraints cover more than 50 per cent of a relevant market (see p 96).

Individual Exemption under Article 81(3)

If a franchising contract includes no clauses infringing Article 81(1), then it should be legal and fully enforceable from the point of view of EU competition law. But if it includes additional restrictions, and does not fit within the terms of a block exemption Regulation, then it can only be exempted from the application of Article 81(1) if it satisfies the four substantive criteria listed in Article 81(3). It is this second type of exemption which is now discussed.[60]

There is no presumption that a franchising agreement falling outside the scope of the block exemption infringes Article 81(1) (Guidelines, para 62). The block exemption and the Commission's Guidelines provide a good source of guidance in assessing what other kinds of agreements may benefit from exemption. They indicate, for example, the degree of territorial protection for franchisees likely to be acceptable. Further, the examples given in the Guidelines of circumstances in which the benefit of exemption may be withdrawn are an indication of the circumstances in which even non-blacklisted clauses are unlikely to benefit from exemption.

As usual, restrictive terms will be judged in the context of the structural and dynamic characteristics of the market in question. In the context of franchising, the Guidelines emphasise that the more important the transfer of knowhow is to the agreement, the more likely the agreement is to be exempted (paras 119/8 and 200). This is in keeping with the ECJ and Commission's tradition of lenient treatment for franchising agreements, as long as they provide for substantial effective assistance to franchisees.

A prohibition on the franchisee's opening further outlets, when combined with territorial exclusivity, will generally need to be exempted (see p 152). In *Computerland*, franchisees were on certain conditions allowed to open 'satellite' stores in other locations. However, even this freedom was not sufficient to take the agreement outside Article 81(1) (para 25).

Also, an obligation to sell only to end-users or other franchisees may violate Article 81(1) in the context of certain types of franchise but merit exemption. One such franchise was the system in *Computerland*, and the Commission explained that:

> the Computerland name and trade mark cover the business format as such, but not the microcomputer products being sold, which bear the name and trade mark of each individual manufacturer. The prohibition on Computerland franchisees to sell the products to otherwise qualified resellers is thus restrictive. (para 26)

---

[60] An example of a franchise arrangement likely to qualify for exemption under Art 81(3) is given by the Commission in its Guidelines on vertical restraints (para 201).

The point seems to be that in these circumstances there is nothing on the goods to connect them with the franchisor, and so its reputation cannot be affected by those goods being sold in outlets or in a way not controlled or approved by it.

However, such a clause may well be exempted, on the grounds that the franchise is based on the premise that franchisees receive training and support which enables them better to serve their customers. This investment would be wasted, or at least diluted, if franchisees were allowed to 'divert their efforts to activities other than retail sales and servicing' according to the Commission in *Computerland*.

Franchising agreements falling outside the block exemption because they only or primarily concern the licensing of intellectual property rights will normally benefit from exemption under Article 81(3) (Guidelines, para 43).

On the other hand, there are certain clauses that will almost certainly not benefit from exemption. Essentially, any clause tending to divide the Community into separate markets in which different prices and conditions can be applied is unlikely to be exempted. Similarly, any attempt indirectly or directly to fix the prices distributors may charge will disqualify an agreement from exemption.

6

Agency

KEY POINTS

- Guidelines set out the Commission's current approach to the application of Article 81 to agency agreements, but these conflict in some respects with the case law of the European Court of Justice, so the law is not clear.
- In order to be characterised as a 'genuine agent' in Community law, a trader must bear no substantial financial risk in respect of the transactions in which it acts as agent. It may also be relevant that the trader be integrated into the business of its principal, rather than trading independently.
- Article 81 will not apply to any agreement between a genuine agent and its principal insofar as it relates to contracts negotiated or concluded by the agent for itsprincipal.
- Other provisions of an agency agreement, such as provision for exclusivity on either side, may infringe Article 81, particularly where the agent may not act for other principals.
- Article 81 applies to agreements of 'non-genuine' agency in the same way as to other distribution agreements.
- If the agreement infringes Article 81 then it will be void and unenforceable unless it benefits from exemption, either by falling within the scope of a block exemption Regulation or by satisfying the four substantive criteria set out in Article 81(3).
- Most agency agreements are also required to conform to the requirements of a Directive intended to protect commercial agents.
- Even if the relevant Member State has not implemented the Directive, or has implemented it incorrectly, it may still be possible to rely on the Directive in that Member State's national courts.

EC Regulation

Commission Regulation (EC) 2790/1999 on the application of Article 81(3) of the
Treaty to categories of vertical agreements and concerted practices (Appendix 4)

EC Directive

Council Directive 86/653/EEC on self-employed commercial agents
(Appendix 3)

EC Notice

Commission Guidelines on vertical restraints (Appendix 7)

ECJ Judgments

Cases 40 etc/73 *Suiker Unie and Others v Commission* [1975] ECR 1663, [1976] 1
CMLR 295
Case 311/85 *Vlaamse Reisbureaus v Sociale Dienst* [1987] ECR 3801, [1989] 4
CMLR 213
Case C-266/93 *Bundeskartellamt v Volkswagen* [1995] ECR I-3477, [1996] 4 CMLR
505

It is essential that this chapter be read in conjunction with Chapter 3 for a full under-standing of the treatment of agency agreements.

6.1 INTRODUCTION

Agency is a relationship between principal and agent in which the agent identifies customers or suppliers and trades with them on behalf of its principal, in return for which the agent earns commission. The principal generally exercises a high degree of control over the agent, in particular over the terms on which it does business.

The Commission defines agency agreements as:

the situation in which a legal or physical person (the agent) is vested with the power to negotiate and/or conclude contracts on behalf of another person (the principal), either in the agent's own name or in the name of the principal, for the:

• purchase of goods or services by the principal, or
• sale of goods or services supplied by the principal.[1]

The prohibition contained in Article 81(1) and discussed in earlier chapters is not applicable to certain types of provisions in agreements between a 'genuine agent' and its principal.[2] There can therefore be considerable advantages to be gained from appointing distribution agents as opposed to independent distributors. It is not clear whether this is because a genuine agent is considered not an independent economic entity, but rather part of the principal's economic entity or business,[3] or whether it is because of an absence of anti-competitive effect.[4]

Whatever the theoretical justification for the favourable treatment of genuine agency agreements, its practical effect is as follows. If the agent is a genuine agent in the eyes of Community law, then any restriction can be imposed on it in relation to the terms on which it conducts the principal's business, just as EU competition law does not apply to restrictions imposed by an employer on the way an employee does business for the employer.[5] The only exception to this freedom applies to dominant undertakings, whose business methods may constitute abuse whether they are distributing through independent dealers or genuine agents (see p 181).

However, it will be seen that in practice the scope for taking advantage of this immunity for agents from the competition rules is fairly limited.

The Commission's Guidelines on vertical restraints (paras 12–20) include a section on the application of Article 81 to agency agreements. However, there are points on which the Guidelines do not mesh with the case law of the European

---

[1] Commission Guidelines on vertical restraints (Appendix 7), para 12.
[2] *Ibid*, para 13.
[3] Cases 40 etc/73 *Suiker Unie v Commission* [1975] ECR 1963, [1976] 1 CMLR 295, para 480.
[4] Opinion of Advocate-General Tesauro, Case C-266/93 *Bundeskartellamt v Volkswagen* [1995] ECR I-3477, [1996] 4 CMLR 505.
[5] However, national rules on restraint of trade may apply to this relationship.

Court of Justice (ECJ), which is a higher authority than the Commission's Guidelines, and so the law in this area remains unclear. In cases where the lack of certainty in the rules causes difficulty, officials in the Commission's Competition Directorate General (DG Comp) should be willing to discuss specific situations and provide an indication of whether the Commission would be likely to consider a particular relationship to be one of genuine agency or not.

These special rules for agency do mean that it is of the utmost importance to know whom the Commission and the ECJ consider to be a genuine agent. In the first part of this chapter, therefore, the definition of this type of agency, which falls, at least for some purposes, outside the scope of Article 81, will be discussed.

Competition rules are not the only source of specific EU-level rules on agency. The Council has also adopted a Directive aimed at the protection of commercial agents.[6] In the second part of this chapter the requirements of this Directive will be considered. Directives require national legislative measures to be taken in each Member State: it will therefore be necessary to consult sources on the relevant national law to find out how implementation has been carried out in the Member State concerned. Further, a Directive may sometimes have legal effects in a Member State even if it has not been implemented, or has been incorrectly implemented, in national law, and this possibility will also be discussed.

6.2 AGENCY AND ARTICLE 81

The following description of the law as it now stands is based on cases decided by the ECJ and on the Commission's most recent statement of its policy, contained in its Guidelines on vertical restraints. As stated above, taken together these are not entirely coherent, and leave the law in an unsatisfactory state of uncertainty.

It is important to notice that here, as always when applying Community competition rules, the legal form of the so-called 'agency' agreement and the designation that the parties give to the relationship are irrelevant. What matters is the real nature of the arrangement in economic terms: this was confirmed explicitly in *Pittsburgh*.[7] Further, national law rules and categories are not conclusive of a party's status as an agent for the purposes of Community law.[8]

'Genuine Agency Agreements'

In its Guidelines the Commission defines 'genuine agency agreements'. These are the agreements that enjoy a special status: in the case of such agency agreements, obligations imposed on the agent *as to contracts negotiated or concluded on behalf of its principal* will not fall within the scope of Article 81. The Guidelines refer to

---

[6] Council Directive 86/653 on self-employed commercial agents, OJ 1986 L382/17 (Appendix 3).
[7] *Re Pittsburgh Corning Europe* OJ 1972 L272/35, [1973] CMLR D2, para 7.
[8] *Ibid*, para 9.

the following types of obligations as being outside the scope of Article 81 in the case of genuine agency:

- limitations on the territory in which the agent may sell these goods or services;
- limitations on the customers to whom the agent may sell these goods or services;
- the prices and conditions at which the agent must sell or purchase these goods or services. (para 18)

Several factors may be relevant in deciding whether a particular agency agreement falls within this category, and they are examined in turn below.

Financial Risk

According to the Commission's Guidelines, the key factor is that of the financial risk assumed by the agent. The essential distinction drawn there and also used by the ECJ[9] is that between an agent and an independent trader who assumes financial risk itself in negotiating and entering into transactions. It was stressed, for example, in *Volkswagen*[10] that the key distinction was between someone bearing 'any of the risks resulting from the contracts negotiated on behalf of the principal' and someone not bearing any such risk.

For the Commission the 'determining factor' in deciding whether Article 81(1) is applicable is 'the financial or commercial risk borne by the agent in relation to the activities for which he has been appointed as agent by the principal' (Guidelines, para 13).

Of course, anyone engaged in trade incurs certain financial risks, and it is not always easy to know precisely what type and degree of risk is meant. The Commission in its Guidelines has developed a definition of relevant 'financial or commercial risk' of two types.[11] If the agent bears no or insignificant risks of either of these types it is a 'genuine agent' and obligations under the agency agreement as to the contracts it negotiates or concludes fall outside the scope of Article 81:

- those 'directly related to the contracts concluded and/or negotiated by the agent on behalf of the principal, such as financing of stocks'; and
- those 'related to market-specific investments. These are investments specifically required for the type of activity for which the agent has been appointed by the principal, i.e. which are required to enable the agent to conclude and/or negotiate this type of contract. Such investments are usually sunk, if upon leaving that particular field of activity the investment cannot be used for other activities or sold other than at a loss. (para 14)

The Guidelines include a long, but not exhaustive, list of the types of risks or costs which are relevant (para 16).

---

[9] *Suiker Unie*, above n 3, at para 482.
[10] Case C-266/93 [1995] ECR I-3477, [1996] 4 CMLR 505.
[11] The two categories of risk are not mentioned in the ECJ's case law or in any previous Commission Decisions.

Other sorts of risk such as those 'related to the activity of providing agency services in general, such as the risk of the agent's income being dependent on his success as an agent or general investments in for instance premises or personnel' are not relevant to this issue.

In the first Commission Decision in which it applied these rules, DaimlerChrysler 'agents' were held not to be genuine agents. Risks held to be of particular relevance arose out of contractual obligations to purchase demonstration and business vehicles, carry out guarantee work, set up maintenance and repair facilities and to supply spare parts.[12]

No Independence of Action

In *Volkswagen*,[13] a relevant factor in deciding whether the agency agreement was within the scope of Article 81 was that the agents' 'principal business of sales and after-sales services is carried on, largely independently, in their own name and for their own account' (para 19). In other words, the agency accounted for a relatively small part of their business.

Independence may be shown in the freedom of a party to act as it chooses: in *Pittsburgh*, one of the elements picked out as showing that the relationship was not one of agency was the fact that the party concerned was in a position to have refused to have taken part in the restrictive practices had it chosen. It was said to make most of its profits from selling both its own goods and those of third parties: thus it was not in a relationship of economic dependence on the other party to the contract (para 11).

Other circumstances that have been considered by the Commission to be indicative of an independent trading relationship are the fact that the sales 'agent' makes out invoices and delivers the goods, and the fact that the 'agent' has a separate account from customers for purchases from his 'principal'.[14]

Companies over a certain size have generally not been characterised as agents. This is explicable on the basis that in practice a large company, even when carrying out the functions of an agent, will always be in a position to exert a certain pressure on its supplier, and therefore will be able to influence the distribution policies of its 'principal'.

However, there is no reference in the Commission's Guidelines to a requirement of independence of action.

---

[12] *DaimlerChrysler* OJ 2002 L257/1, [2003] 4 CMLR 95, para 160. Interestingly, the Commission states that the position would have been different had the 'agent' been given a choice as to whether to assume these risks, or simply to negotiate new vehicle sales contracts. An appeal on the agency point is pending, Case T-352/01, OJ 2002 C68/15.

[13] Case C-266/93 *Bundeskartellamt v Volkswagen* [1995] ECR I-347, [1996] 4 CMLR 505.

[14] *Fisher Price* OJ 1988 L49/19, [1989] 4 CMLR 553, para 18.

Integration into Principal's Business

In *Suiker Unie*, the first case in which the ECJ was called upon to pronounce on the application of Article 81 to agency agreements, the Court explained that if a party acts for the benefit of another party, obeying instructions and behaving generally in a way such as an employee might act, then it will be considered an agent. In such circumstances, it can be seen as an auxiliary organ integrated into the business and forming part of a single economic unity with that business (para 480). In this case the fact that the purported agents worked with a number of different principals was also given as a reason for not characterising them as genuine agents.

In *Vlaamse Reisbureaus v Sociale Dienst*,[15] the claim that travel agents should escape the application of Article 81(1) in their relations with tour operators was rejected. The fact that the travel agents were acting in the name and on behalf of the tour operators was expressly said not to be sufficient. The grounds for regarding the travel agents as independent traders rather than genuine agents were the following:

> a travel agent of the kind referred to . . . must be regarded as an independent agent who provides services on an entirely independent basis. He sells travel organised by a large number of different tour operators and a tour operator sells travel through a very large number of agents. Contrary to the Belgian Government's submissions, a travel agent cannot be treated as an auxiliary organ forming an integral part of a tour operator's undertaking. (para 20)

According to this ECJ judgment,[16] therefore, a true agent works only on behalf of one principal, as well as bearing no commercial risk with respect to the goods being sold: in other words, there must be an exclusive agency provision. The Commission's Guidelines are in direct contradiction to this: after referring to financial or commercial risk as the determining factor, it states that 'it is not material for the assessment [of genuine agency] whether the agent acts for one or several principals'. This is despite the reiteration by the ECJ in *Volkswagen* in 1995[17] of the importance of the integration criterion: in *Volkswagen* it cited the *Suiker Unie* case and stressed the necessity that agents, as well as not bearing certain risks, 'operate as auxiliary organs forming an integrated part of the principal's undertaking'.[18]

Since then the Commission in its *DaimlerChrysler* Decision, citing *Volkswagen*, has said that 'the criterion of integration is, unlike risk allocation, not a separate criterion for distinguishing a commercial agent from a dealer', apparently suggesting that integration *is* a cumulative condition, together with the absence of relevant risks, for genuine agency.

---

[15] Case 311/85 [1987] ECR 3801, [1989] 4 CMLR 213

[16] The judgment has been heavily criticised: see eg Koch and Marenco, 'L'Article 85 du Traité et les Contrats d'Agence' [1987] *Cahiers de Droit Européen* 603. It may be that such criticism of the ECJ's approach has given the Commission the confidence to take a different line in its Guidelines, where it appears to contradict what the Court has said in some cases.

[17] The Guidelines were published in 2000.

[18] It also represents a U-turn from the position adopted in an unpublished but widely circulated Commission Draft Notice on Commercial Agency Agreements dated 1990, which included integration as a key criterion.

Does the Agent Conclude Contracts in its Own Name?

The implication of the Commission's general definition of agency is that whether the contracts are concluded in the agent's name or that of its principal is not in itself relevant to a competition law analysis.

When May Genuine Agency Agreements Infringe Article 81(1)?

According to the Commission's Guidelines, genuine agency agreements fall outside Article 81 only for the purposes of obligations relating to the contracts negotiated or concluded on behalf of the principal. Other restrictions, such as exclusivity provisions which prevent the principal from appointing other agents in respect of a given type of transaction, customer or territory (exclusive agency), or provisions preventing the agent from acting as agent or distributor for its principal's competitors (non-compete clauses), do potentially infringe Article 81, even where the agent bears no significant commercial or financial risk. However, this conflicts with the ECJ cases that suggest that Article 81 does not apply at all to genuine agency relationships.

The Commission's Guidelines state that exclusive agency does not 'in general' have anti-competitive effects, implying that it may sometimes do so. Again, this is in direct conflict with ECJ cases such as *Volkswagen* in which the fact that the agent works only for one principal is seen as an essential characteristic of genuine agency, and therefore of escape from the application of Article 81!

The Guidelines say that non-compete provisions may infringe Article 81 if they lead to foreclosure on the market where the contract goods are sold or purchased. For example, in the Commission Decision *IMA Rules*,[19] the rules of a trade association of Dutch importers, processors and agents dealing in plywood required the agents of the association to work only on the basis of exclusive agency agreements and only to deliver to the association's members. The Commission held that, because these restrictions prevented anyone who might prefer to work through a number of agents, or who was not an IMA member, from engaging the services of agents working through the IMA, Article 81(1) was infringed. Exemption under Article 81(3) was refused because there was no evidence that the restrictions would bring about any improvement in distribution.

Again, the Court's case law suggests that where the agent is integrated into the principal, Article 81 does not apply at all to the agreement between them, so that even foreclosure effects are irrelevant.

Apart from exclusive agency and foreclosure effects, the other factor which may bring any agency agreement within Article 81 is that it facilitates collusion between competitors. The Guidelines give as examples situations in which a number of principals either use the same agents while collectively excluding other principals

---

[19] OJ 1980 L318/1, [1981] 2 CMLR 498. See also Commission Notice *Repsol CPP*, OJ 2004 C258/7.

from using those agents, or use them to collude on marketing strategy or to exchange sensitive market information between the principals.

When May Non-genuine Agency Agreements Infringe Article 81(1)?

If a particular distribution arrangement does not fall within the Community law definition of 'genuine agency', then it may or may not infringe Article 81(1). There is no presumption of infringement. The status of such agreements under Community law depends, just as it does for other distribution agreements with independent dealers, on the terms of the agreement and the market situation both for the goods and services being sold through the agent, and for the services provided by such an agent (see Chapter 3).

Exemption Under Article 81(3)

If there is infringement of Article 81(1), it becomes necessary to decide whether the agreement is nevertheless exempted. Exemption may be conferred by a block exemption Regulation. If no block exemption is applicable then, as in the case of any other agreement, the agreement will be exempted if it satisfies the four substantive requirements of Article 81(3).

Block Exemption

The block exemption on vertical restraints (Appendix 4) states explicitly that agency agreements may, if they satisfy its criteria, benefit from it (Article 1(g)). This will only be possible where the relevant market share does not exceed 30 per cent (see Chapter 3). Where distribution of motor vehicles or their repair and after-sales services is concerned, a sector-specific block exemption may apply (see Chapter 4).

The vertical restraints block exemption may provide exemption for provisions such as the allocation to the agent of an exclusive territory or customer group, non-compete obligations lasting less than five years, or the setting by the principal of maximum or recommended prices.

Exemption Under Article 81(3)

Exemption under Article 81(3) applies where there is an economic efficiency justification for a restriction not exempted by the block exemption: the four substantive criteria of Article 81(3) must be satisfied (see p 30).

Examples of provisions which will probably infringe Article 81 and will not benefit from exemption, either under the block exemption on vertical restraints, or by individual exemption, are obligations preventing or restricting the agent from sharing its commission with the customer,[20] restrictions on its ability to respond to unsolicited orders coming from outside its contract territory, and excessive post-termination clauses.

6.3 AGENCY AND ARTICLE 82

Even an agreement classified as genuine agency under Community law may be prohibited under Article 82 if one of the parties is in a dominant position on the relevant market.

This will be the case in particular either if obligations imposed on the agents by a dominant undertaking, such as non-competition clauses, go further than is warranted by the circumstances, or if other enterprises are prevented from finding agents to distribute their goods because all or too many of the possible agents have been tied up to a dominant undertaking by contracts which prevent them from being available to competitors of the dominant undertaking.[21]

6.4 PROTECTION OF COMMERCIAL AGENTS

Although not part of competition law, one of the main aims of Directive 86/653 on self-employed commercial agents (Appendix 3) is to ensure as far as possible equal competitive conditions throughout Community territory so that principals and agents from one Member State compete on an equal basis with those operating in a different Member State.

The harmonisation of some of the rules applicable to agents also has the effect of giving a minimum level of protection to agents throughout the Community. Although the Directive does not provide any method by which the law applicable to an agency contract is determined, and parties may choose a non-EU law to govern their contracts, an agent carrying on his activity in the Community cannot be deprived of protection under the Directive in this way.[22]

Much fuller protection would have been afforded to agents had the Directive provided some way of preventing differences in national laws being used to unfair advantage by principals. For example, Belgian law provides some elements of protection to agents that do not exist in French law. A supplier may therefore try to avoid application of the more stringent Belgian law by appointing a French agent for the territory of Belgium. Furthermore, in the case of many of the rules appear-

---

[20] Guidelines, para 48.
[21] *Suiker Unie*, above n 3, at para 486.
[22] Case C-381/98 *Ingmar v Eaton Leonard Technologies* [2000] ECR I-9305 concerned an agency agreement between a principal based in California and an agent working within the EU, where the agency was contractually stated to be subject to the law of California. The judgment refers only to rights following termination of the agency contract, but the same principle probably applies to other rights under the Directive.

ing in the Directive, it is not clear whether parties may agree to exclude wholly or in part the application of the rights and obligations provided for. The matter therefore falls to be decided by any mandatory national rule of the governing law of the agency contract.

Definition of Commercial Agent

Not all commercial agents are subject to the Directive. For the purposes of the Directive, 'commercial agent' means a self-employed intermediary who has continuing authority to negotiate[23] the sale or purchase of goods on behalf of another person (its 'principal') or to negotiate and conclude such transactions on behalf of and in the name of that principal (Article 1(2)). A Greek court has asked the ECJ whether this definition encompasses an agent 'who purchases in his own name goods from the principal, deducting his commission from the purchase price, and subsequently sells those goods to third parties, but acting on behalf of the principal'.[24] It is irrelevant how the parties themselves label the relationship: a 'sales representative' may or may not be a 'commercial agent', depending on the nature of his activity.

The definition expressly excludes company officers, partners, receivers, liquidators and trustees in bankruptcy (Article 1(3)). It also excludes unpaid agents and those operating on commodity exchanges or in the commodity market or UK 'Crown Agents' (Article 2(2)).

Given the fact that the definition of commercial agent relates only to the sale or purchase of goods, agents in service industries who are not engaged in the sale of goods also fall outside the scope of the Directive. This excludes many common types of agent; travel and insurance agents, as well as musical, theatrical and sporting agents, for example, are excluded. However, a number of Member States have included service industry agents within the scope of their implementing legislation. Member States also have the freedom when implementing the Directive to exclude those persons 'whose activities as commercial agents are considered secondary by the law of the Member State'. The United Kingdom is one of the few Member States to have taken this option.

Rights and Obligations

Rights and obligations are only addressed in general terms. They provide a basic minimum, and may not be derogated from by the parties (Article 5). On the agent is imposed an obligation to 'look after his principal's interests and act dutifully and

---

[23] The English Court of Appeal has placed a questionably narrow interpretation on the word 'negotiate', holding that it excludes an agent operating a self-service petrol station, *Parks v Esso* [2000] EuLR 531, [2000] 18 TLR 232.
[24] Case C-85/03 *Mavrona v DES* OJ 2003 C112/10.

in good faith' (Article 3(1)). This includes making proper efforts, keeping its principal informed and obeying its reasonable instructions (Article 3(2)).

The principal is also obliged to act dutifully and in good faith (Article 4(1)). In its case this includes providing the agent with all necessary documentation and information. In particular, it should give reasonable notice to the agent if it expects a significantly lower volume of commercial transactions than the agent would normally have expected (Article 4(2)). The agent also has the right to be informed within a reasonable time of the outcome of transactions procured by it for its principal (Article 4(3)).

Remuneration

Member States have the right to retain or enact specific legislation concerning agents' level of remuneration. Principal and agent are also free to agree privately between themselves on payment. However, in the absence of such legislation or agreement, an agent must be entitled to the customary local rate for the kind of goodsit is selling, or to a reasonable rate in the absence of any established custom (Article 6(1)).

The following rules laid down by the Directive apply exclusively to payment by commission and not to other forms of payment. In some Member States these have had the effect of considerably strengthening the position of the agent.

Commission is payable during the contract period on all transactions concluded as a result of the agent's action. If further business is done subsequently with a customer acquired by the agent for the same kind of business, the agent is entitled to commission on that subsequent business during the contract period (Article 7(1)). If the principal receives an order from such a customer during the agent's contract period then it must pay the agent commission on that contract, even if the transaction is not actually concluded until the agency contract has run its term (Article 8(b)).

It may alternatively be provided that where the agent is entrusted with a specific geographical area or group of customers, then during the contract period it is entitled to commission on all transactions with customers belonging to that area or group. Alternatively, similar provision for remuneration may be made in respect of an agent with an exclusive right to such an area or group of customers (Article 7(2)). This applies even when the contract has been concluded without any action on the agent's part. Whether the customer 'belongs' to the area or group is to be determined, where the customer is a legal person, by reference to where it actually carries on its commercial activities, though where this is not a single place, a number of other factors may be taken into account.[25]

Commission must become due to the agent as soon as the transaction has been or should have been executed by the principal according to the agreement made with the customer, or has been executed by the customer. This protects the agent

---

[25] Case C-104/95 *Kontogeorgas v Kartonpak* [1996] ECR I-6643.

against non-performance or breach of contract by its principal. Actual payment shall not be made later than the date on which the customer has executed its part of the transaction or the last day of the month following the quarter during which the commission became due, whichever occurs first.

Even if the transaction is concluded after the end of the contract period, so long as it is not too long after, the agent is entitled to commission if the transaction is mainly attributable to its efforts during the contract period (Article 8(a)).

The above rules could give rise to a situation in which both a current and a previous agent were entitled to commission. In such circumstances it is the earlier agent who is entitled to the payment, 'unless it is equitable because of the circumstances for the commission to be shared between the commercial agents' (Article 9).

Information

The agent is entitled to receive quarterly information on the amounts and breakdown of its commission. If Member States have national rules which permit the agent to inspect the principal's books, these rules are to take precedence over those found in the Directive (Article 12).

Conclusion and Termination of Agency Contracts (Articles 13–16)

Each party has the right to receive a written document relating to the contract. The right to receive such a document cannot be waived. Such a right does not prevent a contract of agency itself being concluded orally, or tacitly. However, Member States may provide that agency contracts not at least evidenced in writing be invalid.

Agency contracts may be concluded for a definite period. However, if such a contract continues to be performed after the expiration of the agreed period, the agreement is transformed automatically into an agreement for an indefinite period which can be terminated by notice. The period of notice cannot be shorter than one month for every expired contract year, with a maximum of three months or, if a Member State so prefers, a maximum of six months for six contract years and longer.

If longer periods of notice are adopted, these should be identical for both agent and principal. Fixed period agreements are also subject to the cumulative notice provisions described above.

However, the Directive does provide for the possibility of immediate termination by either party in certain circumstances. This may happen where one party fails to carry out all or part of its obligations, or when 'exceptional circumstances' arise. 'Exceptional circumstances' probably refer to circumstances which under the law of the Member State concerned give grounds for immediate termination of the contract, such as *force majeure*.

Indemnification and Compensation

The Articles in the Directive which deal with indemnification and compensation for agents (Articles 17–18) represent a political compromise. The principle of indemnification for agents at the termination or expiration of agency agreements was already applied in a number of Member States, including Germany and the Benelux countries. However, to others, such as the United Kingdom, the idea was unwelcome.

These two positions had therefore to be accommodated in the final text of the Directive: eventually indemnification was provided for, but Member States were given the option of providing only for compensation for damage if they preferred. Whichever option applies, there can be no derogation from the rules to the agent's detriment by the parties during the term of the contract (Article 19).

An agent must notify its principal that it intends to make a claim for indemnity or compensation within a limitation period of one year of the termination of the contract. Indemnity or compensation is payable even if the contract ends as a result of the death of the agent.

However, it is not payable either where the principal has terminated the agency contract because of default attributable to the commercial agent which would justify immediate termination of the agency contract under national law, or where the commercial agent has terminated the agency contract, unless such termination is justified by circumstances attributable to the principal or on the grounds of age, infirmity or illness of the commercial agent in consequence of which it cannot reasonably be required to continue its activities, or where, with the agreement of the principal, the commercial agent assigns its rights and duties under the agency contract to another person.

Indemnity

Indemnity refers to payment in respect of business goodwill accumulated by the agent during the period of agency. If the indemnity option is chosen by the relevant Member State, then an agent is entitled to an indemnity if and to the extent that it has brought the principal new customers or has significantly increased the volume of business with existing customers and the principal continues to derive substantial benefits from the business with such customers, and the payment of this indemnity is equitable.

The indemnification may not exceed an amount equivalent to the agent's commissions for one year, calculated from the agent's average annual commissions over the shorter of the preceding five years or the period that the agreement has been in force. However, if the agent thinks it suffers damage that exceeds the indemnification as calculated above, he is entitled to claim additional compensation. The Directive does not clearly indicate what type of damage is envisaged, but it is generally assumed that it refers to situations in which damages are available under national law principles for breach of contract or similar events.

In 1996 the Commission produced a report[26] on the application of Article 17 of the Directive, based on the responses to a questionnaire sent out to a wide variety of interested parties and authorities in each Member State. It reported that most Member States chose the indemnity option, and that problems have arisen as a result of the failure of the Directive to set down a method of calculation of the amount of the indemnity; only a ceiling on the amount is set.

Compensation

The Directive provides an alternative rule that may be selected by Member States in preference to the rules on indemnity outlined above. France, for example, chose the compensation option. The United Kingdom's implementing law allows parties a choice: if no choice is expressed, the compensation rule applies. In practice, application of the law has led to some confusion, as neither concept was previously used in the United Kingdom.[27]

Under this alternative, compensation is granted for actual damage suffered only, and not for goodwill accruing to the principal. This is the case in particular where the agent is deprived of commission which proper performance of the agency contract would have procured him whilst providing the principal with substantial benefits linked to the commercial agent's activities, or in circumstances which have not enabled the commercial agent to amortise the investments and expenses that he had incurred for the performance of the agency.

Post-term Restraint Clauses (Article 20)

Clauses restricting an agent from carrying on its business after termination of the agreement are not generally acceptable, unless the restraint is only imposed on areas, groups of customers and kinds of goods that were covered by the agreement and the restraint lasts no longer than two years. However, Member States' national law takes precedence over these rules if it is more restrictive of such clauses.

National Implementing Measures

Community Directives generally require incorporation into national law in order to be fully effective. Therefore, each Member State was required to enact implementing legislation in order to bring its national legislation into line with the requirements of this Directive.

---

[26] COM(96)364 of 23 July 1996.
[27] In *Douglas King v Tunnock* [2000] EuLR 531, [2000] IRLR 569 the Scottish Court of Appeal expressly relied on French law principles in holding that two years' commission is generally appropriate compensation.

The original deadline for implementation was 1 January 1990, but it was not until 1995 that the Directive was implemented in all the then 15 Member States. As for the 10 Member States that joined on 1 May 2004, they were all required to have implemented the Directive by that date, but it is possible that full and correct implementation may be behind schedule in some of those jurisdictions too.

In a number of Member State jurisdictions, such as France, Germany and the Netherlands, compliance with the Directive involved little change to existing laws giving protection to commercial agents.

In the United Kingdom and Ireland, the concepts involved were completely new. The Directive gave these latter States a correspondingly longer period in which to adapt their legislation to the Directive. Until 1994 when the United Kingdom implemented the Directive, there was no statutory protection for agents there. Implementation represented the introduction of a number of completely new concepts into UK law, some of which UK courts have been called on to interpret.

Some implementing laws go further than required by the Directive: for example, the French definition of an agent is wider than that required by the Directive since it includes agents acting not only in respect of contracts for goods but also contracts for hire and for services.

In some countries an issue arose over national obligations of registration by an agent in a national commercial register. In France, a 1958 Decree requires agents before they can start their activity to register with the Commercial Court of the district in which they are a resident, and the French implementing legislation did not amend this obligation. As the Directive did not provide for any kind of registration, discussion arose in France as to whether such registration was still required and as to whether this registration should be considered as a condition to qualify as an agent. It now seems to be settled in France that registration is only required for agents (French or foreign) with a residence in France, with registration no longer a prerequisite to qualifying as an agent for the purposes of the Directive. Consequently, a non-registered agent operating in France will benefit from the protective measures set out in the Directive and in French implementing legislation.

In Italy, a similar issue arose and came before the European Court of Justice. The Court confirmed that Member States were entitled to maintain a register of commercial agents but said that the Directive precluded a national rule 'which makes the validity of an agency contract conditional upon the commercial agent being entered in the appropriate register'.[28]

Direct Effect of the Directive

It may be that some Member States' implementing legislation does not fully and correctly implement all aspects of the Directive.

---

[28] Case C-215/97 *Bellone v Yokohama* [1998] ECR I-2191, para 18; Case C-456/98 *Centrosteel v Adipol* [2000] ECR I-6007.

If the deadline for implementation of a Directive has passed (as it has for Directive 86/653), then in certain circumstances it may be possible to rely on it even in the absence of implementing legislation. This is also the case where a Directive has been incorrectly implemented.

One important limitation on that principle in this context is that one private party cannot rely on the direct effect of an unimplemented or inadequately implemented Directive in order to establish an obligation on another private party. It would normally be necessary to be invoking the Directive as against the state or a state agency.

However, the ECJ has ruled that national courts should, when interpreting national law, take into account the requirements of an unimplemented Directive (at a time when the state in question should have implemented the Directive). Again, the same applies in the case of an inadequately implemented Directive. In practice, this could be used to create out of an incorrectly implemented Directive an obligation on another private party, provided that a national law in this field already existed to be 'interpreted'. For example, national legislation might provide for the entitlement of an agent to commission in certain circumstances. If the national implementing law was in given circumstances ambiguous then the Directive should be relied on by a national court when interpreting the national law.[29]

---

[29] See further discussion of the direct effect of Directives and liability in damages in Chapter 1.

7

The Future

In the previous edition of this book I referred to the introduction of the single block exemption for vertical restraints and the accompanying Guidelines as a 'revolution'. It seems to have been a bloodless revolution. Since the introduction of the new rules in 2000 there have been no formal Commission Decisions exempting any exclusive distribution or exclusive purchasing arrangements, nor any selective distribution or franchising systems. Nor has the Court of First Instance (CFI) or the European Court of Justice (ECJ) given any judgments interpreting the new rules. Even at an informal level, Commission officials receive relatively few queries in this area.

To a large extent the reform appears to have succeeded in its aim of breaking away from the formalism of the previous regime, and focusing on prohibiting only economically damaging distribution agreements, while still providing a reasonable degree of legal certainty. For those companies falling below the 30 per cent market threshold there is now considerably more commercial flexibility in the EU rules applicable to their distribution arrangements. Freedom of contract has become the general rule, albeit with a number of exceptions, there no longer being any need to fit within the straitjacket of the very detailed old block exemptions. Those with market shares above the 30 per cent threshold, on the other hand, have had to learn to become more circumspect.

Business would appear to have found a way to live with the new rules, and it is therefore not surprising, in the light of the competing demands on its resources, that DG Comp has postponed the review of the vertical restraints Guidelines that was due to take place in 2004.

That is not to say that there are not difficult issues affecting distribution law that will require resolution in the near future. The Commission's crusade to protect parallel trade will continue, with the *Bayer* judgment forcing it to be more rigorous in proving anti-competitive agreements, and pushing it to seek alternative means of achieving its aims, such as the use of Article 82. Linked to this are the specific difficulties faced by the pharmaceutical industry, operating in a highly regulated environment but obliged to observe competition rules which are premised on a single, free market, and these require a solution.

Pressure is also growing for a less formalistic and more economics-based approach to Article 82 cases than has characterised past Commission practice. The

Commission's recent *Microsoft* Decision goes in this direction, and it has indicated that it is seriously considering this general issue internally, with a view to issuing guidance.[1] Such guidance cannot amend the wording of Article 82 or the related CFI and ECJ case law, but it can influence policy choices as to which cases it pursues and how it approaches them. Despite the fact that the CFI recently upheld the Commission's rigidly traditional approach in its *Michelin* Decision, this is an area where significant change can be expected in the medium term.

Those responsible for the new motor vehicles distribution block exemption will be watching anxiously, especially after the prohibition on 'location clauses' enters into force in October 2005, to see if it succeeds in introducing more competition in the market and reducing price differentials across the Community.

In addition, the pace of technological development, and not least the ever-increasing importance of the Internet, have raised a host of issues which have yet to be fully resolved. Many companies are watching for developments in competition policy in response to the growth in electronic communications and the new distribution techniques which they engender.[2] Some of the issues raised by electronic commercial methods were addressed in the Commission's Guidelines on vertical restraints, but a great number still remain to be explored.

At the simplest level, the new technologies are being used to provide a more efficient version of traditional distribution methods, for example where a traditional mail order company introduces electronic ordering. In other cases the changes are more far-reaching. The fact that many products and services such as books, news, videos, music and software can be delivered electronically is leading to the elimination of intermediaries and physical sales outlets by manufacturers which previously relied on networks of wholesalers and retailers or multiple retail outlets. There are even completely new distribution methods, such as websites on which small traders can buy and sell their wares without setting up their own site, and B2B (business to business) systems through which competing businesses co-operate to source their requirements. These horizontal forms of co-operation raise a number of competition law concerns, chief among which are open access and the exchange of confidential market information.

In all cases there are important implications for price transparency and the possibility for price competition, and the problems raised for competition law will be particularly acute where electronic distributors compete with traditional shops. The existence of competing 'new' distributors alongside traditional distributors also introduces 'free-riding' issues: a purchaser may visit a traditional outlet to investigate the book or car he wants to buy, make his decision and then buy it more cheaply from an electronic distributor—or alternatively, the more focused,

---

[1] See speeches by Director-General Philip Lowe and Commissioner Mario Monti at the Fordham Conference, October 2003 (available on DG Comp's website).

[2] The Commission's Green Paper on vertical restraints, COM(96)721, discussed in some detail the changing patterns in the distribution of goods, including the blurring of the traditional distinction between the manufacturing, wholesale and retail functions.

personalised advertising which many electronic traders are in a position to do may lead to traditional suppliers free-riding on them. Market definition is very uncertain in the case of very new or rapidly evolving products as they converge or become differentiated; also, relevant market shares may be changing by the month, making the application of market share thresholds extremely difficult. There is also uncertainty about the impact on geographic market definition of sale via Internet, and existing rules on pricing abuses are not appropriate in respect of products involving high development risks and tiny marginal costs.

In addition the application of competition law rules to other new practices associated with distribution remains untested. 'Category management', for example, involves the provision of advice, by a leading supplier of a particular type of product, to a retailer such as a supermarket. The supplier advises, in respect of its market segment, on the optimum allocation of shelf space to its and to competing products, and on pricing and other aspects of how best to satisfy consumer demand. While the provision of advice may have efficiency benefits and does not in itself infringe competition rules, it is easy to see how such a relationship may raise concerns including information exchange between competing suppliers, foreclosure of other suppliers, enforcement of 'recommended' prices and horizontal price collusion.

However, even taking all these issues into account, the distribution law scene is now a quiet one compared with other areas of EU competition law, and its development over the last four years might not, without more, have justified a new edition of *EU Distribution Law*.

7.2 'MODERNISATION'

But this peaceful scene has now suffered a small earthquake in the form of radical change to the procedural rules governing enforcement of Articles 81 and 82. The implications of this reform, generally known as 'modernisation', are immense. It requires business and its advisers to take much greater responsibility for assessing their own agreements and practices; this was foreshadowed in the Guidelines on vertical restraints, which have as their express aim 'to help companies to make their own assessment of vertical agreements'. It also increases the Commission's enforcement powers, and it grants new powers to and places new responsibilities on national competition authorities and courts.

A host of concerns have been voiced about the new system, and while it is true that many of the potential problems existed prior to modernisation, the reform has made it more likely that they will arise in practice. It will not be until the new system has been in operation for some time that we will know how significant they are in reality. Chief among them are the possible undesirable consequences of the decentralisation involved and in particular the risk to the unity of interpretation of the EU rules posed by diverging decisions taken by the courts and authorities of different Member States, particularly in the light of the recent enlargement of the

EU. The Commission has powers enabling it to some extent to supervise and steer the application and development of the law in this area. Still, avoiding controversy when the Commission is seen to interfere with the work of national courts and authorities represents a considerable challenge.

Relationships between the Commission and national authorities in the European Competition Network will be key, and considerable progress towards establishing the necessary mutual respect and culture of openness has already been made as a result of the face-to-face meetings that started well before the official launch of the new system on 1 May 2004. In practice, the smooth operation of the system will depend as much as anything on the strength and quality of these relationships. This is particularly so given the extent to which this area is governed by non-binding 'soft law' in the form of Commission Guidelines and Notices, and that significant volumes of confidential information will need to be exchanged.

There may be an increase in 'forum shopping', as companies and their advisers learn which Member State's courts are most likely to produce the desired result. There is also a risk of multiple court proceedings since, however good the co-operation within the European Competition Network, decisions of national authorities will not be effective outside their jurisdiction. The same is true of national court proceedings, since although the Brussels Regulation provides for mutual recognition and enforcement of judgments within the EU, it will often not apply to prevent multiple proceedings, for example because the parties may not be identical.

Anxiety has also been voiced about the ability of some national courts to deal with competition cases. Complex economic evaluation is often necessary, as is a full understanding of competition law principles; national judges are not normally trained in economics, and in a number of Member States competition law itself is a relatively new concept.

Another worry is the decrease in legal certainty: companies have always complained at the lack of legal certainty inherent in the Commission's use of comfort letters, but many say the new regime, which requires them to make their own assessment of their conduct, will bring even worse uncertainty. Formal and informal guidance will be available from the Commission, but only where the law (as opposed to the application of the law to the facts) is unclear, and is expected to remain rare. Many Member States have introduced national competition laws modelled on the existing Community approach, including notification and exemption only by decision of the authorities. Some of these have opted to retain these systems, and it may be that companies take this route to achieve indirect comfort as to the legality of their agreements.

The Commission apparently sees no inconsistency in maintaining the block exemption system for those agreements which fall within their scope. This seems unsatisfactory in principle. Since exemption now follows automatically from the fulfilling of the substantive criteria for exemption, without the need for any administrative authorisation or declaration, block exemptions now purport to exempt agreements which are already exempted. More satisfactory from the point of view of principle would be to transform them into guidance notices for the relevant types of agreement. This may yet happen, though admittedly this would not provide the high level of legal certainty afforded by block exemptions, which bind both EU and national institutions.

However, the impact of these changes goes even further. So fundamental are they that, although they are technically procedural, it is already clear that there will also be ramifications for the substance of the law. In particular, there have been signals from the Commission that it will interpret the prohibition in Article 81(1) more narrowly, so as to reduce the number of commercial arrangements falling within its scope. At the same time it is setting the bar high for exemption under Article 81(3), requiring sophisticated economic evidence that the two positive and two negative conditions of that Article are fulfilled. As a result it would appear to be becoming easier to establish that an agreement or practice falls outside Article 81(1) than to be able to show that Article 81(3) applies. We may therefore see the law taking quite a new direction in the coming years.

7.3 DG COMP RESOURCES

A driving motivation for this reform was the need to free up DG Comp's resources to enable it to focus on serious infringements such as major cartels and abuses of dominance. But although it will no longer be dealing with notifications, there are now considerable new calls on its time. These include running the European Competition Network, monitoring national application of Articles 81 and 82 and intervening as necessary, and responding to requests for information and opinions from national courts, and all of this in a Community of 25 Member States instead of 15. It remains to be seen how it will cope and what priorities it will set.

DG Comp was recently reorganised so that notified mergers are dealt with by the appropriate sectoral Directorate, rather than by the specialised Merger Task Force. Though this has many advantages, it does entail the risk that at times when levels of merger activity are high, Article 81 and 82 cases may be neglected, because officials dealing with them are not subject to the strict deadlines that apply to merger review.

7.4 FURTHER PROCEDURAL REFORM

The Commission recognised at the outset of its 'modernisation' project that optimum functioning of the new, more decentralised system, would require a significant degree of harmonisation of national procedural rules. However, in order not to delay adoption of the reforms, it was decided at this first stage only to include a minimum of such procedural harmonisation. Now that Regulation 1/2003 is in place, the Commission is actively considering what additional measures may be needed.

Future reform is likely to cover a broad range of procedural issues and to focus particularly on facilitating private enforcement of Articles 81 and 82 through damages claims before national courts.

7.5 DAMAGES CLAIMS

Although Article 81 is regularly raised as a defence in legal disputes, damages claims are not yet common in EU Member States,[3] in contrast to the situation in the United States. There are a number of reasons for this. One is that the 'damage', such as the higher prices paid as a result of illegal restriction of parallel trade, is often not borne by the immediate purchasers (the wholesalers or distributors), but is passed down the chain to the final consumer. In such a situation an action by the immediate purchasers will be defeated in many jurisdictions by the so-called 'passing-on defence', on the grounds that they themselves have suffered no loss. Actions by those further down the chain who have actually suffered loss may be hampered by the non-existence in some jurisdictions of class or representative actions by which a large number of small plaintiffs, all of whom have suffered loss as a result of the same anti-competitive behaviour, can jointly obtain redress. Moreover, in some jurisdictions an infringement finding by the NCA is not enough to found a damages claim, so that the illegal conduct will have to be proved anew. In others, consumers are barred altogether from claiming damages on the basis of Articles 81 and 82 as this right is confined to businesses.

In 2003, the Commission commissioned a study of the availability of damages for competition law infringements and the barriers facing plaintiffs in all 25 Member States, now available on DG Comp's website. It will serve as a basis for future proposals in this area, to be put forward in a Green Paper by the end of 2005. Wouter Wils, a member of the European Commission's Legal Service, has in his personal capacity put forward some interesting arguments against encouraging private enforcement claims,[4] but it seems clear that the Commission views an increase in such actions as key to the success of competition law enforcement.

---

[3] The first ever award of damages based on infringement of competition rules by a UK court was made in *Crehan v Inntrepreneur* [2004] EWCR 637. The case involved a non-compete obligation imposed by a brewery on a pub tenant which infringed Art 81(1).

[4] He argues essentially that as far as stopping and deterring competition law violations are concerned, public enforcement is more effective because the authorities have greater investigative and sanctioning and prohibition powers, and are motivated by the public interest rather than a private profit motive, and because it is less expensive. As for compensating victims, he argues that in practice private litigation rarely results in those responsible for the violation transferring their gain to those who have in fact been harmed: Should Private Antitrust Enforcement be Encouraged in Europe? (2003) 26(3) World Competition, 473. See also the response in Clifford Jones, 'Private Antitrust Enforcement in Europe: a Policy Analysis and Reality Check', (2004) 27(1) World Competition 13.

7.6 ECONOMICS

The 1996 edition of this book closed with the words: 'it seems clear that arguments based on economic analysis of relevant markets and parties' positions in those markets are likely to play an increasingly crucial role in the resolution of EC competition law questions'. The new policy on vertical restraints more than justified this comment, and yet the prediction still remains valid for this edition. In 2004, DG Comp's first Chief Economist took office, with the avowed intent of ensuring a rigorous approach to economic arguments and evidence. Though much of his and his team's work will be in the merger control field, they are also expected to be active in cases involving allegations of abuse of market dominance, and their existence will undoubtedly influence policy and practice more generally. It is clear that the role of expert economists, both within enforcement bodies and in the private sector, will continue to increase in the years to come.

Bibliography

The books and websites mentioned below represent a personal selection of those which I have found useful. All the books are recent enough to be fairly up to date, and all the online sources listed are accessible free of charge.

EU Distribution Law website

Quarterly updates reporting on legal developments of relevance to the areas covered by *EU Distribution Law* will be available at the Hart Publishing website, www.hartpub.co.uk/updates

EU Law and Institutions

Books

T Hartley, *The Foundations of European Community Law*, 5th edn (Oxford University Press, 2003)
J Steiner and L Woods, *Textbook on EC Law*, 8th edn (Oxford University Press, 2003)

Websites

European Court of Justice and Court of First Instance
http://europa.eu.int/cj/en/transitpage.htm

Eur-Lex
http://europa.eu.int/eur-lex/lex/en/index.htm
This site provides the full text of the Official Journal L series and C series published since 1998. It also includes full text versions of recent preparatory acts (COM docs) treaties and Community legislation in force.

EC Competition Law

Books

A Albors-Llorens, *EC Competition Law and Policy* (Willan Publishing, 2002)
C Bellamy and G Child, *European Community Law of Competition*, 5th edn (Sweet & Maxwell, 2001)
S Bishop and C Walker, *The Economics of Competition Law*, 2nd edn (Sweet & Maxwell, 2002)

D Broomhall and J Goyder (eds), *Modernisation in Europe 2005* (Law Business Research, 2005)

D Goyder, *EC Competition Law*, 4th edn (Oxford University Press, 2003)

A Jones and B Sufrin, *EC Competition Law: Text, Cases and Materials*, 2nd edn (Oxford University Press, 2004)

C Kerse and N Khan, *EC Antitrust Procedure*, 5th edn (Sweet & Maxwell, 2005)

V Korah, *An Introductory Guide to EC Competition Law and Practice*, 8th edn (Hart Publishing, 2003)

V Korah and D O'Sullivan, *Distribution Agreements under the EC Competition Rules* (Hart Publishing, 2002)

L Ritter, D Braun and F Rawlinson, *European Competition Law: a Practitioner's Guide*, 2nd edn (Kluwer Law International, 2000)

R Whish, *Competition Law*, 5th edn (LexisNexis, 2003)

Websites

DG Comp
http://europa.eu.int/comm/competition/index_en.html

Provides information on DG Comp's activities, press releases and publications, speeches and articles by officials, as well as legislation and policy documents, DG Comp's Annual Reports and its Competition Policy Newsletter.

RBB Economics (economics of vertical restraints)
http://www.rbbecon.com/publications/vertical.html

Free Movement of Goods

P Oliver, *Free Movement of Goods in the European Community*, 4th edn (Sweet & Maxwell, 2003)

Appendix 1

ARTICLE 81

1. The following shall be prohibited as incompatible with the common market: all agreements between undertakings, decisions by associations of undertakings and concerted practices which may affect trade between Member States and which have as their object or effect the prevention, restriction or distortion of competition within the common market, and in particular those which:

  (a) directly or indirectly fix purchase or selling prices or any other trading conditions;

  (b) limit or control production, markets, technical development, or investment;

  (c) share markets or sources of supply;

  (d) apply dissimilar conditions to equivalent transactions with other trading parties, thereby placing them at a competitive disadvantage;

  (e) make the conclusion of contracts subject to acceptance by the other parties of supplementary obligations which, by their nature or according to commercial usage, have no connection with the subject of such contracts.

2. Any agreements or decisions prohibited pursuant to this article shall be automatically void.

3. The provisions of paragraph 1 may, however, be declared inapplicable in the case of:

  • any agreement or category of agreements between undertakings,

  • any decision or category of decisions by associations of undertakings,

  • any concerted practice or category of concerted practices,

which contributes to improving the production or distribution of goods or to promoting technical or economic progress, while allowing consumers a fair share of the resulting benefit, and which does not:

(a) impose on the undertakings concerned restrictions which are not indispensable to the attainment of these objectives;

(b) afford such undertakings the possibility of eliminating competition in respect of a substantial part of the products in question.

ARTICLE 82

Any abuse by one or more undertakings of a dominant position within the common market or in a substantial part of it shall be prohibited as incompatible with the common market in so far as it may affect trade between Member States.

Such abuse may, in particular, consist in:

(a) directly or indirectly imposing unfair purchase or selling prices or other unfair trading conditions;

(b) limiting production, markets or technical development to the prejudice of consumers;

(c) applying dissimilar conditions to equivalent transactions with other trading parties, thereby placing them at a competitive disadvantage;

(d) making the conclusion of contracts subject to acceptance by the other parties of supplementary obligations which, by their nature or according to commercial usage, have no connection with the subject of such contracts.

Appendix 2

COUNCIL REGULATION (EC) No 1/2003
OJ 2003, L1/1, [2003] 4 CMLR 551

Council Regulation (EC) No 1/2003of 16 December 2002 on the implementation of the rules on competition laid down in Articles 81 and 82 of the Treaty
(Text with EEA relevance)

THE COUNCIL OF THE EUROPEAN UNION,
Having regard to the Treaty establishing the European Community, and in particular Article 83 thereof,
Having regard to the proposal from the Commission(1),
Having regard to the opinion of the European Parliament(2),
Having regard to the opinion of the European Economic and Social Committee(3),
Whereas:
(1) In order to establish a system which ensures that competition in the common market is not distorted, Articles 81 and 82 of the Treaty must be applied effectively and uniformly in the Community. Council Regulation No 17 of 6 February 1962, First Regulation implementing Articles 81 and 82(4) of the Treaty(5), has allowed a Community competition policy to develop that has helped to disseminate a competition culture within the Community. In the light of experience, however, that Regulation should now be replaced by legislation designed to meet the challenges of an integrated market and a future enlargement of the Community.
(2) In particular, there is a need to rethink the arrangements for applying the exception from the prohibition on agreements, which restrict competition, laid down in Article 81(3) of the Treaty. Under Article 83(2)(b) of the Treaty, account must be taken in this regard of the need to ensure effective supervision, on the one hand, and to simplify administration to the greatest possible extent, on the other.
(3) The centralised scheme set up by Regulation No 17 no longer secures a balance between those two objectives. It hampers application of the Community competition rules by the courts and competition authorities of the Member States, and the system of notification it involves prevents the Commission from concentrating its resources on curbing the most serious infringements. It also imposes considerable costs on undertakings.
(4) The present system should therefore be replaced by a directly applicable exception system in which the competition authorities and courts of the Member States have the power to apply not only Article 81(1) and Article 82 of the Treaty,

which have direct applicability by virtue of the case-law of the Court of Justice of the European Communities, but also Article 81(3) of the Treaty.

(5) In order to ensure an effective enforcement of the Community competition rules and at the same time the respect of fundamental rights of defence, this Regulation should regulate the burden of proof under Articles 81 and 82 of the Treaty. It should be for the party or the authority alleging an infringement of Article 81(1) and Article 82 of the Treaty to prove the existence thereof to the required legal standard. It should be for the undertaking or association of undertakings invoking the benefit of a defence against a finding of an infringement to demonstrate to the required legal standard that the conditions for applying such defence are satisfied. This Regulation affects neither national rules on the standard of proof nor obligations of competition authorities and courts of the Member States to ascertain the relevant facts of a case, provided that such rules and obligations are compatible with general principles of Community law.

(6) In order to ensure that the Community competition rules are applied effectively, the competition authorities of the Member States should be associated more closely with their application. To this end, they should be empowered to apply Community law.

(7) National courts have an essential part to play in applying the Community competition rules. When deciding disputes between private individuals, they protect the subjective rights under Community law, for example by awarding damages to the victims of infringements. The role of the national courts here complements that of the competition authorities of the Member States. They should therefore be allowed to apply Articles 81 and 82 of the Treaty in full.

(8) In order to ensure the effective enforcement of the Community competition rules and the proper functioning of the cooperation mechanisms contained in this Regulation, it is necessary to oblige the competition authorities and courts of the Member States to also apply Articles 81 and 82 of the Treaty where they apply national competition law to agreements and practices which may affect trade between Member States. In order to create a level playing field for agreements, decisions by associations of undertakings and concerted practices within the internal market, it is also necessary to determine pursuant to Article 83(2)(e) of the Treaty the relationship between national laws and Community competition law. To that effect it is necessary to provide that the application of national competition laws to agreements, decisions or concerted practices within the meaning of Article 81(1) of the Treaty may not lead to the prohibition of such agreements, decisions and concerted practices if they are not also prohibited under Community competition law. The notions of agreements, decisions and concerted practices are autonomous concepts of Community competition law covering the coordination of behaviour of undertakings on the market as interpreted by the Community Courts. Member States should not under this Regulation be precluded from adopting and applying on their territory stricter national competition laws which prohibit or impose sanctions on unilateral conduct engaged in by undertakings. These stricter national laws may include provisions which prohibit or impose sanctions on

abusive behaviour toward economically dependent undertakings. Furthermore, this Regulation does not apply to national laws which impose criminal sanctions on natural persons except to the extent that such sanctions are the means whereby competition rules applying to undertakings are enforced.

(9) Articles 81 and 82 of the Treaty have as their objective the protection of competition on the market. This Regulation, which is adopted for the implementation of these Treaty provisions, does not preclude Member States from implementing on their territory national legislation, which protects other legitimate interests provided that such legislation is compatible with general principles and other provisions of Community law. In so far as such national legislation pursues predominantly an objective different from that of protecting competition on the market, the competition authorities and courts of the Member States may apply such legislation on their territory. Accordingly, Member States may under this Regulation implement on their territory national legislation that prohibits or imposes sanctions on acts of unfair trading practice, be they unilateral or contractual. Such legislation pursues a specific objective, irrespective of the actual or presumed effects of such acts on competition on the market. This is particularly the case of legislation which prohibits undertakings from imposing on their trading partners, obtaining or attempting to obtain from them terms and conditions that are unjustified, disproportionate or without consideration.

(10) Regulations such as 19/65/EEC(6), (EEC) No 2821/71(7), (EEC) No 3976/87(8), (EEC) No 1534/91(9), or (EEC) No 479/92(10) empower the Commission to apply Article 81(3) of the Treaty by Regulation to certain categories of agreements, decisions by associations of undertakings and concerted practices. In the areas defined by such Regulations, the Commission has adopted and may continue to adopt so called "block" exemption Regulations by which it declares Article 81(1) of the Treaty inapplicable to categories of agreements, decisions and concerted practices. Where agreements, decisions and concerted practices to which such Regulations apply nonetheless have effects that are incompatible with Article 81(3) of the Treaty, the Commission and the competition authorities of the Member States should have the power to withdraw in a particular case the benefit of the block exemption Regulation.

(11) For it to ensure that the provisions of the Treaty are applied, the Commission should be able to address decisions to undertakings or associations of undertakings for the purpose of bringing to an end infringements of Articles 81 and 82 of the Treaty. Provided there is a legitimate interest in doing so, the Commission should also be able to adopt decisions which find that an infringement has been committed in the past even if it does not impose a fine. This Regulation should also make explicit provision for the Commission's power to adopt decisions ordering interim measures, which has been acknowledged by the Court of Justice.

(12) This Regulation should make explicit provision for the Commission's power to impose any remedy, whether behavioural or structural, which is necessary to bring the infringement effectively to an end, having regard to the principle of proportionality. Structural remedies should only be imposed either where there is no

equally effective behavioural remedy or where any equally effective behavioural remedy would be more burdensome for the undertaking concerned than the structural remedy. Changes to the structure of an undertaking as it existed before the infringement was committed would only be proportionate where there is a substantial risk of a lasting or repeated infringement that derives from the very structure of the undertaking.

(13) Where, in the course of proceedings which might lead to an agreement or practice being prohibited, undertakings offer the Commission commitments such as to meet its concerns, the Commission should be able to adopt decisions which make those commitments binding on the undertakings concerned. Commitment decisions should find that there are no longer grounds for action by the Commission without concluding whether or not there has been or still is an infringement. Commitment decisions are without prejudice to the powers of competition authorities and courts of the Member States to make such a finding and decide upon the case. Commitment decisions are not appropriate in cases where the Commission intends to impose a fine.

(14) In exceptional cases where the public interest of the Community so requires, it may also be expedient for the Commission to adopt a decision of a declaratory nature finding that the prohibition in Article 81 or Article 82 of the Treaty does not apply, with a view to clarifying the law and ensuring its consistent application throughout the Community, in particular with regard to new types of agreements or practices that have not been settled in the existing case-law and administrative practice.

(15) The Commission and the competition authorities of the Member States should form together a network of public authorities applying the Community competition rules in close cooperation. For that purpose it is necessary to set up arrangements for information and consultation. Further modalities for the cooperation within the network will be laid down and revised by the Commission, in close cooperation with the Member States.

(16) Notwithstanding any national provision to the contrary, the exchange of information and the use of such information in evidence should be allowed between the members of the network even where the information is confidential. This information may be used for the application of Articles 81 and 82 of the Treaty as well as for the parallel application of national competition law, provided that the latter application relates to the same case and does not lead to a different outcome. When the information exchanged is used by the receiving authority to impose sanctions on undertakings, there should be no other limit to the use of the information than the obligation to use it for the purpose for which it was collected given the fact that the sanctions imposed on undertakings are of the same type in all systems. The rights of defence enjoyed by undertakings in the various systems can be considered as sufficiently equivalent. However, as regards natural persons, they may be subject to substantially different types of sanctions across the various systems. Where that is the case, it is necessary to ensure that information can only be used if it has been collected in a way which respects the same level of protection

of the rights of defence of natural persons as provided for under the national rules of the receiving authority.

(17) If the competition rules are to be applied consistently and, at the same time, the network is to be managed in the best possible way, it is essential to retain the rule that the competition authorities of the Member States are automatically relieved of their competence if the Commission initiates its own proceedings. Where a competition authority of a Member State is already acting on a case and the Commission intends to initiate proceedings, it should endeavour to do so as soon as possible. Before initiating proceedings, the Commission should consult the national authority concerned.

(18) To ensure that cases are dealt with by the most appropriate authorities within the network, a general provision should be laid down allowing a competition authority to suspend or close a case on the ground that another authority is dealing with it or has already dealt with it, the objective being that each case should be handled by a single authority. This provision should not prevent the Commission from rejecting a complaint for lack of Community interest, as the case-law of the Court of Justice has acknowledged it may do, even if no other competition authority has indicated its intention of dealing with the case.

(19) The Advisory Committee on Restrictive Practices and Dominant Positions set up by Regulation No 17 has functioned in a very satisfactory manner. It will fit well into the new system of decentralised application. It is necessary, therefore, to build upon the rules laid down by Regulation No 17, while improving the effectiveness of the organisational arrangements. To this end, it would be expedient to allow opinions to be delivered by written procedure. The Advisory Committee should also be able to act as a forum for discussing cases that are being handled by the competition authorities of the Member States, so as to help safeguard the consistent application of the Community competition rules.

(20) The Advisory Committee should be composed of representatives of the competition authorities of the Member States. For meetings in which general issues are being discussed, Member States should be able to appoint an additional representative. This is without prejudice to members of the Committee being assisted by other experts from the Member States.

(21) Consistency in the application of the competition rules also requires that arrangements be established for cooperation between the courts of the Member States and the Commission. This is relevant for all courts of the Member States that apply Articles 81 and 82 of the Treaty, whether applying these rules in lawsuits between private parties, acting as public enforcers or as review courts. In particular, national courts should be able to ask the Commission for information or for its opinion on points concerning the application of Community competition law. The Commission and the competition authorities of the Member States should also be able to submit written or oral observations to courts called upon to apply Article 81 or Article 82 of the Treaty. These observations should be submitted within the framework of national procedural rules and practices including those safeguarding the rights of the parties. Steps should therefore be taken to ensure

that the Commission and the competition authorities of the Member States are kept sufficiently well informed of proceedings before national courts.

(22) In order to ensure compliance with the principles of legal certainty and the uniform application of the Community competition rules in a system of parallel powers, conflicting decisions must be avoided. It is therefore necessary to clarify, in accordance with the case-law of the Court of Justice, the effects of Commission decisions and proceedings on courts and competition authorities of the Member States. Commitment decisions adopted by the Commission do not affect the power of the courts and the competition authorities of the Member States to apply Articles 81 and 82 of the Treaty.

(23) The Commission should be empowered throughout the Community to require such information to be supplied as is necessary to detect any agreement, decision or concerted practice prohibited by Article 81 of the Treaty or any abuse of a dominant position prohibited by Article 82 of the Treaty. When complying with a decision of the Commission, undertakings cannot be forced to admit that they have committed an infringement, but they are in any event obliged to answer factual questions and to provide documents, even if this information may be used to establish against them or against another undertaking the existence of an infringement.

(24) The Commission should also be empowered to undertake such inspections as are necessary to detect any agreement, decision or concerted practice prohibited by Article 81 of the Treaty or any abuse of a dominant position prohibited by Article 82 of the Treaty. The competition authorities of the Member States should cooperate actively in the exercise of these powers.

(25) The detection of infringements of the competition rules is growing ever more difficult, and, in order to protect competition effectively, the Commission's powers of investigation need to be supplemented. The Commission should in particular be empowered to interview any persons who may be in possession of useful information and to record the statements made. In the course of an inspection, officials authorised by the Commission should be empowered to affix seals for the period of time necessary for the inspection. Seals should normally not be affixed for more than 72 hours. Officials authorised by the Commission should also be empowered to ask for any information relevant to the subject matter and purpose of the inspection.

(26) Experience has shown that there are cases where business records are kept in the homes of directors or other people working for an undertaking. In order to safeguard the effectiveness of inspections, therefore, officials and other persons authorised by the Commission should be empowered to enter any premises where business records may be kept, including private homes. However, the exercise of this latter power should be subject to the authorisation of the judicial authority.

(27) Without prejudice to the case-law of the Court of Justice, it is useful to set out the scope of the control that the national judicial authority may carry out when it authorises, as foreseen by national law including as a precautionary measure, assistance from law enforcement authorities in order to overcome possible opposition on the part of the undertaking or the execution of the decision to carry out inspections

in non-business premises. It results from the case-law that the national judicial authority may in particular ask the Commission for further information which it needs to carry out its control and in the absence of which it could refuse the authorisation. The case-law also confirms the competence of the national courts to control the application of national rules governing the implementation of coercive measures.

(28) In order to help the competition authorities of the Member States to apply Articles 81 and 82 of the Treaty effectively, it is expedient to enable them to assist one another by carrying out inspections and other fact-finding measures.

(29) Compliance with Articles 81 and 82 of the Treaty and the fulfilment of the obligations imposed on undertakings and associations of undertakings under this Regulation should be enforceable by means of fines and periodic penalty payments. To that end, appropriate levels of fine should also be laid down for infringements of the procedural rules.

(30) In order to ensure effective recovery of fines imposed on associations of undertakings for infringements that they have committed, it is necessary to lay down the conditions on which the Commission may require payment of the fine from the members of the association where the association is not solvent. In doing so, the Commission should have regard to the relative size of the undertakings belonging to the association and in particular to the situation of small and medium-sized enterprises. Payment of the fine by one or several members of an association is without prejudice to rules of national law that provide for recovery of the amount paid from other members of the association.

(31) The rules on periods of limitation for the imposition of fines and periodic penalty payments were laid down in Council Regulation (EEC) No 2988/74(11), which also concerns penalties in the field of transport. In a system of parallel powers, the acts, which may interrupt a limitation period, should include procedural steps taken independently by the competition authority of a Member State. To clarify the legal framework, Regulation (EEC) No 2988/74 should therefore be amended to prevent it applying to matters covered by this Regulation, and this Regulation should include provisions on periods of limitation.

(32) The undertakings concerned should be accorded the right to be heard by the Commission, third parties whose interests may be affected by a decision should be given the opportunity of submitting their observations beforehand, and the decisions taken should be widely publicised. While ensuring the rights of defence of the undertakings concerned, in particular, the right of access to the file, it is essential that business secrets be protected. The confidentiality of information exchanged in the network should likewise be safeguarded.

(33) Since all decisions taken by the Commission under this Regulation are subject to review by the Court of Justice in accordance with the Treaty, the Court of Justice should, in accordance with Article 229 thereof be given unlimited jurisdiction in respect of decisions by which the Commission imposes fines or periodic penalty payments.

(34) The principles laid down in Articles 81 and 82 of the Treaty, as they have been applied by Regulation No 17, have given a central role to the Community bodies. This

central role should be retained, whilst associating the Member States more closely with the application of the Community competition rules. In accordance with the principles of subsidiarity and proportionality as set out in Article 5 of the Treaty, this Regulation does not go beyond what is necessary in order to achieve its objective, which is to allow the Community competition rules to be applied effectively.

(35) In order to attain a proper enforcement of Community competition law, Member States should designate and empower authorities to apply Articles 81 and 82 of the Treaty as public enforcers. They should be able to designate administrative as well as judicial authorities to carry out the various functions conferred upon competition authorities in this Regulation. This Regulation recognises the wide variation which exists in the public enforcement systems of Member States. The effects of Article 11(6) of this Regulation should apply to all competition authorities. As an exception to this general rule, where a prosecuting authority brings a case before a separate judicial authority, Article 11(6) should apply to the prosecuting authority subject to the conditions in Article 35(4) of this Regulation. Where these conditions are not fulfilled, the general rule should apply. In any case, Article 11(6) should not apply to courts insofar as they are acting as review courts.

(36) As the case-law has made it clear that the competition rules apply to transport, that sector should be made subject to the procedural provisions of this Regulation. Council Regulation No 141 of 26 November 1962 exempting transport from the application of Regulation No 17(12) should therefore be repealed and Regulations (EEC) No 1017/68(13), (EEC) No 4056/86(14) and (EEC) No 3975/87(15) should be amended in order to delete the specific procedural provisions they contain.

(37) This Regulation respects the fundamental rights and observes the principles recognised in particular by the Charter of Fundamental Rights of the European Union. Accordingly, this Regulation should be interpreted and applied with respect to those rights and principles.

(38) Legal certainty for undertakings operating under the Community competition rules contributes to the promotion of innovation and investment. Where cases give rise to genuine uncertainty because they present novel or unresolved questions for the application of these rules, individual undertakings may wish to seek informal guidance from the Commission. This Regulation is without prejudice to the ability of the Commission to issue such informal guidance,

HAS ADOPTED THIS REGULATION:

CHAPTER I PRINCIPLES

Article 1 Application of Articles 81 and 82 of the Treaty

1. Agreements, decisions and concerted practices caught by Article 81(1) of the Treaty which do not satisfy the conditions of Article 81(3) of the Treaty shall be prohibited, no prior decision to that effect being required.

2. Agreements, decisions and concerted practices caught by Article 81(1) of the Treaty which satisfy the conditions of Article 81(3) of the Treaty shall not be prohibited, no prior decision to that effect being required.

3. The abuse of a dominant position referred to in Article 82 of the Treaty shall be prohibited, no prior decision to that effect being required.

Article 2   Burden of proof

In any national or Community proceedings for the application of Articles 81 and 82 of the Treaty, the burden of proving an infringement of Article 81(1) or of Article 82 of the Treaty shall rest on the party or the authority alleging the infringement. The undertaking or association of undertakings claiming the benefit of Article 81(3) of the Treaty shall bear the burden of proving that the conditions of that paragraph are fulfilled.

Article 3   Relationship between Articles 81 and 82 of the Treaty and national competition laws

1. Where the competition authorities of the Member States or national courts apply national competition law to agreements, decisions by associations of undertakings or concerted practices within the meaning of Article 81(1) of the Treaty which may affect trade between Member States within the meaning of that provision, they shall also apply Article 81 of the Treaty to such agreements, decisions or concerted practices. Where the competition authorities of the Member States or national courts apply national competition law to any abuse prohibited by Article 82 of the Treaty, they shall also apply Article 82 of the Treaty.

2. The application of national competition law may not lead to the prohibition of agreements, decisions by associations of undertakings or concerted practices which may affect trade between Member States but which do not restrict competition within the meaning of Article 81(1) of the Treaty, or which fulfil the conditions of Article 81(3) of the Treaty or which are covered by a Regulation for the application of Article 81(3) of the Treaty. Member States shall not under this Regulation be precluded from adopting and applying on their territory stricter national laws which prohibit or sanction unilateral conduct engaged in by undertakings.

3. Without prejudice to general principles and other provisions of Community law, paragraphs 1 and 2 do not apply when the competition authorities and the courts of the Member States apply national merger control laws nor do they preclude the application of provisions of national law that predominantly pursue an objective different from that pursued by Articles 81 and 82 of the Treaty.

CHAPTER II POWERS

Article 4 Powers of the Commission

For the purpose of applying Articles 81 and 82 of the Treaty, the Commission shall have the powers provided for by this Regulation.

Article 5 Powers of the competition authorities of the Member States

The competition authorities of the Member States shall have the power to apply Articles 81 and 82 of the Treaty in individual cases. For this purpose, acting on their own initiative or on a complaint, they may take the following decisions:

- requiring that an infringement be brought to an end,

- ordering interim measures,

- accepting commitments,

- imposing fines, periodic penalty payments or any other penalty provided for in their national law.

Where on the basis of the information in their possession the conditions for prohibition are not met they may likewise decide that there are no grounds for action on their part.

Article 6 Powers of the national courts

National courts shall have the power to apply Articles 81 and 82 of the Treaty.

CHAPTER III COMMISSION DECISIONS

Article 7 Finding and termination of infringement

1. Where the Commission, acting on a complaint or on its own initiative, finds that there is an infringement of Article 81 or of Article 82 of the Treaty, it may by decision require the undertakings and associations of undertakings concerned to bring such infringement to an end. For this purpose, it may impose on them any behavioural or structural remedies which are proportionate to the infringement committed and necessary to bring the infringement effectively to an end. Structural remedies can only be imposed either where there is no equally effective behavioural remedy or where any equally effective behavioural remedy would be more burdensome for the undertaking concerned than the structural remedy. If the Commission has a legitimate interest in doing so, it may also find that an infringement has been committed in the past.

2. Those entitled to lodge a complaint for the purposes of paragraph 1 are natural or legal persons who can show a legitimate interest and Member States.

Article 8 Interim measures

1. In cases of urgency due to the risk of serious and irreparable damage to competition, the Commission, acting on its own initiative may by decision, on the basis of a prima facie finding of infringement, order interim measures.

2. A decision under paragraph 1 shall apply for a specified period of time and may be renewed in so far this is necessary and appropriate.

Article 9 Commitments

1. Where the Commission intends to adopt a decision requiring that an infringement be brought to an end and the undertakings concerned offer commitments to meet the concerns expressed to them by the Commission in its preliminary assessment, the Commission may by decision make those commitments binding on the undertakings. Such a decision may be adopted for a specified period and shall conclude that there are no longer grounds for action by the Commission.

2. The Commission may, upon request or on its own initiative, reopen the proceedings:

(a) where there has been a material change in any of the facts on which the decision was based;

(b) where the undertakings concerned act contrary to their commitments; or

(c) where the decision was based on incomplete, incorrect or misleading information provided by the parties.

Article 10 Finding of inapplicability

Where the Community public interest relating to the application of Articles 81 and 82 of the Treaty so requires, the Commission, acting on its own initiative, may by decision find that Article 81 of the Treaty is not applicable to an agreement, a decision by an association of undertakings or a concerted practice, either because the conditions of Article 81(1) of the Treaty are not fulfilled, or because the conditions of Article 81(3) of the Treaty are satisfied.

The Commission may likewise make such a finding with reference to Article 82 of the Treaty.

CHAPTER IV   COOPERATION

Article 11   Cooperation between the Commission and the competition authorities of the Member States

1. The Commission and the competition authorities of the Member States shall apply the Community competition rules in close cooperation.

2. The Commission shall transmit to the competition authorities of the Member States copies of the most important documents it has collected with a view to applying Articles 7, 8, 9, 10 and Article 29(1). At the request of the competition authority of a Member State, the Commission shall provide it with a copy of other existing documents necessary for the assessment of the case.

3. The competition authorities of the Member States shall, when acting under Article 81 or Article 82 of the Treaty, inform the Commission in writing before or without delay after commencing the first formal investigative measure. This information may also be made available to the competition authorities of the other Member States.

4. No later than 30 days before the adoption of a decision requiring that an infringement be brought to an end, accepting commitments or withdrawing the benefit of a block exemption Regulation, the competition authorities of the Member States shall inform the Commission. To that effect, they shall provide the Commission with a summary of the case, the envisaged decision or, in the absence thereof, any other document indicating the proposed course of action. This information may also be made available to the competition authorities of the other Member States. At the request of the Commission, the acting competition authority shall make available to the Commission other documents it holds which are necessary for the assessment of the case. The information supplied to the Commission may be made available to the competition authorities of the other Member States. National competition authorities may also exchange between themselves information necessary for the assessment of a case that they are dealing with under Article 81 or Article 82 of the Treaty.

5. The competition authorities of the Member States may consult the Commission on any case involving the application of Community law.

6. The initiation by the Commission of proceedings for the adoption of a decision under Chapter III shall relieve the competition authorities of the Member States of their competence to apply Articles 81 and 82 of the Treaty. If a competition authority of a Member State is already acting on a case, the Commission shall only initiate proceedings after consulting with that national competition authority.

Article 12   Exchange of information

1. For the purpose of applying Articles 81 and 82 of the Treaty the Commission and the competition authorities of the Member States shall have the power to

provide one another with and use in evidence any matter of fact or of law, including confidential information.

2. Information exchanged shall only be used in evidence for the purpose of applying Article 81 or Article 82 of the Treaty and in respect of the subject-matter for which it was collected by the transmitting authority. However, where national competition law is applied in the same case and in parallel to Community competition law and does not lead to a different outcome, information exchanged under this Article may also be used for the application of national competition law.

3. Information exchanged pursuant to paragraph 1 can only be used in evidence to impose sanctions on natural persons where:

- the law of the transmitting authority foresees sanctions of a similar kind in relation to an infringement of Article 81 or Article 82 of the Treaty or, in the absence thereof,

- the information has been collected in a way which respects the same level of protection of the rights of defence of natural persons as provided for under the national rules of the receiving authority. However, in this case, the information exchanged cannot be used by the receiving authority to impose custodial sanctions.

Article 13 Suspension or termination of proceedings

1. Where competition authorities of two or more Member States have received a complaint or are acting on their own initiative under Article 81 or Article 82 of the Treaty against the same agreement, decision of an association or practice, the fact that one authority is dealing with the case shall be sufficient grounds for the others to suspend the proceedings before them or to reject the complaint. The Commission may likewise reject a complaint on the ground that a competition authority of a Member State is dealing with the case.

2. Where a competition authority of a Member State or the Commission has received a complaint against an agreement, decision of an association or practice which has already been dealt with by another competition authority, it may reject it.

Article 14 Advisory Committee

1. The Commission shall consult an Advisory Committee on Restrictive Practices and Dominant Positions prior to the taking of any decision under Articles 7, 8, 9, 10, 23, Article 24(2) and Article 29(1).

2. For the discussion of individual cases, the Advisory Committee shall be composed of representatives of the competition authorities of the Member States. For meetings in which issues other than individual cases are being discussed, an additional Member State representative competent in competition matters may be appointed. Representatives may, if unable to attend, be replaced by other representatives.

3. The consultation may take place at a meeting convened and chaired by the Commission, held not earlier than 14 days after dispatch of the notice convening it, together with a summary of the case, an indication of the most important documents and a preliminary draft decision. In respect of decisions pursuant to Article 8, the meeting may be held seven days after the dispatch of the operative part of a draft decision. Where the Commission dispatches a notice convening the meeting which gives a shorter period of notice than those specified above, the meeting may take place on the proposed date in the absence of an objection by any Member State. The Advisory Committee shall deliver a written opinion on the Commission's preliminary draft decision. It may deliver an opinion even if some members are absent and are not represented. At the request of one or several members, the positions stated in the opinion shall be reasoned.

4. Consultation may also take place by written procedure. However, if any Member State so requests, the Commission shall convene a meeting. In case of written procedure, the Commission shall determine a time-limit of not less than 14 days within which the Member States are to put forward their observations for circulation to all other Member States. In case of decisions to be taken pursuant to Article 8, the time-limit of 14 days is replaced by seven days. Where the Commission determines a time-limit for the written procedure which is shorter than those specified above, the proposed time-limit shall be applicable in the absence of an objection by any Member State.

5. The Commission shall take the utmost account of the opinion delivered by the Advisory Committee. It shall inform the Committee of the manner in which its opinion has been taken into account.

6. Where the Advisory Committee delivers a written opinion, this opinion shall be appended to the draft decision. If the Advisory Committee recommends publication of the opinion, the Commission shall carry out such publication taking into account the legitimate interest of undertakings in the protection of their business secrets.

7. At the request of a competition authority of a Member State, the Commission shall include on the agenda of the Advisory Committee cases that are being dealt with by a competition authority of a Member State under Article 81 or Article 82 of the Treaty. The Commission may also do so on its own initiative. In either case, the Commission shall inform the competition authority concerned.

A request may in particular be made by a competition authority of a Member State in respect of a case where the Commission intends to initiate proceedings with the effect of Article 11(6).

The Advisory Committee shall not issue opinions on cases dealt with by competition authorities of the Member States. The Advisory Committee may also discuss general issues of Community competition law.

Article 15   Cooperation with national courts

1. In proceedings for the application of Article 81 or Article 82 of the Treaty, courts of the Member States may ask the Commission to transmit to them information in its possession or its opinion on questions concerning the application of the Community competition rules.

2. Member States shall forward to the Commission a copy of any written judgment of national courts deciding on the application of Article 81 or Article 82 of the Treaty. Such copy shall be forwarded without delay after the full written judgment is notified to the parties.

3. Competition authorities of the Member States, acting on their own initiative, may submit written observations to the national courts of their Member State on issues relating to the application of Article 81 or Article 82 of the Treaty. With the permission of the court in question, they may also submit oral observations to the national courts of their Member State. Where the coherent application of Article 81 or Article 82 of the Treaty so requires, the Commission, acting on its own initiative, may submit written observations to courts of the Member States. With the permission of the court in question, it may also make oral observations.

For the purpose of the preparation of their observations only, the competition authorities of the Member States and the Commission may request the relevant court of the Member State to transmit or ensure the transmission to them of any documents necessary for the assessment of the case.

4. This Article is without prejudice to wider powers to make observations before courts conferred on competition authorities of the Member States under the law of their Member State.

Article 16   Uniform application of Community competition law

1. When national courts rule on agreements, decisions or practices under Article 81 or Article 82 of the Treaty which are already the subject of a Commission decision, they cannot take decisions running counter to the decision adopted by the Commission. They must also avoid giving decisions which would conflict with a decision contemplated by the Commission in proceedings it has initiated. To that effect, the national court may assess whether it is necessary to stay its proceedings. This obligation is without prejudice to the rights and obligations under Article 234 of the Treaty.

2. When competition authorities of the Member States rule on agreements, decisions or practices under Article 81 or Article 82 of the Treaty which are already the subject of a Commission decision, they cannot take decisions which would run counter to the decision adopted by the Commission.

CHAPTER V POWERS OF INVESTIGATION

Article 17 Investigations into sectors of the economy and into types of agreements

1. Where the trend of trade between Member States, the rigidity of prices or other circumstances suggest that competition may be restricted or distorted within the common market, the Commission may conduct its inquiry into a particular sector of the economy or into a particular type of agreements across various sectors. In the course of that inquiry, the Commission may request the undertakings or associations of undertakings concerned to supply the information necessary for giving effect to Articles 81 and 82 of the Treaty and may carry out any inspections necessary for that purpose.

The Commission may in particular request the undertakings or associations of undertakings concerned to communicate to it all agreements, decisions and concerted practices.

The Commission may publish a report on the results of its inquiry into particular sectors of the economy or particular types of agreements across various sectors and invite comments from interested parties.

2. Articles 14, 18, 19, 20, 22, 23 and 24 shall apply mutatis mutandis.

Article 18 Requests for information

1. In order to carry out the duties assigned to it by this Regulation, the Commission may, by simple request or by decision, require undertakings and associations of undertakings to provide all necessary information.

2. When sending a simple request for information to an undertaking or association of undertakings, the Commission shall state the legal basis and the purpose of the request, specify what information is required and fix the time-limit within which the information is to be provided, and the penalties provided for in Article 23 for supplying incorrect or misleading information.

3. Where the Commission requires undertakings and associations of undertakings to supply information by decision, it shall state the legal basis and the purpose of the request, specify what information is required and fix the time-limit within which it is to be provided. It shall also indicate the penalties provided for in Article 23 and indicate or impose the penalties provided for in Article 24. It shall further indicate the right to have the decision reviewed by the Court of Justice.

4. The owners of the undertakings or their representatives and, in the case of legal persons, companies or firms, or associations having no legal personality, the persons authorised to represent them by law or by their constitution shall supply the information requested on behalf of the undertaking or the association of undertakings concerned. Lawyers duly authorised to act may supply the information on behalf of their clients. The latter shall remain fully responsible if the information supplied is incomplete, incorrect or misleading.

5. The Commission shall without delay forward a copy of the simple request or of the decision to the competition authority of the Member State in whose territory the seat of the undertaking or association of undertakings is situated and the competition authority of the Member State whose territory is affected.

6. At the request of the Commission the governments and competition authorities of the Member States shall provide the Commission with all necessary information to carry out the duties assigned to it by this Regulation.

Article 19 Power to take statements

1. In order to carry out the duties assigned to it by this Regulation, the Commission may interview any natural or legal person who consents to be interviewed for the purpose of collecting information relating to the subject-matter of an investigation.

2. Where an interview pursuant to paragraph 1 is conducted in the premises of an undertaking, the Commission shall inform the competition authority of the Member State in whose territory the interview takes place. If so requested by the competition authority of that Member State, its officials may assist the officials and other accompanying persons authorised by the Commission to conduct the interview.

Article 20 The Commission's powers of inspection

1. In order to carry out the duties assigned to it by this Regulation, the Commission may conduct all necessary inspections of undertakings and associations of undertakings.

2. The officials and other accompanying persons authorised by the Commission to conduct an inspection are empowered:

(a) to enter any premises, land and means of transport of undertakings and associations of undertakings;

(b) to examine the books and other records related to the business, irrespective of the medium on which they are stored;

(c) to take or obtain in any form copies of or extracts from such books or records;

(d) to seal any business premises and books or records for the period and to the extent necessary for the inspection;

(e) to ask any representative or member of staff of the undertaking or association of undertakings for explanations on facts or documents relating to the subject-matter and purpose of the inspection and to record the answers.

3. The officials and other accompanying persons authorised by the Commission to conduct an inspection shall exercise their powers upon production of a written authorisation specifying the subject matter and purpose of the

inspection and the penalties provided for in Article 23 in case the production of the required books or other records related to the business is incomplete or where the answers to questions asked under paragraph 2 of the present Article are incorrect or misleading. In good time before the inspection, the Commission shall give notice of the inspection to the competition authority of the Member State in whose territory it is to be conducted.

4. Undertakings and associations of undertakings are required to submit to inspections ordered by decision of the Commission. The decision shall specify the subject matter and purpose of the inspection, appoint the date on which it is to begin and indicate the penalties provided for in Articles 23 and 24 and the right to have the decision reviewed by the Court of Justice. The Commission shall take such decisions after consulting the competition authority of the Member State in whose territory the inspection is to be conducted.

5. Officials of as well as those authorised or appointed by the competition authority of the Member State in whose territory the inspection is to be conducted shall, at the request of that authority or of the Commission, actively assist the officials and other accompanying persons authorised by the Commission. To this end, they shall enjoy the powers specified in paragraph 2.

6. Where the officials and other accompanying persons authorised by the Commission find that an undertaking opposes an inspection ordered pursuant to this Article, the Member State concerned shall afford them the necessary assistance, requesting where appropriate the assistance of the police or of an equivalent enforcement authority, so as to enable them to conduct their inspection.

7. If the assistance provided for in paragraph 6 requires authorisation from a judicial authority according to national rules, such authorisation shall be applied for. Such authorisation may also be applied for as a precautionary measure.

8. Where authorisation as referred to in paragraph 7 is applied for, the national judicial authority shall control that the Commission decision is authentic and that the coercive measures envisaged are neither arbitrary nor excessive having regard to the subject matter of the inspection. In its control of the proportionality of the coercive measures, the national judicial authority may ask the Commission, directly or through the Member State competition authority, for detailed explanations in particular on the grounds the Commission has for suspecting infringement of Articles 81 and 82 of the Treaty, as well as on the seriousness of the suspected infringement and on the nature of the involvement of the undertaking concerned. However, the national judicial authority may not call into question the necessity for the inspection nor demand that it be provided with the information in the Commission's file. The lawfulness of the Commission decision shall be subject to review only by the Court of Justice.

Article 21   Inspection of other premises

1. If a reasonable suspicion exists that books or other records related to the business and to the subject-matter of the inspection, which may be relevant to

prove a serious violation of Article 81 or Article 82 of the Treaty, are being kept in any other premises, land and means of transport, including the homes of directors, managers and other members of staff of the undertakings and associations of undertakings concerned, the Commission can by decision order an inspection to be conducted in such other premises, land and means of transport.

2. The decision shall specify the subject matter and purpose of the inspection, appoint the date on which it is to begin and indicate the right to have the decision reviewed by the Court of Justice. It shall in particular state the reasons that have led the Commission to conclude that a suspicion in the sense of paragraph 1 exists. The Commission shall take such decisions after consulting the competition authority of the Member State in whose territory the inspection is to be conducted.

3. A decision adopted pursuant to paragraph 1 cannot be executed without prior authorisation from the national judicial authority of the Member State concerned. The national judicial authority shall control that the Commission decision is authentic and that the coercive measures envisaged are neither arbitrary nor excessive having regard in particular to the seriousness of the suspected infringement, to the importance of the evidence sought, to the involvement of the undertaking concerned and to the reasonable likelihood that business books and records relating to the subject matter of the inspection are kept in the premises for which the authorisation is requested. The national judicial authority may ask the Commission, directly or through the Member State competition authority, for detailed explanations on those elements which are necessary to allow its control of the proportionality of the coercive measures envisaged.

However, the national judicial authority may not call into question the necessity for the inspection nor demand that it be provided with information in the Commission's file. The lawfulness of the Commission decision shall be subject to review only by the Court of Justice.

4. The officials and other accompanying persons authorised by the Commission to conduct an inspection ordered in accordance with paragraph 1 of this Article shall have the powers set out in Article 20(2)(a), (b) and (c). Article 20(5) and (6) shall apply mutatis mutandis.

Article 22 Investigations by competition authorities of Member States

1. The competition authority of a Member State may in its own territory carry out any inspection or other fact-finding measure under its national law on behalf and for the account of the competition authority of another Member State in order to establish whether there has been an infringement of Article 81 or Article 82 of the Treaty. Any exchange and use of the information collected shall be carried out in accordance with Article 12.

2. At the request of the Commission, the competition authorities of the Member States shall undertake the inspections which the Commission considers to be necessary under Article 20(1) or which it has ordered by decision pursuant to Article 20(4). The officials of the competition authorities of the Member States who are

responsible for conducting these inspections as well as those authorised or appointed by them shall exercise their powers in accordance with their national law.

If so requested by the Commission or by the competition authority of the Member State in whose territory the inspection is to be conducted, officials and other accompanying persons authorised by the Commission may assist the officials of the authority concerned.

CHAPTER VI PENALTIES

Article 23 Fines

1. The Commission may by decision impose on undertakings and associations of undertakings fines not exceeding 1 % of the total turnover in the preceding business year where, intentionally or negligently:

(a) they supply incorrect or misleading information in response to a request made pursuant to Article 17 or Article 18(2);

(b) in response to a request made by decision adopted pursuant to Article 17 or Article 18(3), they supply incorrect, incomplete or misleading information or do not supply information within the required time-limit;

(c) they produce the required books or other records related to the business in incomplete form during inspections under Article 20 or refuse to submit to inspections ordered by a decision adopted pursuant to Article 20(4);

(d) in response to a question asked in accordance with Article 20(2)(e),

   • they give an incorrect or misleading answer,

   • they fail to rectify within a time-limit set by the Commission an incorrect, incomplete or misleading answer given by a member of staff, or

   • they fail or refuse to provide a complete answer on facts relating to the subject-matter and purpose of an inspection ordered by a decision adopted pursuant to Article 20(4);

(e) seals affixed in accordance with Article 20(2)(d) by officials or other accompanying persons authorised by the Commission have been broken.

2. The Commission may by decision impose fines on undertakings and associations of undertakings where, either intentionally or negligently:

(a) they infringe Article 81 or Article 82 of the Treaty; or

(b) they contravene a decision ordering interim measures under Article 8; or

(c) they fail to comply with a commitment made binding by a decision pursuant to Article 9.

For each undertaking and association of undertakings participating in the infringement, the fine shall not exceed 10 % of its total turnover in the preceding business year.

Where the infringement of an association relates to the activities of its members, the fine shall not exceed 10 % of the sum of the total turnover of each member active on the market affected by the infringement of the association.

3. In fixing the amount of the fine, regard shall be had both to the gravity and to the duration of the infringement.

4. When a fine is imposed on an association of undertakings taking account of the turnover of its members and the association is not solvent, the association is obliged to call for contributions from its members to cover the amount of the fine.

Where such contributions have not been made to the association within a time-limit fixed by the Commission, the Commission may require payment of the fine directly by any of the undertakings whose representatives were members of the decision-making bodies concerned of the association.

After the Commission has required payment under the second subparagraph, where necessary to ensure full payment of the fine, the Commission may require payment of the balance by any of the members of the association which were active on the market on which the infringement occurred.

However, the Commission shall not require payment under the second or the third subparagraph from undertakings which show that they have not implemented the infringing decision of the association and either were not aware of its existence or have actively distanced themselves from it before the Commission started investigating the case.

The financial liability of each undertaking in respect of the payment of the fine shall not exceed 10 % of its total turnover in the preceding business year.

5. Decisions taken pursuant to paragraphs 1 and 2 shall not be of a criminal law nature.

Article 24 Periodic penalty payments

1. The Commission may, by decision, impose on undertakings or associations of undertakings periodic penalty payments not exceeding 5 % of the average daily turnover in the preceding business year per day and calculated from the date appointed by the decision, in order to compel them:

(a) to put an end to an infringement of Article 81 or Article 82 of the Treaty, in accordance with a decision taken pursuant to Article 7;

(b) to comply with a decision ordering interim measures taken pursuant to Article 8;

(c) to comply with a commitment made binding by a decision pursuant to Article 9;

(d) to supply complete and correct information which it has requested by decision taken pursuant to Article 17 or Article 18(3);

(e) to submit to an inspection which it has ordered by decision taken pursuant to Article 20(4).

2. Where the undertakings or associations of undertakings have satisfied the obligation which the periodic penalty payment was intended to enforce, the Commission may fix the definitive amount of the periodic penalty payment at a figure lower than that which would arise under the original decision. Article 23(4) shall apply correspondingly.

CHAPTER VII LIMITATION PERIODS

Article 25 Limitation periods for the imposition of penalties

1. The powers conferred on the Commission by Articles 23 and 24 shall be subject to the following limitation periods:

(a) three years in the case of infringements of provisions concerning requests for information or the conduct of inspections;

(b) five years in the case of all other infringements.

2. Time shall begin to run on the day on which the infringement is committed. However, in the case of continuing or repeated infringements, time shall begin to run on the day on which the infringement ceases.

3. Any action taken by the Commission or by the competition authority of a Member State for the purpose of the investigation or proceedings in respect of an infringement shall interrupt the limitation period for the imposition of fines or periodic penalty payments. The limitation period shall be interrupted with effect from the date on which the action is notified to at least one undertaking or association of undertakings which has participated in the infringement. Actions which interrupt the running of the period shall include in particular the following:

(a) written requests for information by the Commission or by the competition authority of a Member State;

(b) written authorisations to conduct inspections issued to its officials by the Commission or by the competition authority of a Member State;

(c) the initiation of proceedings by the Commission or by the competition authority of a Member State;

(d) notification of the statement of objections of the Commission or of the competition authority of a Member State.

4. The interruption of the limitation period shall apply for all the undertakings or associations of undertakings which have participated in the infringement.

5. Each interruption shall start time running afresh. However, the limitation period shall expire at the latest on the day on which a period equal to twice the limitation period has elapsed without the Commission having imposed a fine or a periodic penalty payment. That period shall be extended by the time during which limitation is suspended pursuant to paragraph 6.

6. The limitation period for the imposition of fines or periodic penalty payments shall be suspended for as long as the decision of the Commission is the subject of proceedings pending before the Court of Justice.

Article 26 Limitation period for the enforcement of penalties

1. The power of the Commission to enforce decisions taken pursuant to Articles 23 and 24 shall be subject to a limitation period of five years.

2. Time shall begin to run on the day on which the decision becomes final.

3. The limitation period for the enforcement of penalties shall be interrupted:

(a) by notification of a decision varying the original amount of the fine or periodic penalty payment or refusing an application for variation;

(b) by any action of the Commission or of a Member State, acting at the request of the Commission, designed to enforce payment of the fine or periodic penalty payment.

4. Each interruption shall start time running afresh.

5. The limitation period for the enforcement of penalties shall be suspended for so long as:

(a) time to pay is allowed;

(b) enforcement of payment is suspended pursuant to a decision of the Court of Justice.

CHAPTER VIII HEARINGS AND PROFESSIONAL SECRECY

Article 27 Hearing of the parties, complainants and others

1. Before taking decisions as provided for in Articles 7, 8, 23 and Article 24(2), the Commission shall give the undertakings or associations of undertakings which are the subject of the proceedings conducted by the Commission the opportunity of being heard on the matters to which the Commission has taken objection. The Commission shall base its decisions only on objections on which the parties concerned have been able to comment. Complainants shall be associated closely with the proceedings.

2. The rights of defence of the parties concerned shall be fully respected in the proceedings. They shall be entitled to have access to the Commission's file, subject

to the legitimate interest of undertakings in the protection of their business secrets. The right of access to the file shall not extend to confidential information and internal documents of the Commission or the competition authorities of the Member States. In particular, the right of access shall not extend to correspondence between the Commission and the competition authorities of the Member States, or between the latter, including documents drawn up pursuant to Articles 11 and 14. Nothing in this paragraph shall prevent the Commission from disclosing and using information necessary to prove an infringement.

3. If the Commission considers it necessary, it may also hear other natural or legal persons. Applications to be heard on the part of such persons shall, where they show a sufficient interest, be granted. The competition authorities of the Member States may also ask the Commission to hear other natural or legal persons.

4. Where the Commission intends to adopt a decision pursuant to Article 9 or Article 10, it shall publish a concise summary of the case and the main content of the commitments or of the proposed course of action. Interested third parties may submit their observations within a time limit which is fixed by the Commission in its publication and which may not be less than one month. Publication shall have regard to the legitimate interest of undertakings in the protection of their business secrets.

Article 28 Professional secrecy

1. Without prejudice to Articles 12 and 15, information collected pursuant to Articles 17 to 22 shall be used only for the purpose for which it was acquired.

2. Without prejudice to the exchange and to the use of information foreseen in Articles 11, 12, 14, 15 and 27, the Commission and the competition authorities of the Member States, their officials, servants and other persons working under the supervision of these authorities as well as officials and civil servants of other authorities of the Member States shall not disclose information acquired or exchanged by them pursuant to this Regulation and of the kind covered by the obligation of professional secrecy. This obligation also applies to all representatives and experts of Member States attending meetings of the Advisory Committee pursuant to Article 14.

CHAPTER IX EXEMPTION REGULATIONS

Article 29 Withdrawal in individual cases

1. Where the Commission, empowered by a Council Regulation, such as Regulations 19/65/EEC, (EEC) No 2821/71, (EEC) No 3976/87, (EEC) No 1534/91 or (EEC) No 479/92, to apply Article 81(3) of the Treaty by regulation, has declared Article 81(1) of the Treaty inapplicable to certain categories of

agreements, decisions by associations of undertakings or concerted practices, it may, acting on its own initiative or on a complaint, withdraw the benefit of such an exemption Regulation when it finds that in any particular case an agreement, decision or concerted practice to which the exemption Regulation applies has certain effects which are incompatible with Article 81(3) of the Treaty.

2. Where, in any particular case, agreements, decisions by associations of undertakings or concerted practices to which a Commission Regulation referred to in paragraph 1 applies have effects which are incompatible with Article 81(3) of the Treaty in the territory of a Member State, or in a part thereof, which has all the characteristics of a distinct geographic market, the competition authority of that Member State may withdraw the benefit of the Regulation in question in respect of that territory.

CHAPTER X GENERAL PROVISIONS

Article 30 Publication of decisions

1. The Commission shall publish the decisions, which it takes pursuant to Articles 7 to 10, 23 and 24.

2. The publication shall state the names of the parties and the main content of the decision, including any penalties imposed. It shall have regard to the legitimate interest of undertakings in the protection of their business secrets.

Article 31 Review by the Court of Justice

The Court of Justice shall have unlimited jurisdiction to review decisions whereby the Commission has fixed a fine or periodic penalty payment. It may cancel, reduce or increase the fine or periodic penalty payment imposed.

Article 32 Exclusions

This Regulation shall not apply to:

(a) international tramp vessel services as defined in Article 1(3)(a) of Regulation (EEC) No 4056/86;

(b) a maritime transport service that takes place exclusively between ports in one and the same Member State as foreseen in Article 1(2) of Regulation (EEC) No 4056/86;

(c) air transport between Community airports and third countries.

Article 33 Implementing provisions

1. The Commission shall be authorised to take such measures as may be appropriate in order to apply this Regulation. The measures may concern, inter alia:

(a) the form, content and other details of complaints lodged pursuant to Article 7 and the procedure for rejecting complaints;

(b) the practical arrangements for the exchange of information and consultations provided for in Article 11;

(c) the practical arrangements for the hearings provided for in Article 27.

2. Before the adoption of any measures pursuant to paragraph 1, the Commission shall publish a draft thereof and invite all interested parties to submit their comments within the time-limit it lays down, which may not be less than one month. Before publishing a draft measure and before adopting it, the Commission shall consult the Advisory Committee on Restrictive Practices and Dominant Positions.

CHAPTER XI TRANSITIONAL, AMENDING AND FINAL PROVISIONS

Article 34 Transitional provisions

1. Applications made to the Commission under Article 2 of Regulation No 17, notifications made under Articles 4 and 5 of that Regulation and the corresponding applications and notifications made under Regulations (EEC) No 1017/68, (EEC) No 4056/86 and (EEC) No 3975/87 shall lapse as from the date of application of this Regulation.

2. Procedural steps taken under Regulation No 17 and Regulations (EEC) No 1017/68, (EEC) No 4056/86 and (EEC) No 3975/87 shall continue to have effect for the purposes of applying this Regulation.

Article 35 Designation of competition authorities of Member States

1. The Member States shall designate the competition authority or authorities responsible for the application of Articles 81 and 82 of the Treaty in such a way that the provisions of this regulation are effectively complied with. The measures necessary to empower those authorities to apply those Articles shall be taken before 1 May 2004. The authorities designated may include courts.

2. When enforcement of Community competition law is entrusted to national administrative and judicial authorities, the Member States may allocate different powers and functions to those different national authorities, whether administrative or judicial.

3. The effects of Article 11(6) apply to the authorities designated by the Member States including courts that exercise functions regarding the preparation and the adoption of the types of decisions foreseen in Article 5. The effects of Article 11(6) do not extend to courts insofar as they act as review courts in respect of the types of decisions foreseen in Article 5.

4. Notwithstanding paragraph 3, in the Member States where, for the adoption of certain types of decisions foreseen in Article 5, an authority brings an action before a judicial authority that is separate and different from the prosecuting authority and provided that the terms of this paragraph are complied with, the effects of Article 11(6) shall be limited to the authority prosecuting the case which shall withdraw its claim before the judicial authority when the Commission opens proceedings and this withdrawal shall bring the national proceedings effectively to an end.

Article 36 Amendment of Regulation (EEC) No 1017/68

Regulation (EEC) No 1017/68 is amended as follows:

1. Article 2 is repealed;

2. in Article 3(1), the words "The prohibition laid down in Article 2" are replaced by the words "The prohibition in Article 81(1) of the Treaty";

3. Article 4 is amended as follows:

(a) In paragraph 1, the words "The agreements, decisions and concerted practices referred to in Article 2" are replaced by the words "Agreements, decisions and concerted practices pursuant to Article 81(1) of the Treaty";

(b) Paragraph 2 is replaced by the following:

"2. If the implementation of any agreement, decision or concerted practice covered by paragraph 1 has, in a given case, effects which are incompatible with the requirements of Article 81(3) of the Treaty, undertakings or associations of undertakings may be required to make such effects cease."

4. Articles 5 to 29 are repealed with the exception of Article 13(3) which continues to apply to decisions adopted pursuant to Article 5 of Regulation (EEC) No 1017/68 prior to the date of application of this Regulation until the date of expiration of those decisions;

5. in Article 30, paragraphs 2, 3 and 4 are deleted.

Article 37 Amendment of Regulation (EEC) No 2988/74

In Regulation (EEC) No 2988/74, the following Article is inserted:

"Article 7a Exclusion

This Regulation shall not apply to measures taken under Council Regulation (EC) No 1/2003 of 16 December 2002 on the implementation of the rules on competition laid down in Articles 81 and 82 of the Treaty(16)."

Article 38 Amendment of Regulation (EEC) No 4056/86

Regulation (EEC) No 4056/86 is amended as follows:

1. Article 7 is amended as follows:

(a) Paragraph 1 is replaced by the following:

"1. Breach of an obligation

Where the persons concerned are in breach of an obligation which, pursuant to Article 5, attaches to the exemption provided for in Article 3, the Commission may, in order to put an end to such breach and under the conditions laid down in Council Regulation (EC) No 1/2003 of 16 December 2002 on the implementation of the rules on competition laid down in Articles 81 and 82 of the Treaty(17) adopt a decision that either prohibits them from carrying out or requires them to perform certain specific acts, or withdraws the benefit of the block exemption which they enjoyed."

(b) Paragraph 2 is amended as follows:

(i) In point (a), the words "under the conditions laid down in Section II" are replaced by the words "under the conditions laid down in Regulation (EC) No 1/2003";

(ii) The second sentence of the second subparagraph of point (c)(i) is replaced by the following:

"At the same time it shall decide, in accordance with Article 9 of Regulation (EC) No 1/2003, whether to accept commitments offered by the undertakings concerned with a view, inter alia, to obtaining access to the market for non-conference lines."

2. Article 8 is amended as follows:

(a) Paragraph 1 is deleted.

(b) In paragraph 2 the words "pursuant to Article 10" are replaced by the words "pursuant to Regulation (EC) No 1/2003".

(c) Paragraph 3 is deleted;

3. Article 9 is amended as follows:

(a) In paragraph 1, the words "Advisory Committee referred to in Article 15" are replaced by the words "Advisory Committee referred to in Article 14 of Regulation (EC) No 1/2003";

(b) In paragraph 2, the words "Advisory Committee as referred to in Article 15" are replaced by the words "Advisory Committee referred to in Article 14 of Regulation (EC) No 1/2003";

4. Articles 10 to 25 are repealed with the exception of Article 13(3) which continues to apply to decisions adopted pursuant to Article 81(3) of the Treaty prior to the date of application of this Regulation until the date of expiration of those decisions;

5. in Article 26, the words "the form, content and other details of complaints pursuant to Article 10, applications pursuant to Article 12 and the hearings provided for in Article 23(1) and (2)" are deleted.

Article 39 Amendment of Regulation (EEC) No 3975/87

Articles 3 to 19 of Regulation (EEC) No 3975/87 are repealed with the exception of Article 6(3) which continues to apply to decisions adopted pursuant to Article 81(3) of the Treaty prior to the date of application of this Regulation until the date of expiration of those decisions.

Article 40 Amendment of Regulations No 19/65/EEC, (EEC) No 2821/71 and (EEC) No 1534/91

Article 7 of Regulation No 19/65/EEC, Article 7 of Regulation (EEC) No 2821/71 and Article 7 of Regulation (EEC) No 1534/91 are repealed.

Article 41 Amendment of Regulation (EEC) No 3976/87

Regulation (EEC) No 3976/87 is amended as follows:

1. Article 6 is replaced by the following:

"Article 6

The Commission shall consult the Advisory Committee referred to in Article 14 of Council Regulation (EC) No 1/2003 of 16 December 2002 on the implementation of the rules on competition laid down in Articles 81 and 82 of the Treaty(18) before publishing a draft Regulation and before adopting a Regulation."

2. Article 7 is repealed.

Article 42 Amendment of Regulation (EEC) No 479/92

Regulation (EEC) No 479/92 is amended as follows:

1. Article 5 is replaced by the following:

"Article 5

Before publishing the draft Regulation and before adopting the Regulation, the Commission shall consult the Advisory Committee referred to in

Article 14 of Council Regulation (EC) No 1/2003 of 16 December 2002 on the implementation of the rules on competition laid down in Articles 81 and 82 of the Treaty(19)."

2. Article 6 is repealed.

Article 43 Repeal of Regulations No 17 and No 141

1. Regulation No 17 is repealed with the exception of Article 8(3) which continues to apply to decisions adopted pursuant to Article 81(3) of the Treaty prior to the date of application of this Regulation until the date of expiration of those decisions.

2. Regulation No 141 is repealed.

3. References to the repealed Regulations shall be construed as references to this Regulation.

Article 44 Report on the application of the present Regulation

Five years from the date of application of this Regulation, the Commission shall report to the European Parliament and the Council on the functioning of this Regulation, in particular on the application of Article 11(6) and Article 17.

On the basis of this report, the Commission shall assess whether it is appropriate to propose to the Council a revision of this Regulation.

Article 45 Entry into force

This Regulation shall enter into force on the 20th day following that of its publication in the Official Journal of the European Communities.

It shall apply from 1 May 2004.

This Regulation shall be binding in its entirety and directly applicable in all Member States.

Done at Brussels, 16 December 2002.

For the Council
The President
M. Fischer Boel

(1) OJ C 365 E, 19.12.2000, p. 284.
(2) OJ C 72 E, 21.3.2002, p. 305.
(3) OJ C 155, 29.5.2001, p. 73.
(4) The title of Regulation No 17 has been adjusted to take account of the renumbering of the Articles of the EC Treaty, in accordance with Article 12 of the Treaty of Amsterdam; the original reference was to Articles 85 and 86 of the Treaty.

(5) OJ 13, 21.2.1962, p. 204/62. Regulation as last amended by Regulation (EC) No 1216/1999 (OJ L 148, 15.6.1999, p. 5).

(6) Council Regulation No 19/65/EEC of 2 March 1965 on the application of Article 81(3) (The titles of the Regulations have been adjusted to take account of the renumbering of the Articles of the EC Treaty, in accordance with Article 12 of the Treaty of Amsterdam; the original reference was to Article 85(3) of the Treaty) of the Treaty to certain categories of agreements and concerted practices (OJ 36, 6.3.1965, p. 533). Regulation as last amended by Regulation (EC) No 1215/1999 (OJ L 148, 15.6.1999, p. 1).

(7) Council Regulation (EEC) No 2821/71 of 20 December 1971 on the application of Article 81(3) (The titles of the Regulations have been adjusted to take account of the renumbering of the Articles of the EC Treaty, in accordance with Article 12 of the Treaty of Amsterdam; the original reference was to Article 85(3) of the Treaty) of the Treaty to categories of agreements, decisions and concerted practices (OJ L 285, 29.12.1971, p. 46). Regulation as last amended by the Act of Accession of 1994.

(8) Council Regulation (EEC) No 3976/87 of 14 December 1987 on the application of Article 81(3) (The titles of the Regulations have been adjusted to take account of the renumbering of the Articles of the EC Treaty, in accordance with Article 12 of the Treaty of Amsterdam; the original reference was to Article 85(3) of the Treaty) of the Treaty to certain categories of agreements and concerted practices in the air transport sector (OJ L 374, 31.12.1987, p. 9). Regulation as last amended by the Act of Accession of 1994.

(9) Council Regulation (EEC) No 1534/91 of 31 May 1991 on the application of Article 81(3) (The titles of the Regulations have been adjusted to take account of the renumbering of the Articles of the EC Treaty, in accordance with Article 12 of the Treaty of Amsterdam; the original reference was to Article 85(3) of the Treaty) of the Treaty to certain categories of agreements, decisions and concerted practices in the insurance sector (OJ L 143, 7.6.1991, p. 1).

(10) Council Regulation (EEC) No 479/92 of 25 February 1992 on the application of Article 81(3) (The titles of the Regulations have been adjusted to take account of the renumbering of the Articles of the EC Treaty, in accordance with Article 12 of the Treaty of Amsterdam; the original reference was to Article 85(3) of the Treaty) of the Treaty to certain categories of agreements, decisions and concerted practices between liner shipping companies (Consortia) (OJ L 55, 29.2.1992, p. 3). Regulation amended by the Act of Accession of 1994.

(11) Council Regulation (EEC) No 2988/74 of 26 November 1974 concerning limitation periods in proceedings and the enforcement of sanctions under the rules of the European Economic Community relating to transport and competition (OJ L 319, 29.11.1974, p. 1).

(12) OJ 124, 28.11.1962, p. 2751/62; Regulation as last amended by Regulation No 1002/67/EEC (OJ 306, 16.12.1967, p. 1).

(13) Council Regulation (EEC) No 1017/68 of 19 July 1968 applying rules of competition to transport by rail, road and inland waterway (OJ L 175, 23.7.1968, p. 1). Regulation as last amended by the Act of Accession of 1994.

(14) Council Regulation (EEC) No 4056/86 of 22 December 1986 laying down detailed rules for the application of Articles 81 and 82 (The title of the Regulation has been adjusted to take account of the renumbering of the Articles of the EC Treaty, in accordance with Article 12 of the Treaty of Amsterdam; the original reference was to Articles 85 and 86 of the Treaty) of the Treaty to maritime transport (OJ L 378, 31.12.1986, p. 4). Regulation as last amended by the Act of Accession of 1994.

(15) Council Regulation (EEC) No 3975/87 of 14 December 1987 laying down the procedure for the application of the rules on competition to undertakings in the air transport sector (OJ L 374, 31.12.1987, p. 1). Regulation as last amended by Regulation (EEC) No 2410/92 (OJ L 240, 24.8.1992, p. 18).

(16) OJ L 1, 4.1.2003, p. 1.

(17) OJ L 1, 4.1.2003, p. 1.

(18) OJ L 1, 4.1.2003, p. 1.

(19) OJ L 1, 4.1.2003, p. 1.

Appendix 3

Council Directive 86/653/EEC
OJ 1986, L 382/17, [1987] CLE 185

COUNCIL DIRECTIVE of 18 December 1986 on the coordination of the laws of the Member State relating to self-employed commercial agents (86/653/EEC)
THE COUNCIL OF THE EUROPEAN COMMUNITIES,
Having regard to the Treaty establishing the European Economic Community, and in particular Articles 57(2) and 100 thereof,
Having regard to the proposal from the Commission (1),
Having regard to the opinion of the European Parliament (2),
Having regard to the opinion of the Economic and Social Committee (3),
Whereas the restrictions on the freedom of establishment and the freedom to provide services in respect of activities of intermediaries in commerce, industry and small craft industries were abolished by Directive 64/224/EEC (4);
Whereas the differences in national laws concerning commercial representation substantially affect the conditions of competition and the carrying-on of that activity within the Community and are detrimental both to the protection available to commercial agents vis-à-vis their principals and to the security of commercial transactions; whereas moreover those differences are such as to inhibit substantially the conclusion and operation of commerical representation contracts where principal and commercial agents are established in different Member States;
Whereas trade in goods between Member States should be carried on under conditions which are similar to those of a single market, and this necessitates approximation of the legal systems of the Member States to the extent required for the proper functioning of the common market; whereas in this regard the rules concerning conflict of laws do not, in the matter of commercial representation, remove the inconsistencies referred to above, nor would they even if they were made uniform, and accordingly the proposed harmonization is necessary notwithstanding the existence of those rules;
Whereas in this regard the legal relationship between commercial agent and principal must be given priority;
Whereas it is appropriate to be guided by the principles of Article 117 of the Treaty and to maintain improvementsalready made, when harmonizing the laws of the Member States relating to commercial agents;
Whereas additional transitional periods should be allowed for certain Member States which have to make a particular effort to adapt their regulations, especially

those concerning indemnity for termination of contract between the principal and the commercial agent, to the requirements of this Directive,

HAS ADOPTED THIS DIRECTIVE:

CHAPTER I SCOPE

Article 1

1. The harmonization measures prescribed by this Directive shall apply to the laws, regulations and administrative provisions of the Member States governing the relations between commercial agents and their principals.

2. For the purposes of this Directive, 'commercial agent' shall mean a self-employed intermediary who has continuing authority to negotiate the sale or the purchase of goods on behalf of another person, hereinafter called the 'principal', or to negotiate and conclude such transactions on behalf of and in the name of that principal.

3. A commercial agent shall be understood within the meaning of this Directive as not including in particular:

- a person who, in his capacity as an officer, is empowered to enter into commitments binding on a company or association,

- a parter who is lawfully authorized to enter into commitments binding on his partners,

- a receiver, a receiver and manager, a liquidator or a trustee in bankruptcy.

Article 2

1. This Directive shall not apply to:

- commercial agents whose activities are unpaid,

- commercial agents when they operate on commodity exchanges or in the commodity market, or

- the body known is the Crown Agents for Overseas Governments and Administrations, as set up under the Crown Agents Act 1979 in the United Kingdom, or its subsidiaries.

2. Each of the Member States shall have the right to provide that the Directive shall not apply to those persons whose activities as commercial agents are considered secondary by the law of that Member State.

CHAPTER II RIGHTS AND OBLIGATIONS

Article 3

1. In performing has activities a commercial agent must look after his principal's interests and act dutifully and in good faith.

2. In particular, a commercial agent must:

(a) make proper efforts to negotiate and, where appropriate, conclude the transactions he is instructed to take care of;

(b) communicate to his principal all the necessary information available to him;

(c) comply with reasonable instructions given by his principal.

Article 4

1. In his relations with his commercial agent a principal must act dutifully and in good faith.

2. A principal must in particular:

(a) provide his commercial agent with the necessary documentation relating to the goods concerned;

(b) obtain for his commercial agent the information necessary for the performance of the agency contract, and in particular notify the commercial agent within a reasonable period once he anticipates that the volume of commercial transactions will be significantly lower than that which the commercial agent could normally have expected.

3. A principal must, in addition, inform the commercial agent within a reasonable period of his acceptance, refusal, and of any non-execution of a commercial transaction which the commercial agent has procured for the principal.

Article 5

The parties may not derogate from the provisions of Articles 3 and 4.

CHAPTER III REMUNERATION

Article 6

1. In the absence of any agreement on this matter between the parties, and without prejudice to the application of the compulsory provisions of the Member

States concerning the level of remuneration, a commercial agent shall be entitled to the remuneration that commercial agents appointed for the goods forming the subject of his agency contract are customarily allowed in the place where he carries on his activities. If there is no such customary practice a commercial agent shall be entitled to reasonable remuneration taking into account all the aspects of the transaction.

2. Any part of the remuneration which varies with the number or value of business transactions shall be deemed to be commission within the meaning of this Directive.

3. Articles 7 to 12 shall not apply if the commercial agent is not remunerated wholly or in part by commission.

Article 7

1. A commercial agent shall be entitled to commission on commercial transactions concluded during the period covered by the agency contract:

(a) where the transaction has been concluded as a result of his action; or

(b) where the transaction is concluded with a third party whom he has previously acquired as a customer for transactions of the same kind.

2. A commercial agent shall also be entitled to commission on transactions concluded during the period covered by the agency contract:

• either where he is entrusted with a specific geographical area or group of customers,

• or where he has an exclusive right to a specific geographical area or group of customers,
and where the transaction has been entered into with a customer belonging to that area or group.

Member State shall include in their legislation one of the possibilities referred to in the above two indents.

Article 8

A commercial agent shall be entitled to commission on commercial transactions concluded after the agency contract has terminated:

(a) if the transaction is mainly attributable to the commercial agent's efforts during the period covered by the agency contract and if the transaction was entered into within a reasonable period after that contract terminated; or

(b) if, in accordance with the conditions mentioned in Article 7, the order of the third party reached the principal or the commercial agent before the agency contract terminated.

Article 9

A commercial agent shall not be entitled to the commission referred to in Article 7, if that commission is payable, pursuant to Article 8, to the previous commercial agent, unless it is equitable because of the circumstances for the commission to be shared between the commercial agents.

Article 10

1. The commission shall become due as soon as and to the extent that one of the following circumstances obtains:

(a) the principal has executed the transaction; or

(b) the principal should, according to his agreement with the third party, have executed the transaction; or

(c) the third party has executed the transaction.

2. The commission shall become due at the latest when the third party has executed his part of the transaction or should have done so if the principal had executed his part of the transaction, as he should have.

3. The commission shall be paid not later than on the last day of the month following the quarter in which it became due.

4. Agreements to derogate from paragraphs 2 and 3 to the detriment of the commercial agent shall not be permitted.

Article 11

1. The right to commission can be extinguished only if and to the extent that:

• it is established that the contract between the third party and the principal will not be executed, and

• that face is due to a reason for which the principal is not to blame.

2. Any commission which the commercial agent has already received shall be refunded if the right to it is extinguished.

3. Agreements to derogate from paragraph 1 to the detriment of the commercial agent shall not be permitted.

Article 12

1. The principal shall supply his commercial agent with a statement of the commission due, not later than the last day of the month following the quarter in which the commission has become due. This statement shall set out the main components used in calculating the amount of commission.

2. A commercial agent shall be entitled to demand that he be provided with all the information, and in particular an extract from the books, which is available to his principal and which he needs in order to check the amount of the commission due to him.

3. Agreements to derogate from paragraphs 1 and 2 to the detriment of the commercial agent shall not be permitted.

4. This Directive shall not conflict with the internal provisions of Member States which recognize the right of a commercial agent to inspect a principal's books.

CHAPTER IV CONCLUSION AND TERMINATION OF THE AGENCY CONTRACT

Article 13

1. Each party shall be entitled to receive from the other on request a signed written document setting out the terms of the agency contract including any terms subsequently agreed. Waiver of this right shall not be permitted.

2. Notwithstanding paragraph 1 a Member State may provide that an agency contract shall not be valid unless evidenced in writing.

Article 14

An agency contract for a fixed period which continues to be performed by both parties after that period has expired shall be deemed to be converted into an agency contract for an indefinite period.

Article 15

1. Where an agency contract is concluded for an indefinite period either party may terminate it by notice.

2. The period of notice shall be one month for the first year of the contract, two months for the second year commenced, and three months for the third year commenced and subsequent years. The parties may not agree on shorter periods of notice.

3. Member States may fix the period of notice at four months for the fourth year of the contract,five months for the fifth year and six months for the sixth and subsequent years. They may decide that the parties may not agree to shorter periods.

4. If the parties agree on longer periods than those laid down in paragraphs 2 and 3, the period of notice to be observed by the principal must not be shorter than that to be observed by the commercial agent.

5. Unless otherwise agreed by the parties, the end of the period of notice must coincide with the end of a calendar month.

6. The provision of this Article shall apply to an agency contract for a fixed period where it is converted under Article 14 into an agency contract for an indefinite period, subject to the proviso that the earlier fixed period must be taken into account in the calculation of the period of notice.

Article 16

Nothing in this Directive shall affect the application of the law of the Member States where the latter provides for the immediate termination of the agency contract:

(a) because of the failure of one party to carry out all or part of his obligations;

(b) where exceptional circumstances arise.

Article 17

1. Member States shall take the measures necessary to ensure that the commercial agent is, after termination of the agency contract, indemnified in accordance with paragraph 2 or compensated for damage in accordance with paragraph 3.

2. (a) The commercial agent shall be entitled to an indemnity if and to the extent that:

- he has brought the principal new customers or has significantly increased the volume of business with existing customers and the principal continues to derive substantial benefits from the business with such customers, and

- the payment of this indemnity is equitable having regard to all the circumstances and, in particular, the commission lost by the commercial agent on the business transacted with such customers. Member States may provide for such circumstances also to include the application or otherwise of a restraint of trade clause, within the meaning of Article 20;

(b) The amount of the indemnity may not exceed a figure equivalent to an indemnity for one year calculated from the commercial agent's average annual remuneration over the preceding five years and if the contract goes back less than five years the indemnity shall be calculated on the average for the period in question;

(c) The grant of such an indemnity shall not prevent the commercial agent from seeking damages.

3. The commercial agent shall be entitled to compensation for the damage he suffers as a result of the termination of his relations with the principal.
Such damage shall be deemed to occur particularly when the termination takes place in circumstances:

- depriving the commercial agent of the commission which proper performance of the agency contract would have procured him whilst providing the principal with substantial benefits linked to the commercial agent's activities,

• and/or which have not enabled the commercial agent to amortize the costs and expenses that he had incurred for the performance of the agency contract on the principal's advice.

4. Entitlement to the indemnity as provided for in paragraph 2 or to compensation for damage as provided for under paragraph 3, shall also arise where the agency contract is terminated as a result of the commercial agent's death.

5. The commercial agent shall lose his entitlement to the indemnity in the instances provided for in paragraph 2 or to compensation for damage in the instances provided for in paragraph 3, if within one year following termination of the contract he has not notified the principal that he intends pursuing his entitlement.

6. The Commission shall submit to the Council, within eight years following the date of notification of this Directive, a report on the implementation of this Article, and shall if necessary submit to it proposals for amendments.

Article 18

The indemnity or compensation referred to in Article 17 shall not be payable:

(a) where the principal has terminated the agency contract because of default attributable to the commercial agent which would justify immediate termination of the agency contract under national law;

(b) where the commercial agent has terminated the agency contract, unless such termination is justified by circumstances attributable to the principal or on grounds of age, infirmity or illness of the commercial agent in consequence of which he cannot reasonably be required to continue his activities;

(c) where, with the agreement of the principal, the commercial agent assigns his rights and duties under the agency contract to another person.

Article 19

The parties may not derogate from Articles 17 and 18 to the detriment of the commercial agent before the agency contract expires.

Article 20

1. For the purposes of this Directive an agreement restricting the business activities of a commercial agent following termination of the agency contract is hereinafter referred to as a restraint of trade clause.

2. A restraint of trade clause shall be valid only if and to the extent that:

(a) it is concluded in writing; and

(b) it relates to the geographical area or the group of customers and the geographical area entrusted to the commercial agent and to the kind of goods covered by his agency under the contract.

3. A restraint of trade clause shall be valid for not more than two years after termination of the agency contract.

4. This Article shall not affect provisions of national law which impose other restrictions on the validity or enforceability of restraint of trade clauses or which enable the courts to reduce the obligations on the parties resulting from such an agreement.

CHAPTER V GENERAL AND FINAL PROVISIONS

Article 21

Nothing in this Directive shall require a Member State to provide for the disclosure of information where such disclosure would be contrary to public policy.

Article 22

1. Member States shall bring into force the provisions necessary to comply with this Directive before 1 January 1990. They shall for with inform the Commission thereof. Such provisions shall apply at least to contracts concluded after their entry into force. They shall apply to contracts in operation by 1 January 1994 at the latest.

2. As from the notification of this Directive, Member States shall communicate to the Commission the main laws, regulations and administrative provisions which they adopt in the field governed by this Directive.

3. However, with regard to Ireland and the United Kingdom, 1 January 1990 referred to in paragraph 1 shall be replaced by 1 January 1994.

With regard to Italy, 1 January 1990 shall be replaced by 1 January 1993 in the case of the obligations deriving from Article 17.

Article 23

This Directive is addressed to the Member States.

Done at Brussels, 18 December 1986.

For the Council
The President
M.Jopling

(1) OJ No C 13, 18.1.1977, p.2; OJ No C 56, 2.3.1979, p.5.
(2) OJ No C 239, 9.10.1978, p.17.
(3) OJ No C 59, 8.03.1978, p.31.
(4) OJ No 56, 4.4.1964, p.869/64.

Appendix 4

Commision Regulation (EC) 2790/1999
OJ 1999, L336/21, [2000] 4 CMLR 398, [2000] ECLR Supp to May issue

Commission Regulation (EC) No 2790/1999 of 22 December 1999
on the application of Article 81(3) of the Treaty to categories of vertical agreements and concerted practices
(Text with EEA relevance)

THE COMMISSION OF THE EUROPEAN COMMUNITIES,

Having regard to the Treaty establishing the European Community,

Having regard to Council Regulation No 19/65/EEC of 2 March 1965 on the application of Article 85(3) of the Treaty to certain categories of agreements and concerted practices(1), as last amended by Regulation (EC) No 1215/1999(2), and in particular Article 1 thereof,

Having published a draft of this Regulation(3),

Having consulted the Advisory Committee on Restrictive Practices and Dominant Positions,

Whereas:

(1) Regulation No 19/65/EEC empowers the Commission to apply Article 81(3) of the Treaty (formerly Article 85(3)) by regulation to certain categories of vertical agreements and corresponding concerted practices falling within Article 81(1).

(2) Experience acquired to date makes it possible to define a category of vertical agreements which can be regarded as normally satisfying the conditions laid down in Article 81(3).

(3) This category includes vertical agreements for the purchase or sale of goods or services where these agreements are concluded between non-competing undertakings, between certain competitors or by certain associations of retailers of goods; it also includes vertical agreements containing ancillary provisions on the assignment or use of intellectual property rights; for the purposes of this Regulation, the term "vertical agreements" includes the corresponding concerted practices.

(4) For the application of Article 81(3) by regulation, it is not necessary to define those vertical agreements which are capable of falling within Article 81(1); in the individual assessment of agreements under Article 81(1), account has to be taken of several factors, and in particular the market structure on the supply and purchase side.

(5) The benefit of the block exemption should be limited to vertical agreements for which it can be assumed with sufficient certainty that they satisfy the conditions of Article 81(3).

(6) Vertical agreements of the category defined in this Regulation can improve economic efficiency within a chain of production or distribution by facilitating better coordination between the participating undertakings; in particular, they can lead to a reduction in the transaction and distribution costs of the parties and to an optimisation of their sales and investment levels.

(7) The likelihood that such efficiency-enhancing effects will outweigh any anti-competitive effects due to restrictions contained in vertical agreements depends on the degree of market power of the undertakings concerned and, therefore, on the extent to which those undertakings face competition from other suppliers of goods or services regarded by the buyer as interchangeable or substitutable for one another, by reason of the products' characteristics, their prices and their intended use.

(8) It can be presumed that, where the share of the relevant market accounted for by the supplier does not exceed 30 %, vertical agreements which do not contain certain types of severely anti-competitive restraints generally lead to an improvement in production or distribution and allow consumers a fair share of the resulting benefits; in the case of vertical agreements containing exclusive supply obligations, it is the market share of the buyer which is relevant in determining the overall effects of such vertical agreements on the market.

(9) Above the market share threshold of 30 %, there can be no presumption that vertical agreements falling within the scope of Article 81(1) will usually give rise to objective advantages of such a character and size as to compensate for the disadvantages which they create for competition.

(10) This Regulation should not exempt vertical agreements containing restrictions which are not indispensable to the attainment of the positive effects mentioned above; in particular, vertical agreements containing certain types of severely anti-competitive restraints such as minimum and fixed resale-prices, as well as certain types of territorial protection, should be excluded from the benefit of the block exemption established by this Regulation irrespective of the market share of the undertakings concerned.

(11) In order to ensure access to or to prevent collusion on the relevant market, certain conditions are to be attached to the block exemption; to this end, the exemption of non-compete obligations should be limited to obligations which do not exceed a definite duration; for the same reasons, any direct or indirect obligation causing the members of a selective distribution system not to sell the brands of particular competing suppliers should be excluded from the benefit of this Regulation.

(12) The market-share limitation, the non-exemption of certain vertical agreements and the conditions provided for in this Regulation normally ensure that the agreements to which the block exemption applies do not enable the participating undertakings to eliminate competition in respect of a substantial part of the products in question.

(13) In particular cases in which the agreements falling under this Regulation nevertheless have effects incompatible with Article 81(3), the Commission may

withdraw the benefit of the block exemption; this may occur in particular where the buyer has significant market power in the relevant market in which it resells the goods or provides the services or where parallel networks of vertical agreements have similar effects which significantly restrict access to a relevant market or competition therein; such cumulative effects may for example arise in the case of selective distribution or non-compete obligations.

(14) Regulation No 19/65/EEC empowers the competent authorities of Member States to withdraw the benefit of the block exemption in respect of vertical agreements having effects incompatible with the conditions laid down in Article 81(3), where such effects are felt in their respective territory, or in a part thereof, and where such territory has the characteristics of a distinct geographic market; Member States should ensure that the exercise of this power of withdrawal does not prejudice the uniform application throughout the common market of the Community competition rules or the full effect of the measures adopted in implementation of those rules.

(15) In order to strengthen supervision of parallel networks of vertical agreements which have similar restrictive effects and which cover more than 50 % of a given market, the Commission may declare this Regulation inapplicable to vertical agreements containing specific restraints relating to the market concerned, thereby restoring the full application of Article 81 to such agreements.

(16) This Regulation is without prejudice to the application of Article 82.

(17) In accordance with the principle of the primacy of Community law, no measure taken pursuant to national laws on competition should prejudice the uniform application throughout the common market of the Community competition rules or the full effect of any measures adopted in implementation of those rules, including this Regulation,

HAS ADOPTED THIS REGULATION:

Article 1

For the purposes of this Regulation:

(a) "competing undertakings" means actual or potential suppliers in the same product market; the, product market includes goods or services which are regarded by the buyer as interchangeable with or substitutable for the contract goods or services, by reason of the products' characteristics, their prices and their intended use;

(b) "non-compete obligation" means any direct or indirect obligation causing the buyer not to manufacture, purchase, sell or resell goods or services which compete with the contract goods or services, or any direct or indirect obligation on the buyer to purchase from the supplier or from another undertaking designated by the supplier more than 80 % of the buyer's total purchases of the contract goods or services and their substitutes on the relevant market, calculated on the basis of the value of its purchases in the preceding calendar year;

(c) "exclusive supply obligation" means any direct or indirect obligation causing the supplier to sell the goods or services specified in the agreement only to one buyer inside the Community for the purposes of a specific use or for resale;

(d) "Selective distribution system" means a distribution system where the supplier undertakes to sell the contract goods or services, either directly or indirectly, only to distributors selected on the basis of specified criteria and where these distributors undertake not to sell such goods or services to unauthorised distributors;

(e) "intellectual property rights" includes industrial property rights, copyright and neighbouring rights;

(f) "know-how" means a package of non-patented practical information, resulting from experience and testing by the supplier, which is secret, substantial and identified: in this context, "secret" means that the know-how, as a body or in the precise configuration and assembly of its components, is not generally known or easily accessible; "substantial" means that the know-how includes information which is indispensable to the buyer for the use, sale or resale of the contract goods or services; "identified" means that the know-how must be described in a sufficiently comprehensive manner so as to make it possible to verify that it fulfils the criteria of secrecy and substantiality;

(g) "buyer" includes an undertaking which, under an agreement falling within Article 81(1) of the Treaty, sells goods or services on behalf of another undertaking.

Article 2

1. Pursuant to Article 81(3) of the Treaty and subject to the provisions of this Regulation, it is hereby declared that Article 81(1) shall not apply to agreements or concerted practices entered into between two or more undertakings each of which operates, for the purposes of the agreement, at a different level of the production or distribution chain, and relating to the conditions under which the parties may purchase, sell or resell certain goods or services ("vertical agreements").

This exemption shall apply to the extent that such agreements contain restrictions of competition falling within the scope of Article 81(1) ("vertical restraints").

2. The exemption provided for in paragraph 1 shall apply to vertical agreements entered into between an association of undertakings and its members, or between such an association and its suppliers, only if all its members are retailers of goods and if no individual member of the association, together with its

connected undertakings, has a total annual turnover exceeding EUR 50 million; vertical agreements entered into by such associations shall be covered by this Regulation without prejudice to the application of Article 81 to horizontal agreements concluded between the members of the association or decisions adopted by the association.

3. The exemption provided for in paragraph 1 shall apply to vertical agreements containing provisions which relate to the assignment to the buyer or use by the buyer of intellectual property rights, provided that those provisions do not constitute the primary object of such agreements and are directly related to the use, sale or resale of goods or services by the buyer or its customers. The exemption applies on condition that, in relation to the contract goods or services, those provisions do not contain restrictions of competition having the same object or effect as vertical restraints which are not exempted under this Regulation.

4. The exemption provided for in paragraph 1 shall not apply to vertical agreements entered into between competing undertakings; however, it shall apply where competing undertakings enter into a non-reciprocal vertical agreement and:

(a) the buyer has a total annual turnover not exceeding EUR 100 million, or

(b) the supplier is a manufacturer and a distributor of goods, while the buyer is a distributor not manufacturing goods competing with the contract goods, or

(c) the supplier is a provider of services at several levels of trade, while the buyer does not provide competing services at the level of trade where it purchases the contract services.

5. This Regulation shall not apply to vertical agreements the subject matter of which falls within the scope of any other block exemption regulation.

Article 3

1. Subject to paragraph 2 of this Article, the exemption provided for in Article 2 shall apply on condition that the market share held by the supplier does not exceed 30 % of the relevant market on which it sells the contract goods or services.

2. In the case of vertical agreements containing exclusive supply obligations, the exemption provided for in Article 2 shall apply on condition that the market share held by the buyer does not exceed 30 % of the relevant market on which it purchases the contract goods or services.

Article 4

The exemption provided for in Article 2 shall not apply to vertical agreements which, directly or indirectly, in isolation or in combination with other factors under the control of the parties, have as their object:

(a) the restriction of the buyer's ability to determine its sale price, without prejudice to the possibility of the supplier's imposing a maximum sale price or recommending a sale price, provided that they do not amount to a fixed or minimum sale price as a result of pressure from, or incentives offered by, any of the parties;

(b) the restriction of the territory into which, or of the customers to whom, the buyer may sell the contract goods or services, except:

- the restriction of active sales into the exclusive territory or to an exclusive customer group reserved to the supplier or allocated by the supplier to another buyer, where such a restriction does not limit sales by the customers of the buyer,

- the restriction of sales to end users by a buyer operating at the wholesale level of trade,

- the restriction of sales to unauthorised distributors by the members of a selective distribution system, and

- the restriction of the buyer's ability to sell components, supplied for the purposes of incorporation, to customers who would use them to manufacture the same type of goods as those produced by the supplier;

(c) the restriction of active or passive sales to end users by members of a selective distribution system operating at the retail level of trade, without prejudice to the possibility of prohibiting a member of the system from operating out of an unauthorised place of establishment;

(d) the restriction of cross-supplies between distributors within a selective distribution system, including between distributors operating at different level of trade;

(e) the restriction agreed between a supplier of components and a buyer who incorporates those components, which limits the supplier to selling the components as spare parts to end-users or to repairers or other service providers not entrusted by the buyer with the repair or servicing of its goods.

Article 5

The exemption provided for in Article 2 shall not apply to any of the following obligations contained in vertical agreements:

(a) any direct or indirect non-compete obligation, the duration of which is indefinite or exceeds five years. A non-compete obligation which is tacitly renewable beyond a period of five years is to be deemed to have been concluded for an indefinite duration. However, the time limitation of five years shall not apply where the contract goods or services are sold by the buyer from premises and land owned by the supplier or leased by the supplier from third parties not connected with the buyer, provided that the duration of the non-compete obligation does not exceed the period of occupancy of the premises and land by the buyer;

(b) any direct or indirect obligation causing the buyer, after termination of the agreement, not to manufacture, purchase, sell or resell goods or services, unless such obligation:

- relates to goods or services which compete with the contract goods or services, and

- is limited to the premises and land from which the buyer has operated during the contract period, and

- is indispensable to protect know-how transferred by the supplier to the buyer, and provided that the duration of such non-compete obligation is limited to a period of one year after termination of the agreement; this obligation is without prejudice to the possibility of imposing a restriction which is unlimited in time on the use and disclosure of know-how which has not entered the public domain;

(c) any direct or indirect obligation causing the members of a selective distribution system not to sell the brands of particular competing suppliers.

Article 6

The Commission may withdraw the benefit of this Regulation, pursuant to Article 7(1) of Regulation No 19/65/EEC, where it finds in any particular case that vertical agreements to which this Regulation applies nevertheless have effects which are incompatible with the conditions laid down in Article 81(3) of the Treaty, and in particular where access to the relevant market or competition therein is significantly restricted by the cumulative effect of parallel networks of similar vertical restraints implemented by competing suppliers or buyers.

Article 7

Where in any particular case vertical agreements to which the exemption provided for in Article 2 applies have effects incompatible with the conditions laid down in Article 81(3) of the Treaty in the territory of a Member State, or in a part thereof, which has all the characteristics of a distinct geographic market, the competent authority of that Member State may withdraw the benefit of application of this Regulation in respect of that territory, under the same conditions as provided in Article 6.

Article 8

1. Pursuant to Article 1 a of Regulation No 19/65/EEC, the Commission may by regulation declare that, where parallel networks of similar vertical restraints cover more than 50 % of a relevant market, this Regulation shall not apply to vertical agreements containing specific restraints relating to that market.

2. A regulation pursuant to paragraph 1 shall not become applicable earlier than six months following its adoption.

Article 9

1. The market share of 30 % provided for in Article 3(1) shall be calculated on the basis of the market sales value of the contract goods or services and other goods or services sold by the supplier, which are regarded as interchangeable or substitutable by the buyer, by reason of the products' characteristics, their prices and their intended use; if market sales value data are not available, estimates based on other reliable market information, including market sales volumes, may be used to establish the market share of the undertaking concerned. For the purposes of Article 3(2), it is either the market purchase value or estimates thereof which shall be used to calculate the market share.

2. For the purposes of applying the market share, threshold provided for in Article 3 the following rules shall apply:

(a) the market share shall be calculated on the basis of data relating to the preceding calendar year;

(b) the market share shall include any goods or services supplied to integrated distributors for the purposes of sale;

(c) if the market share is initially not more than 30 % but subsequently rises above that level without exceeding 35 %, the exemption provided for in Article 2 shall continue to apply for a period of two consecutive calendar years following the year in which the 30 % market share threshold was first exceeded;

(d) if the market share is initially not more than 30 % but subsequently rises above 35 %, the exemption provided for in Article 2 shall continue to apply for one calendar year following the year in which the level of 35 % was first exceeded;

(e) the benefit of points (c) and (d) may not be combined so as to exceed a period of two calendar years.

Article 10

1. For the purpose of calculating total annual turnover within the meaning of Article 2(2) and (4), the turnover achieved during the previous financial year by

the relevant party to the vertical agreement and the turnover achieved by its connected undertakings in respect of all goods and services, excluding all taxes and other duties, shall be added together. For this purpose, no account shall be taken of dealings between the party to the vertical agreement and its connected undertakings or between its connected undertakings.

2. The exemption provided for in Article 2 shall remain applicable where, for any period of two consecutive financial years, the total annual turnover threshold is exceeded by no more than 10 %.

Article 11

1. For the purposes of this Regulation, the terms "undertaking", "supplier" and "buyer" shall include their respective connected undertakings.

2. "Connected undertakings" are:

(a) undertakings in which a party to the agreement, directly or indirectly:

   - has the power to exercise more than half the voting rights, or

   - has the power to appoint more than half the members of the supervisory board, board of management or bodies legally representing the undertaking, or

   - has the right to manage the undertaking's affairs;

(b) undertakings which directly or indirectly have, over a party to the agreement, the rights or powers listed in (a);

(c) undertakings in which an undertaking referred to in (b) has, directly or indirectly, the rights or powers listed in (a);

(d) undertakings in which a party to the agreement together with one or more of the undertakings referred to in (a), (b) or (c), or in which two or more of the latter undertakings, jointly have the rights or powers listed in (a);

(e) undertakings in which the rights or the powers listed in (a) are jointly held by:

   - parties to the agreement or their respective connected undertakings referred to in (a) to (d), or

   - one or more of the parties to the agreement or one or more of their connected undertakings referred to in (a) to (d) and one or more third parties.

3. For the purposes of Article 3, the market share held by the undertakings referred to in paragraph 2(e) of this Article shall be apportioned equally to each undertaking having the rights or the powers listed in paragraph 2(a).

Article 12

1. The exemptions provided for in Commission Regulations (EEC) No 1983/83(4), (EEC) No 1984/83(5) and (EEC) No 4087/88(6) shall continue to apply until 31 May 2000.

2. The prohibition laid down in Article 81(1) of the EC Treaty shall not apply during the period from 1 June 2000 to 31 December 2001 in respect of agreements already in force on 31 May 2000 which do not satisfy the conditions for exemption provided for in this Regulation but which satisfy the conditions for exemption provided for in Regulations (EEC) No 1983/83, (EEC) No 1984/83 or (EEC) No 4087/88.

Article 13

This Regulation shall enter into force on 1 January 2000.

It shall apply from 1 June 2000, except for Article 12(1) which shall apply from 1 January 2000.

This Regulation shall expire on 31 May 2010.

This Regulation shall be binding in its entirety and directly applicable in all Member States.

Done at Brussels, 22 December 1999.

For the Commission
Mario Monti
Member of the Commission

(1) OJ 36, 6.3.1965, p. 533/65.
(2) OJ L 148, 15.6.1999, p. 1.
(3) OJ C 270, 24.9.1999, p. 7.
(4) OJ L 173, 30.6.1983, p. 1.
(5) OJ L 173, 30.6.1983, p. 5.
(6) OJ L 359, 28.12.1988, p. 46.

Appendix 5

Commission Regulation (EC) 1400/2002
OJ 2002, L203/30, [2002] 5 CMLR 777

Commission Regulation (EC) No 1400/2002 of 31 July 2002 on the application of Article 81(3) of the Treaty to categories of vertical agreements and concerted practices in the motor vehicle sector

THE COMMISSION OF THE EUROPEAN COMMUNITIES,
Having regard to the Treaty establishing the European Community,
Having regard to Council Regulation No 19/65/EEC of 2 March 1965 on the application of Article 85(3) of the Treaty to certain categories of agreements and concerted practices(1), as last amended by Regulation (EC) No 1215/1999(2), and in particular Article 1 thereof,
Having published a draft of this Regulation(3),
Having consulted the Advisory Committee on Restrictive Practices and Dominant Positions,
Whereas:
(1) Experience acquired in the motor vehicle sector regarding the distribution of new motor vehicles, spare parts and after sales services makes it possible to define categories of vertical agreements which can be regarded as normally satisfying the conditions laid down in Article 81(3).
(2) This experience leads to the conclusion that rules stricter than those provided for by Commission Regulation (EC) No 2790/1999 of 22 December 1999 on the application of Article 81(3) of the Treaty to categories of vertical agreements and concerted practices(4) are necessary in this sector.
(3) These stricter rules for exemption by category (the exemption) should apply to vertical agreements for the purchase or sale of new motor vehicles, vertical agreements for the purchase or sale of spare parts for motor vehicles and vertical agreements for the purchase or sale of repair and maintenance services for such vehicles where these agreements are concluded between non-competing undertakings, between certain competitors, or by certain associations of retailers or repairers. This includes vertical agreements concluded between a distributor acting at the retail level or an authorised repairer and a (sub)distributor or repairer. This Regulation should also apply to these vertical agreements when they contain ancillary provisions on the assignment or use of intellectual property rights. The term "vertical agreements" should be defined accordingly to include both such agreements and the corresponding concerted practices.

(4) The benefit of the exemption should be limited to vertical agreements for which it can be assumed with sufficient certainty that they satisfy the conditions of Article 81(3).

(5) Vertical agreements falling within the categories defined in this Regulation can improve economic efficiency within a chain of production or distribution by facilitating better coordination between the participating undertakings. In particular, they can lead to a reduction in the transaction and distribution costs of the parties and to an optimisation of their sales and investment levels.

(6) The likelihood that such efficiency-enhancing effects will outweigh any anti-competitive effects due to restrictions contained in vertical agreements depends on the degree of market power held by the undertakings concerned and therefore on the extent to which those undertakings face competition from other suppliers of goods or services regarded by the buyer as interchangeable or substitutable for one another, by reason of the products' characteristics, prices or intended use.

(7) Thresholds based on market share should be fixed in order to reflect suppliers' market power. Furthermore, this sector-specific Regulation should contain stricter rules than those provided for by Regulation (EC) No 2790/1999, in particular for selective distribution. The thresholds below which it can be presumed that the advantages secured by vertical agreements outweigh their restrictive effects should vary with the characteristics of different types of vertical agreement. It can therefore be presumed that in general, vertical agreements have such advantages where the supplier concerned has a market share of up to 30 % on the markets for the distribution of new motor vehicles or spare parts, or of up to 40 % where quantitative selective distribution is used for the sale of new motor vehicles. As regards after sales services it can be presumed that, in general, vertical agreements by which the supplier sets criteria on how its authorised repairers have to provide repair or maintenance services for the motor vehicles of the relevant make and provides them with equipment and training for the provision of such services have such advantages where the network of authorised repairers of the supplier concerned has a market share of up to 30 %. However, in the case of vertical agreements containing exclusive supply obligations, it is the market share of the buyer which is relevant for determining the overall effects of such vertical agreements on the market.

(8) Above those market share thresholds, there can be no presumption that vertical agreements falling within the scope of Article 81(1) will usually give rise to objective advantages of such a character and magnitude as to compensate for the disadvantages which they create for competition. However, such advantages can be anticipated in the case of qualitative selective distribution, irrespective of the supplier's market share.

(9) In order to prevent a supplier from terminating an agreement because a distributor or a repairer engages in pro-competitive behaviour, such as active or passive sales to foreign consumers, multi-branding or subcontracting of repair and maintenance services, every notice of termination must clearly set out in writing

the reasons, which must be objective and transparent. Furthermore, in order to strengthen the independence of distributors and repairers from their suppliers, minimum periods of notice should be provided for the non-renewal of agreements concluded for a limited duration and for the termination of agreements of unlimited duration.

(10) In order to foster market integration and to allow distributors or authorised repairers to seize additional business opportunities, distributors or authorised repairers have to be allowed to purchase other undertakings of the same type that sell or repair the same brand of motor vehicles within the distribution system. To this end, any vertical agreement between a supplier and a distributor or authorised repairer has to provide for the latter to have the right to transfer all of its rights and obligations to any other undertaking of its choice of the same type that sell or repairs the same brand of motor vehicles within the distribution system.

(11) In order to favour the quick resolution of disputes which arise between the parties to a distribution agreement and which might otherwise hamper effective competition, agreements should only benefit from exemption if they provide for each party to have a right of recourse to an independent expert or arbitrator, in particular where notice is given to terminate an agreement.

(12) Irrespective of the market share of the undertakings concerned, this Regulation does not cover vertical agreements containing certain types of severely anti-competitive restraints (hardcore restrictions) which in general appreciably restrict competition even at low market shares and which are not indispensable to the attainment of the positive effects mentioned above. This concerns in particular vertical agreements containing restraints such as minimum or fixed resale prices and, with certain exceptions, restrictions of the territory into which, or of the customers to whom, a distributor or repairer may sell the contract goods or services. Such agreements should not benefit from the exemption.

(13) It is necessary to ensure that effective competition within the common market and between distributors located in different Member States is not restricted if a supplier uses selective distribution in some markets and other forms of distribution in others. In particular selective distribution agreements which restrict passive sales to any end user or unauthorised distributor located in markets where exclusive territories have been allocated should be excluded from the benefit of the exemption, as should those selective distribution agreements which restrict passive sales to customer groups which have been allocated exclusively to other distributors. The benefit of the exemption should also be withheld from exclusive distribution agreements if active or passive sales to any end user or unauthorised distributor located in markets where selective distribution is used are restricted.

(14) The right of any distributor to sell new motor vehicles passively or, where relevant, actively to end users should include the right to sell such vehicles to end users who have given authorisation to an intermediary or purchasing agent to purchase, take delivery of, transport or store a new motor vehicle on their behalf.

(15) The right of any distributor to sell new motor vehicles or spare parts or of any authorised repairer to sell repair and maintenance services to any end user passively or, where relevant, actively should include the right to use the Internet or Internet referral sites.

(16) Limits placed by suppliers on their distributors' sales to any end user in other Member States, for instance where distributor remuneration or the purchase price is made dependent on the destination of the vehicles or on the place of residence of the end users, amount to an indirect restriction on sales. Other examples of indirect restrictions on sales include supply quotas based on a sales territory other than the common market, whether or not these are combined with sales targets. Bonus systems based on the destination of the vehicles or any form of discriminatory product supply to distributors, whether in the case of product shortage or otherwise, also amount to an indirect restriction on sales.

(17) Vertical agreements that do not oblige the authorised repairers within a supplier's distribution system to honour warranties, perform free servicing and carry out recall work in respect of any motor vehicle of the relevant make sold in the common market amount to an indirect restriction of sales and should not benefit from the exemption. This obligation is without prejudice to the right of a motor vehicle supplier to oblige a distributor to make sure as regards the new motor vehicles that he has sold that the warranties are honoured and that free servicing and recall work is carried out, either by the distributor itself or, in case of subcontracting, by the authorised repairer(s) to whom these services have been subcontracted. Therefore consumers should in these cases be able to turn to the distributor if the above obligations have not been properly fulfilled by the authorised repairer to whom the distributor has subcontracted these services. Furthermore, in order to allow sales by motor vehicle distributors to end users throughout the common market, the exemption should apply only to distribution agreements which require the repairers within the supplier's network to carry out repair and maintenance services for the contract goods and corresponding goods irrespective of where these goods are sold in the common market.

(18) In markets where selective distribution is used, the exemption should apply in respect of a prohibition on a distributor from operating out of an additional place of establishment where he is a distributor of vehicles other than passenger cars or light commercial vehicles. However, this prohibition should not be exempted if it limits the expansion of the distributor's business at the authorised place of establishment by, for instance, restricting the development or acquisition of the infrastructure necessary to allow increases in sales volumes, including increases brought about by Internet sales.

(19) It would be inappropriate to exempt any vertical agreement that restricts the sale of original spare parts or spare parts of matching quality by members of the distribution system to independent repairers which use them for the provision of repair or maintenance services. Without access to such spare parts, these independent repairers would not be able to compete effectively with authorised

repairers, since they could not provide consumers with good quality services which contribute to the safe and reliable functioning of motor vehicles.

(20) In order to give end users the right to purchase new motor vehicles with specifications identical to those sold in any other Member State, from any distributor selling corresponding models and established in the common market, the exemption should apply only to vertical agreements which enable a distributor to order, stock and sell any such vehicle which corresponds to a model within its contract range. Discriminatory or objectively unjustified supply conditions, in particular those regarding delivery times or prices, applied by the supplier to corresponding vehicles, are to be considered a restriction on the ability of the distributor to sell such vehicles.

(21) Motor vehicles are expensive and technically complex mobile goods which require repair and maintenance at regular and irregular intervals. However, it is not indispensable for distributors of new motor vehicles also to carry out repair and maintenance. The legitimate interests of suppliers and end users can be fully satisfied if the distributor subcontracts these services, including the honouring of warranties, free servicing and recall work, to a repairer or to a number of repairers within the supplier's distribution system. It is nevertheless appropriate to facilitate access to repair and maintenance services. Therefore, a supplier may require distributors who have subcontracted repair and maintenance services to one or more authorised repairers to give end users the name and address of the repair shop or shops in question. If any of these authorised repairers is not established in the vicinity of the sales outlet, the supplier may also require the distributor to tell end users how far the repair shop or shops in question are from the sales outlet. However, a supplier can only impose such obligations if he also imposes similar obligations on distributors whose own repair shop is not on the same premises as their sales outlet.

(22) Furthermore, it is not necessary, in order to adequately provide for repair and maintenance services, for authorised repairers to also sell new motor vehicles. The exemption should therefore not cover vertical agreements containing any direct or indirect obligation or incentive which leads to the linking of sales and servicing activities or which makes the performance of one of these activities dependent on the performance of the other; this is in particular the case where the remuneration of distributors or authorised repairers relating to the purchase or sale of goods or services necessary for one activity is made dependent on the purchase or sale of goods or services relating to the other activity, or where all such goods or services are indistinctly aggregated into a single remuneration or discount system.

(23) In order to ensure effective competition on the repair and maintenance markets and to allow repairers to offer end users competing spare parts such as original spare parts and spare parts of matching quality, the exemption should not cover vertical agreements which restrict the ability of authorised repairers within the distribution system of a vehicle manufacturer, independent distributors of spare parts, independent repairers or end users to source spare parts from the

manufacturer of such spare parts or from another third party of their choice. This does not affect spare part manufacturers' liability under civil law.

(24) Furthermore, in order to allow authorised and independent repairers and end users to identify the manufacturer of motor vehicle components or of spare parts and to choose between competing spare parts, the exemption should not cover agreements by which a manufacturer of motor vehicles limits the ability of a manufacturer of components or original spare parts to place its trade mark or logo on these parts effectively and in a visible manner. Moreover, in order to facilitate this choice and the sale of spare parts, which have been manufactured according to the specifications and production and quality standards provided by the vehicle manufacturer for the production of components or spare parts, it is presumed that spare parts constitute original spare parts, if the spare part producer issues a certificate that the parts are of the same quality as the components used for the assembly of a motor vehicle and have been manufactured according to these specifications and standards. Other spare parts for which the spare part producer can issue a certificate at any moment attesting that they match the quality of the components used for the assembly of a certain motor vehicle, may be sold as spare parts of matching quality.

(25) The exemption should not cover vertical agreements which restrict authorised repairers from using spare parts of matching quality for the repair or maintenance of a motor vehicle. However, in view of the vehicle manufacturers' direct contractual involvement in repairs under warranty, free servicing, and recall operations, agreements containing obligations on authorised repairers to use original spare parts supplied by the vehicle manufacturer for these repairs should be covered by the exemption.

(26) In order to protect effective competition on the market for repair and maintenance services and to prevent foreclosure of independent repairers, motor vehicle manufacturers must allow all interested independent operators to have full access to all technical information, diagnostic and other equipment, tools, including all relevant software, and training required for the repair and maintenance of motor vehicles. Independent operators who must be allowed such access include in particular independent repairers, manufacturers of repair equipment or tools, publishers of technical information, automobile clubs, roadside assistance operators, operators offering inspection and testing services and operators offering training for repairers. In particular, the conditions of access must not discriminate between authorised and independent operators, access must be given upon request and without undue delay, and the price charged for the information should not discourage access to it by failing to take into account the extent to which the independent operator uses it. A supplier of motor vehicles should be required to give independent operators access to technical information on new motor vehicles at the same time as such access is given to its authorised repairers and must not oblige independent operators to purchase more than the information necessary to carry out the work in question. Suppliers should be obliged to give access to the technical information necessary for re-programming electronic

devices in a motor vehicle. It is, however, legitimate and proper for them to withhold access to technical information which might allow a third party to bypass or disarm on-board anti-theft devices, to recalibrate electronic devices or to tamper with devices which for instance limit the speed of a motor vehicle, unless protection against theft, re-calibration or tampering can be attained by other less restrictive means. Intellectual property rights and rights regarding know-how including those which relate to the aforementioned devices must be exercised in a manner which avoids any type of abuse.

(27) In order to ensure access to and to prevent collusion on the relevant markets and to give distributors opportunities to sell vehicles of brands from two or more manufacturers that are not connected undertakings, certain specific conditions are attached to the exemption. To this end, the exemption should not be accorded to non-compete obligations. In particular, without prejudice to the ability of the supplier to require the distributor to display the vehicles in brand-specific areas of the showroom in order to avoid brand confusion, any prohibition on sales of competing makes should not be exempted. The same applies to an obligation to display the full range of motor vehicles if it makes the sale or display of vehicles manufactured by undertakings which are not connected impossible or unreasonably difficult. Furthermore, an obligation to have brand-specific sales personnel is considered to be an indirect non-compete obligation and therefore should not be covered by the exemption, unless the distributor decides to have brand-specific sales personnel and the supplier pays all the additional costs involved.

(28) In order to ensure that repairers are able to carry out repairs or maintenance on all motor vehicles, the exemption should not apply to any obligation limiting the ability of repairers of motor vehicles to provide repair or maintenance services for brands of competing suppliers.

(29) In addition, specific conditions are required to exclude certain restrictions, sometimes imposed in the context of a selective distribution system, from the scope of the exemption. This applies in particular to obligations which have the effect of preventing the members of a selective distribution system from selling the brands of particular competing suppliers, which could easily lead to foreclosure of certain brands. Additional conditions are necessary in order to foster intra-brand competition and market integration within the common market, to create opportunities for distributors and authorised repairers who wish to seize business opportunities outside their place of establishment, and to create conditions which allow the development of multi-brand distributors. In particular a restriction on operating out of an unauthorised place of establishment for the distribution of passenger cars and light commercial vehicles or the provision of repair and maintenance services should not be exempted. The supplier may require additional sales or delivery outlets for passenger cars and light commercial vehicles or repair shops to comply with the relevant qualitative criteria applicable for similar outlets located in the same geographic area.

(30) The exemption should not apply to restrictions limiting the ability of a distributor to sell leasing services for motor vehicles.

(31) The market share limitations, the fact that certain vertical agreements are not covered, and the conditions provided for in this Regulation, should normally ensure that the agreements to which the exemption applies do not enable the participating undertakings to eliminate competition in respect of a substantial part of the goods or services in question.

(32) In particular cases in which agreements which would otherwise benefit from the exemption nevertheless have effects incompatible with Article 81(3), the Commission is empowered to withdraw the benefit of the exemption; this may occur in particular where the buyer has significant market power on the relevant market on which it resells the goods or provides the services or where parallel networks of vertical agreements have similar effects which significantly restrict access to a relevant market or competition thereon; such cumulative effects may for example arise in the case of selective distribution. The Commission may also withdraw the benefit of the exemption if competition is significantly restricted on a market due to the presence of a supplier with market power or if prices and conditions of supply to motor vehicle distributors differ substantially between geographic markets. It may also withdraw the benefit of the exemption if discriminatory prices or sales conditions, or unjustifiably high supplements, such as those charged for right hand drive vehicles, are applied for the supply of goods corresponding to the contract range.

(33) Regulation No 19/65/EEC empowers the national authorities of Member States to withdraw the benefit of the exemption in respect of vertical agreements having effects incompatible with the conditions laid down in Article 81(3), where such effects are felt in their territory, or in a part thereof, and where such territory has the characteristics of a distinct geographic market; the exercise of this national power of withdrawal should not prejudice the uniform application throughout the common market of the Community competition rules or the full effect of the measures adopted in implementation of those rules.

(34) In order to allow for better supervision of parallel networks of vertical agreements which have similar restrictive effects and which cover more than 50 % of a given market, the Commission should be permitted to declare the exemption inapplicable to vertical agreements containing specific restraints relating to the market concerned, thereby restoring the full application of Article 81(1) to such agreements.

(35) The exemption should be granted without prejudice to the application of the provisions of Article 82 of the Treaty on the abuse by an undertaking of a dominant position.

(36) Commission Regulation (EC) No 1475/95 of 28 June 1995 on the application of Article 85(3) of the Treaty to certain categories of motor vehicle distribution and servicing agreements(5) is applicable until 30 September 2002. In order to allow all operators time to adapt vertical agreements which are compatible with that regulation and which are still in force when the exemption provided for therein expires, it is appropriate for such agreements to benefit from a transition period until 1 October 2003, during which time they should be exempted from the prohibition laid down in Article 81(1) under this Regulation.

(37) In order to allow all operators within a quantitative selective distribution system for new passenger cars and light commercial vehicles to adapt their business strategies to the non-application of the exemption to location clauses, it is appropriate to stipulate that the condition set out in Article 5(2)(b) shall enter into force on 1 October 2005.

(38) The Commission should monitor the operation of this Regulation on a regular basis, with particular regard to its effects on competition in motor vehicle retailing and in after sales servicing in the common market or relevant parts of it. This should include monitoring the effects of this Regulation on the structure and level of concentration of motor vehicle distribution and any resulting effects on competition. The Commission should also carry out an evaluation of the operation of this Regulation and draw up a report not later than 31 May 2008.

HAS ADOPTED THIS REGULATION:

Article 1 Definitions

1. For the purposes of this Regulation:

(a) "competing undertakings" means actual or potential suppliers on the same product market; the product market includes goods or services which are regarded by the buyer as interchangeable with or substitutable for the contract goods or services, by reason of the products' characteristics, their prices and their intended use;

(b) "non-compete obligation" means any direct or indirect obligation causing the buyer not to manufacture, purchase, sell or resell goods or services which compete with the contract goods or services, or any direct or indirect obligation on the buyer to purchase from the supplier or from another undertaking designated by the supplier more than 30 % of the buyer's total purchases of the contract goods, corresponding goods or services and their substitutes on the relevant market, calculated on the basis of the value of its purchases in the preceding calendar year. An obligation that the distributor sell motor vehicles from other suppliers in separate areas of the showroom in order to avoid confusion between the makes does not constitute a non-compete obligation for the purposes of this Regulation. An obligation that the distributor have brand-specific sales personnel for different brands of motor vehicles constitutes a non-compete obligation for the purposes of this Regulation, unless the distributor decides to have brand-specific sales personnel and the supplier pays all the additional costs involved;

(c) "vertical agreements" means agreements or concerted practices entered into by two or more undertakings, each of which operates, for the purposes of the agreement, at a different level of the production or distribution chain;

(d) "vertical restraints" means restrictions of competition falling within the scope of Article 81(1), when such restrictions are contained in a vertical agreement;

(e) "exclusive supply obligation" means any direct or indirect obligation causing the supplier to sell the contract goods or services only to one buyer inside the common market for the purposes of a specific use or for resale;

(f) "selective distribution system" means a distribution system where the supplier undertakes to sell the contract goods or services, either directly or indirectly, only to distributors or repairers selected on the basis of specified criteria and where these distributors or repairers undertake not to sell such goods or services to unauthorised distributors or independent repairers, without prejudice to the ability to sell spare parts to independent repairers or the obligation to provide independent operators with all technical information, diagnostic equipment, tools and training required for the repair and maintenance of motor vehicles or for the implementation of environmental protection measures;

(g) "quantitative selective distribution system" means a selective distribution system where the supplier uses criteria for the selection of distributors or repairers which directly limit their number;

(h) "qualitative selective distribution system" means a selective distribution system where the supplier uses criteria for the selection of distributors or repairers which are only qualitative in nature, are required by the nature of the contract goods or services, are laid down uniformly for all distributors or repairers applying to join the distribution system, are not applied in a discriminatory manner, and do not directly limit the number of distributors or repairers;

(i) "intellectual property rights" includes industrial property rights, copyright and neighbouring rights;

(j) "know-how" means a package of non-patented practical information, derived from experience and testing by the supplier, which is secret, substantial and identified; in this context, "secret" means that the know-how, as a body or in the precise configuration and assembly of its components, is not generally known or easily accessible; "substantial" means that the know-how includes information which is indispensable to the buyer for the use, sale or resale of the contract goods or services; "identified" means that the know-how must be described in a sufficiently comprehensive manner so as to make it possible to verify that it fulfils the criteria of secrecy and substantiality;

(k) "buyer", whether distributor or repairer, includes an undertaking which sells goods or services on behalf of another undertaking;

(l)   "authorised repairer" means a provider of repair and maintenance services for motor vehicles operating within the distribution system set up by a supplier of motor vehicles;

(m) "independent repairer" means a provider of repair and maintenance services for motor vehicles not operating within the distribution system set up by the supplier of the motor vehicles for which it provides repair or maintenance. An authorised repairer within the distribution system of a given supplier shall be deemed to be an independent repairer for the purposes of this Regulation to the extent that he provides repair or maintenance services for motor vehicles in respect of which he is not a member of the respective supplier's distribution system;

(n)   "motor vehicle" means a self propelled vehicle intended for use on public roads and having three or more road wheels;

(o)   "passenger car" means a motor vehicle intended for the carriage of passengers and comprising no more than eight seats in addition to the driver's seat;

(p)   "light commercial vehicle" means a motor vehicle intended for the transport of goods or passengers with a maximum mass not exceeding 3,5 tonnes; if a certain light commercial vehicle is also sold in a version with a maximum mass above 3,5 tonnes, all versions of that vehicle are considered to be light commercial vehicles;

(q)   the "contract range" means all the different models of motor vehicles available for purchase by the distributor from the supplier;

(r)   a "motor vehicle which corresponds to a model within the contract range" means a vehicle which is the subject of a distribution agreement with another undertaking within the distribution system set up by the manufacturer or with his consent and which is:

• manufactured or assembled in volume by the manufacturer, and

• identical as to body style, drive-line, chassis, and type of motor to a vehicle within the contract range;

(s)   "spare parts" means goods which are to be installed in or upon a motor vehicle so as to replace components of that vehicle, including goods such as lubricants which are necessary for the use of a motor vehicle, with the exception of fuel;

(t)   "original spare parts" means spare parts which are of the same quality as the components used for the assembly of a motor vehicle and which are manufactured according to the specifications and production standards provided by the vehicle manufacturer for the production of components or spare parts for the motor vehicle in question. This includes spare parts which are manufactured on the same production line as these components. It is presumed, unless the contrary is proven, that parts constitute original spare parts if the part manufacturer certifies that the parts match the quality of the components used for the assembly of the vehicle in question and have been manufactured according to the specifications and production standards of the vehicle manufacturer;

(u) "spare parts of matching quality" means exclusively spare parts made by any undertaking which can certify at any moment that the parts in question match the quality of the components which are or were used for the assembly of the motor vehicles in question;

(v) "undertakings within the distribution system" means the manufacturer and undertakings which are entrusted by the manufacturer or with the manufacturer's consent with the distribution or repair or maintenance of contract goods or corresponding goods;

(w) "end user" includes leasing companies unless the leasing contracts used provide for a transfer of ownership or an option to purchase the vehicle prior to the expiry of the contract.

2. The terms "undertaking", "supplier", "buyer", "distributor" and "repairer" shall include their respective connected undertakings.
"Connected undertakings" are:

(a) undertakings in which a party to the agreement, directly or indirectly:

    (i)   has the power to exercise more than half the voting rights, or

    (ii) has the power to appoint more than half the members of the supervisory board, board of management or bodies legally representing the undertaking, or

    (iii) has the right to manage the undertaking's affairs;

(b) undertakings which directly or indirectly have, over a party to the agreement, the rights or powers listed in (a);

(c) undertakings in which an undertaking referred to in (b) has, directly or indirectly, the rights or powers listed in (a);

(d) undertakings in which a party to the agreement together with one or more of the undertakings referred to in (a), (b) or (c), or in which two or more of the latter undertakings, jointly have the rights or powers listed in (a);

(e) undertakings in which the rights or the powers listed in (a) are jointly held by:

    (i)   parties to the agreement or their respective connected undertakings referred to in (a) to (d), or

(ii)   one or more of the parties to the agreement or one or more of their connected undertakings referred to in (a) to (d) and one or more third parties.

Article 2 Scope

1. Pursuant to Article 81(3) of the Treaty and subject to the provisions of this Regulation, it is hereby declared that the provisions of Article 81(1) shall not apply to vertical agreements where they relate to the conditions under which the parties may purchase, sell or resell new motor vehicles, spare parts for motor vehicles or repair and maintenance services for motor vehicles.

The first subparagraph shall apply to the extent that such vertical agreements contain vertical restraints.

The exemption declared by this paragraph shall be known for the purposes of this Regulation as "the exemption".

2. The exemption shall also apply to the following categories of vertical agreements:

(a)   Vertical agreements entered into between an association of undertakings and its members, or between such an association and its suppliers, only if all its members are distributors of motor vehicles or spare parts for motor vehicles or repairers and if no individual member of the association, together with its connected undertakings, has a total annual turnover exceeding EUR 50 million; vertical agreements entered into by such associations shall be covered by this Regulation without prejudice to the application of Article 81 to horizontal agreements concluded between the members of the association or decisions adopted by the association;

(b)   vertical agreements containing provisions which relate to the assignment to the buyer or use by the buyer of intellectual property rights, provided that those provisions do not constitute the primary object of such agreements and are directly related to the use, sale or resale of goods or services by the buyer or its customers. The exemption shall apply on condition that those provisions do not contain restrictions of competition relating to the contract goods or services which have the same object or effect as vertical restraints which are not exempted under this Regulation.

3. The exemption shall not apply to vertical agreements entered into between competing undertakings.

However, it shall apply where competing undertakings enter into a non-reciprocal vertical agreement and:

(a) the buyer has a total annual turnover not exceeding EUR 100 million, or

(b) the supplier is a manufacturer and a distributor of goods, while the buyer is a distributor not manufacturing goods competing with the contract goods, or

(c) the supplier is a provider of services at several levels of trade, while the buyer does not provide competing services at the level of trade where it purchases the contract services.

Article 3   General conditions

1. Subject to paragraphs 2, 3, 4, 5, 6 and 7, the exemption shall apply on condition that the supplier's market share on the relevant market on which it sells the new motor vehicles, spare parts for motor vehicles or repair and maintenance services does not exceed 30 %.

However, the market share threshold for the application of the exemption shall be 40 % for agreements establishing quantitative selective distribution systems for the sale of new motor vehicles.

Those thresholds shall not apply to agreements establishing qualitative selective distribution systems.

2. In the case of vertical agreements containing exclusive supply obligations, the exemption shall apply on condition that the market share held by the buyer does not exceed 30 % of the relevant market on which it purchases the contract goods or services.

3. The exemption shall apply on condition that the vertical agreement concluded with a distributor or repairer provides that the supplier agrees to the transfer of the rights and obligations resulting from the vertical agreement to another distributor or repairer within the distribution system and chosen by the former distributor or repairer.

4. The exemption shall apply on condition that the vertical agreement concluded with a distributor or repairer provides that a supplier who wishes to give notice of termination of an agreement must give such notice in writing and must include detailed, objective and transparent reasons for the termination, in order to prevent a supplier from ending a vertical agreement with a distributor or repairer because of practices which may not be restricted under this Regulation.

5. The exemption shall apply on condition that the vertical agreement concluded by the supplier of new motor vehicles with a distributor or authorised repairer provides

(a) that the agreement is concluded for a period of at least five years; in this case each party has to undertake to give the other party at least six months' prior notice of its intention not to renew the agreement;

(b) or that the agreement is concluded for an indefinite period; in this case the period of notice for regular termination of the agreement has to be at least two years for both parties; this period is reduced to at least one year where:

(i) the supplier is obliged by law or by special agreement to pay appropriate compensation on termination of the agreement, or

(ii) the supplier terminates the agreement where it is necessary to re-organise the whole or a substantial part of the network.

6. The exemption shall apply on condition that the vertical agreement provides for each of the parties the right to refer disputes concerning the fulfilment of their contractual obligations to an independent expert or arbitrator. Such disputes may relate, inter alia, to any of the following:

(a) supply obligations;

(b) the setting or attainment of sales targets;

(c) the implementation of stock requirements;

(d) the implementation of an obligation to provide or use demonstration vehicles;

(e) the conditions for the sale of different brands;

(f) the issue whether the prohibition to operate out of an unauthorised place of establishment limits the ability of the distributor of motor vehicles other than passenger cars or light commercial vehicles to expand its business, or

(g) the issue whether the termination of an agreement is justified by the reasons given in the notice.

The right referred to in the first sentence is without prejudice to each party's right to make an application to a national court.

7. For the purposes of this Article, the market share held by the undertakings referred to in Article 1(2)(e) shall be apportioned equally to each undertaking having the rights or the powers listed in Article 1(2)(a).

Article 4   Hardcore restrictions

(Hardcore restrictions concerning the sale of new motor vehicles, repair and maintenance services or spare parts)

1. The exemption shall not apply to vertical agreements which, directly or indirectly, in isolation or in combination with other factors under the control of the parties, have as their object:

(a) the restriction of the distributor's or repairer's ability to determine its sale price, without prejudice to the supplier's ability to impose a maximum sale price or to recommend a sale price, provided that this does not amount to a fixed or minimum sale price as a result of pressure from, or incentives offered by, any of the parties;

(b) the restriction of the territory into which, or of the customers to whom, the distributor or repairer may sell the contract goods or services; however, the exemption shall apply to:

(i)   the restriction of active sales into the exclusive territory or to an exclusive customer group reserved to the supplier or allocated by the supplier to another distributor or repairer, where such a restriction does not limit sales by the customers of the distributor or repairer;

(ii) the restriction of sales to end users by a distributor operating at the wholesale level of trade;

(iii) the restriction of sales of new motor vehicles and spare parts to unauthorised distributors by the members of a selective distribution system in markets where selective distribution is applied, subject to the provisions of point (i);

(iv) the restriction of the buyer's ability to sell components, supplied for the purposes of incorporation, to customers who would use them to manufacture the same type of goods as those produced by the supplier;

(c) the restriction of cross-supplies between distributors or repairers within a selective distribution system, including between distributors or repairers operating at different levels of trade;

(d) the restriction of active or passive sales of new passenger cars or light commercial vehicles, spare parts for any motor vehicle or repair and maintenance services for any motor vehicle to end users by members of a selective distribution system operating at the retail level of trade in markets where selective distribution is used. The exemption shall apply to agreements containing a prohibition on a member of a selective distribution system from operating out of an unauthorised place of establishment. However, the application of the exemption to such a prohibition is subject to Article 5(2)(b);

(e) the restriction of active or passive sales of new motor vehicles other than passenger cars or light commercial vehicles to end users by members of a selective distribution system operating at the retail level of trade in markets where selective distribution is used, without prejudice to the ability of the supplier to prohibit a member of that system from operating out of an unauthorised place of establishment; (Hardcore restrictions only concerning the sale of new motor vehicles)

(f) the restriction of the distributor's ability to sell any new motor vehicle which corresponds to a model within its contract range;

(g) the restriction of the distributor's ability to subcontract the provision of repair and maintenance services to authorised repairers, without prejudice to the ability of the supplier to require the distributor to give end users the name and address of the authorised repairer or repairers in question before the conclusion of a sales contract and, if any of these authorised repairers is not in the vicinity of the sales outlet, to also tell end users how far the repair shop or repair shops in question are from the sales outlet; however, such obligations may only be imposed provided that similar obligations are imposed on distributors whose repair shop is not on the same premises as their sales outlet; (Hardcore restrictions only concerning the sale of repair and maintenance services and of spare parts)

(h) the restriction of the authorised repairer's ability to limit its activities to the provision of repair and maintenance services and the distribution of spare parts;

(i) the restriction of the sales of spare parts for motor vehicles by members of a selective distribution system to independent repairers which use these parts for the repair and maintenance of a motor vehicle;

(j) the restriction agreed between a supplier of original spare parts or spare parts of matching quality, repair tools or diagnostic or other equipment and a manufacturer of motor vehicles, which limits the supplier's ability to sell these goods or services to authorised or independent distributors or to authorised or independent repairers or end users;

(k) the restriction of a distributor's or authorised repairer's ability to obtain original spare parts or spare parts of matching quality from a third undertaking of its choice and to use them for the repair or maintenance of motor vehicles, without prejudice to the ability of a supplier of new motor vehicles to require the use of original spare parts supplied by it for repairs carried out under warranty, free servicing and vehicle recall work;

(l) the restriction agreed between a manufacturer of motor vehicles which uses components for the initial assembly of motor vehicles and the supplier of such components which limits the latter's ability to place its trade mark or logo effectively and in an easily visible manner on the components supplied or on spare parts.

2. The exemption shall not apply where the supplier of motor vehicles refuses to give independent operators access to any technical information, diagnostic and other equipment, tools, including any relevant software, or training required for the repair and maintenance of these motor vehicles or for the implementation of environmental protection measures.

Such access must include in particular the unrestricted use of the electronic control and diagnostic systems of a motor vehicle, the programming of these systems in accordance with the supplier's standard procedures, the repair and training instructions and the information required for the use of diagnostic and servicing tools and equipment.

Access must be given to independent operators in a non-discriminatory, prompt and proportionate way, and the information must be provided in a usable form. If the relevant item is covered by an intellectual property right or constitutes know-how, access shall not be withheld in any abusive manner.

For the purposes of this paragraph "independent operator" shall mean undertakings which are directly or indirectly involved in the repair and maintenance of motor vehicles, in particular independent repairers, manufacturers of repair equipment or tools, independent distributors of spare parts, publishers of technical information, automobile clubs, roadside assistance operators, operators offering inspection and testing services and operators offering training for repairers.

Article 5 Specific conditions

1. As regards the sale of new motor vehicles, repair and maintenance services or spare parts, the exemption shall not apply to any of the following obligations contained in vertical agreements:

(a) any direct or indirect non-compete obligation;

(b) any direct or indirect obligation limiting the ability of an authorised repairer to provide repair and maintenance services for vehicles from competing suppliers;

(c) any direct or indirect obligation causing the members of a distribution system not to sell motor vehicles or spare parts of particular competing suppliers or not to provide repair and maintenance services for motor vehicles of particular competing suppliers;

(d) any direct or indirect obligation causing the distributor or authorised repairer, after termination of the agreement, not to manufacture, purchase, sell or resell motor vehicles or not to provide repair or maintenance services.

2. As regards the sale of new motor vehicles, the exemption shall not apply to any of the following obligations contained in vertical agreements:

(a) any direct or indirect obligation causing the retailer not to sell leasing services relating to contract goods or corresponding goods;

(b) any direct or indirect obligation on any distributor of passenger cars or light commercial vehicles within a selective distribution system, which limits its ability to establish additional sales or delivery outlets at other locations within the common market where selective distribution is applied.

3. As regards repair and maintenance services or the sale of spare parts, the exemption shall not apply to any direct or indirect obligation as to the place of establishment of an authorised repairer where selective distribution is applied.

Article 6   Withdrawal of the benefit of the Regulation

1. The Commission may withdraw the benefit of this Regulation, pursuant to Article 7(1) of Regulation No 19/65/EEC, where it finds in any particular case that vertical agreements to which this Regulation applies nevertheless have effects which are incompatible with the conditions laid down in Article 81(3) of the Treaty, and in particular:

(a) where access to the relevant market or competition therein is significantly restricted by the cumulative effect of parallel networks of similar vertical restraints implemented by competing suppliers or buyers, or

(b) where competition is restricted on a market where one supplier is not exposed to effective competition from other suppliers, or

(c) where prices or conditions of supply for contract goods or for corresponding goods differ substantially between geographic markets, or

(d) where discriminatory prices or sales conditions are applied within a geographic market.

2. Where in any particular case vertical agreements to which the exemption applies have effects incompatible with the conditions laid down in Article 81(3) of the Treaty in the territory of a Member State, or in a part thereof, which has all the characteristics of a distinct geographic market, the relevant authority of that Member State may withdraw the benefit of application of this Regulation in respect of that territory, under the same conditions as those provided in paragraph 1.

Article 7   Non-application of the Regulation

1. Pursuant to Article 1a of Regulation No 19/65/EEC, the Commission may by regulation declare that, where parallel networks of similar vertical restraints cover more than 50 % of a relevant market, this Regulation shall not apply to vertical agreements containing specific restraints relating to that market.

2. A regulation pursuant to paragraph 1 shall not become applicable earlier than one year following its adoption.

Article 8   Market share calculation

1. The market shares provided for in this Regulation shall be calculated

(a) for the distribution of new motor vehicles on the basis of the volume of the contract goods and corresponding goods sold by the supplier, together with any other goods sold by the supplier which are regarded as interchangeable or substitutable by the buyer, by reason of the products' characteristics, prices and intended use;

(b) for the distribution of spare parts on the basis of the value of the contract goods and other goods sold by the supplier, together with any other goods sold by the supplier which are regarded as interchangeable or substitutable by the buyer, by reason of the products' characteristics, prices and intended use;

(c) for the provision of repair and maintenance services on the basis of the value of the contract services sold by the members of the supplier's distribution network together with any other services sold by these members which are regarded as interchangeable or substitutable by the buyer, by reason of their characteristics, prices and intended use.

If the volume data required for those calculations are not available, value data may be used or vice versa. If such information is not available, estimates based on other reliable market information may be used. For the purposes of Article 3(2), the market purchase volume or the market purchase value respectively, or estimates thereof shall be used to calculate the market share.

2. For the purposes of applying the market share thresholds of 30 % and 40 % provided for in this Regulation the following rules shall apply:

(a) the market share shall be calculated on the basis of data relating to the preceding calendar year;

(b) the market share shall include any goods or services supplied to integrated distributors for the purposes of sale;

(c) if the market share is initially not more than 30 % or 40 % respectively but subsequently rises above that level without exceeding 35 % or 45 % respectively, the exemption shall continue to apply for a period of two consecutive calendar years following the year in which the market share threshold of 30 % or 40 % respectively was first exceeded;

(d) if the market share is initially not more than 30 % or 40 % respectively but subsequently rises above 35 % or 45 % respectively, the exemption shall continue to apply for one calendar year following the year in which the level of 30 % or 40 % respectively was first exceeded;

(e) the benefit of points (c) and (d) may not be combined so as to exceed a period of two calendar years.

Article 9 Turnover calculation

1. For the purposes of calculating total annual turnover figures referred to in Article 2(2)(a) and 2(3)(a) respectively, the turnover achieved during the previous financial year by the relevant party to the vertical agreement and the turnover achieved by its connected undertakings in respect of all goods and services, excluding all taxes and other duties, shall be added together. For this purpose, no account shall be taken of dealings between the party to the vertical agreement and its connected undertakings or between its connected undertakings.

2. The exemption shall remain applicable where, for any period of two consecutive financial years, the total annual turnover threshold is exceeded by no more than 10 %.

Article 10 Transitional period

The prohibition laid down in Article 81(1) shall not apply during the period from 1 October 2002 to 30 September 2003 in respect of agreements already in force on 30 September 2002 which do not satisfy the conditions for exemption provided for in this Regulation but which satisfy the conditions for exemption provided for in Regulation (EC) No 1475/95.

Article 11 Monitoring and evaluation report

1. The Commission shall monitor the operation of this Regulation on a regular basis, with particular regard to its effects on:

(a) competition in motor vehicle retailing and in after sales servicing in the common market or relevant parts of it;

(b) the structure and level of concentration of motor vehicle distribution and any resulting effects on competition.

2. The Commission shall draw up a report on this Regulation not later than 31 May 2008 having regard in particular to the conditions set out in Article 81(3).

Article 12 Entry into force and expiry

1. This Regulation shall enter into force on 1 October 2002.
2. Article 5(2)(b) shall apply from 1 October 2005.
3. This Regulation shall expire on 31 May 2010.

This Regulation shall be binding in its entirety and directly applicable in all Member States.

Done at Brussels, 31 July 2002.

For the Commission
Mario Monti
Member of the Commission

(1) OJ 36, 6.3.1965, p. 533/65.
(2) OJ L 148, 15.6.1999, p. 1.
(3) OJ C 67, 16.3.2002, p. 2.
(4) OJ L 336, 29.12.1999, p. 21.
(5) OJ L 145, 29.6.1995, p. 25.

Appendix 6

Commission Regulation (EC) 773/2004
OJ 2004 L123/8

Commission Regulation (EC) No 773/2004 of 7 April 2004 relating to the conduct of proceedings by the Commission pursuant to Articles 81 and 82 of the EC Treaty (Text with EEA relevance)

THE COMMISSION OF THE EUROPEAN COMMUNITIES,

Having regard to the Treaty establishing the European Community,

Having regard to the Agreement on the European Economic Area,

Having regard to Council Regulation (EC) No 1/2003 of 16 December 2002 on the implementation of the rules on competition laid down in Articles 81 and 82 of the Treaty(1), and in particular Article 33 thereof,

After consulting the Advisory Committee on Restrictive Practices and Dominant Positions,

Whereas:

(1) Regulation (EC) No 1/2003 empowers the Commission to regulate certain aspects of proceedings for the application of Articles 81 and 82 of the Treaty. It is necessary to lay down rules concerning the initiation of proceedings by the Commission as well as the handling of complaints and the hearing of the parties concerned.

(2) According to Regulation (EC) No 1/2003, national courts are under an obligation to avoid taking decisions which could run counter to decisions envisaged by the Commission in the same case. According to Article 11(6) of that Regulation, national competition authorities are relieved from their competence once the Commission has initiated proceedings for the adoption of a decision under Chapter III of Regulation (EC) No 1/2003. In this context, it is important that courts and competition authorities of the Member States are aware of the initiation of proceedings by the Commission. The Commission should therefore be able to make public its decisions to initiate proceedings.

(3) Before taking oral statements from natural or legal persons who consent to be interviewed, the Commission should inform those persons of the legal basis of the interview and its voluntary nature. The persons interviewed should also be informed of the purpose of the interview and of any record which may be made. In order to enhance the accuracy of the statements, the persons interviewed should also be given an opportunity to correct the statements recorded. Where information gathered from oral statements is exchanged pursuant to Article 12 of Regulation (EC) No 1/2003, that information should only be used in evidence to impose sanctions on natural persons where the conditions set out in that Article are fulfilled.

(4) Pursuant to Article 23(1)(d) of Regulation (EC) No 1/2003 fines may be imposed on undertakings and associations of undertakings where they fail to rectify within the time limit fixed by the Commission an incorrect, incomplete or misleading answer given by a member of their staff to questions in the course of inspections. It is therefore necessary to provide the undertaking concerned with a record of any explanations given and to establish a procedure enabling it to add any rectification, amendment or supplement to the explanations given by the member of staff who is not or was not authorised to provide explanations on behalf of the undertaking. The explanations given by a member of staff should remain in the Commission file as recorded during the inspection.

(5) Complaints are an essential source of information for detecting infringements of competition rules. It is important to define clear and efficient procedures for handling complaints lodged with the Commission.

(6) In order to be admissible for the purposes of Article 7 of Regulation (EC) No 1/2003, a complaint must contain certain specified information.

(7) In order to assist complainants in submitting the necessary facts to the Commission, a form should be drawn up. The submission of the information listed in that form should be a condition for a complaint to be treated as a complaint as referred to in Article 7 of Regulation (EC) No 1/2003.

(8) Natural or legal persons having chosen to lodge a complaint should be given the possibility to be associated closely with the proceedings initiated by the Commission with a view to finding an infringement. However, they should not have access to business secrets or other confidential information belonging to other parties involved in the proceedings.

(9) Complainants should be granted the opportunity of expressing their views if the Commission considers that there are insufficient grounds for acting on the complaint. Where the Commission rejects a complaint on the grounds that a competition authority of a Member State is dealing with it or has already done so, it should inform the complainant of the identity of that authority.

(10) In order to respect the rights of defence of undertakings, the Commission should give the parties concerned the right to be heard before it takes a decision.

(11) Provision should also be made for the hearing of persons who have not submitted a complaint as referred to in Article 7 of Regulation (EC) No 1/2003 and who are not parties to whom a statement of objections has been addressed but who can nevertheless show a sufficient interest. Consumer associations that apply to be heard should generally be regarded as having a sufficient interest, where the proceedings concern products or services used by the end-consumer or products or services that constitute a direct input into such products or services. Where it considers this to be useful for the proceedings, the Commission should also be able to invite other persons to express their views in writing and to attend the oral hearing of the parties to whom a statement of objections has been addressed. Where appropriate, it should also be able to invite such persons to express their views at that oral hearing.

(12) To improve the effectiveness of oral hearings, the Hearing Officer should have the power to allow the parties concerned, complainants, other persons invited to the hearing, the Commission services and the authorities of the Member States to ask questions during the hearing.

(13) When granting access to the file, the Commission should ensure the protection of business secrets and other confidential information. The category of "other confidential information" includes information other than business secrets, which may be considered as confidential, insofar as its disclosure would significantly harm an undertaking or person. The Commission should be able to request undertakings or associations of undertakings that submit or have submitted documents or statements to identify confidential information.

(14) Where business secrets or other confidential information are necessary to prove an infringement, the Commission should assess for each individual document whether the need to disclose is greater than the harm which might result from disclosure.

(15) In the interest of legal certainty, a minimum time-limit for the various submissions provided for in this Regulation should be laid down.

(16) This Regulation replaces Commission Regulation (EC) No 2842/98 of 22 December 1998 on the hearing of parties in certain proceedings under Articles 85 and 86 of the EC Treaty(2), which should therefore be repealed.

(17) This Regulation aligns the procedural rules in the transport sector with the general rules of procedure in all sectors. Commission Regulation (EC) No 2843/98 of 22 December 1998 on the form, content and other details of applications and notifications provided for in Council Regulations (EEC) No 1017/68, (EEC) No 4056/86 and (EEC) No 3975/87 applying the rules on competition to the transport sector(3) should therefore be repealed.

(18) Regulation (EC) No 1/2003 abolishes the notification and authorisation system. Commission Regulation (EC) No 3385/94 of 21 December 1994 on the form, content and other details of applications and notifications provided for in Council Regulation No 17(4) should therefore be repealed,

HAS ADOPTED THIS REGULATION:

CHAPTER I SCOPE

Article 1 Subject-matter and scope

This regulation applies to proceedings conducted by the Commission for the application of Articles 81 and 82 of the Treaty.

CHAPTER II INITIATION OF PROCEEDINGS

Article 2 Initiation of proceedings

1. The Commission may decide to initiate proceedings with a view to adopting a decision pursuant to Chapter III of Regulation (EC) No 1/2003 at any point in time, but no later than the date on which it issues a preliminary assessment as referred to in Article 9(1) of that Regulation or a statement of objections or the date on which a notice pursuant to Article 27(4) of that Regulation is published, whichever is the earlier.

2. The Commission may make public the initiation of proceedings, in any appropriate way. Before doing so, it shall inform the parties concerned.

3. The Commission may exercise its powers of investigation pursuant to Chapter V of Regulation (EC) No 1/2003 before initiating proceedings.

4. The Commission may reject a complaint pursuant to Article 7 of Regulation (EC) No 1/2003 without initiating proceedings.

CHAPTER III INVESTIGATIONS BY THE COMMISSION

Article 3 Power to take statements

1. Where the Commission interviews a person with his consent in accordance with Article 19 of Regulation (EC) No 1/2003, it shall, at the beginning of the interview, state the legal basis and the purpose of the interview, and recall its voluntary nature. It shall also inform the person interviewed of its intention to make a record of the interview.

2. The interview may be conducted by any means including by telephone or electronic means.

3. The Commission may record the statements made by the persons interviewed in any form. A copy of any recording shall be made available to the person interviewed for approval. Where necessary, the Commission shall set a time-limit within which the person interviewed may communicate to it any correction to be made to the statement.

Article 4 Oral questions during inspections

1. When, pursuant to Article 20(2)(e) of Regulation (EC) No 1/2003, officials or other accompanying persons authorised by the Commission ask representatives or members of staff of an undertaking or of an association of undertakings for explanations, the explanations given may be recorded in any form.

2. A copy of any recording made pursuant to paragraph 1 shall be made available to the undertaking or association of undertakings concerned after the inspection.

3. In cases where a member of staff of an undertaking or of an association of undertakings who is not or was not authorised by the undertaking or by the association of undertakings to provide explanations on behalf of the undertaking or association of undertakings has been asked for explanations, the Commission shall set a time-limit within which the undertaking or the association of undertakings may communicate to the Commission any rectification, amendment or supplement to the explanations given by such member of staff. The rectification, amendment or supplement shall be added to the explanations as recorded pursuant to paragraph 1.

CHAPTER IV HANDLING OF COMPLAINTS

Article 5 Admissibility of complaints

1. Natural and legal persons shall show a legitimate interest in order to be entitled to lodge a complaint for the purposes of Article 7 of Regulation (EC) No 1/2003.

Such complaints shall contain the information required by Form C, as set out in the Annex. The Commission may dispense with this obligation as regards part of the information, including documents, required by Form C.

2. Three paper copies as well as, if possible, an electronic copy of the complaint shall be submitted to the Commission. The complainant shall also submit a non-confidential version of the complaint, if confidentiality is claimed for any part of the complaint.

3. Complaints shall be submitted in one of the official languages of the Community.

Article 6 Participation of complainants in proceedings

1. Where the Commission issues a statement of objections relating to a matter in respect of which it has received a complaint, it shall provide the complainant with a copy of the non-confidential version of the statement of objections and set a time-limit within which the complainant may make known its views in writing.

2. The Commission may, where appropriate, afford complainants the opportunity of expressing their views at the oral hearing of the parties to which a statement of objections has been issued, if complainants so request in their written comments.

Article 7 Rejection of complaints

1. Where the Commission considers that on the basis of the information in its possession there are insufficient grounds for acting on a complaint, it shall inform the complainant of its reasons and set a time-limit within which the complainant

may make known its views in writing. The Commission shall not be obliged to take into account any further written submission received after the expiry of that time-limit.

2. If the complainant makes known its views within the time-limit set by the Commission and the written submissions made by the complainant do not lead to a different assessment of the complaint, the Commission shall reject the complaint by decision.

3. If the complainant fails to make known its views within the time-limit set by the Commission, the complaint shall be deemed to have been withdrawn.

Article 8   Access to information

1. Where the Commission has informed the complainant of its intention to reject a complaint pursuant to Article 7(1) the complainant may request access to the documents on which the Commission bases its provisional assessment. For this purpose, the complainant may however not have access to business secrets and other confidential information belonging to other parties involved in the proceedings.

2. The documents to which the complainant has had access in the context of proceedings conducted by the Commission under Articles 81 and 82 of the Treaty may only be used by the complainant for the purposes of judicial or administrative proceedings for the application of those Treaty provisions.

Article 9   Rejections of complaints pursuant to Article 13 of Regulation (EC) No 1/2003

Where the Commission rejects a complaint pursuant to Article 13 of Regulation (EC) No 1/2003, it shall inform the complainant without delay of the national competition authority which is dealing or has already dealt with the case.

CHAPTER V   EXERCISE OF THE RIGHT TO BE HEARD

Article 10   Statement of objections and reply

1. The Commission shall inform the parties concerned in writing of the objections raised against them. The statement of objections shall be notified to each of them.

2. The Commission shall, when notifying the statement of objections to the parties concerned, set a time-limit within which these parties may inform it in writing of their views. The Commission shall not be obliged to take into account written submissions received after the expiry of that time-limit.

3. The parties may, in their written submissions, set out all facts known to them which are relevant to their defence against the objections raised by the Commission. They shall attach any relevant documents as proof of the facts set

out. They shall provide a paper original as well as an electronic copy or, where they do not provide an electronic copy, 28 paper copies of their submission and of the documents attached to it. They may propose that the Commission hear persons who may corroborate the facts set out in their submission.

Article 11 Right to be heard

1. The Commission shall give the parties to whom it has addressed a statement of objections the opportunity to be heard before consulting the Advisory Committee referred to in Article 14(1) of Regulation (EC) No 1/2003.

2. The Commission shall, in its decisions, deal only with objections in respect of which the parties referred to in paragraph 1 have been able to comment.

Article 12 Right to an oral hearing

The Commission shall give the parties to whom it has addressed a statement of objections the opportunity to develop their arguments at an oral hearing, if they so request in their written submissions.

Article 13 Hearing of other persons

1. If natural or legal persons other than those referred to in Articles 5 and 11 apply to be heard and show a sufficient interest, the Commission shall inform them in writing of the nature and subject matter of the procedure and shall set a time-limit within which they may make known their views in writing.

2. The Commission may, where appropriate, invite persons referred to in paragraph 1 to develop their arguments at the oral hearing of the parties to whom a statement of objections has been addressed, if the persons referred to in paragraph 1 so request in their written comments.

3. The Commission may invite any other person to express its views in writing and to attend the oral hearing of the parties to whom a statement of objections has been addressed. The Commission may also invite such persons to express their views at that oral hearing.

Article 14 Conduct of oral hearings

1. Hearings shall be conducted by a Hearing Officer in full independence.

2. The Commission shall invite the persons to be heard to attend the oral hearing on such date as it shall determine.

3. The Commission shall invite the competition authorities of the Member States to take part in the oral hearing. It may likewise invite officials and civil servants of other authorities of the Member States.

4. Persons invited to attend shall either appear in person or be represented by legal representatives or by representatives authorised by their constitution as

appropriate. Undertakings and associations of undertakings may also be represented by a duly authorised agent appointed from among their permanent staff.

5. Persons heard by the Commission may be assisted by their lawyers or other qualified persons admitted by the Hearing Officer.

6. Oral hearings shall not be public. Each person may be heard separately or in the presence of other persons invited to attend, having regard to the legitimate interest of the undertakings in the protection of their business secrets and other confidential information.

7. The Hearing Officer may allow the parties to whom a statement of objections has been addressed, the complainants, other persons invited to the hearing, the Commission services and the authorities of the Member States to ask questions during the hearing.

8. The statements made by each person heard shall be recorded. Upon request, the recording of the hearing shall be made available to the persons who attended the hearing. Regard shall be had to the legitimate interest of the parties in the protection of their business secrets and other confidential information.

CHAPTER VI ACCESS TO THE FILE AND TREATMENT OF CONFIDENTIAL INFORMATION

Article 15 Access to the file and use of documents

1. If so requested, the Commission shall grant access to the file to the parties to whom it has addressed a statement of objections. Access shall be granted after the notification of the statement of objections.

2. The right of access to the file shall not extend to business secrets, other confidential information and internal documents of the Commission or of the competition authorities of the Member States. The right of access to the file shall also not extend to correspondence between the Commission and the competition authorities of the Member States or between the latter where such correspondence is contained in the file of the Commission.

3. Nothing in this Regulation prevents the Commission from disclosing and using information necessary to prove an infringement of Articles 81 or 82 of the Treaty.

4. Documents obtained through access to the file pursuant to this Article shall only be used for the purposes of judicial or administrative proceedings for the application of Articles 81 and 82 of the Treaty.

Article 16 Identification and protection of confidential information

1. Information, including documents, shall not be communicated or made accessible by the Commission in so far as it contains business secrets or other confidential information of any person.

2. Any person which makes known its views pursuant to Article 6(1), Article 7(1), Article 10(2) and Article 13(1) and (3) or subsequently submits further information to the Commission in the course of the same procedure, shall clearly identify any material which it considers to be confidential, giving reasons, and provide a separate non-confidential version by the date set by the Commission for making its views known.

3. Without prejudice to paragraph 2 of this Article, the Commission may require undertakings and associations of undertakings which produce documents or statements pursuant to Regulation (EC) No 1/2003 to identify the documents or parts of documents which they consider to contain business secrets or other confidential information belonging to them and to identify the undertakings with regard to which such documents are to be considered confidential. The Commission may likewise require undertakings or associations of undertakings to identify any part of a statement of objections, a case summary drawn up pursuant to Article 27(4) of Regulation (EC) No 1/2003 or a decision adopted by the Commission which in their view contains business secrets.

The Commission may set a time-limit within which the undertakings and associations of undertakings are to:

(a) substantiate their claim for confidentiality with regard to each individual document or part of document, statement or part of statement;

(b) provide the Commission with a non-confidential version of the documents or statements, in which the confidential passages are deleted;

(c) provide a concise description of each piece of deleted information.

4. If undertakings or associations of undertakings fail to comply with paragraphs 2 and 3, the Commission may assume that the documents or statements concerned do not contain confidential information.

CHAPTER VII GENERAL AND FINAL PROVISIONS

Article 17 Time-limits

1. In setting the time-limits provided for in Article 3(3), Article 4(3), Article 6(1), Article 7(1), Article 10(2) and Article 16(3), the Commission shall have regard both to the time required for preparation of the submission and to the urgency of the case.

2. The time-limits referred to in Article 6(1), Article 7(1) and Article 10(2) shall be at least four weeks. However, for proceedings initiated with a view to adopting interim measures pursuant to Article 8 of Regulation (EC) No 1/2003, the time-limit may be shortened to one week.

3. The time-limits referred to in Article 3(3), Article 4(3) and Article 16(3) shall be at least two weeks.

4. Where appropriate and upon reasoned request made before the expiry of the original time-limit, time-limits may be extended.

Article 18 Repeals

Regulations (EC) No 2842/98, (EC) No 2843/98 and (EC) No 3385/94 are repealed.
References to the repealed regulations shall be construed as references to this regulation.

Article 19 Transitional provisions

Procedural steps taken under Regulations (EC) No 2842/98 and (EC) No 2843/98 shall continue to have effect for the purpose of applying this Regulation.

Article 20 Entry into force

This Regulation shall enter into force on 1 May 2004.

This Regulation shall be binding in its entirety and directly applicable in all Member States.

Done at Brussels, 7 April 2004.

For the Commission
Mario Monti
Member of the Commission

(1) OJ L 1, 4.1.2003, p. 1. Regulation as amended by Regulation (EC) No 411/2004 (OJ L 68, 6.3.2004, p. 1).
(2) OJ L 354, 30.12.1998, p. 18.
(3) OJ L 354, 30.12.1998, p. 22.
(4) OJ L 377, 31.12.1994, p. 28.

ANNEX

FORM C COMPLAINT PURSUANT TO ARTICLE 7 OF
REGULATION (EC) No 1/2003

I. Information regarding the complainant and the undertaking(s) or association of undertakings giving rise to the complaint
1. Give full details on the identity of the legal or natural person submitting the complaint. Where the complainant is an undertaking, identify the corporate

group to which it belongs and provide a concise overview of the nature and scope of its business activities. Provide a contact person (with telephone number, postal and e-mail-address) from which supplementary explanations can be obtained.

2. Identify the undertaking(s) or association of undertakings whose conduct the complaint relates to, including, where applicable, all available information on the corporate group to which the undertaking(s) complained of belong and the nature and scope of the business activities pursued by them. Indicate the position of the complainant vis-à-vis the undertaking(s) or association of undertakings complained of (e.g. customer, competitor).

II. Details of the alleged infringement and evidence

3. Set out in detail the facts from which, in your opinion, it appears that there exists an infringement of Article 81 or 82 of the Treaty and/or Article 53 or 54 of the EEA agreement. Indicate in particular the nature of the products (goods or services) affected by the alleged infringements and explain, where necessary, the commercial relationships concerning these products. Provide all available details on the agreements or practices of the undertakings or associations of undertakings to which this complaint relates. Indicate, to the extent possible, the relative market positions of the undertakings concerned by the complaint.

4. Submit all documentation in your possession relating to or directly connected with the facts set out in the complaint (for example, texts of agreements, minutes of negotiations or meetings, terms of transactions, business documents, circulars, correspondence, notes of telephone conversations...). State the names and address of the persons able to testify to the facts set out in the complaint, and in particular of persons affected by the alleged infringement. Submit statistics or other data in your possession which relate to the facts set out, in particular where they show developments in the marketplace (for example information relating to prices and price trends, barriers to entry to the market for new suppliers etc.).

5. Set out your view about the geographical scope of the alleged infringement and explain, where that is not obvious, to what extent trade between Member States or between the Community and one or more EFTA States that are contracting parties of the EEA Agreement may be affected by the conduct complained of.

III. Finding sought from the Commission and legitimate interest

6. Explain what finding or action you are seeking as a result of proceedings brought by the Commission.

7. Set out the grounds on which you claim a legitimate interest as complainant pursuant to Article 7 of Regulation (EC) No 1/2003. State in particular how the conduct complained of affects you and explain how, in your view, intervention by the Commission would be liable to remedy the alleged grievance.

IV. Proceedings before national competition authorities or national courts

8. Provide full information about whether you have approached, concerning the same or closely related subject-matters, any other competition authority

and/or whether a lawsuit has been brought before a national court. If so, provide full details about the administrative or judicial authority contacted and your submissions to such authority.

Declaration that the information given in this form and in the Annexes thereto is given entirely in good faith.

Date and signature.

Appendix 7

Commission Guidelines on vertical restraints
OJ 2000 C291/1

Commission Notice: Guidelines on Vertical Restraints (2000/C 291/01)
(Text with EEA relevance)

I. INTRODUCTION

1. Purpose of the Guidelines

(1) These Guidelines set out the principles for the assessment of vertical agreements under Article 81 of the EC Treaty. What are considered vertical agreements is defined in Article 2(1) of Commission Regulation (EC) No 2790/1999 of 22 December 1999 on the application of Article 81(3) of the Treaty to categories of vertical agreements and concerted practices([1]) (Block Exemption Regulation) (see paragraphs 23 to 45). These Guidelines are without prejudice to the possible parallel application of Article 82 of the Treaty to vertical agreements. The Guidelines are structured in the following way:

- Section II (paragraphs 8 to 20) describes vertical agreements which generally fall outside Article 81(1);

- Section III (paragraphs 21 to 70) comments on the application of the Block Exemption Regulation;

- Section IV (paragraphs 71 to 87) describes the principles concerning the withdrawal of the block exemption and the disapplication of the Block Exemption Regulation;

- Section V (paragraphs 88 to 99) addresses market definition and market share calculation issues;

- Section VI (paragraphs 100 to 229) describes the general framework of analysis and the enforcement policy of the Commission in individual cases concerning vertical agreements.

(2) Throughout these Guidelines the analysis applies to both goods and services, although certain vertical restraints are mainly used in the distribution of goods. Similarly, vertical agreements can be concluded for intermediate and final

---

([1]) OJ L 336, 29.12.1999, p. 21.

goods and services. Unless otherwise stated, the analysis and arguments in the text apply to all types of goods and services and to all levels of trade. The term "products" includes both goods and services. The terms "supplier" and "buyer" are used for all levels of trade.

(3) By issuing these Guidelines the Commission aims to help companies to make their own assessment of vertical agreements under the EC competition rules. The standards set forth in these Guidelines must be applied in circumstances specific to each case. This rules out a mechanical application. Each case must be evaluated in the light of its own facts. The Commission will apply the Guidelines reasonably and flexibly.

(4) These Guidelines are without prejudice to the interpretation that may be given by the Court of First Instance and the Court of Justice of the European Communities in relation to the application of Article 81 to vertical agreements.

2. Applicability of Article 81 to vertical agreements

(5) Article 81 of the EC Treaty applies to vertical agreements that may affect trade between Member States and that prevent, restrict or distort competition (hereinafter referred to as "vertical restraints")([2]). For vertical restraints, Article 81 provides an appropriate legal framework for assessment, recognising the distinction between anti-competitive and pro-competitive effects: Article 81(1) prohibits those agreements which appreciably restrict or distort competition, while Article 81(3) allows for exemption of those agreements which confer sufficient benefits to outweigh the anti-competitive effects.

(6) For most vertical restraints, competition concerns can only arise if there is insufficient inter-brand competition, i.e. if there is some degree of market power at the level of the supplier or the buyer or at both levels. If there is insufficient inter-brand competition, the protection of inter- and intra-brand competition becomes important.

(7) The protection of competition is the primary objective of EC competition policy, as this enhances consumer welfare and creates an efficient allocation of resources. In applying the EC competition rules, the Commission will adopt an economic approach which is based on the effects on the market; vertical agreements have to be analysed in their legal and economic context. However, in the case of restrictions by object as listed in Article 4 of the Block Exemption Regulation, the Commission is not required to assess the actual effects on the market. Market integration is an additional goal of EC competition policy. Market integration enhances competition in the Community. Companies should not be allowed to recreate private barriers between Member States where State barriers have been successfully abolished.

([2]) See inter alia judgment of the Court of Justice of the European Communities in Joined Cases 56/64 and 58/64 Grundig-Consten v Commission [1966] ECR 299; Case 56/65 Technique Minière v Machinenbau Ulm [1966] ECR 235; and of the Court of First Instance of the European Communities in Case T-77/92 Parker Pen v Commission [1994] ECR II 549.

II. VERTICAL AGREEMENTS WHICH GENERALLY FALL OUTSIDE ARTICLE 81(1)

1. Agreements of minor importance and SMEs

(8) Agreements which are not capable of appreciably affecting trade between Member States or capable of appreciably restricting competition by object or effect are not caught by Article 81(1). The Block Exemption Regulation applies only to agreements falling within the scope of application of Article 81(1). These Guidelines are without prejudice to the application of the present or any future "de minimis" notice([3]).

(9) Subject to the conditions set out in points 11, 18 and 20 of the "de minimis" notice concerning hardcore restrictions and cumulative effect issues, vertical agreements entered into by undertakings whose market share on the relevant market does not exceed 10 % are generally considered to fall outside the scope of Article 81(1). There is no presumption that vertical agreements concluded by undertakings having more than 10 % market share automatically infringe Article 81(1). Agreements between undertakings whose market share exceeds the 10 % threshold may still not have an appreciable effect on trade between Member States or may not constitute an appreciable restriction of competition([4]). Such agreements need to be assessed in their legal and economic context. The criteria for the assessment of individual agreements are set out in paragraphs 100 to 229.

(10) As regards hardcore restrictions defined in the "de minimis" notice, Article 81(1) may apply below the 10 % threshold, provided that there is an appreciable effect on trade between Member States and on competition. The applicable case-law of the Court of Justice and the Court of First Instance is relevant in this respect([5]). Reference is also made to the particular situation of launching a new product or entering a new market which is dealt with in these Guidelines (paragraph 119, point 10).

(11) In addition, the Commission considers that, subject to cumulative effect and hardcore restrictions, agreements between small and medium-sized undertakings as defined in the Annex to Commission Recommendation 96/280/EC([6]) are rarely capable of appreciably affecting trade between Member States or of appreciably restricting competition within the meaning of Article 81(1), and therefore generally fall outside the scope of Article 81(1). In cases where such agreements nonetheless meet the conditions for the application of Article 81(1),

---

[3] See Notice on agreements of minor importance of 9 December 1997, OJ C 372, 9.12.1997, p. 13.

[4] See judgment of the Court of First Instance in Case T-7/93 Langnese-Iglo v Commission [1995] ECR II-1533, paragraph 98.

[5] See judgment of the Court of Justice in Case 5/69 Völk v Vervaecke [1969] ECR 295; Case 1/71 Cadillon v Höss [1971] ECR 351 and Case C-306/96 Javico v Yves Saint Laurent [1998] ECR I-1983, paragraphs 16 and 17.

[6] OJ L 107, 30.4.1996, p. 4.

the Commission will normally refrain from opening proceedings for lack of sufficient Community interest unless those undertakings collectively or individually hold a dominant position in a substantial part of the common market.

2. Agency agreements

(12) Paragraphs 12 to 20 replace the Notice on exclusive dealing contracts with commercial agents of 1962([7]). They must be read in conjunction with Council Directive 86/653/EEC([8]).

Agency agreements cover the situation in which a legal or physical person (the agent) is vested with the power to negotiate and/or conclude contracts on behalf of another person (the principal), either in the agent's own name or in the name of the principal, for the:

- purchase of goods or services by the principal, or

- sale of goods or services supplied by the principal.

(13) In the case of genuine agency agreements, the obligations imposed on the agent as to the contracts negotiated and/or concluded on behalf of the principal do not fall within the scope of application of Article 81(1). The determining factor in assessing whether Article 81(1) is applicable is the financial or commercial risk borne by the agent in relation to the activities for which he has been appointed as an agent by the principal. In this respect it is not material for the assessment whether the agent acts for one or several principals. Non-genuine agency agreements may be caught by Article 81(1), in which case the Block Exemption Regulation and the other sections of these Guidelines will apply.

(14) There are two types of financial or commercial risk that are material to the assessment of the genuine nature of an agency agreement under Article 81(1). First there are the risks which are directly related to the contracts concluded and/or negotiated by the agent on behalf of the principal, such as financing of stocks. Secondly, there are the risks related to market-specific investments. These are investments specifically required for the type of activity for which the agent has been appointed by the principal, i.e. which are required to enable the agent to conclude and/or negotiate this type of contract. Such investments are usually sunk, if upon leaving that particular field of activity the investment cannot be used for other activities or sold other than at a significant loss.

(15) The agency agreement is considered a genuine agency agreement and consequently falls outside Article 81(1) if the agent does not bear any, or bears only insignificant, risks in relation to the contracts concluded and/or negotiated on behalf of the principal and in relation to market-specific investments for that field of activity. In such a situation, the selling or purchasing function forms part of the principal's activities, despite the fact that the agent is a separate undertaking. The

[7] OJ 139, 24.12.1962, p. 2921/62.
[8] OJ L 382, 31.12.1986, p. 17.

principal thus bears the related financial and commercial risks and the agent does not exercise an independent economic activity in relation to the activities for which he has been appointed as an agent by the principal. In the opposite situation the agency agreement is considered a non-genuine agency agreement and may fall under Article 81(1). In that case the agent does bear such risks and will be treated as an independent dealer who must remain free in determining his marketing strategy in order to be able to recover his contract- or market-specific investments. Risks that are related to the activity of providing agency services in general, such as the risk of the agent's income being dependent upon his success as an agent or general investments in for instance premises or personnel, are not material to this assessment.

(16) The question of risk must be assessed on a case-by-case basis, and with regard to the economic reality of the situation rather than the legal form. Nonetheless, the Commission considers that Article 81(1) will generally not be applicable to the obligations imposed on the agent as to the contracts negotiated and/or concluded on behalf of the principal where property in the contract goods bought or sold does not vest in the agent, or the agent does not himself supply the contract services and where the agent:

- does not contribute to the costs relating to the supply/purchase of the contract goods or services, including the costs of transporting the goods. This does not preclude the agent from carrying out the transport service, provided that the costs are covered by the principal;

- is not, directly or indirectly, obliged to invest in sales promotion, such as contributions to the advertising budgets of the principal;

- does not maintain at his own cost or risk stocks of the contract goods, including the costs of financing the stocks and the costs of loss of stocks and can return unsold goods to the principal without charge, unless the agent is liable for fault (for example, by failing to comply with reasonable security measures to avoid loss of stocks);

- does not create and/or operate an after-sales service, repair service or a warranty service unless it is fully reimbursed by the principal;

- does not make market-specific investments in equipment, premises or training of personnel, such as for example the petrol storage tank in the case of petrol retailing or specific software to sell insurance policies in case of insurance agents;

- does not undertake responsibility towards third parties for damage caused by the product sold (product liability), unless, as agent, he is liable for fault in this respect;

- does not take responsibility for customers' non-performance of the contract, with the exception of the loss of the agent's commission, unless the agent is liable for fault (for example, by failing to comply with reasonable security or anti-theft measures or failing to comply with reasonable measures to report theft to the principal or police or to communicate to the principal all necessary information available to him on the customer's financial reliability).

(17) This list is not exhaustive. However, where the agent incurs one or more of the above risks or costs, then Article 81(1) may apply as with any other vertical agreement.

(18) If an agency agreement does not fall within the scope of application of Article 81(1), then all obligations imposed on the agent in relation to the contracts concluded and/or negotiated on behalf of the principal fall outside Article 81(1). The following obligations on the agent's part will generally be considered to form an inherent part of an agency agreement, as each of them relates to the ability of the principal to fix the scope of activity of the agent in relation to the contract goods or services, which is essential if the principal is to take the risks and therefore to be in a position to determine the commercial strategy:

- limitations on the territory in which the agent may sell these goods or services;

- limitations on the customers to whom the agent may sell these goods or services;

- the prices and conditions at which the agent must sell or purchase these goods or services.

(19) In addition to governing the conditions of sale or purchase of the contract goods or services by the agent on behalf of the principal, agency agreements often contain provisions which concern the relationship between the agent and the principal. In particular, they may contain a provision preventing the principal from appointing other agents in respect of a given type of transaction, customer or territory (exclusive agency provisions) and/or a provision preventing the agent from acting as an agent or distributor of undertakings which compete with the principal (non-compete provisions). Exclusive agency provisions concern only intra-brand competition and will in general not lead to anti-competitive effects. Non-compete provisions, including post-term non-compete provisions, concern inter-brand competition and may infringe Article 81(1) if they lead to foreclosure on the relevant market where the contract goods or services are sold or purchased (see Section VI.2.1).

(20) An agency agreement may also fall within the scope of Article 81(1), even if the principal bears all the relevant financial and commercial risks, where it facilitates collusion. This could for instance be the case when a number of principals use the same agents while collectively excluding others from using these agents, or when they use the agents to collude on marketing strategy or to exchange sensitive market information between the principals.

III. APPLICATION OF THE BLOCK EXEMPTION REGULATION

1. Safe harbour created by the Block Exemption Regulation

(21) The Block Exemption Regulation creates a presumption of legality for vertical agreements depending on the market share of the supplier or the buyer. Pursuant to Article 3 of the Block Exemption Regulation, it is in general the market share of the supplier on the market where it sells the contract goods or services which determines the applicability of the block exemption. This market share may not exceed the threshold of 30 % in order for the block exemption to apply. Only where the agreement contains an exclusive supply obligation, as defined in Article 1(c) of the Block Exemption Regulation, is it the buyer's market share on the market where it purchases the contract goods or services which may not exceed the threshold of 30 % in order for the block exemption to apply. For market share issues see Section V (paragraphs 88 to 99).

(22) From an economic point of view, a vertical agreement may have effects not only on the market between supplier and buyer but also on markets downstream of the buyer. The simplified approach of the Block Exemption Regulation, which only takes into account the market share of the supplier or the buyer (as the case may be) on the market between these two parties, is justified by the fact that below the threshold of 30 % the effects on downstream markets will in general be limited. In addition, only having to consider the market between supplier and buyer makes the application of the Block Exemption Regulation easier and enhances the level of legal certainty, while the instrument of withdrawal (see paragraphs 71 to 87) remains available to remedy possible problems on other related markets.

2. Scope of the Block Exemption Regulation

(i) Definition of vertical agreements

(23) Vertical agreements are defined in Article 2(1) of the Block Exemption Regulation as "agreements or concerted practices entered into between two or more undertakings each of which operates, for the purposes of the agreement, at a different level of the production or distribution chain, and relating to the conditions under which the parties may purchase, sell or resell certain goods or services".

(24) There are three main elements in this definition:

- the agreement or concerted practice is between two or more undertakings. Vertical agreements with final consumers not operating as an undertaking are not covered; More generally, agreements with final consumers do not fall under Article 81(1), as that article applies only to agreements between undertakings, decisions by associations of undertakings and concerted practices. This is without prejudice to the possible application of Article 82 of the Treaty;

- the agreement or concerted practice is between undertakings each operating, for the purposes of the agreement, at a different level of the production or distribution chain. This means for instance that one undertaking produces a raw material which the other undertaking uses as an input, or that the first is a manufacturer, the second a wholesaler and the third a retailer. This does not

  preclude an undertaking from being active at more than one level of the production or distribution chain;

- the agreements or concerted practices relate to the conditions under which the parties to the agreement, the supplier and the buyer, "may purchase, sell or resell certain goods or services". This reflects the purpose of the Block Exemption Regulation to cover purchase and distribution agreements. These are agreements which concern the conditions for the purchase, sale or resale of the goods or services supplied by the supplier and/or which concern the conditions for the sale by the buyer of the goods or services which incorporate these goods or services. For the application of the Block Exemption Regulation both the goods or services supplied by the supplier and the resulting goods or services are considered to be contract goods or services. Vertical agreements relating to all final and intermediate goods and services are covered.The only exception is the automobile sector, as long as this sector remains covered by a specific block exemption such as that granted by Commission Regulation (EC) No 1475/95[9]. The goods or services provided by the supplier may be resold by the buyer or may be used as an input by the buyer to produce his own goods or services.

(25) The Block Exemption Regulation also applies to goods sold and purchased for renting to third parties. However, rent and lease agreements as such are not covered, as no good or service is being sold by the supplier to the buyer. More generally, the Block Exemption Regulation does not cover restrictions or obligations that do not relate to the conditions of purchase, sale and resale, such as an obligation preventing parties from carrying out independent research and development which the parties may have included in an otherwise vertical agreement. In addition, Articles 2(2) to (5) directly or indirectly exclude certain vertical agreements from the application of the Block Exemption Regulation.

(ii) Vertical agreements between competitors

(26) Article 2(4) of the Block Exemption Regulation explicitly excludes from its application "vertical agreements entered into between competing undertakings".

[9] OJ L 145, 29.6.1995, p. 25.

Vertical agreements between competitors will be dealt with, as regards possible collusion effects, in the forthcoming Guidelines on the applicability of Article 81 to horizontal cooperation([10]). However, the vertical aspects of such agreements need to be assessed under these Guidelines. Article 1(a) of the Block Exemption Regulation defines competing undertakings as "actual or potential suppliers in the same product market", irrespective of whether or not they are competitors on the same geographic market. Competing undertakings are undertakings that are actual or potential suppliers of the contract goods or services or goods or services that are substitutes for the contract goods or services. A potential supplier is an undertaking that does not actually produce a competing product but could and would be likely to do so in the absence of the agreement in response to a small and permanent increase in relative prices. This means that the undertaking would be able and likely to undertake the necessary additional investments and supply the market within 1 year. This assessment has to be based on realistic grounds; the mere theoretical possibility of entering a market is not sufficient([11]).

(27) There are three exceptions to the general exclusion of vertical agreements between competitors, all three being set out in Article 2(4) and relating to non-reciprocal agreements. Non-reciprocal means, for instance, that while one manufacturer becomes the distributor of the products of another manufacturer, the latter does not become the distributor of the products of the first manufacturer. Non-reciprocal agreements between competitors are covered by the Block Exemption Regulation where (1) the buyer has a turnover not exceeding EUR 100 million, or (2) the supplier is a manufacturer and distributor of goods, while the buyer is only a distributor and not also a manufacturer of competing goods, or (3) the supplier is a provider of services operating at several levels of trade, while the buyer does not provide competing services at the level of trade where it purchases the contract services. The second exception covers situations of dual distribution, i.e. the manufacturer of particular goods also acts as a distributor of the goods in competition with independent distributors of his goods. A distributor who provides specifications to a manufacturer to produce particular goods under the distributor's brand name is not to be considered a manufacturer of such own-brand goods. The third exception covers similar situations of dual distribution, but in this case for services, when the supplier is also a provider of services at the level of the buyer.

(iii) Associations of retailers

(28) Article 2(2) of the Block Exemption Regulation includes in its application vertical agreements entered into by an association of undertakings which fulfils

---

([10]) Draft text published in OJ C 118, 27.4.2000, p. 14.

([11]) See Commission Notice on the definition of the relevant market for the purposes of Community competition law, OJ C 372, 9.12.1997, p. 5, at paras. 20–24, the Commission's Thirteenth Report on Competition Policy, point 55, and Commission Decision 90/410/EEC in Case No IV/32.009— Elopak/Metal Box-Odin, OJ L 209, 8.8.1990, p. 15.

certain conditions and thereby excludes from the Block Exemption Regulation vertical agreements entered into by all other associations. Vertical agreements entered into between an association and its members, or between an association and its suppliers, are covered by the Block Exemption Regulation only if all the members are retailers of goods (not services) and if each individual member of the association has a turnover not exceeding EUR 50 million. Retailers are distributors reselling goods to final consumers. Where only a limited number of the members of the association have a turnover not significantly exceeding the EUR 50 million threshold, this will normally not change the assessment under Article 81.

(29) An association of undertakings may involve both horizontal and vertical agreements. The horizontal agreements have to be assessed according to the principles set out in the forthcoming Guidelines on the applicability of Article 81 to horizontal cooperation. If this assessment leads to the conclusion that a co-operation between undertakings in the area of purchasing or selling is acceptable, a further assessment will be necessary to examine the vertical agreements concluded by the association with its suppliers or its individual members. The latter assessment will follow the rules of the Block Exemption Regulation and these Guidelines. For instance, horizontal agreements concluded between the members of the association or decisions adopted by the association, such as the decision to require the members to purchase from the association or the decision to allocate exclusive territories to the members have to be assessed first as a horizontal agreement. Only if this assessment is positive does it become relevant to assess the vertical agreements between the association and individual members or between the association and suppliers.

(iv) Vertical agreements containing provisions on intellectual property rights (IPRs)

(30) Article 2(3) of the Block Exemption Regulation includes in its application vertical agreements containing certain provisions relating to the assignment of IPRs to or use of IPRs by the buyer and thereby excludes from the Block Exemption Regulation all other vertical agreements containing IPR provisions. The Block Exemption Regulation applies to vertical agreements containing IPR provisions when five conditions are fulfilled:

- The IPR provisions must be part of a vertical agreement, i.e. an agreement with conditions under which the parties may purchase, sell or resell certain goods or services;

- The IPRs must be assigned to, or for use by, the buyer;

- The IPR provisions must not constitute the primary object of the agreement;

- The IPR provisions must be directly related to the use, sale or resale of goods or services by the buyer or his customers. In the case of franchising where marketing forms the object of the exploitation of the IPRs, the goods or services are distributed by the master franchisee or the franchisees;

- The IPR provisions, in relation to the contract goods or services, must not contain restrictions of competition having the same object or effect as vertical restraints which are not exempted under the Block Exemption Regulation.

(31) These conditions ensure that the Block Exemption Regulation applies to vertical agreements where the use, sale or resale of goods or services can be performed more effectively because IPRs are assigned to or transferred for use by the buyer. In other words, restrictions concerning the assignment or use of IPRs can be covered when the main object of the agreement is the purchase or distribution of goods or services.

(32) The first condition makes clear that the context in which the IPRs are provided is an agreement to purchase or distribute goods or an agreement to purchase or provide services and not an agreement concerning the assignment or licensing of IPRs for the manufacture of goods, nor a pure licensing agreement. The Block Exemption Regulation does not cover for instance:

- agreements where a party provides another party with a recipe and licenses the other party to produce a drink with this recipe;

- agreements under which one party provides another party with a mould or master copy and licenses the other party to produce and distribute copies;

- the pure licence of a trade mark or sign for the purposes of merchandising;

- sponsorship contracts concerning the right to advertise oneself as being an official sponsor of an event;

- copyright licensing such as broadcasting contracts concerning the right to record and/or the right to broadcast an event.

(33) The second condition makes clear that the Block Exemption Regulation does not apply when the IPRs are provided by the buyer to the supplier, no matter whether the IPRs concern the manner of manufacture or of distribution. An agreement relating to the transfer of IPRs to the supplier and containing possible restrictions on the sales made by the supplier is not covered by the Block Exemption Regulation. This means in particular that subcontracting involving the transfer of know-how to a subcontractor[12] does not fall within the scope of application of the Block Exemption Regulation. However, vertical agreements under which the buyer provides only specifications to the supplier which describe the goods or services to be supplied are covered by the Block Exemption Regulation.

(34) The third condition makes clear that in order to be covered by the Block Exemption Regulation the primary object of the agreement must not be the assignment or licensing of IPRs. The primary object must be the purchase or

---

[12] See Notice on subcontracting, OJ C 1, 3.1.1979, p. 2.

distribution of goods or services and the IPR provisions must serve the implementation of the vertical agreement.

(35) The fourth condition requires that the IPR provisions facilitate the use, sale or resale of goods or services by the buyer or his customers. The goods or services for use or resale are usually supplied by the licensor but may also be purchased by the licensee from a third supplier. The IPR provisions will normally concern the marketing of goods or services. This is for instance the case in a franchise agreement where the franchisor sells to the franchisee goods for resale and in addition licenses the franchisee to use his trade mark and know-how to market the goods. Also covered is the case where the supplier of a concentrated extract licenses the buyer to dilute and bottle the extract before selling it as a drink.

(36) The fifth condition signifies in particular that the IPR provisions should not have the same object or effect as any of the hardcore restrictions listed in Article 4 of the Block Exemption Regulation or any of the restrictions excluded from the coverage of the Block Exemption Regulation by Article 5 (see paragraphs 46 to 61).

(37) Intellectual property rights which may be considered to serve the implementation of vertical agreements within the meaning of Article 2(3) of the Block Exemption Regulation generally concern three main areas: trade marks, copyright and know-how.

Trade mark

(38) A trade mark licence to a distributor may be related to the distribution of the licensor's products in a particular territory. If it is an exclusive licence, the agreement amounts to exclusive distribution.

Copyright

(39) Resellers of goods covered by copyright (books, software, etc.) may be obliged by the copyright holder only to resell under the condition that the buyer, whether another reseller or the end user, shall not infringe the copyright. Such obligations on the reseller, to the extent that they fall under Article 81(1) at all, are covered by the Block Exemption Regulation.

(40) Agreements under which hard copies of software are supplied for resale and where the reseller does not acquire a licence to any rights over the software but only has the right to resell the hard copies, are to be regarded as agreements for the supply of goods for resale for the purpose of the Block Exemption Regulation. Under this form of distribution the licence of the software only takes place between the copyright owner and the user of the software. This may take the form of a "shrink wrap" licence, i.e. a set of conditions included in the package of the hard copy which the end user is deemed to accept by opening the package.

(41) Buyers of hardware incorporating software protected by copyright may be obliged by the copyright holder not to infringe the copyright, for example not to make copies and resell the software or not to make copies and use the software

in combination with other hardware. Such use-restrictions, to the extent that they fall within Article 81(1) at all, are covered by the Block Exemption Regulation.

Know-how

(42) Franchise agreements, with the exception of industrial franchise agreements, are the most obvious example where know-how for marketing purposes is communicated to the buyer. Franchise agreements contain licences of intellectual property rights relating to trade marks or signs and know-how for the use and distribution of goods or the provision of services. In addition to the licence of IPR, the franchisor usually provides the franchisee during the life of the agreement with commercial or technical assistance, such as procurement services, training, advice on real estate, financial planning etc. The licence and the assistance are integral components of the business method being franchised.

(43) Licensing contained in franchise agreements is covered by the Block Exemption Regulation if all five conditions listed in point 30 are fulfilled. This is usually the case, as under most franchise agreements, including master franchise agreements, the franchisor provides goods and/or services, in particular commercial or technical assistance services, to the franchisee. The IPRs help the franchisee to resell the products supplied by the franchisor or by a supplier designated by the franchisor or to use those products and sell the resulting goods or services. Where the franchise agreement only or primarily concerns licensing of IPRs, such an agreement is not covered by the Block Exemption Regulation, but it will be treated in a way similar to those franchise agreements which are covered by the Block Exemption Regulation.

(44) The following IPR-related obligations are generally considered to be necessary to protect the franchisor's intellectual property rights and are, if these obligations fall under Article 81(1), also covered by the Block Exemption Regulation:

(a) an obligation on the franchisee not to engage, directly or indirectly, in any similar business;

(b) an obligation on the franchisee not to acquire financial interests in the capital of a competing undertaking such as would give the franchisee the power to influence the economic conduct of such undertaking;

(c) an obligation on the franchisee not to disclose to third parties the know-how provided by the franchisor as long as this know-how is not in the public domain;

(d) an obligation on the franchisee to communicate to the franchisor any experience gained in exploiting the franchise and to grant it, and other franchisees, a non-exclusive licence for the know-how resulting from that experience;

(e) an obligation on the franchisee to inform the franchisor of infringements of licensed intellectual property rights, to take legal action against infringers or to assist the franchisor in any legal actions against infringers;

(f) an obligation on the franchisee not to use know-how licensed by the franchisor for purposes other than the exploitation of the franchise;

(g) an obligation on the franchisee not to assign the rights and obligations under the franchise agreement without the franchisor's consent.

(v) Relationship to other block exemption regulations

(45) Article 2(5) states that the Block Exemption Regulation does "not apply to vertical agreements the subject matter of which falls within the scope of any other block exemption regulation." This means that the Block Exemption Regulation does not apply to vertical agreements covered by Commission Regulation (EC) No 240/96([13]) on technology transfer, Commission Regulation (EC) No 1475/1995([14]) for car distribution or Regulations (EEC) No 417/85([15]) and (EEC) No 418/85([16]) exempting vertical agreements concluded in connection with horizontal agreements, as last amended by Regulation (EC) No 2236/97([17]) or any future regulations of that kind.

3. Hardcore restrictions under the Block Exemption Regulation

(46) The Block Exemption Regulation contains in Article 4 a list of hardcore restrictions which lead to the exclusion of the whole vertical agreement from the scope of application of the Block Exemption Regulation. This list of hardcore restrictions applies to vertical agreements concerning trade within the Community. In so far as vertical agreements concern exports outside the Community or imports/re-imports from outside the Community see the judgment in Javico v Yves Saint Laurent. Individual exemption of vertical agreements containing such hardcore restrictions is also unlikely.

(47) The hardcore restriction set out in Article 4(a) of the Block Exemption Regulation concerns resale price maintenance (RPM), that is agreements or concerted practices having as their direct or indirect object the establishment of a fixed or minimum resale price or a fixed or minimum price level to be observed by the buyer. In the case of contractual provisions or concerted practices that directly establish the resale price, the restriction is clear cut. However, RPM can also be achieved through indirect means. Examples of the latter are an agreement fixing the distribution margin, fixing the maximum level of discount the distributor can grant from a prescribed price level, making the grant of rebates or reimbursement

of promotional costs by the supplier subject to the observance of a given price level, linking the prescribed resale price to the resale prices of competitors, threats, intimidation, warnings, penalties, delay or suspension of deliveries or contract terminations in relation to observance of a given price level. Direct or indirect means of achieving price fixing can be made more effective when combined with measures to identify price-cutting distributors, such as the implementation of a price monitoring system, or the obligation on retailers to report other members of the distribution network who deviate from the standard price level. Similarly, direct or indirect price fixing can be made more effective when combined with measures which may reduce the buyer's incentive to lower the resale price, such as the supplier printing a recommended resale price on the product or the supplier obliging the buyer to apply a most-favoured-customer clause. The same indirect means and the same "supportive" measures can be used to make maximum or recommended prices work as RPM. However, the provision of a list of recommended prices or maximum prices by the supplier to the buyer is not considered in itself as leading to RPM.

(48) In the case of agency agreements, the principal normally establishes the sales price, as the agent does not become the owner of the goods. However, where an agency agreement falls within Article 81(1) (see paragraphs 12 to 20), an obligation preventing or restricting the agent from sharing his commission, fixed or variable, with the customer would be a hardcore restriction under Article 4(a) of the Block Exemption Regulation. The agent should thus be left free to lower the effective price paid by the customer without reducing the income for the principal([18]).

(49) The hardcore restriction set out in Article 4(b) of the Block Exemption Regulation concerns agreements or concerted practices that have as their direct or indirect object the restriction of sales by the buyer, in as far as those restrictions relate to the territory into which or the customers to whom the buyer may sell the contract goods or services. That hardcore restriction relates to market partitioning by territory or by customer. That may be the result of direct obligations, such as the obligation not to sell to certain customers or to customers in certain territories or the obligation to refer orders from these customers to other distributors. It may also result from indirect measures aimed at inducing the distributor not to sell to such customers, such as refusal or reduction of bonuses or discounts, refusal to supply, reduction of supplied volumes or limitation of supplied volumes to the demand within the allocated territory or customer group, threat of contract termination or profit pass-over obligations. It may further result from the supplier not providing a Community-wide guarantee service, whereby all distributors are obliged to provide the guarantee service and are reimbursed for this service by the supplier, even in relation to products sold by other distributors into their territory. These practices are even more likely to be viewed as a restriction of the buyer's sales when used in conjunction with the implementation by the supplier of a

---

([18]) See, for instance, Commission Decision 91/562/EEC in Case No IV/32.737—Eirpage, OJ L 306, 7.11.1991, p. 22, in particular point (6).

monitoring system aimed at verifying the effective destination of the supplied goods, e.g. the use of differentiated labels or serial numbers. However, a prohibition imposed on all distributors to sell to certain end users is not classified as a hardcore restriction if there is an objective justification related to the product, such as a general ban on selling dangerous substances to certain customers for reasons of safety or health. It implies that also the supplier himself does not sell to these customers. Nor are obligations on the reseller relating to the display of the supplier's brand name classified as hardcore.

(50) There are four exceptions to the hardcore restriction in Article 4(b) of the Block Exemption Regulation. The first exception allows a supplier to restrict active sales by his direct buyers to a territory or a customer group which has been allocated exclusively to another buyer or which the supplier has reserved to itself. A territory or customer group is exclusively allocated when the supplier agrees to sell his product only to one distributor for distribution in a particular territory or to a particular customer group and the exclusive distributor is protected against active selling into his territory or to his customer group by the supplier and all the other buyers of the supplier inside the Community. The supplier is allowed to combine the allocation of an exclusive territory and an exclusive customer group by for instance appointing an exclusive distributor for a particular customer group in a certain territory. This protection of exclusively allocated territories or customer groups must, however, permit passive sales to such territories or customer groups. For the application of Article 4(b) of the Block Exemption Regulation, the Commission interprets "active" and "passive" sales as follows:

• "Active" sales mean actively approaching individual customers inside another distributor's exclusive territory or exclusive customer group by for instance direct mail or visits; or actively approaching a specific customer group or customers in a specific territory allocated exclusively to another distributor through advertisement in media or other promotions specifically targeted at that customer group or targeted at customers in that territory; or establishing a warehouse or distribution outlet in another distributor's exclusive territory.

• "Passive" sales mean responding to unsolicited requests from individual customers including delivery of goods or services to such customers. General advertising or promotion in media or on the Internet that reaches customers in other distributors' exclusive territories or customer groups but which is a reasonable way to reach customers outside those territories or customer groups, for instance to reach customers in non-exclusive territories or in one's own territory, are passive sales.

(51) Every distributor must be free to use the Internet to advertise or to sell products. A restriction on the use of the Internet by distributors could only be compatible with the Block Exemption Regulation to the extent that promotion on the Internet or sales over the Internet would lead to active selling into other distributors' exclusive territories or customer groups. In general, the use of the

Internet is not considered a form of active sales into such territories or customer groups, since it is a reasonable way to reach every customer. The fact that it may have effects outside one's own territory or customer group results from the technology, i.e. the easy access from everywhere. If a customer visits the web site of a distributor and contacts the distributor and if such contact leads to a sale, including delivery, then that is considered passive selling. The language used on the website or in the communication plays normally no role in that respect. Insofar as a web site is not specifically targeted at customers primarily inside the territory or customer group exclusively allocated to another distributor, for instance with the use of banners or links in pages of providers specifically available to these exclusively allocated customers, the website is not considered a form of active selling. However, unsolicited e-mails sent to individual customers or specific customer groups are considered active selling. The same considerations apply to selling by catalogue. Notwithstanding what has been said before, the supplier may require quality standards for the use of the Internet site to resell his goods, just as the supplier may require quality standards for a shop or for advertising and promotion in general. The latter may be relevant in particular for selective distribution. An outright ban on Internet or catalogue selling is only possible if there is an objective justification. In any case, the supplier cannot reserve to itself sales and/or advertising over the Internet.

(52) There are three other exceptions to the second hardcore restriction set out in Article 4(b) of the Block Exemption Regulation. All three exceptions allow for the restriction of both active and passive sales. Thus, it is permissible to restrict a wholesaler from selling to end users, to restrict an appointed distributor in a selective distribution system from selling, at any level of trade, to unauthorised distributors in markets where such a system is operated, and to restrict a buyer of components supplied for incorporation from reselling them to competitors of the supplier. The term "component" includes any intermediate goods and the term "incorporation" refers to the use of any input to produce goods.

(53) The hardcore restriction set out in Article 4(c) of the Block Exemption Regulation concerns the restriction of active or passive sales to end users, whether professional end users or final consumers, by members of a selective distribution network. This means that dealers in a selective distribution system, as defined in Article 1(d) of the Block Exemption Regulation, cannot be restricted in the users or purchasing agents acting on behalf of these users to whom they may sell. For instance, also in a selective distribution system the dealer should be free to advertise and sell with the help of the Internet. Selective distribution may be combined with exclusive distribution provided that active and passive selling is not restricted anywhere. The supplier may therefore commit itself to supplying only one dealer or a limited number of dealers in a given territory.

(54) In addition, in the case of selective distribution, restrictions can be imposed on the dealer's ability to determine the location of his business premises. Selected dealers may be prevented from running their business from different premises or from opening a new outlet in a different location. If the dealer's

outlet is mobile ("shop on wheels"), an area may be defined outside which the mobile outlet cannot be operated.

(55) The hardcore restriction set out in Article 4(d) of the Block Exemption Regulation concerns the restriction of cross-supplies between appointed distributors within a selective distribution system. This means that an agreement or concerted practice may not have as its direct or indirect object to prevent or restrict the active or passive selling of the contract products between the selected distributors. Selected distributors must remain free to purchase the contract products from other appointed distributors within the network, operating either at the same or at a different level of trade. This means that selective distribution cannot be combined with vertical restraints aimed at forcing distributors to purchase the contract products exclusively from a given source, for instance exclusive purchasing. It also means that within a selective distribution network no restrictions can be imposed on appointed wholesalers as regards their sales of the product to appointed retailers.

(56) The hardcore restriction set out in Article 4(e) of the Block Exemption Regulation concerns agreements that prevent or restrict end-users, independent repairers and service providers from obtaining spare parts directly from the manufacturer of these spare parts. An agreement between a manufacturer of spare parts and a buyer who incorporates these parts into his own products (original equipment manufacturer (OEM)), may not, either directly or indirectly, prevent or restrict sales by the manufacturer of these spare parts to end users, independent repairers or service providers. Indirect restrictions may arise in particular when the supplier of the spare parts is restricted in supplying technical information and special equipment which are necessary for the use of spare parts by users, independent repairers or service providers. However, the agreement may place restrictions on the supply of the spare parts to the repairers or service providers entrusted by the original equipment manufacturer with the repair or servicing of his own goods. In other words, the original equipment manufacturer may require his own repair and service network to buy the spare parts from it.

4. Conditions under the Block Exemption Regulation

(57) Article 5 of the Block Exemption Regulation excludes certain obligations from the coverage of the Block Exemption Regulation even though the market share threshold is not exceeded. However, the Block Exemption Regulation continues to apply to the remaining part of the vertical agreement if that part is severable from the non-exempted obligations.

(58) The first exclusion is provided in Article 5(a) of the Block Exemption Regulation and concerns non-compete obligations. Non-compete obligations are obligations that require the buyer to purchase from the supplier or from another undertaking designated by the supplier more than 80 % of the buyer's total purchases during the previous year of the contract goods and services and their substitutes (see the definition in Article 1(b) of the Block Exemption Regulation),

thereby preventing the buyer from purchasing competing goods or services or limiting such purchases to less than 20 % of total purchases. Where for the year preceding the conclusion of the contract no relevant purchasing data for the buyer are available, the buyer's best estimate of his annual total requirements may be used. Such non-compete obligations are not covered by the Block Exemption Regulation when their duration is indefinite or exceeds five years. Non-compete obligations that are tacitly renewable beyond a period of five years are also not covered by the Block Exemption Regulation. However, non-compete obligations are covered when their duration is limited to five years or less, or when renewal beyond five years requires explicit consent of both parties and no obstacles exist that hinder the buyer from effectively terminating the non-compete obligation at the end of the five year period. If for instance the agreement provides for a five-year non-compete obligation and the supplier provides a loan to the buyer, the repayment of that loan should not hinder the buyer from effectively terminating the non-compete obligation at the end of the five-year period; the repayment needs to be structured in equal or decreasing instalments and should not increase over time. This is without prejudice to the possibility, in the case for instance of a new distribution outlet, to delay repayment for the first one or two years until sales have reached a certain level. The buyer must have the possibility to repay the remaining debt where there is still an outstanding debt at the end of the non-compete obligation. Similarly, when the supplier provides the buyer with equipment which is not relationship-specific, the buyer should have the possibility to take over the equipment at its market asset value at the end of the non-compete obligation.

(59) The five-year duration limit does not apply when the goods or services are resold by the buyer "from premises and land owned by the supplier or leased by the supplier from third parties not connected with the buyer." In such cases the non-compete obligation may be of the same duration as the period of occupancy of the point of sale by the buyer (Article 5(a) of the Block Exemption Regulation). The reason for this exception is that it is normally unreasonable to expect a supplier to allow competing products to be sold from premises and land owned by the supplier without his permission. Artificial ownership constructions intended to avoid the five-year limit cannot benefit from this exception.

(60) The second exclusion from the block exemption is provided for in Article 5(b) of the Block Exemption Regulation and concerns post term non-compete obligations. Such obligations are normally not covered by the Block Exemption Regulation, unless the obligation is indispensable to protect know-how transferred by the supplier to the buyer, is limited to the point of sale from which the buyer has operated during the contract period, and is limited to a maximum period of one year. According to the definition in Article 1(f) of the Block Exemption Regulation the know-how needs to be "substantial", meaning "that the know-how includes information which is indispensable to the buyer for the use, sale or resale of the contract goods or services".

(61) The third exclusion from the block exemption is provided for in Article 5(c) of the Block Exemption Regulation and concerns the sale of competing goods

in a selective distribution system. The Block Exemption Regulation covers the combination of selective distribution with a non-compete obligation, obliging the dealers not to resell competing brands in general. However, if the supplier prevents his appointed dealers, either directly or indirectly, from buying products for resale from specific competing suppliers, such an obligation cannot enjoy the benefit of the Block Exemption Regulation. The objective of the exclusion of this obligation is to avoid a situation whereby a number of suppliers using the same selective distribution outlets prevent one specific competitor or certain specific competitors from using these outlets to distribute their products (foreclosure of a competing supplier which would be a form of collective boycott)([19]).

5. No presumption of illegality outside the Block Exemption Regulation

(62) Vertical agreements falling outside the Block Exemption Regulation will not be presumed to be illegal but may need individual examination. Companies are encouraged to do their own assessment without notification. In the case of an individual examination by the Commission, the latter will bear the burden of proof that the agreement in question infringes Article 81(1). When appreciable anti-competitive effects are demonstrated, undertakings may substantiate efficiency claims and explain why a certain distribution system is likely to bring about benefits which are relevant to the conditions for exemption under Article 81(3).

6. No need for precautionary notification

(63) Pursuant to Article 4(2) of Council Regulation No 17 of 6 February 1962, First Regulation implementing Articles 85 and 86 of the Treaty([20]), as last amended by Regulation (EC) No 1216/1999([21]), vertical agreements can benefit from an exemption under Article 81(3) from their date of entry into force, even if notification occurs after that date. This means in practice that no precautionary notification needs to be made. If a dispute arises, an undertaking can still notify, in which case the Commission can exempt the vertical agreement with retroactive effect from the date of entry into force of the agreement if all four conditions of Article 81(3) are fulfilled. A notifying party does not have to explain why the agreement was not notified earlier and will not be denied retroactive exemption simply because it did not notify earlier. Any notification will be reviewed on its merits. This amendment to Article 4(2) of Regulation No 17 should eliminate artificial litigation before national courts and thus strengthen the civil enforceability of contracts. It also takes account of the situation where undertakings have not notified because they assumed the agreement was covered by the Block Exemption Regulation.

[19] An example of indirect measures having such exclusionary effects can be found in Commission Decision 92/428/EEC in Case No IV/33.542—Parfum Givenchy (OJ L 236, 19.8.1992, p. 11).

[20] OJ 13, 21.2.1962, p. 204/62.

[21] OJ L 148, 15.6.1999, p. 5.

(64) Since the date of notification no longer limits the possibility of exemption by the Commission, national courts have to assess the likelihood that Article 81(3) will apply in respect of vertical agreements falling within Article 81(1). If such likelihood exists, they should suspend proceedings pending adoption of a position by the Commission. However, national courts may adopt interim measures pending the assessment by the Commission of the applicability of Article 81(3), in the same way as they do when they refer a preliminary question to the Court of Justice under Article 234 of the EC Treaty. No suspension is necessary in respect of injunction proceedings, where national courts themselves are empowered to assess the likelihood of application of Article 81(3)([22]).

(65) Unless there is litigation in national courts or complaints, notifications of vertical agreements will not be given priority in the Commission's enforcement policy. Notifications as such do not provide provisional validity for the execution of agreements. Where undertakings have not notified an agreement because they assumed in good faith that the market share threshold under the Block Exemption Regulation was not exceeded, the Commission will not impose fines.

7. Severability

(66) The Block Exemption Regulation exempts vertical agreements on condition that no hardcore restriction, as set out in Article 4, is contained in or practised with the vertical agreement. If there are one or more hardcore restrictions, the benefit of the Block Exemption Regulation is lost for the entire vertical agreement. There is no severability for hardcore restrictions.

(67) The rule of severability does apply, however, to the conditions set out in Article 5 of the Block Exemption Regulation. Therefore, the benefit of the block exemption is only lost in relation to that part of the vertical agreement which does not comply with the conditions set out in Article 5.

8. Portfolio of products distributed through the same distribution system

(68) Where a supplier uses the same distribution agreement to distribute several goods/services some of these may, in view of the market share threshold, be covered by the Block Exemption Regulation while others may not. In that case, the Block Exemption Regulation applies to those goods and services for which the conditions of application are fulfilled.

(69) In respect of the goods or services which are not covered by the Block Exemption Regulation, the ordinary rules of competition apply, which means:

- there is no block exemption but also no presumption of illegality;

---

[22] Case C-234/89 Delimitis v Henninger Bräu [1991] ECR I-935, at paragraph 52.

- if there is an infringement of Article 81(1) which is not exemptable, consideration may be given to whether there are appropriate remedies to solve the competition problem within the existing distribution system;

- if there are no such appropriate remedies, the supplier concerned will have to make other distribution arrangements.

This situation can also arise where Article 82 applies in respect of some products but not in respect of others.

9. Transitional period

(70) The Block Exemption Regulation applies from 1 June 2000. Article 12 of the Block Exemption Regulation provides for a transitional period for vertical agreements already in force before 1 June 2000 which do not satisfy the conditions for exemption provided in the Block Exemption Regulation, but which do satisfy the conditions for exemption under the Block Exemption Regulations which expired on 31 May 2000 (Commissions Regulations (EEC) No 1983/83, (EEC) No 1984/83 and (EEC) No 4087/88). The Commission Notice concerning Regulations (EEC) Nos 1983/83 and 1984/83 also ceases to apply on 31 May 2000. The latter agreements may continue to benefit from these outgoing Regulations until 31 December 2001. Agreements of suppliers with a market share not exceeding 30% who signed with their buyers non-compete agreements with a duration exceeding five years are covered by the Block Exemption Regulation if on 1 January 2002 the non-compete agreements have no more than five years to run.

IV. WITHDRAWAL OF THE BLOCK EXEMPTION AND DISAPPLICATION OF THE BLOCK EXEMPTION REGULATION

1. Withdrawal procedure

(71) The presumption of legality conferred by the Block Exemption Regulation may be withdrawn if a vertical agreement, considered either in isolation or in conjunction with similar agreements enforced by competing suppliers or buyers, comes within the scope of Article 81(1) and does not fulfil all the conditions of Article 81(3). This may occur when a supplier, or a buyer in the case of exclusive supply agreements, holding a market share not exceeding 30%, enters into a vertical agreement which does not give rise to objective advantages such as to compensate for the damage which it causes to competition. This may particularly be the case with respect to the distribution of goods to final consumers, who are often in a much weaker position than professional buyers of intermediate goods. In the case of sales to final consumers, the disadvantages caused by a vertical agreement

may have a stronger impact than in a case concerning the sale and purchase of intermediate goods. When the conditions of Article 81(3) are not fulfilled, the Commission may withdraw the benefit of the Block Exemption Regulation under Article 6 and establish an infringement of Article 81(1).

(72) Where the withdrawal procedure is applied, the Commission bears the burden of proof that the agreement falls within the scope of Article 81(1) and that the agreement does not fulfil all four conditions of Article 81(3).

(73) The conditions for an exemption under Article 81(3) may in particular not be fulfilled when access to the relevant market or competition therein is significantly restricted by the cumulative effect of parallel networks of similar vertical agreements practised by competing suppliers or buyers. Parallel networks of vertical agreements are to be regarded as similar if they contain restraints producing similar effects on the market. Similar effects will normally occur when vertical restraints practised by competing suppliers or buyers come within one of the four groups listed in paragraphs 104 to 114. Such a situation may arise for example when, on a given market, certain suppliers practise purely qualitative selective distribution while other suppliers practise quantitative selective distribution. In such circumstances, the assessment must take account of the anti-competitive effects attributable to each individual network of agreements. Where appropriate, withdrawal may concern only the quantitative limitations imposed on the number of authorised distributors. Other cases in which a withdrawal decision may be taken include situations where the buyer, for example in the context of exclusive supply or exclusive distribution, has significant market power in the relevant downstream market where he resells the goods or provides the services.

(74) Responsibility for an anti-competitive cumulative effect can only be attributed to those undertakings which make an appreciable contribution to it. Agreements entered into by undertakings whose contribution to the cumulative effect is insignificant do not fall under the prohibition provided for in Article 81(1)([23]) and are therefore not subject to the withdrawal mechanism. The assessment of such a contribution will be made in accordance with the criteria set out in paragraphs 137 to 229.

(75) A withdrawal decision can only have ex nunc effect, which means that the exempted status of the agreements concerned will not be affected until the date at which the withdrawal becomes effective.

(76) Under Article 7 of the Block Exemption Regulation, the competent authority of a Member State may withdraw the benefit of the Block Exemption Regulation in respect of vertical agreements whose anti-competitive effects are felt in the territory of the Member State concerned or a part thereof, which has all the characteristics of a distinct geographic market. Where a Member State has not enacted legislation enabling the national competition authority to apply Community competition law or at least to withdraw the benefit of the Block

---

[23] Judgment in the Delimitis Case.

Exemption Regulation, the Member State may ask the Commission to initiate proceedings to this effect.

(77) The Commission has the exclusive power to withdraw the benefit of the Block Exemption Regulation in respect of vertical agreements restricting competition on a relevant geographic market which is wider than the territory of a single Member State. When the territory of a single Member State, or a part thereof, constitutes the relevant geographic market, the Commission and the Member State concerned have concurrent competence for withdrawal. Often, such cases lend themselves to decentralised enforcement by national competition authorities. However, the Commission reserves the right to take on certain cases displaying a particular Community interest, such as cases raising a new point of law.

(78) National decisions of withdrawal must be taken in accordance with the procedures laid down under national law and will only have effect within the territory of the Member State concerned. Such national decisions must not prejudice the uniform application of the Community competition rules and the full effect of the measures adopted in implementation of those rules([24]). Compliance with this principle implies that national competition authorities must carry out their assessment under Article 81 in the light of the relevant criteria developed by the Court of Justice and the Court of First Instance and in the light of notices and previous decisions adopted by the Commission.

(79) The Commission considers that the consultation mechanisms provided for in the Notice on cooperation between national competition authorities and the Commission([25]) should be used to avert the risk of conflicting decisions and duplication of procedures.

2. Disapplication of the Block Exemption Regulation

(80) Article 8 of the Block Exemption Regulation enables the Commission to exclude from the scope of the Block Exemption Regulation, by means of regulation, parallel networks of similar vertical restraints where these cover more than 50 % of a relevant market. Such a measure is not addressed to individual undertakings but concerns all undertakings whose agreements are defined in the regulation disapplying the Block Exemption Regulation.

(81) Whereas the withdrawal of the benefit of the Block Exemption Regulation under Article 6 implies the adoption of a decision establishing an infringement of Article 81 by an individual company, the effect of a regulation under Article 8 is merely to remove, in respect of the restraints and the markets concerned, the benefit of the application of the Block Exemption Regulation and to restore the full application of Article 81(1) and (3). Following the adoption of a regulation declaring the Block Exemption inapplicable in respect of certain vertical restraints on a particular market, the criteria developed by the relevant case-law of the Court of Justice and the

---

([24]) Judgment of the Court of Justice in Case 14/68 Walt Wilhelm and Others v Bundeskartellamt [1969] ECR 1, paragraph 4, and judgment in Delimitis.

([25]) OJ C 313, 15.10.1997, p. 3, points 49 to 53.

Court of First Instance and by notices and previous decisions adopted by the Commission will guide the application of Article 81 to individual agreements. Where appropriate, the Commission will take a decision in an individual case, which can provide guidance to all the undertakings operating on the market concerned.

(82) For the purpose of calculating the 50 % market coverage ratio, account must be taken of each individual network of vertical agreements containing restraints, or combinations of restraints, producing similar effects on the market. Similar effects normally result when the restraints come within one of the four groups listed in paragraphs 104 to 114.

(83) Article 8 does not entail an obligation on the part of the Commission to act where the 50 % market-coverage ratio is exceeded. In general, disapplication is appropriate when it is likely that access to the relevant market or competition therein is appreciably restricted. This may occur in particular when parallel networks of selective distribution covering more than 50 % of a market make use of selection criteria which are not required by the nature of the relevant goods or discriminate against certain forms of distribution capable of selling such goods.

(84) In assessing the need to apply Article 8, the Commission will consider whether individual withdrawal would be a more appropriate remedy. This may depend, in particular, on the number of competing undertakings contributing to a cumulative effect on a market or the number of affected geographic markets within the Community.

(85) Any regulation adopted under Article 8 must clearly set out its scope. This means, first, that the Commission must define the relevant product and geographic market(s) and, secondly, that it must identify the type of vertical restraint in respect of which the Block Exemption Regulation will no longer apply. As regards the latter aspect, the Commission may modulate the scope of its regulation according to the competition concern which it intends to address. For instance, while all parallel networks of single-branding type arrangements shall be taken into account in view of establishing the 50 % market coverage ratio, the Commission may nevertheless restrict the scope of the disapplication regulation only to non-compete obligations exceeding a certain duration. Thus, agreements of a shorter duration or of a less restrictive nature might be left unaffected, in consideration of the lesser degree of foreclosure attributable to such restraints. Similarly, when on a particular market selective distribution is practised in combination with additional restraints such as non-compete or quantity-forcing on the buyer, the disapplication regulation may concern only such additional restraints. Where appropriate, the Commission may also provide guidance by specifying the market share level which, in the specific market context, may be regarded as insufficient to bring about a significant contribution by an individual undertaking to the cumulative effect.

(86) The transitional period of not less than six months that the Commission will have to set under Article 8(2) should allow the undertakings concerned to adapt their agreements to take account of the regulation disapplying the Block Exemption Regulation.

(87) A regulation disapplying the Block Exemption Regulation will not affect the exempted status of the agreements concerned for the period preceding its entry into force.

V. MARKET DEFINITION AND MARKET SHARE CALCULATION ISSUES

1. Commission Notice on definition of the relevant market

(88) The Commission Notice on definition of the relevant market for the purposes of Community competition law[26] provides guidance on the rules, criteria and evidence which the Commission uses when considering market definition issues. That Notice will not be further explained in these Guidelines and should serve as the basis for market definition issues. These Guidelines will only deal with specific issues that arise in the context of vertical restraints and that are not dealt with in the general notice on market definition.

2. The relevant market for calculating the 30 % market share threshold under the Block Exemption Regulation

(89) Under Article 3 of the Block Exemption Regulation, it is in general the market share of the supplier that is decisive for the application of the block exemption. In the case of vertical agreements concluded between an association of retailers and individual members, the association is the supplier and needs to take into account its market share as a supplier. Only in the case of exclusive supply as defined in Article 1(c) of the Block Exemption Regulation is it the market share of the buyer, and only that market share, which is decisive for the application of the Block Exemption Regulation.

(90) In order to calculate the market share, it is necessary to determine the relevant market. For this, the relevant product market and the relevant geographic market must be defined. The relevant product market comprises any goods or services which are regarded by the buyer as interchangeable, by reason of their characteristics, prices and intended use. The relevant geographic market comprises the area in which the undertakings concerned are involved in the supply and demand of relevant goods or services, in which the conditions of competition are sufficiently homogeneous, and which can be distinguished from neighbouring geographic areas because, in particular, conditions of competition are appreciably different in those areas.

(91) For the application of the Block Exemption Regulation, the market share of the supplier is his share on the relevant product and geographic market on

---

[26] OJ C 372, 9.12.1997, p. 5.

which he sells to his buyers.([27]) In the example given in paragraph 92, this is market A. The product market depends in the first place on substitutability from the buyers' perspective. When the supplied product is used as an input to produce other products and is generally not recognisable in the final product, the product market is normally defined by the direct buyers' preferences. The customers of the buyers will normally not have a strong preference concerning the inputs used by the buyers. Usually the vertical restraints agreed between the supplier and buyer of the input only relate to the sale and purchase of the intermediate product and not to the sale of the resulting product. In the case of distribution of final goods, what are substitutes for the direct buyers will normally be influenced or determined by the preferences of the final consumers. A distributor, as reseller, cannot ignore the preferences of final consumers when he purchases final goods. In addition, at the distribution level the vertical restraints usually concern not only the sale of products between supplier and buyer, but also their resale. As different distribution formats usually compete, markets are in general not defined by the form of distribution that is applied. Where suppliers generally sell a portfolio of products, the entire portfolio may determine the product market when the portfolios and not the individual products are regarded as substitutes by the buyers. As the buyers on market A are professional buyers, the geographic market is usually wider than the market where the product is resold to final consumers. Often, this will lead to the definition of national markets or wider geographic markets.

(92) In the case of exclusive supply, the buyer's market share is his share of all purchases on the relevant purchase market.([28]) In the example below, this is also market A.

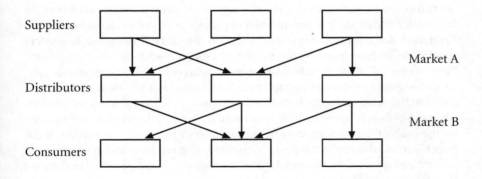

([27]) For example, the Dutch market for new replacement truck and bus tyres in the Michelin case (Case 322/81 Nederlandsche Banden-Industrie Michelinv Commission [1983] ECR 3461), the various meat markets in the Danish slaughter-house case: Commission Decision 2000/42/EC in Case No IV/M.1313—Danish Crown/Vestjyske Slagterier, OJ L 20, 25.1.2000, p. 1.

([28]) For an example of purchase markets, see Commission Decision 1999/674/EC in Case No IV/M.1221—Rewe/Meinl, OJ L 274, 23.10.1999, p. 1.

(93) Where a vertical agreement involves three parties, each operating at a different level of trade, their market shares will have to be below the market share threshold of 30% at both levels in order to benefit from the block exemption. If for instance, in an agreement between a manufacturer, a wholesaler (or association of retailers) and a retailer, a non-compete obligation is agreed, then the market share of both the manufacturer and the wholesaler (or association of retailers) must not exceed 30% in order to benefit from the block exemption.

(94) Where a supplier produces both original equipment and the repair or replacement parts for this equipment, the supplier will often be the only or the major supplier on the after-market for the repair and replacement parts. This may also arise where the supplier (OEM supplier) subcontracts the manufacturing of the repair or replacement parts. The relevant market for application of the Block Exemption Regulation may be the original equipment market including the spare parts or a separate original equipment market and after-market depending on the circumstances of the case, such as the effects of the restrictions involved, the lifetime of the equipment and importance of the repair or replacement costs([29]).

(95) Where the vertical agreement, in addition to the supply of the contract goods, also contains IPR provisions—such as a provision concerning the use of the supplier's trademark—which help the buyer to market the contract goods, the supplier's market share on the market where he sells the contract goods is decisive for the application of the Block Exemption Regulation. Where a franchisor does not supply goods to be resold but provides a bundle of services combined with IPR provisions which together form the business method being franchised, the franchisor needs to take account of his market share as a provider of a business method. For that purpose, the franchisor needs to calculate his market share on the market where the business method is exploited, which is the market where the franchisees exploit the business method to provide goods or services to end users. The franchisor must base his market share on the value of the goods or services supplied by his franchisees on this market. On such a market the competitors may be providers of other franchised business methods but also suppliers of substitutable goods or services not applying franchising. For instance, without prejudice to the definition of such market, if there was a market for fast-food services, a franchisor operating on such a market would need to calculate his market share on the basis of the relevant sales figures of his franchisees on this market. If the franchisor, in addition to the business method, also supplies certain inputs, such as meat and spices, then the franchisor also needs to calculate his market share on the market where these goods are sold.

---

[29] See for example Pelikan/Kyocera in XXV Report on Competition Policy, point 87, and Commission Decision 91/595/EEC in Case No IV/M.12—Varta/Bosch, OJ L 320, 22.11.1991, p. 26, Commission Decision in Case No IV/M.1094—Caterpillar/Perkins Engines, OJ C 94, 28.3.1998, p. 23, and Commission Decision in Case No IV/M.768—Lucas/Varity, OJ C 266, 13.9.1996, p. 6. See also Eastman Kodak Co v Image Technical Services, Inc et al, Supreme Court of the United States, No 90 1029. See also point 56 of the Commission Notice on the definition of relevant market for the purposes of Community competition law.

3. The relevant market for individual assessment

(96) For individual assessment of vertical agreements not covered by the Block Exemption Regulation, additional markets may need to be investigated besides the relevant market defined for the application of the Block Exemption Regulation. A vertical agreement may not only have effects on the market between supplier and buyer but may also have effects on downstream markets. For an individual assessment of a vertical agreement the relevant markets at each level of trade affected by restraints contained in the agreement will be examined:

(i)   For "intermediate goods or services" that are incorporated by the buyer into his own goods or services, vertical restraints generally have effects only on the market between supplier and buyer. A non-compete obligation imposed on the buyer for instance may foreclose other suppliers but will not lead to reduced in-store competition downstream. However, in cases of exclusive supply the position of the buyer on his downstream market is also relevant because the buyer's foreclosing behaviour may only have appreciable negative effects if he has market power on the downstream market.

(ii) For "final products" an analysis limited to the market between supplier and buyer is less likely to be sufficient since vertical restraints may have negative effects of reduced inter-brand and/or intra-brand competition on the resale market, that is on the market downstream of the buyer. For instance, exclusive distribution may not only lead to foreclosure effects on the market between the supplier and the buyer, but may above all lead to less intra-brand competition in the resale territories of the distributors. The resale market is in particular important if the buyer is a retailer selling to final consumers. A non-compete obligation agreed between a manufacturer and a wholesaler may foreclose this wholesaler to other manufacturers but a loss of in-store competition is not very likely at the wholesale level. The same agreement concluded with a retailer may however cause this added loss of in-store inter-brand competition on the resale market.

(iii) In cases of individual assessment of an "after-market", the relevant market may be the original equipment market or the after-market depending on the circumstances of the case. In any event, the situation on a separate after-market will be evaluated taking account of the situation on the original equipment market. A less significant position on the original equipment market will normally reduce possible anti-competitive effects on the after-market.

4. Calculation of the market share under the Block Exemption Regulation

(97) The calculation of the market share needs to be based in principle on value figures. Where value figures are not available substantiated estimates can be made. Such estimates may be based on other reliable market information such as volume figures (see Article 9(1) of the Block Exemption Regulation).

(98) In-house production, that is production of an intermediate product for own use, may be very important in a competition analysis as one of the competitive constraints or to accentuate the market position of a company. However, for the purpose of market definition and the calculation of market share for intermediate goods and services, in-house production will not be taken into account.

(99) However, in the case of dual distribution of final goods, i.e. where a producer of final goods also acts as a distributor on the market, the market definition and market share calculation need to include the goods sold by the producer and competing producers through their integrated distributors and agents (see Article 9(2)(b) of the Block Exemption Regulation). "Integrated distributors" are connected undertakings within the meaning of Article 11 of the Block Exemption Regulation.

VI. ENFORCEMENT POLICY IN INDIVIDUAL CASES

(100) Vertical restraints are generally less harmful than horizontal restraints. The main reason for treating a vertical restraint more leniently than a horizontal restraint lies in the fact that the latter may concern an agreement between competitors producing identical or substitutable goods or services. In such horizontal relationships the exercise of market power by one company (higher price of its product) may benefit its competitors. This may provide an incentive to competitors to induce each other to behave anti-competitively. In vertical relationships the product of the one is the input for the other. This means that the exercise of market power by either the upstream or downstream company would normally hurt the demand for the product of the other. The companies involved in the agreement therefore usually have an incentive to prevent the exercise of market power by the other.

(101) However, this self-restraining character should not be over-estimated. When a company has no market power it can only try to increase its profits by optimising its manufacturing and distribution processes, with or without the help of vertical restraints. However, when it does have market power it can also try to increase its profits at the expense of its direct competitors by raising their costs and at the expense of its buyers and ultimately consumers by trying to appropriate some of their surplus. This can happen when the upstream and downstream company share the extra profits or when one of the two uses vertical restraints to appropriate all the extra profits.

(102) In the assessment of individual cases, the Commission will adopt an economic approach in the application of Article 81 to vertical restraints. This will limit the scope of application of Article 81 to undertakings holding a certain degree of market power where inter-brand competition may be insufficient. In those cases, the protection of inter-brand and intra-brand competition is important to ensure efficiencies and benefits for consumers.

1. The framework of analysis

1.1. Negative effects of vertical restraints

(103) The negative effects on the market that may result from vertical restraints which EC competition law aims at preventing are the following:

(i) foreclosure of other suppliers or other buyers by raising barriers to entry;

(ii) reduction of inter-brand competition between the companies operating on a market, including facilitation of collusion amongst suppliers or buyers; by collusion is meant both explicit collusion and tacit collusion (conscious parallel behaviour);

(iii) reduction of intra-brand competition between distributors of the same brand;

(iv) the creation of obstacles to market integration, including, above all, limitations on the freedom of consumers to purchase goods or services in any Member State they may choose.

(104) Such negative effects may result from various vertical restraints. Agreements which are different in form may have the same substantive impact on competition. To analyse these possible negative effects, it is appropriate to divide vertical restraints into four groups: a single branding group, a limited distribution group, a resale price maintenance group and a market partitioning group. The vertical restraints within each group have largely similar negative effects on competition.

(105) The classification into four groups is based upon what can be described as the basic components of vertical restraints. In paragraphs 103 to 136, the four different groups are analysed. In 137 to 229, vertical agreements are analysed as they are used in practice because many vertical agreements make use of more than one of these components.

Single branding group

(106) Under the heading of "single branding" come those agreements which have as their main element that the buyer is induced to concentrate his orders for a particular type of product with one supplier. This component can be found amongst others in non-compete and quantity-forcing on the buyer, where an obligation or incentive scheme agreed between the supplier and the buyer makes the latter purchase his requirements for a particular product and its substitutes only, or mainly, from one supplier. The same component can be found in tying,

where the obligation or incentive scheme relates to a product that the buyer is required to purchase as a condition of purchasing another distinct product. The first product is referred to as the "tied" product and the second is referred to as the "tying" product.

(107) There are four main negative effects on competition: (1) other suppliers in that market cannot sell to the particular buyers and this may lead to foreclosure of the market or, in the case of tying, to foreclosure of the market for the tied product; (2) it makes market shares more rigid and this may help collusion when applied by several suppliers; (3) as far as the distribution of final goods is concerned, the particular retailers will only sell one brand and there will therefore be no inter-brand competition in their shops (no in-store competition); and (4) in the case of tying, the buyer may pay a higher price for the tied product than he would otherwise do. All these effects may lead to a reduction in inter-brand competition.

(108) The reduction in inter-brand competition may be mitigated by strong initial competition between suppliers to obtain the single branding contracts, but the longer the duration of the non-compete obligation, the more likely it will be that this effect will not be strong enough to compensate for the reduction in inter-brand competition.

Limited distribution group

(109) Under the heading of "limited distribution" come those agreements which have as their main element that the manufacturer sells to only one or a limited number of buyers. This may be to restrict the number of buyers for a particular territory or group of customers, or to select a particular kind of buyers. This component can be found amongst others in:

- exclusive distribution and exclusive customer allocation, where the supplier limits his sales to only one buyer for a certain territory or class of customers;

- exclusive supply and quantity-forcing on the supplier, where an obligation or incentive scheme agreed between the supplier and the buyer makes the former sell only or mainly to one buyer;

- selective distribution, where the conditions imposed on or agreed with the selected dealers usually limit their number;

- after-market sales restrictions which limit the component supplier's sales possibilities.

(110) There are three main negative effects on competition: (1) certain buyers within that market can no longer buy from that particular supplier, and this may lead in particular in the case of exclusive supply, to foreclosure of the purchase market, (2) when most or all of the competing suppliers limit the number of retailers, this may facilitate collusion, either at the distributor's level or at the supplier's level, and (3) since fewer distributors will offer the product it will also lead to a reduction of intra-brand competition. In the case of wide exclusive territories or

exclusive customer allocation the result may be total elimination of intra-brand competition. This reduction of intra-brand competition can in turn lead to a weakening of inter-brand competition.

Resale price maintenance group

(111) Under the heading of "resale price maintenance" (RPM) come those agreements whose main element is that the buyer is obliged or induced to resell not below a certain price, at a certain price or not above a certain price. This group comprises minimum, fixed, maximum and recommended resale prices. Maximum and recommended resale prices, which are not hardcore restrictions, may still lead to a restriction of competition by effect.

(112) There are two main negative effects of RPM on competition: (1) a reduction in intra-brand price competition, and (2) increased transparency on prices. In the case of fixed or minimum RPM, distributors can no longer compete on price for that brand, leading to a total elimination of intra-brand price competition. A maximum or recommended price may work as a focal point for resellers, leading to a more or less uniform application of that price level. Increased transparency on price and responsibility for price changes makes horizontal collusion between manufacturers or distributors easier, at least in concentrated markets. The reduction in intra-brand competition may, as it leads to less downward pressure on the price for the particular goods, have as an indirect effect a reduction of inter-brand competition.

Market partitioning group

(113) Under the heading of "market partitioning" come agreements whose main element is that the buyer is restricted in where he either sources or resells a particular product. This component can be found in exclusive purchasing, where an obligation or incentive scheme agreed between the supplier and the buyer makes the latter purchase his requirements for a particular product, for instance beer of brand X, exclusively from the designated supplier, but leaving the buyer free to buy and sell competing products, for instance competing brands of beer. It also includes territorial resale restrictions, the allocation of an area of primary responsibility, restrictions on the location of a distributor and customer resale restrictions.

(114) The main negative effect on competition is a reduction of intra-brand competition that may help the supplier to partition the market and thus hinder market integration. This may facilitate price discrimination. When most or all of the competing suppliers limit the sourcing or resale possibilities of their buyers this may facilitate collusion, either at the distributors' level or at the suppliers' level.

1.2. Positive effects of vertical restraints

(115) It is important to recognise that vertical restraints often have positive effects by, in particular, promoting non-price competition and improved quality of services. When a company has no market power, it can only try to increase its

profits by optimising its manufacturing or distribution processes. In a number of situations vertical restraints may be helpful in this respect since the usual arm's length dealings between supplier and buyer, determining only price and quantity of a certain transaction, can lead to a sub-optimal level of investments and sales.

(116) While trying to give a fair overview of the various justifications for vertical restraints, these Guidelines do not claim to be complete or exhaustive. The following reasons may justify the application of certain vertical restraints:

(1) To "solve a 'free-rider' problem". One distributor may free-ride on the promotion efforts of another distributor. This type of problem is most common at the wholesale and retail level. Exclusive distribution or similar restrictions may be helpful in avoiding such free-riding. Free-riding can also occur between suppliers, for instance where one invests in promotion at the buyer's premises, in general at the retail level, that may also attract customers for its competitors. Non-compete type restraints can help to overcome this situation of free-riding.

For there to be a problem, there needs to be a real free-rider issue. Free-riding between buyers can only occur on pre-sales services and not on after-sales services. The product will usually need to be relatively new or technically complex as the customer may otherwise very well know what he or she wants, based on past purchases. And the product must be of a reasonably high value as it is otherwise not attractive for a customer to go to one shop for information and to another to buy. Lastly, it must not be practical for the supplier to impose on all buyers, by contract, effective service requirements concerning pre-sales services.

Free-riding between suppliers is also restricted to specific situations, namely in cases where the promotion takes place at the buyer's premises and is generic, not brand specific.

(2) To "open up or enter new markets". Where a manufacturer wants to enter a new geographic market, for instance by exporting to another country for the first time, this may involve special "first time investments" by the distributor to establish the brand in the market. In order to persuade a local distributor to make these investments it may be necessary to provide territorial protection to the distributor so that he can recoup these investments by temporarily charging a higher price. Distributors based in other markets should then be restrained for a limited period from selling in the new market. This is a special case of the free-rider problem described under point (1).

(3) The "certification free-rider issue". In some sectors, certain retailers have a reputation for stocking only "quality" products. In such a case, selling through these retailers may be vital for the introduction of a new product. If the manufacturer cannot initially limit his sales to the premium stores, he runs the risk of being de-listed and the product introduction may fail. This means that there may be a reason for allowing for a limited duration a restriction such as exclusive distribution or selective distribution. It must be enough to guarantee introduction of the new product but not so long as to hinder large-scale dissemination. Such benefits are more likely with "experience" goods or complex goods that represent a relatively large purchase for the final consumer.

(4) The so-called "hold-up problem". Sometimes there are client-specific investments to be made by either the supplier or the buyer, such as in special equipment or training. For instance, a component manufacturer that has to build new machines and tools in order to satisfy a particular requirement of one of his customers. The investor may not commit the necessary investments before particular supply arrangements are fixed.

However, as in the other free-riding examples, there are a number of conditions that have to be met before the risk of under-investment is real or significant. Firstly, the investment must be relationship-specific. An investment made by the supplier is considered to be relationship-specific when, after termination of the contract, it cannot be used by the supplier to supply other customers and can only be sold at a significant loss. An investment made by the buyer is considered to be relationship-specific when, after termination of the contract, it cannot be used by the buyer to purchase and/or use products supplied by other suppliers and can only be sold at a significant loss. An investment is thus relationship-specific because for instance it can only be used to produce a brand-specific component or to store a particular brand and thus cannot be used profitably to produce or resell alternatives. Secondly, it must be a long-term investment that is not recouped in the short run. And thirdly, the investment must be asymmetric; i.e. one party to the contract invests more than the other party. When these conditions are met, there is usually a good reason to have a vertical restraint for the duration it takes to depreciate the investment. The appropriate vertical restraint will be of the non-compete type or quantity-forcing type when the investment is made by the supplier and of the exclusive distribution, exclusive customer allocation or exclusive supply type when the investment is made by the buyer.

(5) The "specific hold-up problem that may arise in the case of transfer of substantial know-how". The know-how, once provided, cannot be taken back and the provider of the know-how may not want it to be used for or by his competitors. In as far as the know-how was not readily available to the buyer, is substantial and indispensable for the operation of the agreement, such a transfer may justify a non-compete type of restriction. This would normally fall outside Article 81(1).

(6) "Economies of scale in distribution". In order to have scale economies exploited and thereby see a lower retail price for his product, the manufacturer may want to concentrate the resale of his products on a limited number of distributors. For this he could use exclusive distribution, quantity forcing in the form of a minimum purchasing requirement, selective distribution containing such a requirement or exclusive purchasing.

(7) "Capital market imperfections". The usual providers of capital (banks, equity markets) may provide capital sub-optimally when they have imperfect information on the quality of the borrower or there is an inadequate basis to secure the loan. The buyer or supplier may have better information and be able, through an exclusive relationship, to obtain extra security for his investment. Where the supplier provides the loan to the buyer this may lead to non-compete or quantity forcing on the buyer. Where the buyer provides the loan to the

supplier this may be the reason for having exclusive supply or quantity forcing on the supplier.

(8) "Uniformity and quality standardisation". A vertical restraint may help to increase sales by creating a brand image and thereby increasing the attractiveness of a product to the final consumer by imposing a certain measure of uniformity and quality standardisation on the distributors. This can for instance be found in selective distribution and franchising.

(117) The eight situations mentioned in paragraph 116 make clear that under certain conditions vertical agreements are likely to help realise efficiencies and the development of new markets and that this may offset possible negative effects. The case is in general strongest for vertical restraints of a limited duration which help the introduction of new complex products or protect relationship-specific investments. A vertical restraint is sometimes necessary for as long as the supplier sells his product to the buyer (see in particular the situations described in paragraph 116, points (1), (5), (6) and (8).

(118) There is a large measure of substitutability between the different vertical restraints. This means that the same inefficiency problem can be solved by different vertical restraints. For instance, economies of scale in distribution may possibly be achieved by using exclusive distribution, selective distribution, quantity forcing or exclusive purchasing. This is important as the negative effects on competition may differ between the various vertical restraints. This plays a role when indispensability is discussed under Article 81(3).

1.3. General rules for the evaluation of vertical restraints

(119) In evaluating vertical restraints from a competition policy perspective, some general rules can be formulated:

(1) For most vertical restraints competition concerns can only arise if there is insufficient inter-brand competition, i.e. if there exists a certain degree of market power at the level of the supplier or the buyer or both. Conceptually, market power is the power to raise price above the competitive level and, at least in the short term, to obtain supra-normal profits. Companies may have market power below the level of market dominance, which is the threshold for the application of Article 82. Where there are many firms competing in an unconcentrated market, it can be assumed that non-hardcore vertical restraints will not have appreciable negative effects. A market is deemed unconcentrated when the HHI index, i.e. the sum of the squares of the individual market shares of all companies in the relevant market, is below 1000.

(2) Vertical restraints which reduce inter-brand competition are generally more harmful than vertical restraints that reduce intra-brand competition. For instance, non-compete obligations are likely to have more net negative effects than exclusive distribution. The former, by possibly foreclosing the market to other brands, may prevent those brands from reaching the market. The latter, while limiting intra-brand competition, does not prevent goods from reaching the final consumer.

(3) Vertical restraints from the limited distribution group, in the absence of sufficient inter-brand competition, may significantly restrict the choices available to consumers. They are particularly harmful when more efficient distributors or distributors with a different distribution format are foreclosed. This can reduce innovation in distribution and denies consumers the particular service or price-service combination of these distributors.

(4) Exclusive dealing arrangements are generally worse for competition than non-exclusive arrangements. Exclusive dealing makes, by the express language of the contract or its practical effects, one party fulfil all or practically all its requirements from another party. For instance, under a non-compete obligation the buyer purchases only one brand. Quantity forcing, on the other hand, leaves the buyer some scope to purchase competing goods. The degree of foreclosure may therefore be less with quantity forcing.

(5) Vertical restraints agreed for non-branded goods and services are in general less harmful than restraints affecting the distribution of branded goods and services. Branding tends to increase product differentiation and reduce substitutability of the product, leading to a reduced elasticity of demand and an increased possibility to raise price. The distinction between branded and non-branded goods or services will often coincide with the distinction between intermediate goods and services and final goods and services.

Intermediate goods and services are sold to undertakings for use as an input to produce other goods or services and are generally not recognisable in the final goods or services. The buyers of intermediate products are usually well-informed customers, able to assess quality and therefore less reliant on brand and image. Final goods are, directly or indirectly, sold to final consumers who often rely more on brand and image. As distributors (retailers, wholesalers) have to respond to the demand of final consumers, competition may suffer more when distributors are foreclosed from selling one or a number of brands than when buyers of intermediate products are prevented from buying competing products from certain sources of supply.

The undertakings buying intermediate goods or services normally have specialist departments or advisers who monitor developments in the supply market. Because they effect sizeable transactions, search costs are in general not prohibitive. A loss of intra-brand competition is therefore less important at the intermediate level.

(6) In general, a combination of vertical restraints aggravates their negative effects. However, certain combinations of vertical restraints are better for competition than their use in isolation from each other. For instance, in an exclusive distribution system, the distributor may be tempted to increase the price of the products as intra-brand competition has been reduced. The use of quantity forcing or the setting of a maximum resale price may limit such price increases.

(7) Possible negative effects of vertical restraints are reinforced when several suppliers and their buyers organise their trade in a similar way. These so-called cumulative effects may be a problem in a number of sectors.

(8) The more the vertical restraint is linked to the transfer of know-how, the more reason there may be to expect efficiencies to arise and the more a vertical restraint may be necessary to protect the know-how transferred or the investment costs incurred.

(9) The more the vertical restraint is linked to investments which are relationship-specific, the more justification there is for certain vertical restraints. The justified duration will depend on the time necessary to depreciate the investment.

(10) In the case of a new product, or where an existing product is sold for the first time on a different geographic market, it may be difficult for the company to define the market or its market share may be very high. However, this should not be considered a major problem, as vertical restraints linked to opening up new product or geographic markets in general do not restrict competition. This rule holds, irrespective of the market share of the company, for two years after the first putting on the market of the product. It applies to all non-hardcore vertical restraints and, in the case of a new geographic market, to restrictions on active and passive sales imposed on the direct buyers of the supplier located in other markets to intermediaries in the new market. In the case of genuine testing of a new product in a limited territory or with a limited customer group, the distributors appointed to sell the new product on the test market can be restricted in their active selling outside the test market for a maximum period of 1 year without being caught by Article 81(1).

1.4. Methodology of analysis

(120) The assessment of a vertical restraint involves in general the following four steps:

(1) First, the undertakings involved need to define the relevant market in order to establish the market share of the supplier or the buyer, depending on the vertical restraint involved (see paragraphs 88 to 99, in particular 89 to 95).

(2) If the relevant market share does not exceed the 30 % threshold, the vertical agreement is covered by the Block Exemption Regulation, subject to the hardcore restrictions and conditions set out in that regulation.

(3) If the relevant market share is above the 30 % threshold, it is necessary to assess whether the vertical agreement falls within Article 81(1).

(4) If the vertical agreement falls within Article 81(1), it is necessary to examine whether it fulfils the conditions for exemption under Article 81(3).

1.4.1. Relevant factors for the assessment under Article 81(1)

(121) In assessing cases above the market share threshold of 30 %, the Commission will make a full competition analysis. The following factors are the most important to establish whether a vertical agreement brings about an appreciable restriction of competition under Article 81(1):

(a) market position of the supplier;

(b) market position of competitors;

(c) market position of the buyer;

(d) entry barriers;

(e) maturity of the market;

(f) level of trade;

(g) nature of the product;

(h) other factors.

(122) The importance of individual factors may vary from case to case and depends on all other factors. For instance, a high market share of the supplier is usually a good indicator of market power, but in the case of low entry barriers it may not indicate market power. It is therefore not possible to provide strict rules on the importance of the individual factors. However the following can be said: Market position of the supplier

(123) The market position of the supplier is established first and foremost by his market share on the relevant product and geographic market. The higher his market share, the greater his market power is likely to be. The market position of the supplier is further strengthened if he has certain cost advantages over his competitors. These competitive advantages may result from a first mover advantage (having the best site, etc.), holding essential patents, having superior technology, being the brand leader or having a superior portfolio.

Market position of competitors

(124) The same indicators, that is market share and possible competitive advantages, are used to describe the market position of competitors. The stronger the established competitors are and the greater their number, the less risk there is that the supplier or buyer in question will be able to foreclose the market individually and the less there is a risk of a reduction of inter-brand competition. However, if the number of competitors becomes rather small and their market position (size, costs, R& D potential, etc.) is rather similar, this market structure may increase the risk of collusion. Fluctuating or rapidly changing market shares are in general an indication of intense competition.

Market position of the buyer

(125) Buying power derives from the market position of the buyer. The first indicator of buying power is the market share of the buyer on the purchase market. This share reflects the importance of his demand for his possible suppliers. Other indicators focus on the market position of the buyer on his resale market including characteristics such as a wide geographic spread of his outlets, own

brands of the buyer/distributor and his image amongst final consumers. The effect of buying power on the likelihood of anti-competitive effects is not the same for the different vertical restraints. Buying power may in particular increase the negative effects in case of restraints from the limited distribution and market partitioning groups such as exclusive supply, exclusive distribution and quantitative selective distribution.

Entry barriers

(126) Entry barriers are measured by the extent to which incumbent companies can increase their price above the competitive level, usually above minimum average total cost, and make supra-normal profits without attracting entry. Without any entry barriers, easy and quick entry would eliminate such profits. In as far as effective entry, which would prevent or erode the supra-normal profits, is likely to occur within one or two years, entry barriers can be said to be low.

(127) Entry barriers may result from a wide variety of factors such as economies of scale and scope, government regulations, especially where they establish exclusive rights, state aid, import tariffs, intellectual property rights, ownership of resources where the supply is limited due to for instance natural limitations([30]), essential facilities, a first mover advantage and brand loyalty of consumers created by strong advertising. Vertical restraints and vertical integration may also work as an entry barrier by making access more difficult and foreclosing (potential) competitors. Entry barriers may be present at only the supplier or buyer level or at both levels.

(128) The question whether certain of these factors should be described as entry barriers depends on whether they are related to sunk costs. Sunk costs are those costs that have to be incurred to enter or be active on a market but that are lost when the market is exited. Advertising costs to build consumer loyalty are normally sunk costs, unless an exiting firm could either sell its brand name or use it somewhere else without a loss. The more costs are sunk, the more potential entrants have to weigh the risks of entering the market and the more credibly incumbents can threaten that they will match new competition, as sunk costs make it costly for incumbents to leave the market. If, for instance, distributors are tied to a manufacturer via a non-compete obligation, the foreclosing effect will be more significant if setting up its own distributors will impose sunk costs on the potential entrant.

(129) In general, entry requires sunk costs, sometimes minor and sometimes major. Therefore, actual competition is in general more effective and will weigh more in the assessment of a case than potential competition.

---

[30] See Commission Decision 97/26/EC (Case No IV/M.619—Gencor/Lonrho), (OJ L 11, 14.1.1997, p. 30).

Maturity of the market

(130) A mature market is a market that has existed for some time, where the technology used is well known and widespread and not changing very much, where there are no major brand innovations and in which demand is relatively stable or declining. In such a market negative effects are more likely than in more dynamic markets.

Level of trade

(131) The level of trade is linked to the distinction between intermediate and final goods and services. As indicated earlier, negative effects are in general less likely at the level of intermediate goods and services.

Nature of the product

(132) The nature of the product plays a role in particular for final products in assessing both the likely negative and the likely positive effects. When assessing the likely negative effects, it is important whether the products on the market are more homogeneous or heterogeneous, whether the product is expensive, taking up a large part of the consumer's budget, or is inexpensive and whether the product is a one-off purchase or repeatedly purchased. In general, when the product is more heterogeneous, less expensive and resembles more a one-off purchase, vertical restraints are more likely to have negative effects.

Other factors

(133) In the assessment of particular restraints other factors may have to be taken into account. Among these factors can be the cumulative effect, i.e. the coverage of the market by similar agreements, the duration of the agreements, whether the agreement is "imposed" (mainly one party is subject to the restrictions or obligations) or "agreed" (both parties accept restrictions or obligations), the regulatory environment and behaviour that may indicate or facilitate collusion like price leadership, pre-announced price changes and discussions on the "right" price, price rigidity in response to excess capacity, price discrimination and past collusive behaviour.

1.4.2. Relevant factors for the assessment under Article 81(3)

(134) There are four cumulative conditions for the application of Article 81(3):

- the vertical agreement must contribute to improving production or distribution or to promoting technical or economic progress;

- the vertical agreement must allow consumers a fair share of these benefits;

- the vertical agreement must not impose on the undertakings concerned vertical restraints which are not indispensable to the attainment of these benefits;

- the vertical agreement must not afford such undertakings the possibility of eliminating competition in respect of a substantial part of the products in question.

(135) The last criterion of elimination of competition for a substantial part of the products in question is related to the question of dominance. Where an undertaking is dominant or becoming dominant as a consequence of the vertical agreement, a vertical restraint that has appreciable anti-competitive effects can in principle not be exempted. The vertical agreement may however fall outside Article 81(1) if there is an objective justification, for instance if it is necessary for the protection of relationship-specific investments or for the transfer of substantial know-how without which the supply or purchase of certain goods or services would not take place.

(136) Where the supplier and the buyer are not dominant, the other three criteria become important. The first, concerning the improvement of production or distribution and the promotion of technical or economic progress, refers to the type of efficiencies described inparagraphs 115 to 118. These efficiencies have to be substantiated and must produce a net positive effect. Speculative claims on avoidance of free-riding or general statements on cost savings will not be accepted. Cost savings that arise from the mere exercise of market power or from anti-competitive conduct cannot be accepted. Secondly, economic benefits have to favour not only the parties to the agreement, but also the consumer. Generally the transmission of the benefits to consumers will depend on the intensity of competition on the relevant market. Competitive pressures will normally ensure that cost-savings are passed on by way of lower prices or that companies have an incentive to bring new products to the market as quickly as possible. Therefore, if sufficient competition which effectively constrains the parties to the agreement is maintained on the market, the competitive process will normally ensure that consumers receive a fair share of the economic benefits. The third criterion will play a role in ensuring that the least anti-competitive restraint is chosen to obtain certain positive effects.

2. Analysis of specific vertical restraints

(137) Vertical agreements may contain a combination of two or more of the components of vertical restraints described in paragraphs 103 to 114. The most common vertical restraints and combinations of vertical restraints are analysed below following the methodology of analysis developed in paragraphs 120 to 136.

2.1. Single branding

(138) A non-compete arrangement is based on an obligation or incentive scheme which makes the buyer purchase practically all his requirements on a particular market from only one supplier. It does not mean that the buyer can only buy directly from the supplier, but that the buyer will not buy and resell or incorporate competing goods or services. The possible competition risks are foreclosure of the market to competing suppliers and potential suppliers, facilitation of collusion between suppliers in case of cumulative use and, where the buyer is a retailer selling to final consumers, a loss of in-store inter-brand competition. All three restrictive effects have a direct impact on inter-brand competition.

(139) Single branding is exempted by the Block Exemption Regulation when the supplier's market share does not exceed 30 % and subject to a limitation in time of five years for the non-compete obligation. Above the market share threshold or beyond the time limit of five years, the following guidance is provided for the assessment of individual cases.

(140) The "market position of the supplier" is of main importance to assess possible anti-competitive effects of non-compete obligations. In general, this type of obligation is imposed by the supplier and the supplier has similar agreements with other buyers.

(141) It is not only the market position of the supplier that is of importance but also the extent to and the duration for which he applies a non-compete obligation. The higher his tied market share, i.e. the part of his market share sold under a single branding obligation, the more significant foreclosure is likely to be. Similarly, the longer the duration of the non-compete obligations, the more significant foreclosure is likely to be. Non-compete obligations shorter than one year entered into by non-dominant companies are in general not considered to give rise to appreciable anti-competitive effects or net negative effects. Non-compete obligations between one and five years entered into by non-dominant companies usually require a proper balancing of pro- and anti-competitive effects, while non-compete obligations exceeding five years are for most types of investments not considered necessary to achieve the claimed efficiencies or the efficiencies are not sufficient to outweigh their foreclosure effect. Dominant companies may not impose non-compete obligations on their buyers unless they can objectively justify such commercial practice within the context of Article 82.

(142) In assessing the supplier's market power, the "market position of his competitors" is important. As long as the competitors are sufficiently numerous and strong, no appreciable anti-competitive effects can be expected. It is only likely that competing suppliers will be foreclosed if they are significantly smaller than the supplier applying the non-compete obligation. Foreclosure of competitors is not very likely where they have similar market positions and can offer similarly attractive products. In such a case foreclosure may however occur for potential entrants when a number of major suppliers enter into non-compete contracts with a significant number of buyers on the relevant market (cumulative effect situation). This is also a situation where non-compete agreements may facilitate collusion between competing suppliers. If individually these suppliers are covered by the Block Exemption Regulation, a withdrawal of the block exemption may be necessary to deal with such a negative cumulative effect. A tied market share of less than 5 % is not considered in general to contribute significantly to a cumulative foreclosure effect.

(143) In cases where the market share of the largest supplier is below 30 % and the market share of the five largest suppliers (concentration rate (CR) 5) is below 50 %, there is unlikely to be a single or a cumulative anti-competitive effect situation. If a potential entrant cannot penetrate the market profitably, this is likely to be due to factors other than non-compete obligations, such as consumer

preferences. A competition problem is unlikely to arise when, for instance, 50 companies, of which none has an important market share, compete fiercely on a particular market.

(144) "Entry barriers" are important to establish whether there is real foreclosure. Wherever it is relatively easy for competing suppliers to create new buyers or find alternative buyers for the product, foreclosure is unlikely to be a real problem. However, there are often entry barriers, both at the manufacturing and at the distribution level.

(145) "Countervailing power" is relevant, as powerful buyers will not easily allow themselves to be cut off from the supply of competing goods or services. Foreclosure which is not based on efficiency and which has harmful effects on ultimate consumers is therefore mainly a risk in the case of dispersed buyers. However, where non-compete agreements are concluded with major buyers this may have a strong foreclosure effect.

(146) Lastly, "the level of trade" is relevant for foreclosure. Foreclosure is less likely in case of an intermediate product. When the supplier of an intermediate product is not dominant, the competing suppliers still have a substantial part of demand that is "free". Below the level of dominance a serious foreclosure effect may however arise for actual or potential competitors where there is a cumulative effect. A serious cumulative effect is unlikely to arise as long as less than 50 % of the market is tied. When the supplier is dominant, any obligation to buy the products only or mainly from the dominant supplier may easily lead to significant foreclosure effects on the market. The stronger his dominance, the higher the risk of foreclosure of other competitors.

(147) Where the agreement concerns supply of a final product at the wholesale level, the question whether a competition problem is likely to arise below the level of dominance depends in large part on the type of wholesaling and the entry barriers at the wholesale level. There is no real risk of foreclosure if competing manufacturers can easily establish their own wholesaling operation. Whether entry barriers are low depends in part on the type of wholesaling, i.e. whether or not wholesalers can operate efficiently with only the product concerned by the agreement (for example ice cream) or whether it is more efficient to trade in a whole range of products (for example frozen foodstuffs). In the latter case, it is not efficient for a manufacturer selling only one product to set up his own wholesaling operation. In that case anti-competitive effects may arise below the level of dominance. In addition, cumulative effect problems may arise if several suppliers tie most of the available wholesalers.

(148) For final products, foreclosure is in general more likely to occur at the retail level, given the significant entry barriers for most manufacturers to start retail outlets just for their own products. In addition, it is at the retail level that non-compete agreements may lead to reduced in-store inter-brand competition. It is for these reasons that for final products at the retail level, significant anti-competitive effects may start to arise, taking into account all other relevant factors, if a non-dominant supplier ties 30 % or more of the relevant market. For a domin-

ant company, even a modest tied market share may already lead to significant anti-competitive effects. The stronger its dominance, the higher the risk of foreclosure of other competitors.

(149) At the retail level a cumulative foreclosure effect may also arise. When all companies have market shares below 30 % a cumulative foreclosure effect is unlikely if the total tied market share is less than 40 % and withdrawal of the block exemption is therefore unlikely. This figure may be higher when other factors like the number of competitors, entry barriers etc. are taken into account. When not all companies have market shares below the threshold of the Block Exemption Regulation but none is dominant, a cumulative foreclosure effect is unlikely if the total tied market share is below 30 %.

(150) Where the buyer operates from premises and land owned by the supplier or leased by the supplier from a third party not connected with the buyer, the possibility of imposing effective remedies for a possible foreclosure effect will be limited. In that case intervention by the Commission below the level of dominance is unlikely.

(151) In certain sectors the selling of more than one brand from a single site may be difficult, in which case a foreclosure problem can better be remedied by limiting the effective duration of contracts.

(152) A so-called "English clause", requiring the buyer to report any better offer and allowing him only to accept such an offer when the supplier does not match it, can be expected to have the same effect as a non-compete obligation, especially when the buyer has to reveal who makes the better offer. In addition, by increasing the transparency of the market it may facilitate collusion between the suppliers. An English clause may also work as quantity-forcing. Quantity-forcing on the buyer is a weaker form of non-compete, where incentives or obligations agreed between the supplier and the buyer make the latter concentrate his purchases to a large extent with one supplier. Quantity-forcing may for example take the form of minimum purchase requirements or non-linear pricing, such as quantity rebate schemes, loyalty rebate schemes or a two-part tariff (fixed fee plus a price per unit). Quantity-forcing on the buyer will have similar but weaker foreclosure effects than a non-compete obligation. The assessment of all these different forms will depend on their effect on the market. In addition, Article 82 specifically prevents dominant companies from applying English clauses or fidelity rebate schemes.

(153) Where appreciable anti-competitive effects are established, the question of a possible exemption under Article 81(3) arises as long as the supplier is not dominant. For non-compete obligations, the efficiencies described in paragraph 116, points 1 (free riding between suppliers), 4, 5 (hold-up problems) and 7 (capital market imperfections) may be particularly relevant.

(154) In the case of an efficiency as described in paragraph 116, points 1, 4 and 7, quantity forcing on the buyer could possibly be a less restrictive alternative. A non-compete obligation may be the only viable way to achieve an efficiency as described in paragraph 116, point 5 (hold-up problem related to the transfer of know-how).

(155) In the case of a relationship-specific investment made by the supplier (see efficiency 4 in paragraph 116), a non-compete or quantity forcing agreement for the period of depreciation of the investment will in general fulfil the conditions of Article 81(3). In the case of high relationship-specific investments, a non-compete obligation exceeding five years may be justified. A relationship-specific investment could, for instance, be the installation or adaptation of equipment by the supplier when this equipment can be used afterwards only to produce components for a particular buyer. General or market-specific investments in (extra) capacity are normally not relationship-specific investments. However, where a supplier creates new capacity specifically linked to the operations of a particular buyer, for instance a company producing metal cans which creates new capacity to produce cans on the premises of or next to the canning facility of a food producer, this new capacity may only be economically viable when producing for this particular customer, in which case the investment would be considered to be relationship-specific.

(156) Where the supplier provides the buyer with a loan or provides the buyer with equipment which is not relationship-specific, this in itself is normally not sufficient to justify the exemption of a foreclosure effect on the market. The instances of capital market imperfection, whereby it is more efficient for the supplier of a product than for a bank to provide a loan, will be limited (see efficiency 7 in paragraph 116). Even if the supplier of the product were to be the more efficient provider of capital, a loan could only justify a non-compete obligation if the buyer is not prevented from terminating the non-compete obligation and repaying the outstanding part of the loan at any point in time and without payment of any penalty. This means that the repayment of the loan should be structured in equal or decreasing instalments and should not increase over time and that the buyer should have the possibility to take over the equipment provided by the supplier at its market asset value. This is without prejudice to the possibility, in case for example of a new point of distribution, to delay repayment for the first one or two years until sales have reached a certain level.

(157) The transfer of substantial know-how (efficiency 5 in paragraph 116) usually justifies a non-compete obligation for the whole duration of the supply agreement, as for example in the context of franchising.

(158) Below the level of dominance the combination of non-compete with exclusive distribution may also justify the non-compete obligation lasting the full length of the agreement. In the latter case, the non-compete obligation is likely to improve the distribution efforts of the exclusive distributor in his territory (see paragraphs 161 to 177).

(159) Example of non-compete

The market leader in a national market for an impulse consumer product, with a market share of 40 %, sells most of its products (90 %) through tied retailers (tied market share 36 %). The agreements oblige the retailers to purchase only from the market leader for at least four years. The market leader is especially strongly represented in the more densely populated areas like the capital. Its competitors, 10 in number, of which some are only locally available, all have much smaller market shares, the biggest having 12 %. These 10 competitors together supply another 10 % of the market via tied outlets. There is strong brand and product differentiation in the market. The market leader has the strongest brands. It is the only one with regular national advertising campaigns. It provides its tied retailers with special stocking cabinets for its product.

The result on the market is that in total 46 % (36 % + 10 %) of the market is foreclosed to potential entrants and to incumbents not having tied outlets. Potential entrants find entry even more difficult in the densely populated areas where foreclosure is even higher, although it is there that they would prefer to enter the market. In addition, owing to the strong brand and product differentiation and the high search costs relative to the price of the product, the absence of in-store inter-brand competition leads to an extra welfare loss for consumers. The possible efficiencies of the outlet exclusivity, which the market leader claims result from reduced transport costs and a possible hold-up problem concerning the stocking cabinets, are limited and do not outweigh the negative effects on competition. The efficiencies are limited, as the transport costs are linked to quantity and not exclusivity and the stocking cabinets do not contain special know-how and are not brand specific. Accordingly, it is unlikely that the conditions for exemption are fulfilled.

(160) Example of quantity forcing

A producer X with a 40 % market share sells 80 % of its products through contracts which specify that the reseller is required to purchase at least 75 % of its requirements for that type of product from X. In return X is offering financing and equipment at favourable rates. The contracts have a duration of five years in which repayment of the loan is foreseen in equal instalments. However, after the first two years buyers have the possibility to terminate the contract with a six-month notice period if they repay the outstanding loan and take over the equipment at its market asset value. At the end of the five-year period the equipment becomes the property of the buyer. Most of the competing producers are small, twelve in total with the biggest having a market share of 20 %, and engage in similar contracts with different durations. The producers with market shares below 10 % often have contracts with longer durations and with less generous termination clauses. The contracts of producer X leave 25 % of requirements free to be supplied by competitors. In the last three years, two new producers have entered the market and gained a combined market share of around 8 %, partly by taking over the loans of a number of resellers in return for contracts with these resellers.

Producer X's tied market share is 24 % (0,75 x 0,80 x 40 %). The other producers' tied market share is around 25 %. Therefore, in total around 49 % of the market is foreclosed to potential entrants and to incumbents not having tied outlets for at least the first two years of the supply contracts. The market shows that the resellers often have difficulty in obtaining loans from banks and are too small in general to obtain capital through other means like the issuing of shares. In addition, producer X is able to demonstrate that concentrating his sales on a limited number of resellers allows him to plan his sales better and to save transport costs. In the light of the 25 % non-tied part in the contracts of producer X, the real possibility for early termination of the contract, the recent entry of new producers and the fact that around half the resellers are not tied, the quantity forcing of 75 % applied by producer X is likely to fulfil the conditions for exemption.

2.2. Exclusive distribution

(161) In an exclusive distribution agreement the supplier agrees to sell his products only to one distributor for resale in a particular territory. At the same time the distributor is usually limited in his active selling into other exclusively allocated territories. The possible competition risks are mainly reduced intra-brand competition and market partitioning, which may in particular facilitate price discrimination. When most or all of the suppliers apply exclusive distribution this may facilitate collusion, both at the suppliers' and distributors' level.

(162) Exclusive distribution is exempted by the Block Exemption Regulation when the supplier's market share does not exceed 30 %, even if combined with other non-hardcore vertical restraints, such as a non-compete obligation limited to five years, quantity forcing or exclusive purchasing. A combination of exclusive distribution and selective distribution is only exempted by the Block Exemption Regulation if active selling in other territories is not restricted. Above the 30 % market share threshold, the following guidance is provided for the assessment of exclusive distribution in individual cases.

(163) The market position of the supplier and his competitors is of major importance, as the loss of intra-brand competition can only be problematic if inter-brand competition is limited. The stronger the "position of the supplier", the more serious is the loss of intra-brand competition. Above the 30 % market share threshold there may be a risk of a significant reduction of intra-brand competition. In order to be exemptable, the loss of intra-brand competition needs to be balanced with real efficiencies.

(164) The "position of the competitors" can have a dual significance. Strong competitors will generally mean that the reduction in intra-brand competition is outweighed by sufficient inter-brand competition. However, if the number of competitors becomes rather small and their market position is rather similar in terms of market share, capacity and distribution network, there is a risk of collusion. The loss of intra-brand competition can increase this risk, especially when several suppliers operate similar distribution systems. Multiple exclusive dealer-ships, i.e. when different suppliers appoint the same exclusive distributor in a given territory, may further increase the risk of collusion. If a dealer is granted the exclusive right to distribute two or more important competing products in the same territory, inter-brand competition is likely to be substantially restricted for those brands. The higher the cumulative market share of the brands distributed by the multiple dealer, the higher the risk of collusion and the more inter-brand com-petition will be reduced. Such cumulative effect situations may be a reason to withdraw the benefit of the Block Exemption Regulation when the market shares of the suppliers are below the threshold of the Block Exemption Regulation.

(165) "Entry barriers" that may hinder suppliers from creating new distributors or finding alternative distributors are less important in assessing the possible anti-competitive effects of exclusive distribution. Foreclosure of other suppliers does not arise as long as exclusive distribution is not combined with single branding.

(166) Foreclosure of other distributors is not a problem if the supplier which operates the exclusive distribution system appoints a high number of exclusive distributors in the same market and these exclusive distributors are not restricted in selling to other non-appointed distributors. Foreclosure of other distributors may however become a problem where there is "buying power" and market power downstream, in particular in the case of very large territories where the exclusive distributor becomes the exclusive buyer for a whole market. An example would be a supermarket chain which becomes the only distributor of a leading brand on a national food retail market. The foreclosure of other distributors may be aggravated in the case of multiple exclusive dealership. Such a case, covered by the Block Exemption Regulation when the market share of each supplier is below 30 %, may give reason for withdrawal of the block exemption.

(167) "Buying power" may also increase the risk of collusion on the buyers' side when the exclusive distribution arrangements are imposed by important buyers, possibly located in different territories, on one or several suppliers.

(168) "Maturity of the market" is important, as loss of intra-brand competition and price discrimination may be a serious problem in a mature market but may be less relevant in a market with growing demand, changing technologies and changing market positions.

(169) "The level of trade" is important as the possible negative effects may differ between the wholesale and retail level. Exclusive distribution is mainly applied in the distribution of final goods and services. A loss of intra-brand competition is especially likely at the retail level if coupled with large territories, since final consumers may be confronted with little possibility of choosing between a high price/high service and a low price/low service distributor for an important brand.

(170) A manufacturer which chooses a wholesaler to be his exclusive distributor will normally do so for a larger territory, such as a whole Member State. As long as the wholesaler can sell the products without limitation to downstream retailers there are not likely to be appreciable anti-competitive effects if the manufacturer is not dominant. A possible loss of intra-brand competition at the wholesale level may be easily outweighed by efficiencies obtained in logistics, promotion etc, especially when the manufacturer is based in a different country. Foreclosure of other wholesalers within that territory is not likely as a supplier with a market share above 30 % usually has enough bargaining power not to choose a less efficient wholesaler. The possible risks for inter-brand competition of multiple exclusive dealerships are however higher at the wholesale than at the retail level.

(171) The combination of exclusive distribution with single branding may add the problem of foreclosure of the market to other suppliers, especially in case of a dense network of exclusive distributors with small territories or in case of a

cumulative effect. This may necessitate application of the principles set out above on single branding. However, when the combination does not lead to significant foreclosure, the combination of exclusive distribution and single branding may be pro-competitive by increasing the incentive for the exclusive distributor to focus his efforts on the particular brand. Therefore, in the absence of such a foreclosure effect, the combination of exclusive distribution with non-compete is exemptable for the whole duration of the agreement, particularly at the wholesale level.

(172) The combination of exclusive distribution with exclusive purchasing increases the possible competition risks of reduced intra-brand competition and market partitioning which may in particular facilitate price discrimination. Exclusive distribution already limits arbitrage by customers, as it limits the number of distributors and usually also restricts the distributors in their freedom of active selling. Exclusive purchasing, requiring the exclusive distributors to buy their supplies for the particular brand directly from the manufacturer, eliminates in addition possible arbitrage by the exclusive distributors, who are prevented from buying from other distributors in the system. This enhances the possibilities for the supplier to limit intra-brand competition while applying dissimilar conditions of sale. The combination of exclusive distribution and exclusive purchasing is therefore unlikely to be exempted for suppliers with a market share above 30 % unless there are very clear and substantial efficiencies leading to lower prices to all final consumers. Lack of such efficiencies may also lead to withdrawal of the block exemption where the market share of the supplier is below 30 %.

(173) The "nature of the product" is not very relevant to assessing the possible anti-competitive effects of exclusive distribution. It is, however, relevant when the issue of possible efficiencies is discussed, that is after an appreciable anti-competitive effect is established.

(174) Exclusive distribution may lead to efficiencies, especially where investments by the distributors are required to protect or build up the brand image. In general, the case for efficiencies is strongest for new products, for complex products, for products whose qualities are difficult to judge before consumption (so-called experience products) or of which the qualities are difficult to judge even after consumption (so-called credence products). In addition, exclusive distribution may lead to savings in logistic costs due to economies of scale in transport and distribution.

(175) Example of exclusive distribution at the wholesale level

In the market for a consumer durable, A is the market leader. A sells its product through exclusive wholesalers. Territories for the wholesalers correspond to the entire Member State for small Member States, and to a region for larger Member States. These exclusive distributors take care of sales to all the retailers in their territories. They do not sell to final consumers. The wholesalers are in charge of promotion in their markets. This includes sponsoring of local events, but also explaining and promoting the new products to the retailers in their territories. Technology and product innovation are evolving fairly quickly on this market, and pre-sale service to retailers and to final consumers plays an important role.

The wholesalers are not required to purchase all their requirements of the brand of supplier A from the producer himself, and arbitrage by wholesalers or retailers is practicable because the transport costs are relatively low compared to the value of the product. The wholesalers are not under a non-compete obligation. Retailers also sell a number of brands of competing suppliers, and there are no exclusive or selective distribution agreements at the retail level. On the European market of sales to wholesalers A has around 50 % market share. Its market share on the various national retail markets varies between 40 % and 60 %. A has between 6 and 10 competitors on every national market: B, C and D are its biggest competitors and are also present on each national market, with market shares varying between 20 % and 5 %. The remaining producers are national producers, with smaller market shares. B, C and D have similar distribution networks, whereas the local producers tend to sell their products directly to retailers.

On the wholesale market described above, the risk of reduced intra-brand competition and price discrimination is low. Arbitrage is not hindered, and the absence of intra-brand competition is not very relevant at the wholesale level. At the retail level neither intra- nor inter-brand competition are hindered. Moreover, inter-brand competition is largely unaffected by the exclusive arrangements at the wholesale level. This makes it likely, if anti-competitive effects exist, that the conditions for exemption are fulfilled.

(176) Example of multiple exclusive dealerships in an oligopolistic market

In a national market for a final product, there are four market leaders, who each have a market share of around 20 %. These four market leaders sell their product through exclusive distributors at the retail level. Retailers are given an exclusive territory which corresponds to the town in which they are located or a district of the town for large towns. In most territories, the four market leaders happen to appoint the same exclusive retailer ("multiple dealership"), often centrally located and rather specialised in the product. The remaining 20 % of the national market is composed of small local producers, the largest of these producers having a market share of 5 % on the national market. These local producers sell their products in general through other retailers, in particular because the exclusive distributors of the four largest suppliers show in general little interest in selling less well-known and cheaper brands. There is strong brand and product differentiation on the market. The four market leaders have large national advertising campaigns and strong brand images, whereas the fringe producers do not advertise their products at the national level. The market is rather mature, with stable demand and no major product and technological innovation. The product is relatively simple.

In such an oligopolistic market, there is a risk of collusion between the four market leaders. This risk is increased through multiple dealerships. Intra-brand competition is limited by the territorial exclusivity. Competition between the four leading brands is reduced at the retail level, since one retailer fixes the price of all four brands in each territory. The multiple dealership implies that, if one producer cuts the price for its brand, the retailer will not be eager to transmit this price cut to the final consumer as it would reduce its sales and profits made with the other brands. Hence, producers have a reduced interest in entering into price competition with one another. Inter-brand price competition exists mainly with the low brand image goods of the fringe producers. The possible efficiency arguments for (joint) exclusive distributors are limited, as the product is relatively simple, the resale does not require any specific investments or training and advertising is mainly carried out at the level of the producers.

Even though each of the market leaders has a market share below the threshold, exemption under Article 81(3) may not be justified and withdrawal of the block exemption may be necessary.

(177) Example of exclusive distribution combined with exclusive purchasing

Manufacturer A is the European market leader for a bulky consumer durable, with a market share of between 40 % and 60 % in most national retail markets. In every Member State, it has about seven competitors with much smaller market shares, the largest of these competitors having a market share of 10 %. These competitors are present on only one or two national markets. A sells its product through its national subsidiaries to exclusive distributors at the retail level, which are not allowed to sell actively into each other's territories. In addition, the retailers are obliged to purchase manufacturer A's products exclusively from the national subsidiary of manufacturer A in their own country. The retailers selling the brand of manufacturer A are the main resellers of that type of product in their territory. They handle competing brands, but with varying degrees of success and enthusiasm. A applies price differences of 10 % to 15 % between markets and smaller differences within markets. This is translated into smaller price differences at the retail level. The market is relatively stable on the demand and the supply side, and there are no significant technological changes.

In these markets, the loss of intra-brand competition results not only from the territorial exclusivity at the retail level but is aggravated by the exclusive purchasing obligation imposed on the retailers. The exclusive purchase obligation helps to keep markets and territories separate by making arbitrage between the exclusive retailers impossible. The exclusive retailers also cannot sell actively into each other's territory and in practice tend to avoid delivering outside their own territory. This renders price discrimination possible. Arbitrage by consumers or independent traders is limited due to the bulkiness of the product.

The possible efficiency arguments of this system, linked to economies of scale in transport and promotion efforts at the retailers' level, are unlikely to outweigh the negative effect of price discrimination and reduced intra-brand competition. Consequently, it is unlikely that the conditions for exemption are fulfilled.

2.3. Exclusive customer allocation

(178) In an exclusive customer allocation agreement, the supplier agrees to sell his products only to one distributor for resale to a particular class of customers. At the same time, the distributor is usually limited in his active selling to other exclusively allocated classes of customers. The possible competition risks are mainly

reduced intra-brand competition and market partitioning, which may in particular facilitate price discrimination. When most or all of the suppliers apply exclusive customer allocation, this may facilitate collusion, both at the suppliers' and the distributors' level.

(179) Exclusive customer allocation is exempted by the Block Exemption Regulation when the supplier's market share does not exceed the 30 % market share threshold, even if combined with other non-hardcore vertical restraints such as non-compete, quantity-forcing or exclusive purchasing. A combination of exclusive customer allocation and selective distribution is normally hardcore, as active selling to end-users by the appointed distributors is usually not left free. Above the 30 % market share threshold, the guidance provided in paragraphs 161 to 177 applies mutatis mutandis to the assessment of exclusive customer allocation, subject to the following specific remarks.

(180) The allocation of customers normally makes arbitrage by the customers more difficult. In addition, as each appointed distributor has his own class of customers, non-appointed distributors not falling within such a class may find it difficult to obtain the product. This will reduce possible arbitrage by non-appointed distributors. Therefore, above the 30 % market share threshold of the Block Exemption Regulation exclusive customer allocation is unlikely to be exemptable unless there are clear and substantial efficiency effects.

(181) Exclusive customer allocation is mainly applied to intermediate products and at the wholesale level when it concerns final products, where customer groups with different specific requirements concerning the product can be distinguished.

(182) Exclusive customer allocation may lead to efficiencies, especially when the distributors are required to make investments in for instance specific equipment, skills or know-how to adapt to the requirements of their class of customers. The depreciation period of these investments indicates the justified duration of an exclusive customer allocation system. In general the case is strongest for new or complex products and for products requiring adaptation to the needs of the individual customer. Identifiable differentiated needs are more likely for intermediate products, that is products sold to different types of professional buyers. Allocation of final consumers is unlikely to lead to any efficiencies and is therefore unlikely to be exempted.

(183) Example of exclusive customer allocation

A company has developed a sophisticated sprinkler installation. The company has currently a market share of 40 % on the market for sprinkler installations. When it started selling the sophisticated sprinkler it had a market share of 20 % with an older product. The installation of the new type of sprinkler depends on the type of building that it is installed in and on the use of the building (office, chemical plant, hospital etc.). The company has appointed a number of distributors to sell and install the sprinkler installation. Each distributor needed to train its employees for the general and specific requirements of installing the sprinkler installation for a particular class of customers. To ensure that distributors would specialise the company assigned to each distributor an exclusive class of customers and prohibited active sales to each others' exclusive customer classes. After five years, all the exclusive distributors will be allowed to sell actively to all classes of customers, thereby ending the system of exclusive customer allocation. The supplier may then also start selling to new distributors. The market is quite dynamic, with two recent entries and a number of technological developments. Competitors, with market shares between 25 % and 5 %, are also upgrading their products.

As the exclusivity is of limited duration and helps to ensure that the distributors may recoup their investments and concentrate their sales efforts first on a certain class of customers in order to learn the trade, and as the possible anti-competitive effects seem limited in a dynamic market, the conditions for exemption are likely to be fulfilled.

2.4. Selective distribution

(184) Selective distribution agreements, like exclusive distribution agreements, restrict on the one hand the number of authorised distributors and on the other the possibilities of resale. The difference with exclusive distribution is that the restriction of the number of dealers does not depend on the number of territories but on selection criteria linked in the first place to the nature of the product. Another difference with exclusive distribution is that the restriction on resale is not a restriction on active selling to a territory but a restriction on any sales to non-authorised distributors, leaving only appointed dealers and final customers as possible buyers. Selective distribution is almost always used to distribute branded final products.

(185) The possible competition risks are a reduction in intra-brand competition and, especially in case of cumulative effect, foreclosure of certain type(s) of distributors and facilitation of collusion between suppliers or buyers. To assess the possible anti-competitive effects of selective distribution under Article 81(1), a distinction needs to be made between purely qualitative selective distribution and quantitative selective distribution. Purely qualitative selective distribution selects dealers only on the basis of objective criteria required by the nature of the product such as training of sales personnel, the service provided at the point of sale, a certain range of the products being sold etc([31]). The application of such criteria does not put a direct limit on the number of dealers. Purely qualitative selective distribution is in general considered to fall outside Article 81(1) for lack of anti-competitive effects, provided that three conditions are satisfied. First, the nature of the product in question must necessitate a selective distribution system, in the sense that such a system must constitute a legitimate requirement, having regard to the nature of the product concerned, to preserve its quality and ensure its proper use. Secondly, resellers must be chosen on the basis of objective criteria of a qualitative nature which are laid down uniformly for all potential resellers and

---

([31]) See for example judgment of the Court of First Instance in Case T-88/92 Groupement d'achat Édouard Leclerc v Commission [1996] ECR II-1961.

are not applied in a discriminatory manner. Thirdly, the criteria laid down must not go beyond what is necessary([32]). Quantitative selective distribution adds further criteria for selection that more directly limit the potential number of dealers by, for instance, requiring minimum or maximum sales, by fixing the number of dealers, etc.

(186) Qualitative and quantitative selective distribution is exempted by the Block Exemption Regulation up to 30 % market share, even if combined with other non-hardcore vertical restraints, such as non-compete or exclusive distribution, provided active selling by the authorised distributors to each other and to end users is not restricted. The Block Exemption Regulation exempts selective distribution regardless of the nature of the product concerned. However, where the nature of the product does not require selective distribution, such a distribution system does not generally bring about sufficient efficiency enhancing effects to counterbalance a significant reduction in intra-brand competition. If appreciable anti-competitive effects occur, the benefit of the Block Exemption Regulation is likely to be withdrawn. In addition, the following guidance is provided for the assessment of selective distribution in individual cases which are not covered by the Block Exemption Regulation or in the case of cumulative effects resulting from parallel networks of selective distribution.

(187) The market position of the supplier and his competitors is of central importance in assessing possible anti-competitive effects, as the loss of intra-brand competition can only be problematic if inter-brand competition is limited. The stronger the position of the supplier, the more problematic is the loss of intra-brand competition. Another important factor is the number of selective distribution networks present in the same market. Where selective distribution is applied by only one supplier in the market which is not a dominant undertaking, quantitative selective distribution does not normally create net negative effects provided that the contract goods, having regard to their nature, require the use of a selective distribution system and on condition that the selection criteria applied are necessary to ensure efficient distribution of the goods in question. The reality, however, seems to be that selective distribution is often applied by a number of the suppliers in a given market.

(188) The position of competitors can have a dual significance and plays in particular a role in case of a cumulative effect. Strong competitors will mean in general that the reduction in intra-brand competition is easily outweighed by sufficient inter-brand competition. However, when a majority of the main suppliers apply selective distribution there will be a significant loss of intra-brand competition and possible foreclosure of certain types of distributors as well as an increased risk of collusion between those major suppliers. The risk of foreclosure of more efficient distributors has always been greater with selective distribution

---

([32]) See judgments of the Court of Justice in Case 31/80 L'Oréal v PVBA [1980] ECR 3775, paragraphs 15 and 16; Case 26/76 Metro I [1977] ECR 1875, paragraphs 20 and 21; Case 107/82 AEG [1983] ECR 3151, paragraph 35; and of the Court of First Instance in Case T-19/91 Vichy v Commission [1992] ECR II-415, paragraph 65.

than with exclusive distribution, given the restriction on sales to non-authorised dealers in selective distribution. This is designed to give selective distribution systems a closed character, making it impossible for non-authorised dealers to obtain supplies. This makes selective distribution particularly well suited to avoid pressure by price discounters on the margins of the manufacturer, as well as on the margins of the authorised dealers.

(189) Where the Block Exemption Regulation applies to individual networks of selective distribution, withdrawal of the block exemption or disapplication of the Block Exemption Regulation may be considered in case of cumulative effects. However, a cumulative effect problem is unlikely to arise when the share of the market covered by selective distribution is below 50 %. Also, no problem is likely to arise where the market coverage ratio exceeds 50 %, but the aggregate market share of the five largest suppliers (CR5) is below 50 %. Where both the CR5 and the share of the market covered by selective distribution exceed 50 %, the assessment may vary depending on whether or not all five largest suppliers apply selective distribution. The stronger the position of the competitors not applying selective distribution, the less likely the foreclosure of other distributors. If all five largest suppliers apply selective distribution, competition concerns may in particular arise with respect to those agreements that apply quantitative selection criteria by directly limiting the number of authorised dealers. The conditions of Article 81(3) are in general unlikely to be fulfilled if the selective distribution systems at issue prevent access to the market by new distributors capable of adequately selling the products in question, especially price discounters, thereby limiting distribution to the advantage of certain existing channels and to the detriment of final consumers. More indirect forms of quantitative selective distribution, resulting for instance from the combination of purely qualitative selection criteria with the requirement imposed on the dealers to achieve a minimum amount of annual purchases, are less likely to produce net negative effects, if such an amount does not represent a significant proportion of the dealer's total turnover achieved with the type of products in question and it does not go beyond what is necessary for the supplier to recoup his relationship-specific investment and/or realise economies of scale in distribution. As regards individual contributions, a supplier with a market share of less than 5 % is in general not considered to contribute significantly to a cumulative effect.

(190) "Entry barriers" are mainly of interest in the case of foreclosure of the market to non-authorised dealers. In general entry barriers will be considerable as selective distribution is usually applied by manufacturers of branded products. It will in general take time and considerable investment for excluded retailers to launch their own brands or obtain competitive supplies elsewhere.

(191) "Buying power" may increase the risk of collusion between dealers and thus appreciably change the analysis of possible anti-competitive effects of selective distribution. Foreclosure of the market to more efficient retailers may especially result where a strong dealer organisation imposes selection criteria on the supplier aimed at limiting distribution to the advantage of its members.

(192) Article 5(c) of the Block Exemption Regulation provides that the supplier may not impose an obligation causing the authorised dealers, either directly or indirectly, not to sell the brands of particular competing suppliers. This condition aims specifically at avoiding horizontal collusion to exclude particular brands through the creation of a selective club of brands by the leading suppliers. This kind of obligation is unlikely to be exemptable when the CR5 is equal to or above 50 %, unless none of the suppliers imposing such an obligation belongs to the five largest suppliers in the market.

(193) Foreclosure of other suppliers is normally not a problem as long as other suppliers can use the same distributors, i.e. as long as the selective distribution system is not combined with single branding. In the case of a dense network of authorised distributors or in the case of a cumulative effect, the combination of selective distribution and a non-compete obligation may pose a risk of foreclosure to other suppliers. In that case the principles set out above on single branding apply. Where selective distribution is not combined with a non-compete obligation, foreclosure of the market to competing suppliers may still be a problem when the leading suppliers apply not only purely qualitative selection criteria, but impose on their dealers certain additional obligations such as the obligation to reserve a minimum shelf-space for their products or to ensure that the sales of their products by the dealer achieve a minimum percentage of the dealer's total turnover. Such a problem is unlikely to arise if the share of the market covered by selective distribution is below 50 % or, where this coverage ratio is exceeded, if the market share of the five largest suppliers is below 50 %.

(194) Maturity of the market is important, as loss of intra-brand competition and possible foreclosure of suppliers or dealers may be a serious problem in a mature market but is less relevant in a market with growing demand, changing technologies and changing market positions.

(195) Selective distribution may be efficient when it leads to savings in logistical costs due to economies of scale in transport and this may happen irrespective of the nature of the product (efficiency 6 in paragraph 116). However, this is usually only a marginal efficiency in selective distribution systems. To help solve a free-rider problem between the distributors (efficiency 1 in paragraph 116) or to help create a brand image (efficiency 8 in paragraph 116), the nature of the product is very relevant. In general the case is strongest for new products, for complex products, for products of which the qualities are difficult to judge before consumption (so-called experience products) or of which the qualities are difficult to judge even after consumption (so-called credence products). The combination of selective and exclusive distribution is likely to infringe Article 81 if it is applied by a supplier whose market share exceeds 30 % or in case of cumulative effects, even though active sales between the territories remain free. Such a combination may exceptionally fulfil the conditions of Article 81(3) if it is indispensable to protect substantial and relationship-specific investments made by the authorised dealers (efficiency 4 in paragraph 116).

(196) To ensure that the least anti-competitive restraint is chosen, it is relevant to see whether the same efficiencies can be obtained at a comparable cost by for instance service requirements alone.

(197) Example of quantitative selective distribution:

In a market for consumer durables, the market leader (brand A), with a market share of 35 %, sells its product to final consumers through a selective distribution network. There are several criteria for admission to the network: the shop must employ trained staff and provide pre-sales services, there must be a specialised area in the shop devoted to the sales of the product and similar hi-tech products, and the shop is required to sell a wide range of models of the supplier and to display them in an attractive manner. Moreover, the number of admissible retailers in the network is directly limited through the establishment of a maximum number of retailers per number of inhabitants in each province or urban area. Manufacturer A has 6 competitors in this market. Its largest competitors, B, C and D, have market shares of respectively 25, 15 and 10 %, whilst the other producers have smaller market shares. A is the only manufacturer to use selective distribution. The selective distributors of brand A always handle a few competing brands. However, competing brands are also widely sold in shops which are not member of A's selective distribution network. Channels of distribution are various: for instance, brands B and C are sold in most of A's selected shops, but also in other shops providing a high quality service and in hypermarkets. Brand D is mainly sold in high service shops. Technology is evolving quite rapidly in this market, and the main suppliers maintain a strong quality image for their products through advertising.

In this market, the coverage ratio of selective distribution is 35 %. Inter-brand competition is not directly affected by the selective distribution system of A. Intra-brand competition for brand A may be reduced, but consumers have access to low service/low price retailers for brands B and C, which have a comparable quality image to brand A. Moreover, access to high service retailers for other brands is not foreclosed, since there is no limitation on the capacity of selected distributors to sell competing brands, and the quantitative limitation on the number of retailers for brand A leaves other high service retailers free to distribute competing brands. In this case, in view of the service requirements and the efficiencies these are likely to provide and the limited effect on intra-brand competition the conditions for exempting A's selective distribution network are likely to be fulfilled.

(198) Example of selective distribution with cumulative effects:

On a market for a particular sports article, there are seven manufacturers, whose respective market shares are: 25 %, 20 %, 15 %, 15 %, 10 %, 8 % and 7 %. The five largest manufacturers distribute their products through quantitative selective distribution, whilst the two smallest use different types of distribution systems, which results in a coverage ratio of selective distribution of 85 %. The criteria for access to the selective distribution networks are remarkably uniform amongst manufacturers: shops are required to have trained personnel and to provide pre-sale services, there must be a specialised area in the shop devoted to the sales of the article and a minimum size for this area is specified. The shop is required to sell a wide range of the brand in question and to display the article in an attractive manner, the shop must be located in a commercial street, and this type of article must represent at least 30 % of the total turnover of the shop. In general, the same dealer is appointed selective distributor for all five brands. The two brands which do not use selective distribution usually sell through less specialised retailers with lower service levels. The market is stable, both on the supply and on the demand side, and there is strong brand image and product differentiation. The five market leaders have strong brand images, acquired through advertising and sponsoring, whereas the two smaller manufacturers have a strategy of cheaper products, with no strong brand image.

In this market, access by general price discounters to the five leading brands is denied. Indeed, the requirement that this type of article represents at least 30 % of the activity of the dealers and the criteria on presentation and pre-sales services rule out most price discounters from the network of authorised dealers. As a consequence, consumers have no choice but to buy the five leading brands in high service/high price shops. This leads to reduced inter-brand competition between the five leading brands. The fact that the two smallest brands can be bought in low service/low price shops does not compensate for this, because the brand image of the five market leaders is much better. Inter-brand competition is also limited through multiple dealership. Even though there exists some degree of intra-brand competition and the number of retailers is not directly limited, the criteria for admission are strict enough to lead to a small number of retailers for the five leading brands in each territory.

The efficiencies associated with these quantitative selective distribution systems are low: the product is not very complex and does not justify a particularly high service. Unless the manufacturers can prove that there are clear efficiencies linked to their network of selective distribution, it is probable that the block exemption will have to be withdrawn because of its cumulative effects resulting in less choice and higher prices for consumers.

2.5. Franchising

(199) Franchise agreements contain licences of intellectual property rights relating in particular to trade marks or signs and know-how for the use and distribution of goods or services. In addition to the licence of IPRs, the franchisor usually provides the franchisee during the life of the agreement with commercial or technical assistance. The licence and the assistance are integral components of the business method being franchised. The franchisor is in general paid a franchise fee by the franchisee for the use of the particular business method. Franchising may enable the franchisor to establish, with limited investments, a uniform network for the distribution of his products. In addition to the provision of the business method, franchise agreements usually contain a combination of different vertical restraints concerning the products being distributed, in particular selective distribution and/or non-compete and/or exclusive distribution or weaker forms thereof.

(200) The coverage by the Block Exemption Regulation of the licensing of IPRs contained in franchise agreements is dealt with in paragraphs 23 to 45. As for the vertical restraints on the purchase, sale and resale of goods and services within a franchising arrangement, such as selective distribution, non-compete or exclusive distribution, the Block Exemption Regulation applies up to the 30 % market share threshold for the franchisor or the supplier designated by the franchisor[33]. The guidance provided earlier in respect of these types of restraints applies also to franchising, subject to the following specific remarks:

(1) In line with general rule 8 (see paragraph 119), the more important the transfer of know-how, the more easily the vertical restraints fulfil the conditions for exemption.

(2) A non-compete obligation on the goods or services purchased by the franchisee falls outside Article 81(1) when the obligation is necessary to maintain the common identity and reputation of the franchised network. In such cases, the duration of the non-compete obligation is also irrelevant under Article 81(1), as long as it does not exceed the duration of the franchise agreement itself.

(201) Example of franchising:

A manufacturer has developed a new format for selling sweets in so-called fun shops where the sweets can be coloured specially on demand from the consumer. The manufacturer of the sweets has also developed the machines to colour the sweets. The manufacturer also produces the colouring liquids. The quality and freshness of the liquid is of vital importance to producing good sweets. The manufacturer made a success of its sweets through a number of own retail outlets all operating under the same trade name and with the uniform fun image (style of layout of the shops, common advertising etc.). In order to expand sales the manufacturer started a franchising system. The franchisees are obliged to buy the sweets, liquid and colouring machine from the manufacturer, to have the same image and operate under the trade name, pay a franchise fee, contribute to common advertising and ensure the confidentiality of the operating manual prepared by the franchisor. In addition, the franchisees are only allowed to sell from the agreed premises, are only allowed to sell to end users or other franchisees and are not allowed to sell other sweets. The franchisor is obliged not to appoint another franchisee nor operate a retail outlet himself in a given contract territory. The franchisor is also under the obligation to update and further develop its products, the business outlook and the operating manual and make these improvements available to all retail franchisees. The franchise agreements are concluded for a duration of 10 years.

Sweet retailers buy their sweets on a national market from either national producers that cater for national tastes or from wholesalers which import sweets from foreign producers in addition to selling products from national producers. On this

---

[33] See also paragraphs AEG [1983] ECR 3151, paragraph 35; and of the Court of First Instance in Case T-19/91 Vichy v Commission [1992] ECR II-415, paragraph 65. See also paragraphs 89 to 95, in particular paragraph 95.

market the franchisor's products compete with other brands of sweets. The franchisor has a market share of 30 % on the market for sweets sold to retailers. Competition comes from a number of national and international brands, sometimes produced by large diversified food companies. There are many potential points of sale of sweets in the form of tobacconists, general food retailers, cafeterias and specialised sweet shops. On the market for machines for colouring food the franchisor's market share is below 10 %.

Most of the obligations contained in the franchise agreements can be assessed as being necessary to protect the intellectual property rights or maintain the common identity and reputation of the franchised network and fall outside Article 81(1). The restrictions on selling (contract territory and selective distribution) provide an incentive to the franchisees to invest in the colouring machine and the franchise concept and, if not necessary for, at least help to maintain the common identity, thereby offsetting the loss of intra-brand competition. The non-compete clause excluding other brands of sweets from the shops for the full duration of the agreements does allow the franchisor to keep the outlets uniform and prevent competitors from benefiting from its trade name. It does not lead to any serious foreclosure in view of the great number of potential outlets available to other sweet producers. The franchise agreements of this franchisor are likely to fulfil the conditions for exemption under Article 81(3) in as far as the obligations contained therein fall under Article 81(1).

2.6. Exclusive supply

(202) Exclusive supply as defined in Article 1(c) of the Block Exemption Regulation is the extreme form of limited distribution in as far as the limit on the number of buyers is concerned: in the agreement it is specified that there is only one buyer inside the Community to which the supplier may sell a particular final product. For intermediate goods or services, exclusive supply means that there is only one buyer inside the Community or that there is only one buyer inside the Community for the purposes of a specific use. For intermediate goods or services, exclusive supply is often referred to as industrial supply.

(203) Exclusive supply as defined in Article 1(c) of the Block Exemption Regulation is exempted by Article 2(1) read in conjunction with Article 3(2) of the Block Exemption Regulation up to 30 % market share of the buyer, even if combined with other non-hardcore vertical restraints such as non-compete. Above the market share threshold the following guidance is provided for the assessment of exclusive supply in individual cases.

(204) The main competition risk of exclusive supply is foreclosure of other buyers. The market share of the buyer on the upstream purchase market is obviously important for assessing the ability of the buyer to "impose" exclusive supply which forecloses other buyers from access to supplies. The importance of the buyer on the downstream market is however the factor which determines whether a competition problem may arise. If the buyer has no market power downstream,

then no appreciable negative effects for consumers can be expected. Negative effects can however be expected when the market share of the buyer on the downstream supply market as well as the upstream purchase market exceeds 30 %. Where the market share of the buyer on the upstream market does not exceed 30 %, significant foreclosure effects may still result, especially when the market share of the buyer on his downstream market exceeds 30 %. In such cases withdrawal of the block exemption may be required. Where a company is dominant on the downstream market, any obligation to supply the products only or mainly to the dominant buyer may easily have significant anti-competitive effects.

(205) It is not only the market position of the buyer on the upstream and downstream market that is important but also the extent to and the duration for which he applies an exclusive supply obligation. The higher the tied supply share, and the longer the duration of the exclusive supply, the more significant the foreclosure is likely to be. Exclusive supply agreements shorter than five years entered into by non-dominant companies usually require a balancing of pro- and anti-competitive effects, while agreements lasting longer than five years are for most types of investments not considered necessary to achieve the claimed efficiencies or the efficiencies are not sufficient to outweigh the foreclosure effect of such long-term exclusive supply agreements.

(206) The market position of the competing buyers on the upstream market is important as it is only likely that competing buyers will be foreclosed for anti-competitive reasons, i.e. to increase their costs, if they are significantly smaller than the foreclosing buyer. Foreclosure of competing buyers is not very likely where these competitors have similar buying power and can offer the suppliers similar sales possibilities. In such a case, foreclosure could only occur for potential entrants, who may not be able to secure supplies when a number of major buyers all enter into exclusive supply contracts with the majority of suppliers on the market. Such a cumulative effect may lead to withdrawal of the benefit of the Block Exemption Regulation.

(207) Entry barriers at the supplier level are relevant to establishing whether there is real foreclosure. In as far as it is efficient for competing buyers to provide the goods or services themselves via upstream vertical integration, foreclosure is unlikely to be a real problem. However, often there are significant entry barriers.

(208) Countervailing power of suppliers is relevant, as important suppliers will not easily allow themselves to be cut off from alternative buyers. Foreclosure is therefore mainly a risk in the case of weak suppliers and strong buyers. In the case of strong suppliers the exclusive supply may be found in combination with non-compete. The combination with non-compete brings in the rules developed for single branding. Where there are relationship-specific investments involved on both sides (hold-up problem) the combination of exclusive supply and non-compete i.e. reciprocal exclusivity in industrial supply agreements is usually justified below the level of dominance.

(209) Lastly, the level of trade and the nature of the product are relevant for foreclosure. Foreclosure is less likely in the case of an intermediate product or

where the product is homogeneous. Firstly, a foreclosed manufacturer that uses a certain input usually has more flexibility to respond to the demand of his customers than the wholesaler/retailer has in responding to the demand of the final consumer for whom brands may play an important role. Secondly, the loss of a possible source of supply matters less for the foreclosed buyers in the case of homogeneous products than in the case of a heterogeneous product with different grades and qualities.

(210) For homogeneous intermediate products, anti-competitive effects are likely to be exemptable below the level of dominance. For final branded products or differentiated intermediate products where there are entry barriers, exclusive supply may have appreciable anti-competitive effects where the competing buyers are relatively small compared to the foreclosing buyer, even if the latter is not dominant on the downstream market.

(211) Where appreciable anti-competitive effects are established, an exemption under Article 81(3) is possible as long as the company is not dominant. Efficiencies can be expected in the case of a hold-up problem (paragraph 116, points 4 and 5), and this is more likely for intermediate products than for final products. Other efficiencies are less likely. Possible economies of scale in distribution (paragraph 116, point 6) do not seem likely to justify exclusive supply.

(212) In the case of a hold-up problem and even more so in the case of scale economies in distribution, quantity forcing on the supplier, such as minimum supply requirements, could well be a less restrictive alternative.

(213) Example of exclusive supply:

On a market for a certain type of components (intermediate product market) supplier A agrees with buyer B to develop, with his own know-how and considerable investment in new machines and with the help of specifications supplied by buyer B, a different version of the component. B will have to make considerable investments to incorporate the new component. It is agreed that A will supply the new product only to buyer B for a period of five years from the date of first entry on the market. B is obliged to buy the new product only from A for the same period of five years. Both A and B can continue to sell and buy respectively other versions of the component elsewhere. The market share of buyer B on the upstream component market and on the downstream final goods market is 40 %. The market share of the component supplier is 35 %. There are two other component suppliers with around 20-25 % market share and a number of small suppliers.

Given the considerable investments, the agreement is likely to fulfil the conditions for exemption in view of the efficiencies and the limited foreclosure effect. Other buyers are foreclosed from a particular version of a product of a supplier with 35 % market share and there are other component suppliers that could develop similar new products. The foreclosure of part of buyer B's demand to other suppliers is limited to maximum 40 % of the market.

(214) Exclusive supply is based on a direct or indirect obligation causing the supplier only to sell to one buyer. Quantity forcing on the supplier is based on

incentives agreed between the supplier and the buyer that make the former concentrate his sales mainly with one buyer. Quantity forcing on the supplier may
have similar but more mitigated effects than exclusive supply. The assessment of
quantity forcing will depend on the degree of foreclosure of other buyers on the
upstream market.

2.7. Tying

(215) Tying exists when the supplier makes the sale of one product conditional
upon the purchase of another distinct product from the supplier or someone designated by the latter. The first product is referred to as the tying product and the
second is referred to as the tied product. If the tying is not objectively justified by
the nature of the products or commercial usage, such practice may constitute an
abuse within the meaning of Article 82([34]). Article 81 may apply to horizontal
agreements or concerted practices between competing suppliers which make the
sale of one product conditional upon the purchase of another distinct product.
Tying may also constitute a vertical restraint falling under Article 81 where it
results in a single branding type of obligation (see paragraphs 138 to 160) for the
tied product. Only the latter situation is dealt with in these Guidelines.

(216) What is to be considered as a distinct product is determined first of all by
the demand of the buyers. Two products are distinct if, in the absence of tying,
from the buyers' perspective, the products are purchased by them on two different markets. For instance, since customers want to buy shoes with laces, it has
become commercial usage for shoe manufacturers to supply shoes with laces.
Therefore, the sale of shoes with laces is not a tying practice. Often combinations
have become accepted practice because the nature of the product makes it technically difficult to supply one product without the supply of another product.

(217) The main negative effect of tying on competition is possible foreclosure
on the market of the tied product. Tying means that there is at least a form of
quantity-forcing on the buyer in respect of the tied product. Where in addition a
non-compete obligation is agreed in respect of the tied product, this increases the
possible foreclosure effect on the market of the tied product. Tying may also lead
to supra-competitive prices, especially in three situations. Firstly, when the tying
and tied product are partly substitutable for the buyer. Secondly, when the tying
allows price discrimination according to the use the customer makes of the tying
product, for example the tying of ink cartridges to the sale of photocopying
machines (metering). Thirdly, when in the case of long-term contracts or in the
case of after-markets with original equipment with a long replacement time, it
becomes difficult for the customers to calculate the consequences of the tying.
Lastly, tying may also lead to higher entry barriers both on the market of the tying
and on the market of the tied product.

---

[34] Judgment of the Court of Justice in Case C-333/94 P Tetrapak v Commission[1996] ECR I-
5951, paragraph 37.

(218) Tying is exempted by Article 2(1) read in conjunction with Article 3 of the Block Exemption Regulation when the market share of the supplier on both the market of the tied product and the market of the tying product does not exceed 30 %. It may be combined with other non-hardcore vertical restraints such as non-compete or quantity forcing in respect of the tying product, or exclusive purchasing. Above the market share threshold the following guidance is provided for the assessment of tying in individual cases.

(219) The market position of the supplier on the market of the tying product is obviously of main importance to assess possible anti-competitive effects. In general this type of agreement is imposed by the supplier. The importance of the supplier on the market of the tying product is the main reason why a buyer may find it difficult to refuse a tying obligation.

(220) To assess the supplier's market power, the market position of his competitors on the market of the tying product is important. As long as his competitors are sufficiently numerous and strong, no anti-competitive effects can be expected, as buyers have sufficient alternatives to purchase the tying product without the tied product, unless other suppliers are applying similar tying. In addition, entry barriers on the market of the tying product are relevant to establish the market position of the supplier. When tying is combined with a non-compete obligation in respect of the tying product, this considerably strengthens the position of the supplier.

(221) Buying power is relevant, as important buyers will not easily be forced to accept tying without obtaining at least part of the possible efficiencies. Tying not based on efficiency is therefore mainly a risk where buyers do not have significant buying power.

(222) Where appreciable anti-competitive effects are established, the question of a possible exemption under Article 81(3) arises as long as the company is not dominant. Tying obligations may help to produce efficiencies arising from joint production or joint distribution. Where the tied product is not produced by the supplier, an efficiency may also arise from the supplier buying large quantities of the tied product. For tying to be exemptable, it must, however, be shown that at least part of these cost reductions are passed on to the consumer. Tying is therefore normally not exemptable when the retailer is able to obtain, on a regular basis, supplies of the same or equivalent products on the same or better conditions than those offered by the supplier which applies the tying practice. Another efficiency may exist where tying helps to ensure a certain uniformity and quality standardisation (see efficiency 8 in paragraph 116). However, it needs to be demonstrated that the positive effects cannot be realised equally efficiently by requiring the buyer to use or resell products satisfying minimum quality standards, without requiring the buyer to purchase these from the supplier or someone designated by the latter. The requirements concerning minimum quality standards would not normally fall within Article 81(1). Where the supplier of the tying product imposes on the buyer the suppliers from which the buyer must purchase the tied product, for instance because the formulation of minimum quality standards is not possible,

this may also fall outside Article 81(1), especially where the supplier of the tying product does not derive a direct (financial) benefit from designating the suppliers of the tied product.

(223) The effect of supra-competitive prices is considered anti-competitive in itself. The effect of foreclosure depends on the tied percentage of total sales on the market of the tied product. On the question of what can be considered appreciable foreclosure under Article 81(1), the analysis for single branding can be applied. Above the 30 % market share threshold exemption of tying is unlikely, unless there are clear efficiencies that are transmitted, at least in part, to consumers. Exemption is even less likely when tying is combined with non-compete, either in respect of the tied or in respect of the tying product.

(224) Withdrawal of the block exemption is likely where no efficiencies result from tying or where such efficiencies are not passed on to the consumer (see paragraph 222). Withdrawal is also likely in the case of a cumulative effect where a majority of the suppliers apply similar tying arrangements without the possible efficiencies being transmitted at least in part to consumers.

2.8. Recommended and maximum resale prices

(225) The practice of recommending a resale price to a reseller or requiring the reseller to respect a maximum resale price is—subject to the comments in paragraphs 46 to 56 concerning RPM—covered by the Block Exemption Regulation when the market share of the supplier does not exceed the 30 % threshold. For cases above the market share threshold and for cases of withdrawal of the block exemption the following guidance is provided.

(226) The possible competition risk of maximum and recommended prices is firstly that the maximum or recommended price will work as a focal point for the resellers and might be followed by most or all of them. A second competition risk is that maximum or recommended prices may facilitate collusion between suppliers.

(227) The most important factor for assessing possible anti-competitive effects of maximum or recommended resale prices is the market position of the supplier. The stronger the market position of the supplier, the higher the risk that a maximum resale price or a recommended resale price leads to a more or less uniform application of that price level by the resellers, because they may use it as a focal point. They may find it difficult to deviate from what they perceive to be the preferred resale price proposed by such an important supplier on the market. Under such circumstances the practice of imposing a maximum resale price or recommending a resale price may infringe Article 81(1) if it leads to a uniform price level.

(228) The second most important factor for assessing possible anti-competitive effects of the practice of maximum and recommended prices is the market position of competitors. Especially in a narrow oligopoly, the practice of using or publishing maximum or recommended prices may facilitate collusion between the suppliers by exchanging information on the preferred price level and by reducing the likelihood of lower resale prices. The practice of imposing a

maximum resale price or recommending resale prices leading to such effects may also infringe Article 81(1).

2.9. Other vertical restraints

(229) The vertical restraints and combinations described above are only a selection. There are other restraints and combinations for which no direct guidance is provided here. They will however be treated according to the same principles, with the help of the same general rules and with the same emphasis on the effect on the market.

Appendix 8

Commission Notice on agreements of minor importance
OJ 2001 C368/13

Commission Notice on agreements of minor importance which do not appreciably restrict competition under Article 81(1) of the Treaty establishing the European Community (*de minimis*)[1] (2001/C 368/07) (Text with EEA relevance)

I

1. Article 81(1) prohibits agreements between undertakings which may affect trade between Member States and which have as their object or effect the prevention, restriction or distortion of competition within the common market. The Court of Justice of the European Communities has clarified that this provision is not applicable where the impact of the agreement on intra-Community trade or on competition is not appreciable.

2. In this notice the Commission quantifies, with the help of market share thresholds, what is not an appreciable restriction of competition under Article 81 of the EC Treaty. This negative definition of appreciability does not imply that agreements between undertakings which exceed the thresholds set out in this notice appreciably restrict competition. Such agreements may still have only a negligible effect on competition and may therefore not be prohibited by Article 81(1)[2].

3. Agreements may in addition not fall under Article 81(1) because they are not capable of appreciably affecting trade between Member States. This notice does not deal with this issue. It does not quantify what does not constitute an appreciable effect on trade. It is however acknowledged that agreements between small and medium-sized undertakings, as defined in the Annex to Commission

---

[1] This notice replaces the notice on agreements of minor importance published in OJ C 372, 9.12.1997.

[2] See, for instance, the judgment of the Court of Justice in Joined Cases C-215/96 and C-216/96 Bagnasco (Carlos) v Banca Popolare di Novara and Casa di Risparmio di Genova e Imperia (1999) ECR I-135, points 34–35. This notice is also without prejudice to the principles for assessment under Article 81(1) as expressed in the Commission notice 'Guidelines on the applicability of Article 81 of the EC Treaty to horizontal cooperation agreements', OJ C 3, 6.1.2001, in particular points 17–31 inclusive, and in the Commission notice 'Guidelines on vertical restraints', OJ C 291, 13.10.2000, in particular points 5-20 inclusive.

Recommendation 96/280/EC([3]), are rarely capable of appreciably affecting trade between Member States. Small and medium-sized undertakings are currently defined in that recommendation as undertakings which have fewer than 250 employees and have either an annual turnover not exceeding EUR 40 million or an annual balance-sheet total not exceeding EUR 27 million.

4. In cases covered by this notice the Commission will not institute proceedings either upon application or on its own initiative. Where undertakings assume in good faith that an agreement is covered by this notice, the Commission will not impose fines. Although not binding on them, this notice also intends to give guidance to the courts and authorities of the Member States in their application of Article 81.

5. This notice also applies to decisions by associations of undertakings and to concerted practices.

6. This notice is without prejudice to any interpretation of Article 81 which may be given by the Court of Justice or the Court of First Instance of the European Communities.

II

7. The Commission holds the view that agreements between undertakings which affect trade between Member States do not appreciably restrict competition within the meaning of Article 81(1):

(a) if the aggregate market share held by the parties to the agreement does not exceed 10 % on any of the relevant markets affected by the agreement, where the agreement is made between undertakings which are actual or potential competitors on any of these markets (agreements between competitors)([4]); or

(b) if the market share held by each of the parties to the agreement does not exceed 15 % on any of the relevant markets affected by the agreement, where the agreement is made between undertakings which are not actual or potential competitors on any of these markets (agreements between non-competitors).

[3] OJ L 107, 30.4.1996, p. 4. This recommendation will be revised. It is envisaged to increase the annual turnover threshold from EUR 40 million to EUR 50 million and the annual balance-sheet total threshold from EUR 27 million to EUR 43 million.

[4] On what are actual or potential competitors, see the Commission notice 'Guidelines on the applicability of Article 81 of the EC Treaty to horizontal cooperation agreements', OJ C 3, 6.1.2001, paragraph 9. A firm is treated as an actual competitor if it is either active on the same relevant market or if, in the absence of the agreement, it is able to switch production to the relevant products and market them in the short term without incurring significant additional costs or risks in response to a small and permanent increase in relative prices (immediate supply-side substitutability). A firm is treated as a potential competitor if there is evidence that, absent the agreement, this firm could and would be likely to undertake the necessary additional investments or other necessary switching costs so that it could enter the relevant market in response to a small and permanent increase in relative prices.

In cases where it is difficult to classify the agreement as either an agreement between competitors or an agreement between non-competitors the 10 % threshold is applicable.

8. Where in a relevant market competition is restricted by the cumulative effect of agreements for the sale of goods or services entered into by different suppliers or distributors (cumulative foreclosure effect of parallel networks of agreements having similar effects on the market), the market share thresholds under point 7 are reduced to 5 %, both for agreements between competitors and for agreements between non-competitors. Individual suppliers or distributors with a market share not exceeding 5 % are in general not considered to contribute significantly to a cumulative foreclosure effect([5]). A cumulative foreclosure effect is unlikely to exist if less than 30 % of the relevant market is covered by parallel (networks of) agreements having similar effects.

9. The Commission also holds the view that agreements are not restrictive of competition if the market shares do not exceed the thresholds of respectively 10 %, 15 % and 5 % set out in point 7 and 8 during two successive calendar years by more than 2 percentage points.

10. In order to calculate the market share, it is necessary to determine the relevant market. This consists of the relevant product market and the relevant geographic market. When defining the relevant market, reference should be had to the notice on the definition of the relevant market for the purposes of Community competition law([6]). The market shares are to be calculated on the basis of sales value data or, where appropriate, purchase value data. If value data are not available, estimates based on other reliable market information, including volume data, may be used.

11. Points 7, 8 and 9 do not apply to agreements containing any of the following hardcore restrictions:

(1) as regards agreements between competitors as defined in point 7, restrictions which, directly or indirectly, in isolation or in combination with other factors under the control of the parties, have as their object([7]):

(a) the fixing of prices when selling the products to third parties;

(b) the limitation of output or sales;

(c) the allocation of markets or customers;

([5]) See also the Commission notice 'Guidelines on vertical restraints', OJ C 291, 13.10.2000, in particular paragraphs 73, 142, 143 and 189. While in the guidelines on vertical restraints in relation to certain restrictions reference is made not only to the total but also to the tied market share of a particular supplier or buyer, in this notice all market share thresholds refer to total market shares.

([6]) OJ C 372, 9.12.1997, p. 5.

([7]) Without prejudice to situations of joint production with or without joint distribution as defined in Article 5, paragraph 2, of Commission Regulation (EC) No 2658/2000 and Article 5, paragraph 2, of Commission Regulation (EC) No 2659/2000, OJ L 304, 5.12.2000, pp. 3 and 7 respectively.

(2) as regards agreements between non-competitors as defined in point 7, restrictions which, directly or indirectly, in isolation or in combination with other factors under the control of the parties, have as their object:

(a) the restriction of the buyer's ability to determine its sale price, without prejudice to the possibility of the supplier imposing a maximum sale price or recommending a sale price, provided that they do not amount to a fixed or minimum sale price as a result of pressure from, or incentives offered by, any of the parties;

(b) the restriction of the territory into which, or of the customers to whom, the buyer may sell the contract goods or services, except the following restrictions which are not hardcore:

- the restriction of active sales into the exclusive territory or to an exclusive customer group reserved to the supplier or allocated by the supplier to another buyer, where such a restriction does not limit sales by the customers of the buyer,

- the restriction of sales to end users by a buyer operating at the wholesale level of trade,

- the restriction of sales to unauthorised distributors by the members of a selective distribution system, and

- the restriction of the buyer's ability to sell components, supplied for the purposes of incorporation, to customers who would use them to manufacture the same type of goods as those produced by the supplier;

(c) the restriction of active or passive sales to end users by members of a selective distribution system operating at the retail level of trade, without prejudice to the possibility of prohibiting a member of the system from operating out of an unauthorised place of establishment;

(d) the restriction of cross-supplies between distributors within a selective distribution system, including between distributors operating at different levels of trade;

(e) the restriction agreed between a supplier of components and a buyer who incorporates those components, which limits the supplier's ability to sell the components as spare parts to end users or to repairers or other service providers not entrusted by the buyer with the repair or servicing of its goods;

(3) as regards agreements between competitors as defined in point 7, where the competitors operate, for the purposes of the agreement, at a different level of the production or distribution chain, any of the hardcore restrictions listed in paragraph (1) and (2) above.

12. (1) For the purposes of this notice, the terms "undertaking", "party to the agreement", "distributor", "supplier" and "buyer" shall include their respective connected undertakings.

(2) "Connected undertakings" are:

(a) undertakings in which a party to the agreement, directly or indirectly:

- has the power to exercise more than half the voting rights, or

- has the power to appoint more than half the members of the supervisory board, board of management or bodies legally representing the undertaking, or

- has the right to manage the undertaking's affairs;

(b) undertakings which directly or indirectly have, over a party to the agreement, the rights or powers listed in (a);

(c) undertakings in which an undertaking referred to in (b) has, directly or indirectly, the rights or powers listed in (a);

(d) undertakings in which a party to the agreement together with one or more of the undertakings referred to in (a), (b) or (c), or in which two or more of the latter undertakings, jointly have the rights or powers listed in (a);

(e) undertakings in which the rights or the powers listed in (a) are jointly held by:

- parties to the agreement or their respective connected undertakings referred to in (a) to (d), or

- one or more of the parties to the agreement or one or more of their connected undertakings referred to in (a) to (d) and one or more third parties.

(3) For the purposes of paragraph 2(e), the market share held by these jointly held undertakings shall be apportioned equally to each undertaking having the rights or the powers listed in paragraph 2(a).

Index